Universiade'83

Pictorial Record

Edmonton Alberta Canada

Universiade '83 Edmonton Corp.
c/o Hurtig Publishers, Distributor
10560 - 105 Street
Edmonton, Alberta

ISBN 0-9691570-0-2

Printed and bound in Canada by D.W. Friesen & Sons Ltd.

Universiade'83

Edmonton·Alberta·Canada

FISU

Acknowledgments

Publisher	Universiade '83 Edmonton Corp.
Administration	Ed Zemrau, *President* Bruce Cleveley, *Executive Vice President* John Russell, *V. P. Communications Division*
Written by	Ernie Miller
Art Production	Tim Radford
Research Assistants	Bill France Marsha Mah Poy Barbara Chaffey Mark W. Miller Robert Paddon
Photographic Direction	Bob Peterson
Photographers	Ottmar Bierwagen Bill Brennan Denis Brodeur Crombie McNeil Jim Merrithew Tim O'lett Colin Price Ray Smith Davis Strong Victor Post Photography Merle Prosofsky Photography Ltd. Penny Dubberlee Terry Elinski Al Girard Grant Johnson Voya Mikulic Wendy Nelson Tim Radford
Photo Assistants	Stephina-Anne Fridel Sophia Graham Winnie Kaptein Colin McIsaac James Mah Fred Solylo
With Special Thanks to:	Kodak, Canada Inc., Canon Canada Inc., The Edmonton Journal; The Edmonton Sun; D.W. Friesen and Sons Ltd., Altona Manitoba; Hurtig Publishing, Edmonton, Alberta; Trendsetters Typographers Ltd., Edmonton, Alberta; Superior Typesetting Ltd., Edmonton, Alberta.

Contents

President's Message

Universiade '83 was a window to the world for Canada, Alberta, and the City of Edmonton. It was a mirror for our unique multiculturism and a reflection of the spirit, enthusiasm, and expertise that more than nineteen thousand Albertans gave freely to the Games.

It was a magnificent portrait which fully captured the pagentry of a Royal Visit, the colour of a spectacular Opening Ceremonies and a quality of athletic and artistic excellence unparalleled in our history.

More important perhaps, Universiade '83 was a festival of friendship which gave fresh impetus to the noble ideals of brotherhood and mutual understanding.

Universiade '83 · The Pictorial Record, is intended to reflect all of these things and to serve as a lasting memento of those eleven joyous days in July, 1983 when Edmonton "Welcomed the World".

We cared for each other.

We cared for the young Peruvian basketball team beset by a bizarre series of financial and transportation problems ... and won their hearts forever by rallying to their aid.

We cared for the young students from Rwanda who had never before played on a hardwood floor and brought along their own volleyball. The joy that lit their faces during a shopping visit to a sporting goods store was a picture to be savoured. Canadians were the Games' finest ambassadors.

The diving accident which claimed the life of twenty-one-year-old Sergei Shalibaswili was indeed tragic. The outpouring of concern expressed by Canadians for Sergei's mother back home in Tblisi, deeply touched the entire Soviet delegation.

We cared for each other.

The swelling of emotion which engulfed Commonwealth Stadium when swimmer Alex Bauman of Laurentian University marched onto the track carrying Canada's flag will always retain a special place in our memories. So will the gritty performances of our Canadian student-athletes: Dave Steen, Molly Killingbeck, Guillaume Leblanc, Phillipe Chartrand, Madeline Philion, Mike West and Jack Donohue's men's basketball team.

Kaleidoscope '83, the cultural component of the Games, was a magnificent experience and an unqualified success. The traditions and cultures of fifty-six countries and hundreds of artists, musicians and street performers native to our own country, came to life on the stages, parks and street corners of our city and contributed immeasurably to the festival of friendship that was Universiade '83.

The FISU-CESU conference, which attracted sports scholars and historians from around the world, made a valued contribution to university sports, the impact of which will be felt for many years. The co-operation extended to the Organizing Committee by the International University Sports Federation was most appreciated.

It was an honour to host the first World University Games awarded to Canada. The pleasure was made even more unforgettable by the opportunity to welcome the world on the 116th birthday of our country and to extend at the same time our fondest wishes to the Princess of Wales on her twenty-second birthday.

To the citizens of Canada, may I take this opportunity on behalf of the Organizing Committee to express our profound appreciation for the contributions you made to these very enjoyable and successful World University Games.

Sincerely,

Ed Zemrau
President, Universiade '83

Board of Governors

Alex Fallow, *Chairman*
Ted Allan
Marg Andrekson
Max Berretti
Art Clough
Jim Hole
Lynn Karas, *Secretary*

Larry Kelly
Dr. Herb McLachlin
Hon. Tevie Miller
Doreen Ryan
John Schlosser
Don H. Sprague
Erskine Williams

Ed Zemrau
Dr. Myer Horowitz
Mayor, Cec J. Purves
Don Carlson
Julian J. Nowicki
Robert Pugh
Doug Burrows

Management Committee

Ed Zemrau
President and Chairman

Pam Freeman
Exec. Assistant

Carol Gilfillan
VP Special Events

Murray Smith
VP Venues

Rod Stutchbury
VP Administration

Ross Macnab
U of A Liaison (VP)

Bruce Cleveley
Executive VP

John Russell
VP Communications

Bob Steadward
VP Accommodation

Hank Tatarchuk
VP Sports

Richard Gaul
VP Revenues

Jack Boddington
City of Edmonton Liaison (VP)

Not pictured: Jim Acton, Provincial Government Liaison

The Games Bid

Edmonton, Alberta, Canada was a fresh, pivotal chapter in the history of World University Games, broadening the horizons of growth for the International University Sports Federation while solidifying its own world presence as a city with not only the facilities to host major games but also one with a proven record to deliver them.

These were the milestones attained in Edmonton during the 1983 Games:

- Thirty-three Universiade records in swimming and athletics
- First major multi-sport participation by China since the 1932 Olympics
- First World University Games held in Canada
- First Women's marathon in a World University Games
- First cycling event in a world games
- Largest television viewing audience in World University Games history
- Largest cultural participation in World University Games' history

"The future of FISU and the Games as a major force in international sport was dramatically enhanced, in my view, as a result of the Games in Edmonton," said Canadian Interuniversity Athletic Union VicePresident, Bob Pugh.

"You can't escape the fact these Games had little or no awareness in Canada or the United States before they came to Edmonton," said Nick Rodis, a past Vice-President of FISU representing the United States. "The media in North America simply had little perception of what they were all about -- and justifiably so when you consider they've never been exposed to our large media markets before this year. Many athletes in the U.S. had never heard of them either and that's one of the reasons our athletes in a couple of sports, such as swimming, opted to stay home and get ready for the Pan-Am Games. But having come, seen, and been conquered in the pool, I guarantee the U.S. Swimming Federation won't underestimate the competition again."

"There's no question in my mind Edmonton put these Games on the map. There's never been in all my years in FISU an Opening Ceremonies like you had in Edmonton. It was as good or better than any I've ever seen in any Games including the Olympics. Everything was first rate. It was world class and it certainly opened a lot of eyes in my country."

Rodis said lack of awareness of the Games in North America is no longer a heavy chain around the organizational neck of FISU. The Games received national coverage in both Canada and the U.S. via the CBC and CBS television networks and was fed to nine other countries including the People's Republic of China. More than eleven hundred print and electronic journalists reported on the Games from Edmonton.

There were many ancillary benefits. Canada's athletes won international respect with their performances in Edmonton. They won thirty-eight medals -- more medals than they won at eight previous Universiades combined.

The Games at Edmonton also opened the doors to a large number of sports and cultural exchanges and future trade talks with countries represented at Universiade '83.

"It was a shot in the arm for many people," said Edmonton Mayor Cec Purves. "It manifested a tremendous feeling of goodwill throughout the City, and at a time of economic downturn across the country, the Games generated considerable spending in the business community, not only in Edmonton but throughout the Province."

The Games' legacy to the City was a large number of new and improved sports facilities. Commonwealth Stadium was expanded by eighteen thousand seats, increasing its capacity to sixty-one thousand. Minor improvements were made to the cycling track at Argyll Velodrome and to Kinsmen Aquatic Centre. A new two-million dollar scoreboard is now a stadium showpiece. The University of Alberta benefitted by the addition of a ten thousand-seat all-purpose pavilion, an outdoor tennis centre, and new housing facilities for hundreds of students.

While the first formal step towards a bid for the Games wasn't taken until 1979, City administrators had discussed the possibility of seeking a major games as far back as 1970 when Edmonton hosted the World Wrestling Championships.

City Council initiated a design plan for a new sports stadium in 1975 as a condition of hosting the 1978 Commonwealth Games. The Commonwealth Games heightened discussions about other major events. At the same time, the Canadian Interuniversity Athletic Union was being badgered by Ed Zemrau, who served both as CIAU President and Chairman of Athletics at The University of Alberta, to consider supporting a bid by one of its member universities for the World University Games.

"The CIAU was interested in 1979 to bid for the FISU games even though they weren't well known in Canada at the time," Mr. Zemrau said. "It was felt that an event of this magnitude would raise the stature of university sport in Canada and allow our university athletes a rare opportunity to compete at an international games in their own country."

Member universities were asked to prepare submissions of interest for the 1981, 1983 and 1985 Games. Seven universities replied: McGill and the University of Montreal in Montreal, York University and the University of Toronto in Toronto, the University of Manitoba in Winnipeg, the University of British Columbia in Vancouver and the University of Alberta in Edmonton. The choice was soon narrowed down to the University of Montreal and the University of Alberta. Montreal, however, was firm in its preference to bid for the '85 Games, leaving Alberta the only candidate for an '83 bid. It was at that point Mr. Zemrau sought and received the endorsement of University President Dr. Myer Horowitz and Edmonton Mayor Cec Purves to pursue the CIAU's request for a formal submission.

A joint eight-man committee representing the City and University was charged with preparing and presenting the submission. Those members were Ed Zemrau, Ross Macnab, Herb McLachlin and Mel Poole from the University, and Commissioner Alf Savage, Ron Ferguson, Hugh Monroe and Jim Armstrong representing the City of Edmonton.

The bid received the blessing of City council on November 14, 1979, and the funding approval by the Province of Alberta was secured on January 9, 1980. City council gave its financial support two days later and on January 18, the CIAU endorsed Edmonton's bid.

Politics and the infamous boycott of the 1980 Moscow Olympics worked both against and for Edmonton's application to the International University Sports Federation (FISU) for the right to host the '83 Games on Canada's behalf. Two other countries, Brazil and Yugoslavia, would also present bids to FISU at meetings scheduled for April 1980 in Moscow.

The CIAU was confident it had the support of the Soviets and Eastern Block countries as a result of their intensive lobbying at previous meetings of FISU. Shock, however, greeted Mr. Zemrau when he attended the Moscow meeting. The Canadian government had just announced it would boycott the Moscow Olympics. FISU, as a result of the turmoil caused by the mounting boycott pressures, postponed its decision to award the Games.

The postponement, however, turned out to be a blessing in disguise. It afforded Mr. Zemrau more time to lobby the FISU delegates who were already in Moscow. Brazil and Yugoslavia were not there. The final decision by FISU at its meeting in Rome six months later proved

academic for Canada. Edmonton was unanimously endorsed as host city for the 1983 World University Games.

Thirty three months and seventeen days!

That was the time frame remaining for Edmonton to put together an organizational structure, hire its staff, secure its volunteers and implement its program for a world event which few people had heard about.

Above: Raising of FISU, Universiade '83 and flags of three governments October 19, 1981 launched the formal beginning of operations for the Edmonton Organizing Committee

The organization would revolve around a board of governors representing the interests of the city, university and public-at-large. A president would be hired to be responsible for the day-to-day operation of the Games. Those appointments were made by a steering committee representing the city and the university. Jim Hole, Larry Kelly and Don Sprague were selected to represent the interests of the public. John Schlosser, Max Berretti and Dr. Herb McLachlin were appointed to represent the university while Alex Fallow, Hon. Tevie Miller and Doreen Ryan were appointed to represent the City of Edmonton. Dr. Horowitz and Mayor Purves were also appointed as ex-officio members of the Board. Mr. Fallow was elected chairman of the board which in turn hired Mr.

Zemrau to be President of the Organizing Committee.

The board of governors voted to increase its membership to 14 persons and added Marg Andrekson, Art Clough, Ted Allan and Erskine Williams from the public sector. The board then structured a management committee to oversee the operation of seven working divisions. The committee comprised seven vice-presidents in charge of Administration, Special Events, Venues, Accommodation, Sports, Communications and Revenues along with liaison representation from the City, University, CIAU, Provincial and Federal governments.

This key committee implemented the working policies for a full-time staff of 196 persons and 19,000 volunteers.

Torch Relay

The telephone ring from Sofia, Bulgaria to historic Signal Hill in St. John's Newfoundland appeared to be several seconds ahead of schedule. For more than five hundred school children, civic leaders, provincial dignitaries and university officials who had gathered at the precise spot where Marconi received the first telephone transmission eighty-one years earlier, the moment they so eagerly anticipated had arrived.

"Hello, is Charlie there?"

The crowd broke into laughter and understanding applause. They'd been upstaged by a local resident who dialed the wrong number.

It was the ring of the telephone, ironically, that ignited the Cross-Canada Torch Relay for the 1983 World University Games. The crowd cheered and the twenty-six athletes from Memorial University who would alternately carry the flame on the first leg of its ten thousand-kilometre journey across the country, escorted the flame to the streets below.

Enthusiasm was the byword at each of the fifty-three communities the torch passed on its thirty-six-day journey from The Atlantic to The Pacific -- through all ten provinces and the two territories.

It was met by university presidents, provincial premiers, and on the steps of Parliament in the nation's capital by the Minister for Fitness and Amateur Sport, Senator Ray Perrault.

In Granby, Quebec, more than six hundred school children who had been excused for the day, formed a human wall behind runners representing seven Quebec universities and escorted the entourage to the highway leading to Montreal. Here, a crowd of thirty thousand welcomed the runners at Olympic Stadium in the midst of an Expos' baseball game. The torch was symbolically passed from ten former Canadian Olympians to ten children representative of the new guard in Canadian sport.

A special ceremony was celebrated near Thunder Bay, Ontario, at the site where Canadian folk hero Terry Fox ended his gallant coast-to-coast effort in support of cancer research. His parents officiated at yet another ceremony at the Terry Fox Plaza in Vancouver, sending the flame on its way to the host province of Alberta.

Lethbridge. Fort Macleod. High River. Calgary. Olds. Red Deer. Millet.

The spirit engendered for thousands of Canadians by the 1480 athletes from forty-two Canadian universities swelled at each community milepost.

Edmonton. July 1, 3:10 p.m.

Graham Smith, a former world record swimmer, and Tracy Mills, a member of Canada's Universiade volleyball team, emerged from the tunnel at Commonwealth Stadium, greeted by a tumultuous standing ovation from the crowd of sixty-one thousand which included the Prince and Princess of Wales.

At precisely 3:15 p.m., the two young Edmonton athletes ignited the flame which would burn for the duration of the Games, culminating the longest, most ambitious undertaking of its kind for an international games.

The message on the giant scoreboard at Commonwealth Stadium said it best for the volunteers, athletes, officials and spectators in a special welcome for Prince Charles and Princess Diana on their first visit to Edmonton. More than 60,000 spectators at the Opening Ceremonies for the Games turned the occasion into the city's biggest birthday party in celebrating the 116th birthday of Canada, the 22nd birthday of Princess Diana and 60th anniversary of the World University Games.

WELCOME TO EDMONTON

A Royal Visit

A future king and queen ignited a stampede of Canadian patriotism and touched the hearts of thousands of visitors during their three-day visit to Edmonton for the 1983 World University Games.

The city was wrapped in ribbons and banners for the first visit by their Royal Highnesses Prince Charles and Princess Diana. It coincided with the opening of the Games, Canada's 116th birthday, and the twenty-second birthday of Princess Diana, all on July 1.

Above: Visit by Prince Charles to Village delighted the athletes

Right: Royal couple in their Klondike finest at historic Fort Edmonton

Edmonton was the last stop on an eighteen-day visit to Canada and for the fifty-eight hours they were here, the Royal couple was showered with unbridled affection wherever they went: during a walk across Churchill Square; at a lively Fort Edmonton barbeque for which the Royal couple dressed in Klondike Days costume; on a visit to city hall; during a drive through city streets jammed by an estimated one hundred thousand persons seeking to catch even a glimpse of Prince Charles and Princess Diana on their way to a formal dinner with Premier Lougheed at Government House.

Prince Charles was the recipient of an honorary Doctor of Laws degree from the University of Alberta, the second such degree conferred by the university upon a Prince of Wales. On September 13, 1919, another young prince who reigned briefly as King Edward VIII, received the same degree.

Opposite, upper: A gracious Princess Diana won the hearts of thousands along parade route

Opposite, lower: Prince Charles often stopped to chat with young and old alike

Below: A standing Happy Birthday salute to Princess Diana

Prince Charles also unveiled a plaque commemorating the opening of Edmonton's new Convention Centre and with Princess Diana, toured the Athlete's Village at the University of Alberta. For many of the athletes, this was their first look at the handsome prince and the young lady with the shy smile.

Linda Saunders, a member of the Canadian swimming team, was accorded one of the most coveted souvenirs when Prince Charles kissed her check.

"It was heaven," she said. "I haven't stopped smiling since."

Prince Charles and Princess Diana good-naturedly tried on matching wraparound punk sunglasses presented by Canadian volleyball player Dave Wilson. They stopped to chat with a group of athletes from Great Britain who said it wasn't possible to get this close to royalty back home. The princess seemed slightly embarrassed when a group of U.S. athletes sang a rousing chorus of "Isn't She Beautiful".

At Government House, Prince Charles took the opportunity to reflect on the warmth and devotion shown to him and his wife.

"We have both, I think, quite truthfully, been overwhelmed by the kindness we have come across in Canada," he said. "I think overwhelmed is an understatement. We have been spoiled thoroughly."

"My wife has been enormously moved by the wealth of love and affection seen by us in the last two weeks. We've been showered by flowers from small people, from medium-sized people. My wife has been inundated with presents of every kind for herself, and one or two for me. There were a large number for our son who is becoming increasingly fortunate as time goes by. One day we'll have to tell him the truth about what's in store for him."

Above: Prince Charles received honorary Doctor of Laws degree from The University of Alberta

Canons roared a twenty-one-gun salute and the King's Own Calgary Regiment Marching Band struck up "O Canada" when Prince Charles and Princess Diana, clutching her navy plumed hat in a stiff wind, boarded a 707 at CFB Edmonton for their return to London.

Opposite: Stadium infield was a maze of flags and colour during march-in of the athletes

Opening Ceremonies

under the escort of one hundred and sixty pipers and drummers from twenty Northern Alberta communities.

The Chimes of Westminster struck 2 p.m. Sixty trumpeters heralded the arrival of their Royal Highnesses the Prince and Princess of Wales, and Dr. Primo Nebiolo, President of the International Federation of University Sports.

A hush of anticipation engulfed Commonwealth Stadium.

Billowy, grey clouds which had hung menacingly over the city since late morning, posed an ominous threat to the Opening Ceremonies of the 1983 World University Games and to the special birthday salutes planned for Canada and Princess Diana. They parted almost majestically, however, when the open white convertibles bearing the Royal couple and the FISU president, crawled onto the stadium track

The portent of rain dissipated immediately amid the electricity of the moment and the thunderous applause of sixty-one thousand spectators. For the next two hours and ten minutes, a ceremony two years in the making and involving sixty-five hundred volunteers, transformed the stadium into a river of blazing color and a sea of friendly warmth.

It was a ceremony steeped in the pomp of a royal visit and the traditions of a Games sixty years old.

Prince Charles provided a ray of disarming humour to the solemnity of the occasion.

"It is the birthday of my dear wife. She had the good sense and the excellent taste to be born on Canada's national day, which we celebrate today -- the 116th anniversary of the Confederation."

Left: His Royal Highness declares Games open

Above: Ed Zemrau, Dr. Nebiolo welcomed Games' athletes and dignitaries

Opposite, lower: Edmonton was the centrepiece for national celebration of our 116th birthday

Royal Couple at Games' Opening -- Their Royal Highnesses the Prince and Princess of Wales were the honoured guests for the Opening Ceremonies of Universiade '83. The official family included, from the left, Alex Fallow, chairman of the Board of Governors; International Olympic Committee President, Juan Antonio Samaranch; Mayor Cec Purves; FISU President Dr. Primo Nebiolo; Prince Charles; Hon. Serge Joyal, Secretary of State; Princess Diana; Premier Peter Lougheed; Dr. Myer Horowitz, President, University of Alberta; Ed Zemrau, President, Universiade '83.

Prince Charles, Princess Diana arrive in an open, white convertible

Prince Charles, Princess Diana and Dr. Nebiolo, arrive for Opening Ceremonies

Princess Diana and Premier Lougheed enjoy lighter moment during Opening Ceremonies

His Highness wished "good fortune" to the competitors and urged them to preserve "those qualities of good sportsmanship which are the essence of such amateur games."

In thanking Canadians for their hospitality, Prince Charles said: "It is our last event in Canada before we return to Britain, and we shall leave here with our hearts overflowing with the warmth, friendliness, and hospitality showered on us the past seventeen days."

The Honourable Serge Joyal, Secretary of State, representing Prime Minister Trudeau, paid tribute to the Organizing Committee for bringing the Games to Canada and stressed the importance of the event as a vehicle to spread the ideals of peace, fraternity, sharing, and mutual respect.

Far left: And there were pretty girls everywhere

Left: Decorated pipe major led massed band from 20 Alberta communities

Right: Princess Diana reflects acute interest in ceremonies

Below: Scarlet-coated Mounties from Ottawa carried Canada's flag into stadium

The Secretary of State then invited His Royal Highness to officially declare the Games open.

There was an almost reverent silence when twenty-two members of the Royal Canadian Mounted Police detachment from Ottawa raised the flag of the host country and the crowd stood as one to sing O'Canada. It was sharply contrasted by the appearance of several hundred young dancers in brightly colored skirts in a light, yet moving musical salute to Kaleidoscope '83, the cultural component of the Games. They were accompanied by a massed choir of three hundred children.

Take my hand brother, take my hand sister
Take my hand and together we will see
That the sun will shine above
And we'll build a new world of love
A world of peace where every man is free
Take my hand, little children, take my hand
EVERYBODY
Life is grand when you're walking hand in hand...

"Ladies and Gentlemen... The Entrance of the Athletes!"

Rhythmic applause greeted Mihai Simion, a member of Romania's waterpolo team, when he led his sixty-three member delegation onto the track. Romania, as host country for the previous Universiade at Bucharest, was accorded the honour of leading the athletes into the stadium.

The Belgians broke ranks to photograph Princess Diana. Members of the British team unveiled individual cards spelling out HAPPY BIRTHDAY DIANA as they passed the Royal box. A fresh wave of applause greeted each new team, and each in turn waved back. There was an extended, polite ovation for the Soviets and a boisterous reception for the large United States team.

CANADA! The host country was entering the Stadium.

Patriotism ran wild. The emotion of the moment was choking. Even the protocol-conscious Japanese stepped out of line to applaud the host team. The Americans charged to the edge of the track to clap and cheer their northern neighbours home.

The formal welcome to the athletes, dignitaries, and guests was extended by FISU President, Dr. Nebiolo and Ed Zemrau, President of the Edmonton Organizing Committee. Mr. Zemrau paid special tribute to the participating countries for their support of the Games and to the nineteen thousand volunteers whose "generosity and heart contributed immeasurably to the success and enjoyment of the Games."

Left: Dr. Nebiolo, Prince Charles, Hon. Serge Joyal applaude arrival of the athletes

Below: Spectators, Athletes, Performers all in place for the Opening festivities

23

Dr. Nebiolo, beginning his twenty-second year as FISU President, emphasized the ideals underlying the Games.

"Students of all races and religions and political creeds are assembled here to participate in a friendly, peaceful festival of sport... to demonstrate once again the desire of youth to meet and compete in a spirit of good will. This is the message our movement wants to give the whole world."

The arrival of the ceremonial torch, carried into the stadium by Graham Smith, swimming star of the 1978 Commonwealth Games, and Tracy Mills, a member of Canada's national volleyball team, generated another standing ovation. The flame tower, located high on the north concourse, was donated to the Games by the Sawridge Indian Band of Slave Lake, Alberta. It was constructed in the shape of a dove, a symbol of the Games and of international peace. The two young Edmonton athletes touched the flame to the ceremonial urn, capping a thirteen thousand-kilometre journey from Sofia, Bulgaria, site of the 1983 Winter Universiade, to St. John's Newfoundland and across all ten Canadian provinces and two territories to its final destination at Edmonton thirty-six days later.

The raising of the FISU flag to the accompaniment of the Universiade Hymn, Gaudeamus Igitur, added yet another wave of emotion to the ceremony. The Athletes' Oath was taken by Ian Newhouse of Edmonton and Sylvie Bernier of Montreal.

The Canadian Brass, one of the foremost bands in the country, paid a special musical salute to the athletes. WUGIE, the wise athletic owl whose promotional appearances across the country endeared him to young and old alike, was centre stage for his final formal appearance.

The finale was a stirring, hand-clappin' foot-stompin' salute to Canada. Sports and entertainment celebrities representing the 10 provinces and two territories -- Wayne Gretzky, Karen Magnussen, Toller Cranston, Gordie Howe, Don Herron, Karen Baldwin, John Allan Cameron, Diane Jones Konihowski, Eric Fryer, Susan Nattrass, Wilf Paiement, and Expo Ernie, sent good luck messages via the stadium scoreboard. The Cathy Hauptman Dancers skipped into Manitoba; the McDade Family Band marched into Newfoundland and the Calgary Fiddlers paid a roaring musical salute to host Alberta.

Left: Edmonton natives Graham Smith and Tracy Mills carry ceremonial Torch into stadium

Below: Sylvie Bernier, Alex Bauman, Ian Newhouse took oath on behalf of the athletes

A solemn moment when the flag of FISU is escorted past the Royal box

Dove of Peace flame tower was special project of Sawridge Indian Band

A colourful salute to International Federation of University Sports

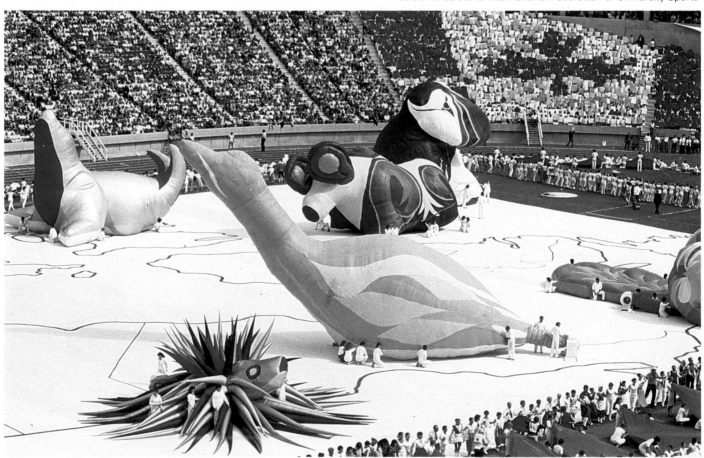

Giant, inflatible animals native to Provinces and Territories were a 'big' hit

Volunteers and colorful parasols were part of the spectacular opening

Cape Breton Symphony marched into Nova Scotia for musical salute

A dozen gigantic inflatible animals native to the provinces and territories -- a mammoth salmon representing British Columbia; a New Brunswick moose; polar bear from the Yukon; beaver from Quebec; puffin from Nova Scotia; Prince Edward Island lobster; walrus from the Northwest Territories; Saskatchewan porcupine; Ontario snow goose -- was a multi-coloured, nylon sensation.

The entire production cast of sixty-five hundred performers including almost three thousand student flashcard holders, formed a border for the magnificent infield portrait. Nine Snowbird jets passed in ceremonial salute and the sky filled with a crackling, colorful display of fireworks in a final tribute to Canada Day.

Canada is the Rocky Mountains
Canada is Prince Edward Island
Canada is a country made for love
Canada is a Prairie cowboy
Canada is a Yukon miner
Canada is a country made for love

Left: WUGIE has his place in the sun during Games' Opening Ceremonies

Right: Michael Spottel (388) of France took early lead over Italy's Giovanni D'Aleo and Evgeny Okorokov of the Soviet Union in the gruelling marathon. Spottel finished third. D'Aleo was second while the Soviet was fifth. The race was won by another Italian, Alessio Faustini.

Athletics

The agony of victory etched into Dave Steen's face was the joy that triggered a spontaneous, standing ovation at Commonwealth Stadium.

It was an emotional salute to an athlete who fought off the pain of a sprained left ankle and an aching back to run the fastest 1500-metre race of his life. Steen finished second in this final event of the men's decathlon but his time earned him 703 points and the gold medal by a scant 45 points over Herbert Peter of the Federal Republic of Germany.

Right: Canada's Dave Steen wins long jump event in decathlon

Below: A proud Dave Steen wears decathlon gold

Mexico's Premio Sebastian waddles into the lead of the 20km walk but it was Canada's Guillaume Leblanc (28) who was first the next time the field entered the stadium. The first seven finishers bettered the existing Games' record.

Canada's Molly Killingbeck steps over fallen Easter Gabriel of the United States (679) on her way to a silver medal in the women's 4 × 100 relay.

Steen's effort was representative of the grit Canada's track and field athletes displayed at the 1983 World University Games. They won thirteen medals; they set two Universiade records, eight Canadian Open records and two Commonwealth Games marks. It was Canada's best performance at an international games.

There was Guillaume Leblanc, a twenty-one-year-old University of Montreal student from Sept-Iles, Quebec who bolted from international obscurity to win the twenty-kilometre walk and Canada's first gold medal in athletics since 1965.

Leblanc set a blistering pace to win the event in one hour, twenty-four minutes and 2.89 seconds to establish records for the University Games, Commonwealth, and Canada. This was two minutes faster than his previous best time despite a brief stop at the seventeen-kilometre mark.

Below: Sergei Pougach of USSR displays shot put form

Right: John Amabile of the U.S. prepares javelin throw

Far right: Strained facial expression of Orville Peterson from U.S. reflects effort in discus

36

"The cramps in my stomach were very bad," said Guillaume. "I just couldn't go on. I knew when I stopped that I had to do it fast..."

Leblanc did it fast enough to defeat 1980 Olympic champion Maurizio Damilano of Italy by ninety metres.

The heat, the hills and the loneliness took its toll in the women's marathon, -- the first marathon for women at an international games -- but Kathy Roberts of London, Ontario, found fresh strength in the cheering of Canadian spectators along the forty-two-kilometre route and persevered for a silver medal. Three of her teammates dropped out.

"It's hard to describe how much it hurts," Roberts said following the race, "but there were people out there cheering for me and Canada and I didn't want to let them down."

And Molly Killingbeck of York University in Toronto..

Opposite upper: Gerald Heinrich of France clears the pole vault

Opposite lower: Edmonton's Ian Newhouse displays form in men's 400m hurdles

Left: Tightly-bunched field in women's 100m hurdles

Below: Italy's Fredrico Secchi gave it his all in long jump

Gerardo Alcala of Mexico (871) has the inside track on the field in the men's 5000m final. Fathi Baccouche of Tunisia (270) was first declared the winner as a result of disqualifications to Stephen Harris of Great Britain, Canada's Paul Williams (20) and Agapius Amo of Tanzania. The International Jury later reversed its decision and awarded the race to Harris.

Ekaterina Smirnova managed only a fifth place in the long jump of the women's heptathlon but did exceedingly better in six other events to win the gold medal.

Molly had become accustomed to the back spasms which set in AFTER a race but didn't count on their happening DURING the final of the women's 400-metre race. Killingbeck simply gritted her teeth and ran flat out over the last thirty metres. She won a silver medal.

Killingbeck and Maritia Payne, who had just finished winning her heat in the women's 200-metre race, teamed with Charmaine Crooks and Jillian Richardson to run the 4x400 metre relay together for the first time... and won yet another silver, chasing the Soviet Union to a Games' record.

Nigeria's track and field contingent - all eight of them -- set the major powers on their heels by winning five gold medals. They swept the sprint titles. Chidi Imoh won the prestigous 100-metre race with Canada's Desai Williams nipping favoured Sam Graddy of the United States for the silver. Ino Egunike won the 200-metre race over Elliott Quow of the U.S., who would later win the silver at the Helsinki World Championships. Sunday Uti pulled off the biggest upset in winning the gold medal for the 400-metre race, beating 1980 Olympic champion Victor Markin of the Soviet Union and Sunder Nix of the U.S., who was ranked No. 1 in the world. Nix also finished third at Helsinki.

Anisoara Cusmir of Romania couldn't duplicate the world record she set in the women's long jump just three weeks prior to the Edmonton Universiade but she bettered the Games' record on her first three jumps to win the gold medal over Zvetlana Zorina of the Soviet Union and Valy Ionesc of Romania. Ionescu was ranked No. 1 in the world.

Cuba's Luis Marino Delis, No. 1 in the world in the men's discus, easily won the gold with a Games' record throw but Willie Gault of the U.S., ranked No. 2 in the world in the 110-metre hurdles, was upset by Andrei Prokofyev of the Soviet Union. Canada's Mark McCoy finished .08 seconds behind Gault to claim the bronze.

Tamara Bykova, who would go on to win the women's high jump at the World Championships and follow it up with a world record performance two weeks later, won the gold at Edmonton, adding two metres to the Universiade record but missing on her attempt for the world record.

Opposite, upper: Four young Canadian gals celebrate their silver medal victory in the 4 × 100m relay. From the left are Angella Taylor, Molly Killingbeck, Tanya Brothers and Marita Payne.

Opposite, lower: Soviet Alexander Kharlov leads tightly-bunched field in 400m hurdles final

Below: Christopher Bunyan of Great Britain (566) took the lead midway through the men's marathon over Mike Spottel of France and Yakov Tolstikov of the Soviet Union. Bunyan fell back to eighth at the finish with Spottel hanging on for third and Tolstikov sixth.

Canada's Milt Ottey was virtually conceded the gold in the men's high jump. He had ranked No. 1 in the world in 1982. It was obvious however, that Ottey had not fully recovered from a hairline ankle fracture he incurred six months earlier. He finished eleventh in the twenty-man field. Igor Paklin won the event with a Games' record leap of 2.31 metres.

Canada's Angella Taylor was a blink shy of winning the women's 100-metre event. Taylor finished third behind Beverley King of Great Britain and Randy Givens of the U.S. A mere .04 seconds separated the first three finishers. Surprisingly, the men's 10,000-metre was even closer. It required a television replay to show that a twenty-two-year old University of Tokyo student, Shuichi Yoneshinge, had out-lunged Agapius Amo of Tanzania by .02 seconds.

Above: Canada's Denise Fillion clears the high jump bar in women's heptathlon

Left: Great Britain's Judith Livermore won bronze medal in women's heptathlon

Kang Giang Weng of China bends into the pole vault during men's decathlon

The camera frames the start of the men's 110m hurdles event in the decathlon

Poland's Ryszard Ostrowski (320) nips Graham Williamson of Britain and Mohamed Alouini of Tunisia in the men's 800m final. The first five finishers were separated by 0.58 seconds.

Canada's Desai Williams (13) turns it on for silver medal in men's 4 × 100 relay

Charles Barkley (4) of the U.S. leaps to block shot by Canada's Danny Meagher (right) while Gerald Kazanowski (8) and Greg Wiltjer (14) wait for a rebound during exciting Canada-U.S. semifinal.

Basketball

A big Canadian flag was unfurled and fifteen exhilarated Canadian basketball players zoomed it around the floor at the new Universiade Pavilion.

The yet-standing crowd of ten thousand who watched Canada defeat Olympic champion Yugoslavia 83-68 in the gold medal game, was drunk with joy.

Gathered under their basket, the Canadians hoisted each other rim-high to snip a cord in a symbolic gesture of victory.

One strand remained.

In a touching, fitting tribute to their coach and architect of Canada's first gold medal in basketball at a World University Games, the players charged to the sidelines and pulled Jack Donohue onto the floor. Then they stood him twelve feet tall to make the final cut.

Moments later, Coach Donohue, his eyes swollen with tears of pride, stood with his players on the victory podium, flanked by Yugoslavia and the United States, to receive his gold medal.

It was a moment to be savoured.

This was one of Canada's finest hours in international basketball. Not since the 1936 Berlin Olympics had Canada won a medal in men's basketball at a world games. Except for that silver medal, Canada had never finished better than tenth at either the Olympics or the World Championships until Donohue was hired to coach the national team in 1972. Two years later, Canada placed eighth at the world championships, and in 1976, caught the attention of the international community by finishing fourth at the Montreal Olympics, losing the bronze medal game to Yugoslavia.

Right: The defensive dominance of Canada's Eli Pasquale (6) over Yugoslavia's young scoring star Drazen Petrovic was a key to Canada's gold medal victory.

Below, left: Deborah Lee of U.S. prepares for foul shot

Below: Paul Ramirez of Cuba puts move on Andre Goode of U.S. in bronze medal game

Donohue's teams had consistently courted international victory since 1976 but even while his teams were upsetting the Americans and the Soviets, losing only to the Soviets in the ten games they played at the 1981 Bucharest Universiade, there remained an air of indifference to basketball and Donohue's team across the country. That was why Canada's victory at Edmonton meant more than just a gold medal to Coach Donohue.

Finally, eleven years after this transplanted New York Irishman arrived in Canada to coach the national team, he had made believers of a doubting Canadian public.

"It's been an enjoyable but often frustrating eleven years," offered Donohue. "Even while we were beating the world powers, it seemed the Canadian public didn't care or perhaps didn't understand the significance of it all. I often chided Canadians whenever I spoke on the banquet circuit about their lack of patriotism. I think what they really needed was an opportunity to see for themselves just how good their national basketball team was and how much they had to be proud of.

Opposite: Kit Wing Ug (9) and Vicky Chung (10) of Hong Kong battle for ball against Tresa Spaulding of the U.S. The Americans went on to a gold medal victory over Romania.

Right: Canada-U.S. semifinal was close affair

Below: Deborah Huband (7) of Canada defends against Spain

Britain's Robert Donaldson (12) and Zhaoguang Ji (14) of China can only wait on Donaldson's shot as it spins around the rim. The ball didn't go in and China went on to a victory which clinched fifth place.

Canada's Anna Pendergast (6) battles Biljana Majsrorovic of Yugoslavia for possession

"There wasn't anything wrong with their national pride in Edmonton. It was fantastic. And now that they've had a taste, I think basketball can do nothing but prosper in this country."

In Edmonton, Donohue's team had whipped up a large measure of patriotic fervour by upsetting the favoured United States 85-77 in a semi-final game. It set the euphoric stage for the final against Yugoslavia, which had beaten Canada by nine points earlier in the tournament.

The Miracle on Wood was never in doubt. The Canadians, fueled by the emotion of the moment, raced to a 47-28 halftime lead and limited Yugoslavia's brilliant eighteen-year-old guard, Drazel Petrovic, to a meagre four points. He was completely overshadowed by an equally brilliant Canadian guard, Eli Pasquale. Yugoslavia never came closer than thirteen points, and with ten minutes remaining, the countdown to gold had already begun.

Canada's women's team came into the tournament with a string of international bronze-medal successes behind it and was considered a shoo-in for a medal. Controversy, however, shredded their medal aspirations.

Coach Don McCrae was relieved of his job only days before the tournament and eight of his players quit in protest. McCrae was eventually reinstated -- after the Games -- but by then the United States had overcome an early-game deficit against Romania and posted an 83-61 victory for the gold medal. Yugoslavia won the bronze, defeating the Peoples' Republic of China 59-46.

Right: Eric Turner of U.S. drives for basket against Cuba's Alberto Maturell Ramos

Below: Fish eye lens of the camera catches crowd and court during U.S.-Canada semifinal

Opposite upper: FISU President Dr. Primo Nebiolo presented gold medals to Canadian basketball team

Opposite lower: Canada's men's basketball team acknowledges the ovation of the partisan Canadian spectators following their gold medal victory over Yugoslavia. It was the first gold medal won by Canada in Universiade basketball play.

Above: It was a golden moment for Canada in international basketball when coach Jack Donohue was lifted twelve feet into the air by his players and handed the scissors to cut the final strand of net, symbolic of their victory over Yugoslavia in the gold medal game.

Cycling

Cycle: a recurrent pattern of events ...

This definition particularly suited the performance of twenty-five Soviet cyclists at the 1983 World University Games.

The regularity with which Soviets were called to the victory podium was indeed recurrent. It was almost monotonous. They won twenty-one medals, six more than all of the other countries combined. Ten gold. Five silver. Six bronze ... in 12 races!

Left: The pack begins to thin in gruelling men's road race

Below: France's Isabelle Nicoloso (167) and Canada's Beth Tabor (084) play cat and mouse in women's sprint. Nicoloso went on to win the silver medal while Tabor finished a credible sixth.

Right: Costica Paraschiv (088) of Romania drafts behind Bernardus Zoont Jens of Holland (067) as the field in men's road race winds uphill through Groat Road portion of the course.

Stephane Wernimont of Belgium takes the short route in individual points race

A victorious Sergio Scremin of Italy in the men's road race

Twisted frames and skinned knees punctuated road race

61

Only Italy's Sergio Scremin and French champion Isabella Nicoloso were able to crack the Soviet juggernaut and avert their sweep of victories.

Scremin, however, won the most prestigious event of all, the gruelling 170-kilometre road race on a challenging and punishing 11.3-kilometre circuit. For almost four hours, Scremin drafted behind Pavel Muzhitsky, the race favourite and best sprinter for the Soviets. Fully cognizant of the blocking tactics of the Soviets which elicited complaints by other competitors, Scremin took the wide side of the road and blasted out of a jostling pack two hundred metres from the finish. He nipped Muzhitsky by half a wheel.

Nicoloso won the women's individual points race over Soviet double gold medalist Erika Salouimaee, who had earlier beaten Nicoloso in a hotly-contested women's sprint final. The Soviet took Nicoloso high on the steep bank, twice rammed her front wheel and broke away with a hundred and twenty metres remaining to win the gold. The French protest was sustained, forcing a rerun which the Soviet won easily.

Nadejda Kibardina, 1981 world champion in the women's pursuit, was the predominant medalist. She won two gold and two bronze. Tamara Poliakova, also of the Soviet Union, won gold, silver, and bronze while Viktor Manakov, a member of the Soviet gold medal pursuit team at the 1980 Olympics, won the individual men's points title and added a silver in the men's pursuit behind Alexander Krasnov, a member of the 1982 Soviet world champion pursuit team.

Canada's Alex Stieda and Guiling Yang of China each won bronze medals, Steida in the individual men's pursuit and Yang in the women's sprint. These were the first medals won by their countries in cycling at the University Games and for China, it was its first cycling medal in any international games.

Two other Canadians performed extremely well. Twenty-year-old Marie Claude Audet of La Salle, Quebec, and twenty-one-year-old Ross Chafe of Greenfield Park, Quebec, finished fourth in the women's sprint and men's road race respectively.

Right: Gold medalist Erika Saloumiaee (141) of USSR and Cristy Hegg of USA in women's sprint

Below: Mexico's Rafael Gonzdiez (101) leads the Road Race pack

Left: Canada's Garry Altwasser in Individual Pursuit
Right: Canada's Randy Sageman shows form in 3 metre Springboard

Diving

It was a special moment in international sport when Greg Louganis, Nikolay Drozhzhin and Tan Liangde stepped onto the victory platform to receive their diving medals at the 1983 World University Games.

It marked the first time athletes from the United States, Soviet Union and the Peoples' Republic of China stood together for a medals presentation at a world games. It was an occurrence twice repeated in three other diving events.

Below: Canada's Elizabeth McKay prepares for platform dive

Right: Wei Lu of China shows gold medal form in women's platform event

Opposite,upper: Greg Louganis of USA was premier diver at Universiade

Opposite, lower: The People's Republic of China won four medals in diving at Universiade '83 including gold in the two events for women.

66

China didn't enter world competition, save for a token appearance at the 1932 Los Angeles Olympics, until the 1978 World University Games in Mexico City. However, its divers have been attracting world attention for almost ten years. They first won four gold medals at the seventh Asian Games in 1974, then four gold and four silver medals at the 1978 Asian Games. In 1980, the Chinese participated in five major international games, winning sixteen gold medals in twenty events against the U.S.A., the U.S.S.R. and the Democratic Republic of Germany. In 1981 at the University Games in Bucharest, China won three of four gold medals.

In Edmonton, however, they faced the stiffest competition of all. The field included Louganis, the premier men's diver in the world and reigning champion in both the 3-metre springboard and the 10-metre platform events; Alexander Portnov who won the 3-metre springboard gold at the Moscow Olympics. Vladimir Alemik, silver medalist in the 10-metre platform at the Moscow Olympics; Wendy Wyland and Megan Neyer, current world champions in the 10-metre platform and 3 metre springboard respectively, and Irina Kalinina, the 1980 Olympics gold medalist and world champion in the 10-metre tower event from 1975 to 1979.

Louganis performed brilliantly to retain his titles. He won the 3-metre springboard gold by a

whopping 55 points over Drozhzhin with Liangde and a second Chinese diver, Li Kongzehng, finishing third and fourth. Louganis had a more difficult time in the platform event. He trailed Tong Hui of China by 19.29 points after eight of ten dives but pulled off two exceptional dives worth 82.17 and 81.60 points respectively to win the title by a scant seven points.

The Chinese pulled major upsets in both women's events. Shi Meiquin, 23, of Shanghai, who was second in the springboard event at the 1982 World Cup, defeated Neyer by 25 points to win the gold medal. Canada's Sylvie Bernier narrowly missed winning the silver, finishing only 2.8 points behind Neyer for the bronze.

Lu Wei, 18, winner of the women's platform title at the ninth Asian Games in New Delhi last December, outclassed the field at Edmonton. Despite scoring a mediocre 32.19 points on her final dive, she finished 31 points better than Wyland and 39 points more than bronze medalist Tatiana Beliakova of the U.S.S.R.

Right: Minimum of 'splash' reflects a perfect entry.

Below: The diving grace of platform champion Wei Lu

Opposite, top-left: Culture Minister Mary LeMessurier presents bronze to Sylvie Bernier

Opposite, top-right: International judges found competition keen in women's diving

Opposite lower: Jennifer Tysdale of Canada scored high on this dive

Fencing

Philion rose slowly to her feet.
Bing. Bing.
It was over.
Madeline Philion. Champion in the hearts of all.

There were tears of joy and cries of anguish, shouts of encouragement and gestures of defiance. Spectators dodged security personnel to embrace victors, and losers threatened to hurdle barricades to do verbal battle with the spectators

Such was the emotional roller coaster called fencing at the 1983 World University Games.

Italy ruled the competition almost as though by divine right. The country that played a major role in the development of fencing three hundred years ago, won nine medals including five gold. The Italians, bent on skinning the proverbial Russian bear which had been their long-standing international nemesis, sent their strongest team to these Games. It included Mauro Numa, National and European champion and defending gold medalist in the foil at Bucharest in 1981. He led Italy to a resounding 9-1 victory over the Soviets in the team foil and successfully defended his Universiade title in the individual foil over Didier Lemange of France.

Surprisingly, however, it was a twenty-year-old Canadian who stood above the fencing giants of Europe, winning a bronze medal in the individual foil -- the first medal won by a Canadian in the history on international fencing.

Madeline Philion was the heroine of the Games. The lithesome university physical education student from Laval, Quebec, shed a few tears of frustration after losing two matches in the morning elimination pool but bounced back to win an exciting quarter-final fight, 8-7, against Clara Alfonso Freire of Cuba. In the semi-final, Philion came from behind a 5-3 deficit to tie Qungyuan Zhu of China 5-5 and win the fight 5-4 when Zhu was penalized a point for a second body infraction just as time ran out. That victory thrust Philion into the medal round. She lost to No. 1 seed Elizabeth Guzganu of Romania but scored a stunning 6-5 victory over 1980 Olympic gold medalist Pascale Trinquet of France in the bronze medal fight.

Philion fell behind 3-2, twice came back to tie the fight at 5-5 and went ahead 6-5 late in the match. Philion fell to the floor, rocked on her knees and grabbed her head. The reality of a possible medal struck her that hard.

Above: Italy's Mauro Numa was numero uno in men's foil

Opposite: Didier Lemenage of France won the silver medal in men's individual foil

71

Canada's Madeline Philion reflects the exhilaration of her bronze
medal victory over 1980 Olympic champion Pascale Trinquet of France
in the individual foil. It was the first medal won by a Canadian in
international fencing.

Cuba's Clara Alfonso Freire, left, defends against Tatiana Petrova of USSR

Gymnastics

World champion Yuri Korolev and Natalia Yurchenko of the Soviet Union were the dominant gymnasts at the 1983 World University Games, but for another champion, all that glittered wasn't gold, silver or bronze.

While Korolev and Yurchenko gave brilliant performances, amassing nine of a possible fourteen medals, including seven of twelve in the individual events, the shiniest, most treasured 'medal' of all went to Phillipe Chartrand, an unheralded Canadian substitute who didn't learn he would compete until four days prior to the Games.

Chartrand, 19, of Laval, Quebec, 'won' the complete horizontal bar he competed on. It was given to him by the apparatus manufacturers as a memento of the most outstanding performance by a Canadian in the history of gymnastics. Not only did Chartrand win the gold medal in a stunning upset of the world champion, he gave Canada its first gold medal for gymnastics in an international games and served due notice on the gymnastics fraternity of a Canadian presence in future world events.

His mark of 9.95 on the horizontal bars was the highest awarded at the Games.

Chartrand remembers the "explosion" when he landed a faultless triple sommersault on his dismount.

"I knew in my mind I did well but I couldn't believe the explosion by the crowd. It was ... fantastic," he said. "I couldn't believe the standing ovation -- again - after the marks were announced."

Left: Romania's Octavian Loansiu displays form on still rings

Right: Anita Botnen won bronze for Canada on the balance beam

Valentin Pintea of Romania performs on the horizontal bar

Emilian Nicula of Romania works floor exercise routine

Canada's Brad Peters on the Pommel horse

Cuba's Elsa Chivas Cleger performs on the balance beam

It was a fitting reward for a young gymnast who rides the streetcar and bus six days a week -- sometimes twice a day -- from his home in Laval to the Immaculate Conception gymnasium in Montreal where he trains four to six hours almost daily.

Chartrand was a late replacement for Dan Gaudet, Canada's No. 1 men's gymnast, who injured a thumb while training for the Games.

"This was by far the best we've ever done in international competition," said Canadian men's coach Andre Simard. Canadian gymnasts won three other medals. They went to seventeen-year-old Anita Botnen from West Vancouver who was just 0.5 points shy of a silver and won a bronze on the balance beam; Warren Long, who won a silver in the men's vault; and the Canadian women's team, which won a bronze for the team event.

Opposite, right: Wen Jia of China won silver medal on the balance beam

Right: The athletic grace of Canada's Elfi Schlegel

Below: Roni Lynn Barrios of USA performs floor exercise

Phillipe Chartrand of Canada stunned the gymnastics world with a
gold medal performance on the horizontal bars

Alaxender Pogorelov of USSR performs difficult Jaegar Salto on horizontal bars

Jana Gajdosova of Czechoslovakia on the uneven bars

Yurchenko, the 1982 World Cup Champion from Norilsk, north of the Arctic Circle, was the class of the women's competition, winning five of a possible six golds while finishing fourth in the floor exercises. She won the all-around title with first-place scores in each of the four disciplines. Her points total was .65 ahead of Mihaela Riciu of Romania and Olympic Games silver medalist Emilia Eberle, also of Romania, who tied for second.

Korolev led the Soviet men to a sweep of the medals in the all-around competition and repeated as all-around Universiade champion with four golds and a silver.

Chartrand, meanwhile, donated his coveted horizontal bar award to the Immaculate Conception Gym Club in Montreal for the training of other potential champions.

Opposite, Left: Canada's Frank Nutzenberger is a study of concentration on the parallel bars

Left: Jim Hartung of USA scored high on parallel bars

Below: Romania's Nadia Comaneci, the perfect '10' at the 1976 Montreal Olympics and premier women's gymnast for five years, served as an assistant trainer for the Romanian team at Edmonton

Swimming

The story of swimming at the 1984 Los Angeles Olympics may have been foretold in Edmonton during the 1983 World University Games.

The Soviet Union simply blew everybody out of the water, leaving in their wake at the Kinsmen Aquatic Centre eighteen records; twenty-two gold medals in the twenty-nine events, while achieving the largest medal haul for one event -- thirty-four -- in the sixty-year history of the Games. It augurs well for their chances at Los Angeles.

The quality of competition provided by two hundred and sixty-one swimmers from thirty-three countries was the highest in Games history, reflected in the fact that fifty-seven individuals and teams bettered previous records, wiping out all fifteen men's records and ten of fourteen women's marks. The first five finishers in the men's 400-metre freestyle bettered the existing record and the first four finishers surpassed the existing games' record in six other events.

The Soviets were awesome. Not since the United States won a then-record twenty-two medals in the pool at the 1967 Tokyo Games, has one country dominated an event as the Soviets dominated swimming at Edmonton.

Vladimir Salnikov, twenty-one-year-old world record holder in the 400-metre and 1500-metre freestyle events, did as he was expected to do with record gold medal performances in his specialties, obliterating existing marks by twenty seconds in both races.

It was two comparative Soviet unknowns, however, who ruled the waves in Edmonton. Irini Laricheva, 19, of Moscow, stamped herself one of the favourites for the Olympics in the freestyle events with a smashing five-gold-medal effort which included record performances in 200-metre, 400-metre and 4x100-metre freestyle relay.

Left: Irina Larichiva from Moscow won five gold medals in swimming. Here she stands for medal ceremony with Annelies Kraus of Holland, left, and Tammy Thomas of the United States, right, following the women's 100-metre freestyle final.

Below: The Soviets won the 4 × 100 freestyle women's relay in Games record time. From the left are Irinia Gerasimova, Irina Sergeeva, Tatiana Kurnikova and Irina Laricheva. The U.S. won the silver, also beating the Games record and Canada won the bronze.

Irina Gerasimova, twenty-one-year-old Soviet champion in three freestyle events, emerged with four golds and a bronze and four Games' records. Larisa Gorchakova and Larisa Belokon each won three golds with Belokon setting records in all three events. The only 'outsider' to crack the Soviet domination was Australia's Susie Woodhouse with record swims in the 100-metre and 200-metre butterfly races.

Canada's thirty-member team generated most of the excitement for the partisan crowds which jammed the Kinsmen Centre to capacity throughout the competition.

Canadians won fourteen medals in the pool, only four fewer than the United States whose medal count dropped by almost fifty percent from the 1981 Bucharest Games.

Alex Bauman from Laurentian University at Sudbury won six medals but more significantly for him, clearly proved to the swimming world that a nagging shoulder injury which threatened to end his young career eighteen months earlier, no longer was a factor in his quest for Olympic gold.

Right: Canada's Ken Fitzpatrick in 100-metre breaststroke

Below: Sergei Smiryagin of the USSR clenches fist in victory after winning men's 100-metre freestyle in record time.

Opposite: Valdimir Salnikov of the Soviet Union, centre, re-confirmed his ranking as No. 1 1500-metre swimmer in the world by winning the gold at Universiade '83. Countryman Svyatosal Semenov, left, was second and Lawrence Hayes of the United States third in the exciting final.

Bauman, accorded the honour of carrying the Canadian flag in the Opening Ceremonies, raised the patriotic fervor of the host Canadian spectators by stepping to the starting pads with the maple leaf tatooed over his heart.

He won two golds in record times, a silver and three bronze. His most glittering performance came in the 200-metre individual medley over 1980 Olympic champion Alexandre Siderenko of the Soviet Union and Brazil's Ricardo Prado, who holds the world record in the 400-metre medley. Bauman drove the wall in two minutes, 2.29 seconds -- 0.04 seconds off the world record he established at a tri-meet with the Soviets and West Germany at Heidleberg in July 1982.

In April, Bauman's right shoulder popped during training in Sudbury. The incessant throbbing of pain forced him to quit training for two months. He attempted a comeback but was forced out again for another three-month period while he visited doctors looking for a cure.

Below: Alex Bauman and maple leaf tatoo over his heart

Right: Alex Bauman of Canada set Games' record in 400-metre individual medley. Here he stands for Games' Hymn flanked by silver medalist Lawrence Hayes, left, of the United States and Brazil's Ricardo Prado who won bronze.

Opposite, upper: Alexei Markovsky of the USSR, set a new record in the 100-metre butterfly

Opposite, lower: Christy Woolger of the U.S., Canada's Natalie Gingras and Grazyna of Poland off to good start in women's 400-metre individual medley

"I saw a doctor in London, Ontario. He said to keep swimming to pain level. He gave me a lot of exercises to do and since that time I haven't had the problem," said Bauman.

Canada's third gold in the pool -- two more that the U.S. team won here -- went to Mike West, 18, of Kitchener-Waterloo. He won the 100-metre backstroke with a 56.64 clocking that gave him the Games record, Canadian record, and Commonwealth record. He finished a mere 0.07 seconds ahead of Vladimir Shemetov and Victor Kuznetsov, who was only one-tenth of one second shy of the gold.

Opposite: Canada's Lori Borsholt won a bronze in the women's 200-metre breaststroke

Left: Julie Daigneault of Canada won bronze in women's 800-metre freestyle

Below: Robertas Zhulpa of the USSR edged Japan's Shigehiro Takahashi in men's 200-metre breaststroke

Tennis

The tallest trees in the forest were felled early and often in an amazing string of tennis upsets at the 1983 World University Games.

These were the casualties:

Lucia Romanov, Romania; No. 1 seed in the women's singles. Silver medalist at the 1981 Games at Bucharest.

Vladim Borisov, Soviet Union; No. 2 seed nationally, No. 2 seed men's singles at Universiade '83. Gold medalist 1979 Mexico Universiade.

Alexander Zverev, Soviet Union; No. 1 seed nationally, No. 1 seed Universiade in the men's singles.

Martin Wostenholme, Canada's No. 1 seed men's singles and No. 1 amateur in Canada.

Lucia and Maria Romanov, Romania; No. 1 seeds women's doubles.

Li Shuhua and Ma Kegin; People's Republic of China; Gold medalists men's doubles 1983 Asian Games; ranked No. 2 and No. 3 in China.

Laurentia Bucur and Adrian Marcu, Romania; No. 1 seeds men's doubles Universiade '83.

Svetlana Cherneva and Yuri Filev, Soviet Union; No. 1 seeds mixed doubles Universiade '83.

Cherneva and Olga Zaytseva, Soviet Union; No. 1 seeds women's doubles Universiade '83.

Three young Canadians headed the list of giant killers in an event punctuated by two days of heavy rain, four days of unbridled spectator enthusiasm and an unending collapse of top – seeded players who didn't win an event.

Upset followed upset. Unseeded Jill Heatherington of Peterborough, Ontario, and Karen Dewis of London, Ontario, the No. 183-ranked women's amateur in the world, pulled off

Left: Canada's Nina Bland, foreground, returns backhand against Korea's Ya-Yang Park

Below: Cecilia Fernandez of the United States, centre, won the women's singles title over Olga Zaytseva, left, of the USSR and Romania's Lucia Romanov

one of the major surprises with a stunning 6-4, 6-3 victory over the No. 1 seeded Romanov sisters in the quarter-final round of women's doubles play. They went on to defeat Cornelia Dries and Kerstein Haas of West Germany in straight sets in the semi-final. That put them into the final against unseeded Kumiko Okamoto and Junko Kimura of Japan, who upset the No. 2 seeds, Zaytseva and Cherneva, in their semi-final.

Canada came from behind to win the first medal within their grasp after trailing the third set 4-1. Heatherington and Dewis battled desperately for survival and tied the set, 4-4. Japan took a one-game lead three times only to have the Canadians come back and tie the set at seven games each. The flag-waving and cheering among supporters from both countries died out in a dramatic tie-breaker which went to a fifteenth game before Canada won, giving them an 8-7 lead in sets. Heatherington and Dewis won the sixteenth game with comparative ease and claimed Canada's first gold medal in tennis at the University Games.

Opposite: Romania's No. 1 seed Lucia Romanov won bronze medal in women's singles

Right: Serve by Korea's Ya-Yang Park

Below: The United States dominated the men's singles. Fourth-seeded Richard Gallien, centre, won the gold medal while teammate Daniel Goldie won the silver and Alexander Zverev of the Soviet Union the bronze.

Angelo Binaghi helped Italy win silver medal in men's doubles

Karen Dewis, left, and Jill Heatherington struck gold for Canada in women's doubles

Moments later, Heatherington was back on the centre court again, teaming with Bill Jenkins of Toronto for another cliffhanger in the mixed doubles against West Germany. Canada won 7-6, 7-6 with both games going to a tie-breaker before a winner was determined.

Heatherington and Jenkins, who needed three sets to get past Romanov and Marcu in the quarterfinal, defeated Jennifer Goodling and Daniel Goldie of the United States in straight sets before scoring two exciting 7-6 victories over Dries and Jochen Settlemayer of France for Canada's second tennis gold.

U.S. players won three golds: the men's singles title by Richard Gallien, the No. 4 seed, over countryman Daniel Goldie; the women's singles by Cecilia Fernandez in three sets over Zaytseva; and the men's doubles with Jeff Arons and John Seveley winning a five-set thriller over Angelo Binaghi and Raimondo Bitti of Italy.

Opposite: Shuhdia Liu of China prepares return in men's singles play

Left: Germany's Jochen Settlemayer returns serve

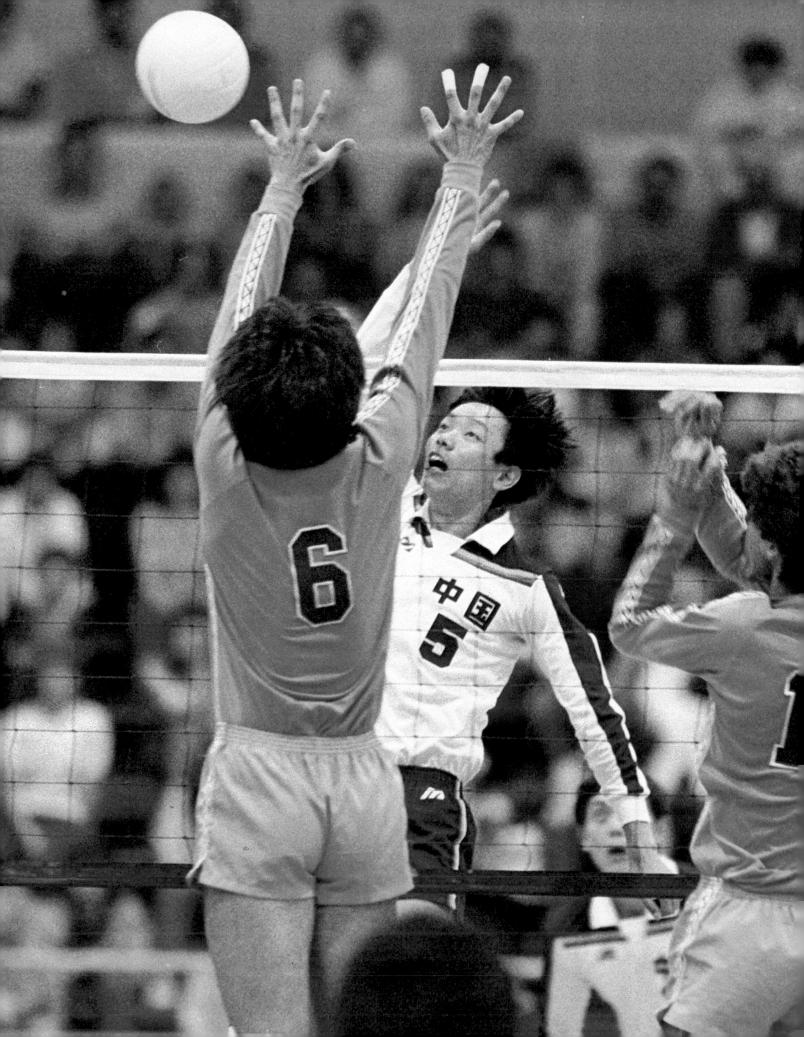

Volleyball

The speed of Korea.
The power of the Soviets.
The jumping of Cuba.
The team work of Japan.
These have been the distinctive playing styles of the countries that have dominated international volleyball since it was introduced as an Olympic discipline in 1964 at Tokyo.

Left: Ai Sheng Bad (5) of China made good on this shot against Mexico's J. Salvador Gonzalez

Right: Score point for Japan's Yasunori Kumada

Below: Brazil blocks against Japan in key men's match

They have also contributed immeasurably to the popularity of the game, which was developed in the United States just before the turn of the century and introduced to Europe by American troops during the First World War. Today there are more than one hundred and twenty countries which compete internationally and about sixty-three million players participating at the recreational level.

Variety was the spice which characterized the 1983 World University Games at Edmonton. Some fresh faces emerged to challenge the world's best. The People's Republic of China, gold medal winners in women's volleyball at the 1981 Bucharest Universiade and winners of the world championship at Lima, Peru, in 1982, were upset 3-1 in games by an aggressive, quick, and highly emotional team from Brazil. The disciplined team play of Japan, which won the gold medal at the 1976 Montreal Olympics and finished fourth behind China, Peru, and the United States at the 1982 world championship, prevailed in the bronze medal game against an inexperienced but aggressive Canadian team, 15-6, 15-10, and 15-7. It was the best performance by a Canadian women's team in international play. They finished ninth at Bucharest.

The freshest face and newest threat to the world powers in men's volleyball belonged to Canada. The Canadian team didn't win a set at the Montreal Olympics, but in Edmonton it rode a winning streak of twenty-five games -- a Universiade record -- into the gold medal game against Cuba.

Canada advanced to the final with a 3-0 victory over Korea while Cuba, fourth in the world championships in 1982, squeaked past Italy with the help of a controversial call in the final set with the score tied at thirteen. The referee ruled an Italian player was the last to touch an out-of-bounds ball. Cuba was awarded service and they went on to score the two points required for the win.

The Canadians started quickly in the final before an emotional crowd of thirteen-thousand at the Coliseum, winning the first game, losing the second, but leading 14-7 in the third before the Cubans, led by an awesome display of power by spiker Carlos Ruiz Lagargue, scored nine straight points to win the game and steal the momentum of the match.

Right: Luis Oviedo Bonilla (5) rises to occasion for Cuba in men's final against Canada

Below: Alan Coulter (6) and Tom Jones (7) of Canada in action against Cuba

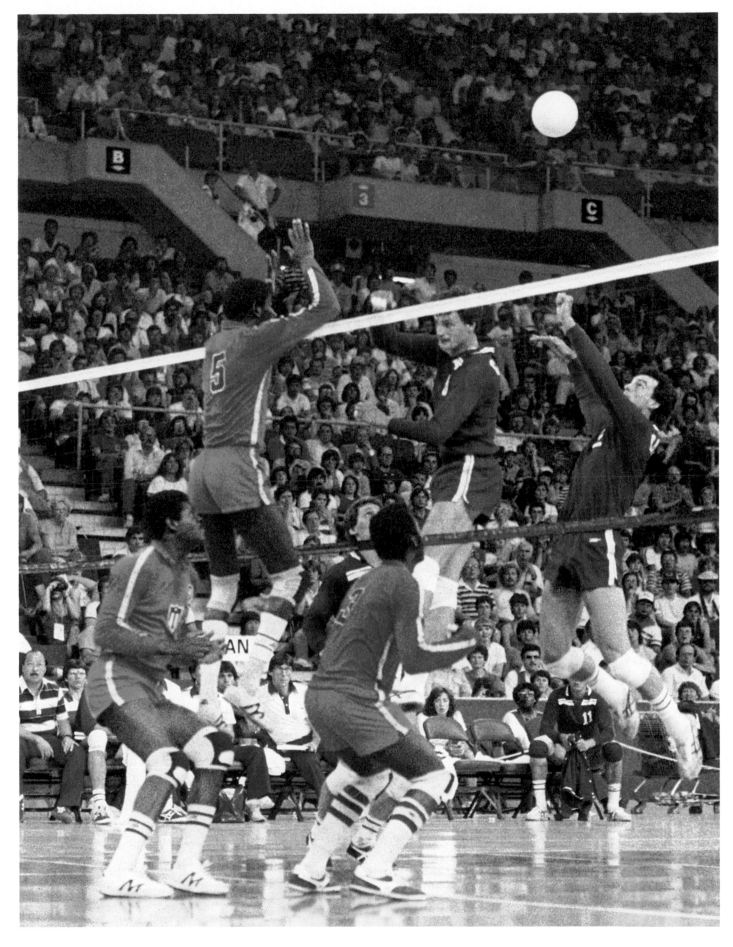

While the international community viewed Canada's performance with surprise, the Canadians viewed it as a slow but calculated rise to international prominence.

"We've been improving steadily since Ken Maeda came to us from Japan to coach the national team in 1978," said John Paulson of Volleyball Canada. "Ken's influence and the establishment of a national training centre in Calgary has done wonders for the program all across the country.

"Maeta introduced a unique style: the best features of good technical play which the Czechs are noted for; the power of the Soviets; the speed of the Koreans; and the team play of the Japanese. More important, Ken has allowed the individual strengths of the players to dictate the style of our game. The other qualities are built around this facet of our game. I guess you might call this particular style unorthodox by some standards but there isn't any question it's different. It's strictly Canadian ... and it's effective."

Opposite upper: Lucrecia Aragon (1) of Guatemala defends against silver medalist team from China

Opposite lower: The net was no barrier to conversation for Brigitte Lesage (8) of the U.S.!

Below: Canada turns back Japanese volley at the net

Right: Guiying Wang of China sets for spike

Switzerland in action against Mexico

Yasunori Kumada of Japan (11) drives point home against Canada

Above: Evgeny Shoumov (6) and Alexander Ivanov (4) of USSR missed this spike by Jordan

Opposite: Erlan Aiapbergenov of USSR and Italy's Riccardo Tempestini (3) swim for loose ball. The Soviets won the game 12-10 and went on to claim the gold medal.

Waterpolo

It was the classic confrontation.
United States against the Soviet Union.
The No. 1-ranked waterpolo team in the world against the defending Olympic champions, a team of international veterans motivated by one more fling at an Olympic medal in 1984, against a team of comparative youngsters being groomed to defend the title their countrymen won in 1980.

Right: Australian goaltender Christopher Fenech at work against Cuba

Below: This is one the goaltender didn't stop

Opposite: Holland's Renier Yskes (2) readies for shot at Canadian goaltender Richard Zayonc. Canada went on to defeat Holland 6-5.

Above: Canada's Rene Bol (10) comes to aid of goaltender Zayonc

Opposite, upper: Canadian goaltender Richard Zayonc faced 30 shots in key game against Cuba. Here, Zayonc is about to stop shot by Cuba's Nelson Avila. Cuba went on to win 12-6.

Opposite, lower: Canadian forward swims away from Dutch defender

The luck of the draw brought these two waterpolo giants together prematurely at the 1983 World University Games. They were included in a pool with defending Universiade champion Cuba and the Romanian silver medalists at the 1981 Games.

The Soviets finished first. The United States and Cuba tied for second place only two points behind but Cuba was accorded the higher finish by virtue of a better goals for-against record during the tournament.

The Soviets won what was ostensibly the 'gold medal game' in a semi-final against the U.S., coming from behind three times to defeat the Americans 11-10. Cuba defeated Romania by the same score to advance against the Soviets in the second round of medal play while the U.S. faced Romania in its final game. The Americans required a win over Romania along with a Cuban upset over the Soviets in order to sneak in for the gold. It didn't happen. The U.S., despite holding a four-goal advantage over Romania with only three minutes to play, was hard pressed to escape with an 11-10 victory. The Soviets had already beaten Cuba 10-7 to secure the gold, forcing the Americans to settle for the silver.

Canada's team wound up in a tie with Italy for first place in the second pool. Canada defeated China 10-6 while Italy trimmed Holland 11-7. Italy and Canada tied 8-8 in their head-on game to finish at the top of the draw with three points each. Italy was accorded the high placing by virtue of a better goals for-against ratio. The sixth place finish by the Canadians was their best at the University Games.

Below: Clear sailing for Chinese attacker

113

Kaleidoscope '83

Kaleidoscope '83 was a cultural Pied Piper which banded together more than twenty-five hundred performers and artisans from fifty-six countries and led thousands of followers on a spree of unabashed merriment during the 1983 World University Games.

An entire city was the backdrop for the ten-day extravaganza of music, dance and art played out on the stages of local galleries, city parks and streets, hotel lobbies, banks, stores, escalators, rooftops and civic institutions.

Left: Gumboot Lollipop was a favorite with the children

Right: And there were clowns with big red noses

Below: 'Ksan peoples brought friendship and a mammoth totem pole

Kaleidoscope was music - the stirring marches of Souza performed by the Royal Canadian Mounted Police band from Ottawa and the gypsy music of Romania's Balada Folk Dance troupe. Kaleidoscope was an afternoon in the sun with the renowned Canadian Brass playing a slow New Orleans street march and an evening with the classics for a Mahler symphony and a Chopin concerto by The Group. There was the amplified rock by the Spoons, Darkroom and The Touch and the pulsating log drums and answer chants of the Te Ivi Maori Cultural Dance troupe from the Cook Islands.

The rhythms of the West Indies echoed throughout the city while two dancers with the Exodus Steel Band of Trinidad cleared a limbo pole by twenty centimetres. A shy, nine-year-old master drummer with the Odomankoma Kyerema Cultural Troupe of Ghana, proved himself a master of the talking drums.

Left: Kevin Cohen was a Pied Piper for the small fry

Right: City aldermen wrapped in red tape celebration

Below: A clear plastic sheet interwoven among the trees at Borden Park became the canvas for these small-fry artists. Indeed, Kaleidoscope '83 was for kids.

117

The Keichin Girls Marching Band and the Kobe Women's Cultural Group dancers performed a special salute to Japan, host country for the 1985 Summer Universiade.

Kaleidoscope '83 was ... sea gods riding chariots in city parks and giant puppets manipulated by the eight members of the Mettawee River Company from Salem, N.Y., delighting the small fry. It was the Fools Theatre from Vancouver, a wandering troupe of professional loons, performing mime, magic, music, juggling and fireblowing throughout the city. It was the vaudvillian diversity of street magician Jeff Sheridan and a trio of clowns known as Stringbean, Melba Toast and Shadow.

Kaleidoscope '83 was an exhibition of more than one thousand works of native crafts representing twenty countries around the world. More than two hundred thousand visitors attended the exhibition at the Convention Centre. The works included a reed boat from Bolivia; contemporary jewellery from Great Britain; traditional woodwork, basketry, embroidery and pottery from Cyprus; Sicilian glassware; carved reindeer and moose horn and pewter-threaded embroidery from Sweden.

Right: Carol Gilfillan conducts crafts tour for the Royal couple

Below: Indian soap stone carvers attracted the interest of Prince Charles and Princess Diana

Opposite: Giant murals brightened downtown buildings

Live drama and dance performances augmented an exhibition of masks, illustrating their use in maintaining traditions and rituals. A special exhibit of Canadian Indian masks was featured in the display. A Healthy Mind in a Healthy Body was the theme of an international poster competition which attracted submissions from around the world. Thirty countries submitted one hundred and twenty-five entries in four categories of an international student film festival while more than four hundred entries from post secondary students around the world competed for cash and prizes in an international photography competition.

Kaleidoscope '83 was ... Ballet Naucalpan of Mexico warming crowds to the pleasant rhythm of their mariachi music and the Balloon Man whipping up rubber pets. It was kids hanging from the nylon lingerie fabric transformed into nets by artist-in-residence Evelyn Roth.

Right: Inuit crafts attracted large crowds

Below: Kaleidoscope '83 has special attraction for kids as well as grown-ups

Opposite upper: City Celebration breathed life into downtown buildings

Opposite lower: Alberta's school children made more than 3,000 banners for city decoration

The Spirit of Universiade rose 11.2 metres high while an Indian chant drifted through the trees on the grounds of the Provincial Museum and a totem pole which was carved for Universiade by the people of 'Ksan from Hazelton, B.C., was slowly raised off the ground in an ancient and solemn ceremony.

Totem poles were the first visible language for the 'Ksan peoples. Initially, they were legal documents, describing the area of land belonging to a specific family. The 37-foot pole was carved in rough at Hazelton then transferred to Borden Park and Winston Churchill Square in Edmonton for its final carving. It was designated by the 'Ksan peoples to be a gesture of their friendship and as an ambassador of their unique culture. The totem pole will stand permanently on the Provincial Museum grounds.

Kaleidoscope '83 was ... the conservative madness of Chrome, a three-man Australian dance troupe arriving unannounced at shopping malls and city parks to the tune of a tin whistle and the beat of their chrome drums, performing as modern jesters. They contradicted the inherent reverence of a massive outdoor church service which attracted more than six thousand visitors. The featured speaker was Dr. Charles Malik, first President of the United Nations Security Council.

Kaleidoscope was a city festooned in the paint box colors of three thousand banners produced by Alberta's school children. It was ballerinas in limousines and antique cars and the Mar Mac dancers in decorated rickshaws -- bikes, trikes, wagons, carriages, stilts, roller skates, crazy dancers and figures of fear bursting out of alleys. Kaleidoscope was a mammoth street parade and illusions of fire breathing out of downtown buildings.

In the end, Kaleidoscope '83 was a spectacular ethnic farewell featuring a massed performance by the host Edmonton ethno-cultural entertainers in a salute to the guests from fifty-five other countries. It rendered valid the idealism of mutual understanding among peoples whose cultural customs were as widely separated as Sri Lanka and Sweden.

Above: The city celebrated in music and dance

Opposite: Figures of fear burst out of tall buildings during City Celebration

Nine-year-old master drummer from Ghana was a scene stealer

Mariachi music of Mexico's Ballet Naucalpan warmed audiences

Chrome troupe was conservative madness

A salute to 1985 Summer Games at Kobe Japan

Meet the Lion Dancers from Hong Kong

FISU Conference; General Assembly

The University Role in the Development of Modern Sport: Past, Present and Future was the common theme for a historic meeting of sports scientists, academics and historians during the 1983 World University Games at Edmonton.

The joint conference which attracted three hundred delegates from thirty-seven countries, focused on four major interest areas: Issues Concerning University Sport; Sports Medicine in University Sport; University Sport in Emerging Nations Sport Programs, and History of University Sport.

It was the first time delegates to the Congress for the History of Physical Education and Sport (HISPA), and representatives to the Commission for University Sport Study (CESU) met jointly to present papers on a singular theme.

The three-day conference during which one hundred and forty-six presenters delved into subjects ranging from "The Crisis of University Sports in Nigeria" to "The Evolution and Future of Sport in Great Britain," was lauded as the most intense examination of university sport ever held.

The General Assembly of FISU which conducted its bi-annual meeting in conjunction with the Games, re-elected Dr. Primo Nebiolo of Italy as its president and for the first time in its history elected a Canadian, Ed Zemrau, president of the Edmonton Organizing Committee, to its Executive Committee.

The assembly also appointed Zang Jian of the People's Republic of China as an Assessor, marking the first time FISU has accepted either a woman or a representative from China to its top committee. Other new Assessors named were Sylvio Coelho of Brazil, Georghe Copos of Romania, and Walter Ronmark of Sweden.

Personnel changes included the election of Leonid Drachevsky of the Soviet Union as first vice-president, replacing countryman Sergei Ivanov. Warren Giese of the United States was elected Vice-President, replacing Nick Rodis.

Dr. Nebiolo also announced a restructuring of the sports program, adding football as a compulsory sport starting with the 1985 Summer Universiade in Kobe, Japan. The next

Universiade will encompass 12 sports, including Judo as an optional discipline at Kobe.

"We don't want gigantism, but we will include football because it is popular with students," explained Dr. Nebiolo.

While recognizing the efforts of both organizing committees at Kobe and at Belluno, Italy, the site of the 1985 Winter Universiade, Dr. Nebiolo also announced that three cities have bid for the 1987 Summer Universiade: Brisbane, Australia; New Delhi, India; and Zagreb, Yugoslavia. A fourth, Indianapolis, U.S.A., has also made representation to the committee.

"We were most pleased to receive these bids," said Dr. Nebiolo. "To us, it indicates international acceptance of the Games, especially in these adverse economic conditions."

Opposite: The General Assembly of FISU elected a Canadian to the Executive Committee and gave representation to the People's Republic of China on it's top committee for the first time

Below: Dr. Primo Nebiolo, left, with Secretary-General Roch Campana. Dr. Nebiolo begins his 22nd year as President of the International University Sports Federation.

FISU Executive Committee Members

Primo Nebiolo, *President*	Italy
Leonid Drachevsky, *1st Vice-President*	Soviet Union
Constantin Anastassov, *Vice-President*	Bulgaria
Gunter Eglin, *Vice-President*	Federal Republic of Germany
Warren Giese, *Vice-President*	United States
Gilbert Schwaar, *Vice-President*	Switzerland
Roch Campana, *Secretary General*	Belgium
Charles Wenden, *Treasurer*	Great Britain
Jesus Hermida, *Senior Assessor*	Spain
Silvio Coelho, *Assessor*	Brazil
Georghe Copos, *Assessor*	Romania
Werner Czisek, *Assessor*	Austria
Hironoshin Furuhashi, *Assessor*	Japan
Boghdan Kolodziejek, *Assessor*	Poland
Walter Ronmark, *Assessor*	Sweden
Ben Ali Sekkal, *Assessor*	Algeria
Bohuslav Sykora, *Assessor*	Czechoslovakia
Jean Talbot, *Assessor*	France
Erkki Tervo, *Assessor*	Finland
Jian Zang, *Assessor*	China
Ed Zemrau, *Assessor*	Canada
Alf Lazer, *Senior Auditor*	Australia

Commission Presidents

Emanuel Scarpiello, *International Technical Committee*	Italy
Ludovik Komadel, *Medical Committee*	Czechoslovakia
Constantin Anastassov, *International Control Committee*	Bulgaria
Werner Czisek, *Committee for the Study of University Sport*	Austria
Gunther Eglin, *Committee for Sports Regulations*	Federal Republic of Germany

Opposite: Pom Pom girls and flashcard holders ring in Closing Ceremonies

Closing Ceremonies

The starter's gun was silent.
The race was over.
No more medals to chase. No more drama to unfold.

The tears and cheers inherent to the competitive struggles had dried and died -- surrendering now to that precise moment on July 11 at Commonwealth Stadium when the curtain closed on the 1983 World University Games and Edmonton said goodbye to more than six thousand new friends from eighty-seven countries.

Opposite: Young Korean athletes wrapped up in balloons

Right: Brazil brought more than good athletes

Below: Canadian flags hold pigtails in place for this happy athlete

130

Governor-General Ed Schreyer paid tribute to the athletes and performers on behalf of Canada. Mayor Cec Purves toasted the magnificent volunteer efforts of his citizens. Alex Fallow, Chairman of the Board of Governors for Universiade '83, saluted the three levels of government for their invaluable contributions, and Dr. Myer Horowitz, President of the University of Alberta, heaped praise upon the university community across the country which provided not only the 280 athletes which made up Canada's team, but hundreds of volunteers who rallied behind the Games in a multitude of roles.

There was a special introduction and salute to nineteen thousand volunteers and another for the performing artists and officials from Kobe, Japan, where the 1985 Summer Universiade will be staged. The flag of FISU was presented by President Nebiolo to the President of the Organizing Committee from Belluno, Italy, where the 1985 Winter Universiade will be held.

Right: Clowns, musicians, pom pom girls, dancers and marching bands were all part of the Closing Ceremonies program.

Opposite: A salute to the 1985 Summer Universiade '85 in Kobe, Japan

Below: Many got to hold historic flag of FISU

Dance troupes from twenty countries performed mini-routines. There were balloons -- thousands of balloons -- and hundreds of nylon streamers decorating the infield. Japan won the hearts of all with a spectacular display of fireworks.

The athletes, however, said it best.

They marched into the stadium, not as Romania, Kenya, China, or Peru, but as a virtual army of one. The Brits wore bowler hats painted to resemble the Union Jack. Decathlon champion Dave Steen of Toronto was wrapped in a flag of Canada. There were athletes from the United States wearing Nigerian robes and a vivacious Hawaiian dancer who had mysteriously traded her grass skirt for a Scottish kilt.

Right: A tear says it all at Closing Ceremonies

Opposite: Pretty Australian lady brought her own mascot

Below: The old and the new joined as one in a celebration of their friendship during the Closing Ceremonies for Universiade '83, Canada, host country for the 1983 World University Summer Games, presented the FISU flag to Japan which will host the 1985 Games.

136

It was a sea of frivolity -- an unsolicited testimonial for brotherhood as the athletes snake-danced in long lines and boogied in small circles without benefit of music. The always-smiling Angolans waved Canadian flags. A young Chinese girl giggled as she was dragged into the dance circle. The Cubans were having a field day trading the tops of their sweat suits with the Germans. The Japanese just smiled.

There were no cold wars at Commonwealth Stadium.

No racial or religious disparities.

But there were cheers and there were tears to the tune of Auld Lang Syne.

It ended all too soon.

Opposite, upper: Great Britain had a special message for citizens of Edmonton

Opposite, lower: Athletes and volunteers joined in singing our anthem

Left: Auld Lang Syne took its toll

Below: Ed Zemrau, left, president of the Edmonton Organizing Committee, turned over the flag of FISU to international president Dr. Primo Nebiolo for formal presentation to Ignazio Lojacono, president of the Italian University Sports Federation. The 1985 Winter Universiade will be held in Belluno, Italy.

Athletics

Event	Place	Country	Name	Time
Men's 100m	**Gold**	Nigeria	IMOH, Chidi	00:10.33
	Silver	Canada	WILLIAMS, Desai	00:10.37
	Bronze	United States	GRADDY, Sam	00:10.42
			Universiade Record 00:10.08	
Men's 110m Hurdles	**Gold**	U.S.S.R.	PROKOFYEV, Andrei	00:13.46
	Silver	United States	GAULT, Willie	00:13.49
	Bronze	Canada	MCKOY, Marc	00:13.57
			Universiade Record 00:13.21	
Men's 200m	**Gold**	Nigeria	EGUNIKE, I.	00:20.42
	Silver	United States	QUOW, Elliott	00:20.46
	Bronze	United States	JACKSON, Bernard	00:20.57
			Universiade Record 00:19.72	
Men's 400m	**Gold**	Nigeria	UTI, Sunday	00:45.32
	Silver	U.S.S.R.	MARKIN, Victor	00:45.38
	Bronze	United States	NIX, Sunder	00:45.53
			Universiade Record 00:44.98	
Men's 400m Hurdles	**Gold**	U.S.S.R.	KHARLOV, Alexander	00:49.41
	Silver	Senegal	BA, E.H. Amadou Dia	00:49.94
	Bronze	United States	PATRICK, Mark	00:50.28
			Universiade Record 00:48.44	
Men's 4 × 100m Relay	**Gold**	United States	SCOTT, Terry GRADDY, Sam ROBINSON, Ken GAULT, Willie	00:38.50
	Silver	Canada	WILLIAMS, Desai HINDS, Sterling SHARPE, Tony JOHNSON, Ben	00:38.69
	Bronze	U.S.S.R.	PROKOFYEV, Andrei SIDOROV, Nickolay MURAVYEV, Vladimir ZOLOTAREV, Alexander	00:39.04
			Universiade Record 00:38.42	
Men's 4 × 400m Relay	**Gold**	United States	NIX, Sunder TABRON, Elliott BABERS, Alonzo WILEY, Cliff	03:01.24

Event	Place	Country	Name	Time
Men's 4 × 400m Relay	Silver	U.S.S.R.	MARKIN, Victor KUTSEBO, Sergey LOMTEV, Evgeny TROSCILO, Alexandre	03:01.58
	Bronze	France	CANTI, Aldo LLASTER, CHICHIGNOUD, Pascal QUENTREC, Yann	03:04.89
			Universiade Record	03:00.98
Men's 800m	Gold	Poland	OSTROWSKI, Ryszard	01:46.29
	Silver	Great Britain	WILLIAMSON, Graham	01:46.66
	Bronze	Tunisia	ALOUINI, Mohamed	01:46.75
			Universiade Record	01:43.40
Men's 1500m	Gold	Italy	PATRIGNANI, Claudio	03:41.02
	Silver	Fed. Rep. of Germany	BARANSKI, Andreas	03:41.21
	Bronze	Great Britain	TURNBULL, Geoffrey	03:41.24
			Universiade Record	03:38.43
Men's 3000m Steeplechase	Gold	Belgium	DAENENS, Peter	08:28.86
	Silver	United States	GERBER, Farley	08:29.07
	Bronze	Japan	AIKYO, Shigeyuki	08:33.44
			Universiade Record	08:21.26
Men's 5000m	Gold	Great Britain	HARRIS, Stephen John	13:46.99
	Silver	Tunisia	BACCOUCHE, Fathi	13:47.69
	Bronze	Japan	YONESHIGE, Shuichi	13:48.13
			Universiade Record	0:13:37.56
Men's 10 000m	Gold	Japan	YONESHIGE, Shuichi	28:55.37
	Silver	Tanzania	AMO, Agapius	28:55.39
	Bronze	Tunisia	BACCOUCHE, Fathi	28:55.76
			Universiade Record	28:37.92
Men's 20km Walk	Gold	Canada	LEBLANC, Guillaume	01:24.02.9
	Silver	Italy	DAMILANO, Maurizio	01:24:21.0
	Bronze	U.S.S.R.	MATVEEV, Nickolay	01:25:06.5
			Universiade Best Performance	01:26:47.00
Men's Marathon	Gold	Italy	FAUSTINI, Alessio	02:17:09.5
	Silver	Italy	D'ALEO, Giovanni	02:17:19.7
	Bronze	Fed. Rep. of Germany	SPOTTEL, Michael	02:18:11.6
Men's High Jump	Gold	U.S.S.R.	PAKLIN, Igor	2.31
	Silver	Belgium	ANNYS, Eddy	2.29
	Bronze	Bermuda	SAUNDERS, Clarance	2.26
			Universiade Record	2.28
Men's Pole Vault	Gold	U.S.S.R.	VOLKOV, Konstantin	05.65
	Silver	France	VIGNERON, Thierry	05.60
	Bronze	United States	WARD, Jeff	05.50
			Universiade Record	05.75

Event	Place	Country	Name	
Men's Long Jump	Gold	Nigeria	ALLI, Yussuf	8.21
	Silver	United States	SPRY, Ralph	7.91
	Bronze	U.S.S.R.	RODIN, Sergei	7.85
			Universiade Record 8.23	
Men's Triple Jump	Gold	Nigeria	AGBEBAKU, Ajayi	17.26
	Silver	United States	CONLEY, Mike	17.20
	Bronze	Great Britain	HERBERT, John	17.05
			Universiade Record 17.32	
Men's Shot Put	Gold	United States	CARTER, Mike	19.74
	Silver	Yugoslavia	SARACEVIC, Zlatko	19.66
	Bronze	U.S.S.R.	SMIRNOV, Sergei	19.61
			Universiade Record 20.49	
Men's Discus	Gold	Cuba	DELIS FOURNIER, Luis Mariano	69.46
	Silver	Poland	JUZYSZYN, Dariusz	63.32
	Bronze	Italy	BUCCI, Marco	60.62
			Universiade Record 65.90	
Men's Javelin	Gold	U.S.S.R.	KOULA, Dainis	87.80
	Silver	Fed. Rep. of Germany	SCHREIBER, Helmut	84.12
	Bronze	Poland	GORAK, Stanislaw	83.20
			Universiade Record 89.52	
Men's Hammer	Gold	U.S.S.R.	TAMM, Yuri	76.82
	Silver	Great Britain	WEIR, Robert	74.10
	Bronze	U.S.S.R.	PASTUKHOV, Yuri	73.38
			Universiade Record 77.74	
Men's Decathlon	Gold	Canada	STEEN, David	8205
	Silver	Fed. Rep. of Germany	PETER, Herbert	8160
	Bronze	Australia	WERTHNER, Georg	7905
			Universiade Record 8203	

Event	Place	Country	Name	Time
Women's 100m	Gold	Great Britain	KINCH, Beverley	00:11.13
	Silver	United States	GIVENS, Randy	00:11.16
	Bronze	Canada	TAYLOR, Angella	00:11:17
			Universiade Record 00:11.00	
Women's 100m Hurdles	Gold	U.S.S.R.	PETROVA, Natalya	00:13.04
	Silver	U.S.S.R.	BISEROVA, Elena	00:13.07
	Bronze	United States	FITZGERALD, Benita	00:13:24
			Universiade Record 00:12.62	
Women's 200m	Gold	United States	GIVENS, Randy	00:22.47
	Silver	Canada	PAYNE, Marita	00:22.62
	Bronze	Jamaica	JACKSON, Grace	00:22:69
			Universiade Record 00:21.91	
Women's 400m	Gold	U.S.S.R.	PINIGINA, Maria	00:50.47
	Silver	Canada	KILLINGBECK, Molly	00:51.94
	Bronze	U.S.S.R.	KORBAN, Elena	00:52:07
			Universiade Record 00:50.08	

Event	Place	Country	Name	Time
Women's 400m Hurdles	Gold	U.S.S.R.	FESENKO, Ekaterina	00:54.97
	Silver	U.S.S.R.	FILIPISHINA, Elena	00:56.10
	Bronze	Canada	WALL, Gwen	00:56:10

Universiade Record 00:55.52

Event	Place	Country	Name	Time
Women's 800m	Gold	U.S.S.R.	PODYALOVSKAYA, Irena	01:59.29
	Silver	United States	CAMPBELL, Robin	01:59.81
	Bronze	Romania	MELINTE, Doina Ofelia	01:59:93

Universiade Record 01:57.60

Event	Place	Country	Name	Time
Women's 1500m	Gold	Italy	DORIO, Gabriella	04:07.26
	Silver	Romania	MELINTE, Doina Ofelia	04:07.34
	Bronze	Romania	RADU, Maria	04:08:41

Universiade Record 04:05.35

Event	Place	Country	Name	Time
Women's 3000m	Gold	Romania	RADU, Maria	09:04.32
	Silver	U.S.S.R.	MALYCHINA, Elena	09:06.17
	Bronze	Canada	WILLIAMS, Lynn	09:07.74

Universiade Record 08:53.78

Event	Place	Country	Name	Time
Women's 4 × 100m Relay	Gold	United States	NEDD, Lashion WASHINGTON, Jackie CLIETTE, Brenda GIVENS, Randy	00:42.82
	Silver	Canada	TAYLOR, Angella BROTHERS, Tanya PAYNE, Marita KILLINGBECK, Molly	00:43.21
	Bronze	U.S.S.R.	ROMANOVA, Marina MOLOKOVA, Marina OLHHOVNIKOVA, Irina ANTONOVA, Olga	00:44:20

Universiade Record 00:43.14

Event	Place	Country	Name	Time
Women's 4 × 400m Relay	Gold	U.S.S.R.	BORISOVA, Loujdmila KRYLOVA, Iarysa PINIGINA, Maria KORBAN, Elena	03:24.97
	Silver	Canada	KILLINGBECK, Molly PAYNE, Marita CROOKS, Charmaine RICHARDSON, Jillian	03:25.26
	Bronze	United States	BOLTON, Kelia GABRIEL, Easter DABNEY, Sharon EMERSON, Arlise	03:34.64

Universiade Record 03:26.25

Event	Place	Country	Name	Time
Women's Marathon	Gold	Great Britain	ROWELL, Sarah	02:47:36.2
	Silver	Canada	ROBERTS, Katherine	02:52:46.1
	Bronze	United States	KAPUT, Margie	02:54:02.7

Not previously staged in Universiade

Event	Place	Country	Name	
Women's High Jump	Gold	U.S.S.R.	BYKOVA, Tamara	1.98
	Silver	Cuba	COSTA ACOSTA, Silvia	1.98
	Bronze	France	EWANGE-EPEE, Maryse	1.92

Universiade Record 1.96

Women's Long Jump	Gold	Romania	CUSHMIR, Anisoara	7.06
	Silver	U.S.S.R.	ZORINA, Svetlana	6.81
	Bronze	Romania	IONESCU, Valy	6.56

Universiade Record 6.83

Women's Shot Put	Gold	U.S.S.R.	LISOVSKAYA, Natalya	20.46
	Silver	Fed. Rep. of Germany	LOSCH, Claudia	18.81
	Bronze	U.S.S.R.	AKHREMENKO, Natalya	18.67

Universiade Record 20.82

Women's Discus	Gold	Romania	CRACIUNESCU, Florenta	64.56
	Silver	U.S.S.R.	AKHREMENKO, Natalya	62.62
	Bronze	U.S.S.R.	URAKOVA, Lubov	58.28

Universiade Record 67.48

Women's Javelin	Gold	Fed. Rep. of Germany	PETERS, Beate	66.86
	Silver	Italy	QUINTAVALLA, Fausta	63.06
	Bronze	Cuba	VILA MACHADO, Mayra	62.34

Universiade Record 67.20

Women's Heptathlon	Gold	U.S.S.R.	SMIRNOVA, Ekaterina	6350
	Silver	Fed. Rep. of Germany	EVERTS, Sabine	6291
	Bronze	Great Britain	LIVERMORE, Judith	6184

Universiade Record 6198

Basketball

Event	Place	Country	Name
Men's Basketball	Gold	Canada	DUKESHIRE, Kelly
			HATCH, John
			HERBERT, Gordon
			KAZANOWSKI, Gerald
			KELSEY, William
			MEAGHER, Danny
			PASQUALE, Ilario
			SIMMS, Tony
			TILLEMAN, Karl
			TRIANO, Howard
			WENNINGTON, William
			WILTUER, Gregory

Event	Place	Country	Name
Men's Basketball	Silver	Yugoslavia	CVJETICANIN, Danko
			GRBOVIC, Goran
			IVANOVIC, Marko
			MUTAPCIC, Emir
			PERASOVIC, Velimir
			PETROVIC, Drazen
			SAVOVIC, Milenko
			SUNARA, Ivan
			VUCUROVIC, Zarko
			VUJACIC, Jadranko
			ZIZIC, Rajko
			ZORKIC, Nebojsa
	Bronze	United States	BARKLEY, Charles Wade
			CAVENER, Gregory Kent
			DAWKINS, Johnny Earl
			DURRANT, Devin George
			GOODE, Andre L.
			HUMPHRIES, John Jay
			MALONE, Karl A.
			PINCKNEY, Edward
			THOMAS, Malcolm
			THOMPSON, Bernard Louis
			TURNER, Eric C.
			WILLIS, Kevin Alvin

Event	Place	Country	Name
Women's Basketball	Gold	United States	BOSWELL, Cathy
			COLLINS, Sheila
			HENRY, Lea
			LACEY, Trudi
			LAMB, Monica Van Dora
			LEE, Deborah Ann
			MENKEN-SCHAUDT, Carol Jean
			OSTROWSKI, Mary Lynne
			SCOTT, Lori Anne
			SMITH, Annette Marie
			SPAULDING, Tresa Dawn
			WALKER, Joyce Denise
	Silver	Romania	BADINICI, Maria
			BOSR, Stefania
			CIUBANCAN, Mandica
			FILIP, Elena
			GRIGORAS, Constanta
			HINDA, Camelia
			HOSSZU, Csilla
			KISS, Gabriela
			PALL, Maria Magdalena
			POPA, Virgina
			STOCHITA, Cornelia
			TOCALA, Carmen
	Bronze	Yugoslavia	BOZINOVIC, Snezana
			CANGALOVIC, Olivera
			DEKLEVA, Cvetana
			DORNIK, Polona

Event	Place	Country	Name
Women's Basketball	**Bronze**	Yugoslavia	GOLIC, Sladjana KOMNENOVICH, Jelica KRIVOKAPIC, Olivera MAJSTOROVIC, Biljana PERAZIC, Jasmina SHUKA, Slavica UZELAC, Marija VANGELOVSKA, Totjna

Cycling

Event	Place	Country	Name
Men's 1000m Time Trial	**Gold** **Silver** **Bronze**	U.S.S.R. Italy U.S.S.R.	PANFILOV, Alexandre BAUDINO, Stefano ZELCH-LOTCHMELIS, Andris
Men's Team Time Trial	**Gold** **Silver** **Bronze**	U.S.S.R. Netherlands Italy	KASHIRIN, Yury NAVOLOKIN, Sergei VORONIN, Sergei KOROLKOV, Evgeniy BOEVE, Henk DUCROT, Martinus JENNEN, Wilhelmus KOLKHUIS TANKE, Paschalis MINELLO, Ennio PAOLETTI, Roberto SCIAMANNA, Fabio SCREMIN, Sergio
Men's Sprint	**Gold** **Silver** **Bronze**	U.S.S.R. U.S.S.R. Cuba	DOTSENKO, Alexey GUELACHWILI, Emzar TRIANA ALMENARES, Adolfo
Men's Individual Road Race	**Gold** **Silver** **Bronze**	Italy U.S.S.R. Korea	SCREMIN, Sergio MUZHITSKY, Pavel SHIN, Dea-Cheul
Men's Individual Points Race	**Gold** **Silver** **Bronze**	U.S.S.R. Romania France	MANAKOV, Viktor LAUTARA, Gheorghe SPEZZATTI, Robert
Men's Individual Pursuit	**Gold** **Silver** Bronze	U.S.S.R. U.S.S.R. Canada	KRASNOV, Alexandre MANAKOV, Viktor STIEDA, Alex

Event	Place	Country	Name
Women's 1000m Time Trial	**Gold**	U.S.S.R.	SALOUMIAEE, Erika
	Silver	France	Nicoloso, Isabelle
	Bronze	U.S.S.R.	KIBARDIAN, Nadegeda
Women's Individual Time Trial	**Gold**	U.S.S.R.	POLIAKOVA, Tamara
	Silver	U.S.S.R.	SLEPOKOUROVA, Lubov
	Bronze	U.S.S.R.	KIBARDINA, Nadegeda
Women's Sprint	**Gold**	U.S.S.R.	SALOUMIAEE, Erika
	Silver	France	NICOLOSO, Isabelle
	Bronze	People's Rep. of China	YANG, Guiling
Women's Individual Road Race	**Gold**	U.S.S.R.	KIBARDINA, Nadegeda
	Silver	U.S.S.R.	POLIAKOVA, Tamara
	Bronze	France	LONGO, Jeannie
Women's Individual Points Race	**Gold**	France	NICOLOSO, Isabelle
	Silver	U.S.S.R.	SALOUMIAEE, Erika
	Bronze	U.S.S.R.	STARIKOVA, Ekaterina
Women's Individual Pursuit	**Gold**	U.S.S.R.	KIBARDINA, Nadejda
	Silver	France	LONGO, Jeannie
	Bronze	U.S.S.R.	POLIAKOVA, Tamara

Event	Place	Country	Name
Men's 3m Springboard	**Gold**	United States	LOUGANIS, Gregory
	Silver	U.S.S.R.	DROZHZHIN, Nikolay
	Bronze	People's Rep. of China	TAN, Liangde
Men's 10m Platform	**Gold**	United States	LOUGANIS, Gregory
	Silver	U.S.S.R.	TROSHIN, Viaecheslav
	Bronze	People's Rep. of China	TONG, Hui

Event	Place	Country	Name
Women's 3m Springboard	**Gold**	People's Rep. of China	SHI, Meigin
	Silver	United States	NEYER, Megan
	Bronze	Canada	BERNIER, Sylvie
Women's 10m Platform	**Gold**	People's Rep. of China	LU, Wei
	Silver	United States	WYLAND, Wendy
	Bronze	U.S.S.R.	BELIAKOVA, Tatiana

Fencing

Event	Place	Country	Name
Men's Individual Foil	Gold	Italy	NUMA, Mauro
	Silver	France	LEMENAGE, Didier
	Bronze	Italy	BORELLA, Andrea
Men's Individual Sabre	Gold	Italy	MARIN, Marco
	Silver	Italy	SCALZO, Giovanni
	Bronze	Italy	DALLA BARBA, Gianfranco
Men's Individual Epee	Gold	Italy	Bellone, Stefano
	Silver	Romania	BODOCZI, Miklos
	Bronze	U.S.S.R.	SOKOLOV, Vladimir
Men's Team Foil	Gold	Italy	BORELLA, Andrea
			CERVI, Federico
			CIPRESSA, Andrea
			NUMA, Mauro
			SCURI, Angelo
	Silver	U.S.S.R.	CHVETSOV, Alexei
			KALININE, Andrei
			KLIOUCHINE, Andrei
			LOGVINE, Vitali
			SOMOV, Serguei
	Bronze	Cuba	DIAZ BABIER, Tulio
			FAVIEL SANDO, Efigenio
			GARCIA GARCIA, Angel
			GONZALEZ ZIQUES, Herberto
			MERENCIO GIRON, Pedro
Men's Team Sabre	Gold	U.S.S.R.	KORIAJKINE, Serguei
			MINDIGRASSOV, Serguei
			PAITCHADZE, Evgueni
			TSUKHLO, Yvegeny
			VINNIK, Alexandre
	Silver	Italy	CAVALIERE, Massimo
			DALLA BARBA, Gianfranco
			MARIN, Marco
			MEGLIO, Ferdinando
			SCALZO, Giovanni
	Bronze	Hungary	CSONGRADI, Laszlo
			GEMESI, Dr. Gyorgy
			SZABO, Bence
			SZETEY, Andras

Event	Place	Country	Name
Men's Team Epee	Gold	Italy	BELLONE, Stefano CUOMO, Alessandro FALCONE, Marco MANZI, Roberto PANTANO, Stefano
	Silver	Poland	CHRONOWSKI, Ludomir JABLKOWSKI, Piotr PIASECKI, Mariusz STRZALKA, Mariusz SWORNOWSKI, Leszek
	Bronze	U.S.S.R.	AGEER, Vitaly ALENINE, Sergei KOUTCHERIAVYI, Igor LOUKIANOV, Jouzy SOKOLOV, Vladimir

Event	Place	Country	Name
Women's Individual Foil	Gold	Romania	GUZGANU, Elisabeta
	Silver	Romania	OROS, Rozalita
	Bronze	Canada	PHILION, Madeleine
Women's Team Foil	Gold	People's Rep. of China	LI, Huahua LUAN, Jujie SUE, Lianfeng WU, Qiuhua ZHU, Qingyuan
	Silver	Romania	DAN, Aurora GUZGANU, Elisabeta OROS, Rozalia RUPARCSICS, Csilla ZSAK, Marcela
	Bronze	France	BOUGNOL, Florence CABANE, Marie MEYGET, Anne TRINQUET, Pascale

Gymnastics

Event	Place	Country	Name	Points
Men's Team Results	Gold	U.S.S.R.	ARTIEMOV, Vladimir KOROLEV, Yuri MARTSINKIV, Stephan POGORELOV, Alexander	174.80

Event	Place	Country	Name	Points
Men's Team Results	Silver	People's Rep. of China	LIMIN, Zou WOFU, Huang YUN, Lou ZHIQIANG, Xu	173.20
	Bronze	United States	BABCOCK, Brian GAYLORD, Mitchell HARTUNG, James VIDMAR, Peter	172.60
Men's Individual All-Around	Gold	U.S.S.R.	KOROLEV, Yuri	58.30
	Silver	U.S.S.R.	ARTIEMOV, Vladimir	58.20
	Bronze	U.S.S.R.	POGORELOV, Alexander	58.10
Men's Floor Exercises	Gold	U.S.S.R.	KOROLEV, Yuri	19.80
	Silver	U.S.S.R.	ARTIEMOV, Vladimir	19.45
	Bronze	People's Rep. of China	WOFU, Huang	19.40
	Bronze	France	VATUONE, Philippe	19.40
Men's Pommel Horse	Gold	U.S.S.R.	KOROLEV, Yuri	19.60
	Silver	U.S.S.R.	POGORELOV, Alexander	19.60
	Bronze	Romania	MOLNAR, Levente	19.25
	Bronze	Japan	MURAMATSU, Toshiya	19.25
Men's Rings	Gold	Romania	MOLNAR, Levente	19.60
	Silver	United States	HARTUNG, James	19.50
	Bronze	Japan	OKADA, Taichi	19.40
	Bronze	United States	VIDMAR, Peter	19.40
Men's Vault	Gold	People's Rep. of China	YUN, Lou	19.65
	Silver	Canada	LONG, Warren	19.55
	Bronze	Romania	PINTEA, Valentin	19.50
Men's Parallel Bars	Gold	U.S.S.R.	ARTIEMOV, Vladimir	19.50
	Silver	People's Rep. of China	WOFU, Huang	19.50
	Bronze	United States	HARTUNG, James	19.35
Men's High Bar	Gold	Canada	CHARTRAND, Phillipe	19.85
	Silver	U.S.S.R.	KOROLEV, Yuri	19.70
	Bronze	United States	HARTUNG, James	19.60
	Bronze	U.S.S.R.	POGORELOV, Alexander	19.60

Event	Place	Country	Name	Points
Women's Team Results	Gold	U.S.S.R.	POLEVAYA, Elena PONOMARENKO, Elena VESELOVA, Elena YURCHENKO, Natalia	115.35
	Silver	Romania	BALAN, Liliana DUNCA, Rodica EBERLE, Emilia RICIU, Mihaela	114.50
	Bronze	Canada	AGGISS, Sara BOTNEN, Anita DE SERRES, Anne Marie SCHLEGEL, Elfi	113.95
Women's Individual All-Around	Gold	U.S.S.R.	YURCHENKO, Natalia	39.05
	Silver	Romania	EBERLE, Emilia	38.40
	Bronze	Romania	RICIU, Mihaela	38.40

Event	Place	Country	Name	Points
Women's Vault	Gold	U.S.S.R.	YURCHENKO, Natalia	19.40
	Silver	U.S.S.R.	VESELOVA, Elena	19.325
	Bronze	Romania	RICIU, Mihaela	19.30
Women's Uneven Bars	Gold	U.S.S.R.	YURCHENKO, Natalia	19.60
	Silver	Czechoslovakia	GAJDOSOVA, Jana	19.35
	Bronze	Romania	RICIU, Mihaela	19.30
Women's Balance Beam	Gold	U.S.S.R.	YURCHENKO, Natalia	19.50
	Silver	People's Rep. of China	JIA, Wen	19.30
	Bronze	Canada	BOTNEN, Anita	19.25
Women's Floor Exercises	Gold	Romania	BALAN, Liliana	19.60
	Silver	Romania	RICIU, Mihaela	19.50
	Bronze	U.S.S.R.	VESELOVA, Elena	19.35

Swimming

Event	Place	Country	Name	Time
Men's 100m Freestyle	Gold	U.S.S.R.	SMIRYAGIN, Sergey	50.51
	Silver	United States	JAGER, Thomas	51.02
	Bronze	Fed. Rep. of Germany	SCHMIDT, Andreas	51.60

Universiade Record 51.39

Men's 200m Freestyle	Gold	United States	HAYES, Lawrence	01:51.19
	Silver	U.S.S.R.	FILONOV, Alexei	01:51.90
	Bronze	Canada	BAUMANN, Alex	01:51.97

Universiade Record 01:51.44

Men's 400m Freestyle	Gold	U.S.S.R.	SALNIKOV, Vladimir	03:49.38
	Silver	United States	HAYES, Lawrence	03:54.93
	Bronze	U.S.S.R.	SEMENOV, Svyatoslal	03:56.57

Universiade Record 03:58.08

Men's 1500m Freestyle	Gold	U.S.S.R	SALNIKOV, Vladimir	15:02.83
	Silver	U.S.S.R.	SEMENOV, Svyatoslal	15:28.36
	Bronze	United States	HAYES, Lawrence	15:37.97

Universiade Record 15:22.25

Men's 100m Backstroke	Gold	Canada	WEST, Mike	56.64
	Silver	U.S.S.R.	SHEMETOV, Vladimir	56.71
	Bronze	U.S.S.R.	KUZNETSOV, Victor	56.74

Universiade Record 57.05

Event	Place	Country	Name	Time
Men's 200m Backstroke	Gold	U.S.S.R.	ZABOLOTNOV, Sergey	02:00.42
	Silver	U.S.S.R.	SHEMETOV, Vladimir	02:01.27
	Bronze	Canada	West, Mike	02:01.63

Universiade Record 02:03.65

Event	Place	Country	Name	Time
Men's 100m Breaststroke	Gold	Japan	TAKAHASHI, Shigehiro	01:04.13
	Silver	U.S.S.R.	KIS, Uriy	01:04.21
	Bronze	Australia	EVANS, Peter	01:04.32

Universiade Record 01:03.95

Event	Place	Country	Name	Time
Men's 200m Breaststroke	Gold	U.S.S.R.	ZHULPA, Robertas	2:15.93
	Silver	Japan	TAKAHASHI, Shigehiro	2:19.72
	Bronze	U.S.S.R.	UTENKOV, Gennadiy	2:19.80

Universiade Record 02:19.42

Event	Place	Country	Name	Time
Men's 100m Butterfly	Gold	U.S.S.R.	MARKOVSKY, Alexei	54.65
	Silver	United States	JAGER, Thomas	55.45
	Bronze	Canada	PONTING, Thomas	55.55

Universiade Record 00:55.37

Event	Place	Country	Name	Time
Men's 200m Butterfly	Gold	U.S.S.R.	FESENKO, Sergey	02:00.38
	Silver	Great Britain	HUBBLE, Philip	02:01.36
	Bronze	New Zealand	MOSSE, Anthony	02:02.03

Universiade Record 02:01.86

Event	Place	Country	Name	Time
Men's 200m Individual Medley	Gold	Canada	BAUMANN, Alex	02:02.29
	Silver	U.S.S.R.	SIDORENKO, Aleksandre	02:04.21
	Bronze	Brazil	PRADO, Ricardo	02:05.50

Universiade Record 02:06.34

Event	Place	Country	Name	Time
Men's 400m Individual Medley	Gold	Canada	BAUMANN, Alex	04:19.80
	Silver	United States	HAYES, Lawrence	04:26.05
	Bronze	Brazil	PRADO, Ricardo	04:26.87

Universiade Record 04:25.53

Event	Place	Country	Name	Time
Men's 4 × 100m Freestyle Relay	Gold	U.S.S.R.	SMIRYAGIN, Sergey TKACHENKO, Vladimir KRASUK, Sergey MARKOVSKY, Alexei	03:21.72
	Silver	United States	JAGER, Thomas SILVA, Christopher KYLE, Dallas HAYES, Lawrence	03:21:82
	Bronze	Canada	WELBOURNE, Graham SHEEHAN, Jeffrey KELLY, Wayne BAUMANN, Alex	03:26.38

Universiade Record 03:27.84

Event	Place	Country	Name	Time
Men's 4 × 200m Freestyle Relay	Gold	U.S.S.R.	SMIRYAGIN, Sergey SEMENOV, Svyatoslal CHAEV, Aleksandre FILONOU, Alexei	07:27.22
	Silver	United States	MACDONALD, Stuart BODOR, R. HAYES, Lawrence SAEGER, Richard	07:30.18

Event	Place	Country	Name	Time
Men's 4 × 200m Freestyle Relay	Bronze	Canada	BAUMANN, Alex SZMIDT, Peter KELLY, Wayne WELBOURNE, Graham	07:31.40
			Universiade Record 07:33.96	
Men's 4 × 100m Medley Relay	Gold	U.S.S.R.	SHEMETOV, Vladimir KIS, Uriy MARKOVSKY, Alexei SMIRYAGIN, Sergey	03:44.33
	Silver	Canada	WEST, Mike FITZPATRICK, Kenneth PONTING, Thomas BAUMANN, Alex	03:46.49
	Bronze	United States	ERICSON, Eric BAUER, Andrew JAGER, Thomas KYLE, Dallas	03:46.65
			Universiade Record 03:48.75	

Event	Place	Country	Name	Time
Women's 100m Freestyle	Gold Silver Bronze	U.S.S.R. Netherlands United States	LARICHEVA, Irina KRAUS, Annelies THOMAS, Tammy	00:58.15 00:58.27 00:58.45
			Universiade Record 00:57.17	
Women's 200m Freestyle	Gold Silver Bronze	U.S.S.R. Netherlands U.S.S.R.	LARICHEVA, Irina KRAUS, Annelies GERASIMOVA, Irina	02:02.17 02:02.78 02:02.84
			Universiade Record 02:03.97	
Women's 400m Freestyle	Gold Silver Bronze	U.S.S.R. United States Canada	LARICHEVA, Irina LINZMEIER, Marybeth DAIGNEAULT, Julie	04:13.41 04:15.36 04:17.77
			Universiade Record 04:15.26	
Women's 800m Freestyle	Gold Silver Bronze	U.S.S.R United States Canada	LARICHEVA, Irina LINZMEIER, Marybeth DAIGNEAULT, Julie	08:40.31 08:41.43 08:53.52
			Universiade Record 08:37.50	
Women's 100m Backstroke	Gold Silver Bronze	U.S.S.R. Romania United States	GORCHAKOVA, Larisa BUNACIU, Carmen WALSH, Susan	01:03.28 01:03.77 01:03.80
			Universiade Record 01:02.47	
Women's 200m Backstroke	Gold Silver Bronze	U.S.S.R. Romania United States	GORCHAKOVA, Larisa BUNACIU, Carmen WALSH, Susan	02:15.37 02:15.96 02:16.41
			Universiade Record 02:13.21	
Women's 100m Breaststroke	Gold Silver Bronze	U.S.S.R. U.S.S.R. Italy	BELOKON, Larisa BUZELITE, Ishkute DALLA VALLE, Manuela	01:12.17 01:13.08 01:13.90
			Universiade Record 01:14.20	

Event	Place	Country	Name	Time
Women's 200m Breaststroke	Gold	U.S.S.R.	BELOKON, Larisa	02:34.02
	Silver	U.S.S.R.	BUZELITE, Ishkute	02:34.58
	Bronze	Canada	BORSHOLT, Lisa	02:36.22

Universiade Record 02:35.85

Event	Place	Country	Name	Time
Women's 100m Butterfly	Gold	Australia	WOODHOUSE, Susie	01:01.79
	Silver	Italy	SAVI SCARPONI, Cinzia	01:02.31
	Bronze	Japan	KUME, Naoko	01:02.48

Universiade Record 01:01.91

Event	Place	Country	Name	Time
Women's 200m Butterfly	Gold	Australia	WOODHOUSE, Susie	02:13.50
	Silver	Japan	KUME, Naoko	02:15.02
	Bronze	Australia	FORD, Michelle	02:15.38

Universiade Record 02:15.71

Event	Place	Country	Name	Time
Women's 200m Individual Medley	Gold	U.S.S.R.	GERASIMOVA, Irina	02:18.23
	Silver	Italy	SAVI SCARPONI, Cinzi	02:19.73
	Bronze	United States	BARKER, Vera	02:20.63

Universiade Record 02:20.43

Event	Place	Country	Name	Time
Women's 400m Individual Medley	Gold	U.S.S.R.	GERASIMOVA, Irina	04:52.27
	Silver	Italy	SAVI SCARPONI, Cinzia	04:55.77
	Bronze	United States	WOOLGER, Christy	04:56.70

Universiade Record 04:54.83

Event	Place	Country	Name	Time
Women's 4 × 100m Freestyle Relay	Gold	U.S.S.R.	GERASIMOVA, Irina SERGEEVA, Irina KURNIKOVA, Tatiana LARICHEVA, Irina	03:49.64
	Silver	United States	EMERY, Elizabeth WILLIAMS, J. LAWRENCE, Ingrid THOMAS, Tammy	03:50.19
	Bronze	Canada	MARUBASHI, Naomi SANDERS, Linda CORCORAN, Erin NEW, Maureen	03:54.67

Universiade Record 03:53.70

Event	Place	Country	Name	Time
Women's 4 × 100m Medley Relay	Gold	U.S.S.R.	GORCHAKOVA, Larisa BELOKON, Larisa KURNIKOVA, Tatiana GERASIMOVA, Irina	04:14.10
	Silver	United States	WALSH, Susan CHILDS, Jeanne WAGSTAFF, Jennifer WILLIAMS, J.	04:16.29
	Bronze	Canada	ABDO, Reema WATSON, Megan VANDYKE, Anita MARUBASHI, Naomi	04:22.46

Universiade Record 04:18.84

Tennis

Event	Place	Country	Name
Men's Singles	Gold	United States	GALLIEN, Richard Adam
	Silver	United States	GOLDIE, Daniel Clyde
	Bronze	U.S.S.R.	ZVEREV, Alexandr
Men's Doubles	Gold	United States	ARONS, Jeff Steven
			SEVELY, John Vincent
	Silver	Italy	BINAGHI, Angelo
			BITTI, Raimondo Ricci
	Bronze	Romania	BUCUR, Laurentiv
			MARCU, Adrian

Event	Place	Country	Name
Women's Singles	Gold	United States	FERNANDEZ, Cecilia
	Silver	U.S.S.R.	ZAYTSEVA, Olga
	Bronze	Romania	ROMANOV, Lucia
Women's Doubles	Gold	Canada	DEWIS, Karen
			HETHERINGTON, Jill
	Silver	Japan	KIMURA, Junko
			OKAMOTO, Kumiko
	Bronze	U.S.S.R.	CHERNEVA, Svetland
			ZAYTSEVA, Olga
Mixed	Gold	Canada	HETHERINGTON, Jill
			JENKINS, Bill
	Silver	Fed. Rep. of Germany	DRIES, Cornelia
			SETTLEMAYER, Jochen
	Bronze	U.S.S.R.	CHERNEVA, Svetlana
			VILEV, Yuri

Volleyball

Event	Place	Country	Name
Men's Volleyball	Gold	Cuba	ALFONSO ABREU, Emilo
			BELTRAN, RIZO, Lazaro
			GUILLEN PEDROSO, Rodolfo

Event	Place	Country	Name
Men's Volleyball	**Gold**	Cuba	LEYVA BORRERO, Richard
			OVIEDO BONILLA, Luis
			PAEZ ROJAS, Aguedo
			PEREZ HERRERA, Roberto
			PEREZ LOPEZ, Antonio
			RUIZ LAGARGUE, Carlos
			SARMIENTOS BIOS, Abel
			SILIE TABARES, Leonardo
			TORRES TORRES, Gonzalo
	Silver	Canada	BACON, Richard
			BARRETT, John
			COULTER, Allan
			DANYLUK, Taras
			GRATTON, Paul
			HITCHCOCK, Dean
			HOAG, Glenn
			JONES, Thomas
			KETRZYNSKI, Alexander
			SAXTON, Donald
			WAGNER, Randolph
			YOUNG, Daryl
	Bronze	Italy	BERTOLI, Franco
			DAMETTO, Giancarlo
			DIBERNARDO, Mauro
			ERRICHIELLO, Giovanni
			LANFRANCO, Giovanni
			LAZZERONI, Alessandro
			LUCCHETTA, Andrea
			NEGRI, Marco
			NINFA, Maurizio
			REBAUDENGO, Piero
			SACCHETTI, Gianluigi
			VECCHI, Paolo

Event	Place	Country	Name
Women's	**Gold**	Brazil	CARVALHO, Dulce
			LEME, Vera
			MACHADO, Luiza
			NEVES DE SOUZA, Ivonette
			ROESE, Heloisa
			SALGADO, Maria
			SILVA, Fernanda
			SILVA, Jacqueline
			SILVA, Martha
			SUFFERT, Helga
			TEIXEIRA, Rita
			VCHOA, Regina
	Silver	People's Rep. of China	CHEN, Xiao Qi
			CHEN, Yahui
			HE, Ping
			HUANG, Xiuqin
			LIN, Hui
			PU, Ziaoxia
			WANG, Guiying
			WANG, Meina
			XU, Li
			YANG, Rongxin
			YIN, Qin
			YU, Cuizhi

Event	Place	Country	Name
Women's Volleyball	**Bronze**	Japan	HIRO, Miwako
			HISHIKO, Etsuko
			KATSUNO, Mariko
			KAWAKITA, Rika
			OGAWA, Yumi
			OZAKI, Akiko
			SATO, Ichiko
			SHIMA, Keiko
			TAKIZAMA, Reinko
			WATANABE, Ikuyo
			YAMAMOTO, Yoko
			YOSHIDA, Miwako

Waterpolo

Event	Place	Country	Name
Men's Waterpolo	**Gold**	U.S.S.R.	AIAPBERGENOV, Erlan
			BERENDUGA, Victor
			GIORGADZE, Mihail
			GVAHARIA, Davy
			KRUPIN, Georgi
			MOROZOV, Sergey
			NAUMOV, Sergey
			ORAZALINOV, Askar
			PROCOPCHUK, Pavel
			PUZANKOV, Oleg
			SEDOV, Igor
			VOLKOV, Pavel
	Silver	United States	BERGESON, James
			BURKE, Douglas
			CAMPBELL, Jeff
			CAMPBELL, Peter
			CUTINO, Peter Jr.
			DORST, Chris
			GENSEL, John
			GRESHAM, Alan
			GRIER, Michael
			ROBINSON, Edward
			SCHROEDER, Terry
			SPICER, Mike
			VARGAS, John
	Bronze	Cuba	BENITEZ SUAREZ, Carlos
			COSTA MENDEZ, Lazaro
			CUESTA ZULUETA, Pablo
			DEROUVILLE DE LA CRUZ, Jesus
			DIAZ CERVANTES, Barbaro

Event	Place	Country	Name
Men's Waterpolo	**Bronze**	Cuba	DOMINGUES AVILA, Nelson DOMINGUEZ AVILA, Juan GONZALEZ ALONSO, Sergio NUNEZ LEYVA, Miguel PEREZ LEMUS, Enrique RAMOS HERNANDEZ, Auturo RAMOS SOLER, Jose RUIZ LORENZO, Fabio

Final Medal Standings

Country	Gold	Silver	Bronze	Total
U.S.S.R.	59	29	27	115
United States	12	22	20	54
Canada	9	10	19	38
Romania	6	12	9	27
Italy	9	10	6	25
France	1	5	6	12
Peoples Republic of China	5	3	4	12
Japan	2	3	6	11
Great Britain	3	3	3	9
Federal Republic of Germany	1	6	2	9
Cuba	2	1	4	7
Nigeria	5	–	–	5
Poland	1	2	1	4
Australia	2	–	2	4
Tunisia	–	1	2	3
Yugoslavia	–	2	1	3
Netherlands	–	3	–	3
Brazil	1	–	2	3
Belgium	1	1	–	2
Austria	–	–	1	1
Czechoslovakia	–	1	–	1
Tanzania	–	1	–	1
Senegal	–	1	–	1
New Zealand	–	–	1	1
Korea	–	–	1	1
Jamaica	–	–	1	1
Hungary	–	–	1	1
Bermuda	–	–	1	1

Athletes

Algeria

AFANE, Mimoun; AMIER, Yacine; AMOUR, Brahim; AZZI, Halim; BELBACHIR, El Hocain; BENHADDAD, Mohamed-Riad; BERKANE, Houredine; BOUABDELLAH, Mohamed; FERUGUENE, Abdelouhab; GRICHE, Ilham; HAMMOU, Tahar; KOUIDRI, Soumaya; KRIM, Abdenour; MAHAMED, Amine; MAHOUR BACHA, Ahmed; MEFOU, Brahim; SI-MOHAMED, Nafissa; TAYEBI, Dalila; YAHIOUCHE, Djamel;

Angola

ALEXIXO, Amaral; ASSIS, Faustina; BAIAO, Adriano; BONIFACIO, Orlando; CARVALHO, Maria; CONCEICAO, Jean; COSTA, Agostinho; CRUZ, Filomena; DAIO, Ana; FERNANDES, Gaspar; FERRAZ, Afonso; FONSECA, Fernando; GARRIDO, Luis; GONCALVES, Carols; GONCALVES, Fernando; GOURGEL, Maria; GUIMARAES, Jose; INACIO, Ruben; INGLES, Augusto; JOAO, Armando; JUNIOR, Manmel; KOLL, Joao; MCCAMBA, Jacinto; MATAMBA, Agostinho; PAQUETE, Gualberto; PEREIRA, Domingos; SANTOS, Antonio; SEPULVEDA, Gertrudes; TAVARES, Sara;

Argentina

BARRIOPEDRO, Carlos Alberto; BLANCO, Alejandro; CALLIGARO, Guillermo Eduardo; GIANCOLA, Silvana Ines; GIOIOSO, Felix Maria; LECOT, Alejandro; LUCCHETTI, Marcos Flavio; LUCCHETTI, Sergio Alejandro; LUTOTOVICH, Claudio; MAGNASCO, Marcelo Mariano; MULERO, Gabriel E.; ORIANI, Coustanza; REMETE, Tomas Antonia; SINIGAGLIA, Maria Alicia; URIZAR, M.; URIZAR, Marcelo;

Australia

ALLISON, Gary; APPLEBY, Christopher T.; BARRALET, Heather O.; BARRATT, Mark R.; BIRNBAUM, Werner; BOGNAR, Jane; BYNG, Shaw; CAIRNS, Brett; CARLYON, Grant; CARRIGAN, Christopher J.; CLOSE, Ross A.; COOKING, Doug; COTEN, Edward J.; COTTRELL, Simon G.; CREW, Brett J.; CURTIN, John; DEDMAN, Lisa; EVANS, Leanne; EVANS, Peter; FENECH, Christopher; FENTON, Scott A.; FORD, Michelle; FORD, Richard; GILBERT, Paul L.; JOHNSON, Lance; LEE, Michael P.; LUKE, Karl A.; MCGUFFICKE, Graeme; MCKAY, Christopher; MIDDLETON, James; O'REGAN, Denis; OPHEL, John L.; PANAYI, Shaun; POTOK, Richard; RAWSON, Bruce; RODDA, David; ROYAL, Glen; TERRELL, Kim; TOTH, Magdalena; VADIVELOO, Michael T.; WAIN, Peter T.; WILSON, Andrew; WOODHOUSE, Susie;

Austria

BAYER, Herwig; BLASCHKA, Robert; BLUMEL, Andreas; BLUMEL, Harald; DITTRICH, Kurt; HUBER, Norbert; JOKL, Roland; KATZELBERGER, Florian; LEMBACHER, Hannes; PACHTA, Georg; PETUTSHNIG, Elisabeth; PILHATSCH, Alexander; PRENNER, Petra; PROHASKA, Gerhard; STROHMEYER, Arno; TSCHIRK, Wolfgang; WERTHNER, Georg;

Bangladesh

SARDARIFTEKAR, Ahmed;

Barbados

BAYLEY, Ruben; FORDE, Elvis; INNISS, Henry;

Belgium

ANNYS, Eddy; BODEUX, Marc; BOTTELBERGHS, Peter; CAMBRE, Peter; CAUTAERTS, Patrick Louis Felix; CLAES, Carl; DAENES, Peter; DE BRANDT, Jan; DE RUYSSCHER, Isle; DUCHATEAU, Myriam; FLAMENT, Luc; HOORENS, Jan; JAMMAERT, Jan; JASPAR, Jean Paul; KWASPEN, Jos; LARDINOIT, Thierry; MUSHIETE, Olivier; PLATEAU, Carl; REDANT, Hendrik; ROUSSEAUX, Emile; SCHELLEKENS, Daniel; SCHELLEKENS, Kris; SOETEWEY, Peter; STEVENS, Eric; TEURLINGS, Luc; VAN HEMELRYCK, Rudi; WERNIMONT, Stephane; WILLEN, Luc;

Benin

ADJANOHOUN, Alphonse Evariste; AHLINVI, Maxime; AMLON, Georges; BANKOLE, Yves; DARBOUX, David Jean; GAGLOZOUN, Alphonse; GANSOU, Luc; KARL, Kenneth; OUSSOU, Augustin; VIGNISSY, Dossou Germain Modeste; ZIME, Ali;

Bermuda

BURGESS, Steven; SAUNDERS, Clarence; SMITH, Sonya;

Bolivia

AGUAYO ALMAROZ, Edgar; AUZA, Eduardo; AUZA, Luis; CHIRI AVALOS, Laura; CRIALES ESTRUGO, Jose Antonio; FLORES CASTRO, Javier; HERRERA LLANQUE, Marcelino; MOREJON LOPEZ, Osvaldo; ROJAS VILLANUEVA, Maria; SAUCEDO VACA, Guillermo Javier; VAZQUEZ, Luis Dario;

Brazil

AMARL CHAVES, Orlando; ANCHIETA, Ana Keilh; ANDREATTA, Virginia; ARAUJO NOBREGA, Wellington; BECKER LOTUFO, Mario Sergio; BORTOLOCCI FERREIRA, Renato; CAMPOS DO NASCIMENTO, Rui; CARVALHO, Carlos Eduardo; CARVALHO, Dulce; CARVALHO, Luiz; CLAUDIO DE CASTRO FIGUEIREDO, Luis; CORREIA, Paulo Roberto; DA MATTA FREIRE, Claudio; DE ANDRADE SOUTO, Mario Eduardo; DE ANDRADE SOUZA, Gerson; DE CAMPOS, Andre Nicolas; DE FREITAS GUIMARAES, Gilberto; DE OLIVERIA BOHRER, Walter Carlos; DIAS FERREIRA, Antonio; DOS SANTOS, Solon; FERNANDES, Jorge; FRANCA MAGALHAES, Marcus Vinicius; FREITAS GARCIA, Esmeralda de Jesus; GOLDENSTEIN, Marcos; GOMES, Claudia; GUEIROZ RIBEIRO, Antonio Carlos; JUCA, Marcelo; LAMPARIELLO NETO, Domingos; LEME, Vera; LINS OLIVEIRA CHAVES NETTO, Franciscolins; LOURENCO, Marcus; MACHADO, Luiza; MADRUGA, Djan; MADRUGA, Roger; MANFRED, Silvio; MARTINS LIMA, Paulo Antonio; MATTA, Maria; MENEZES, Ronald; MIRANDA, Isabel; NAKAYA, Katsuhico; NEVES DE SOUZA, Ivonete; PASQUALI DE PRA FILHO, Leonidio; PEREIRA, Adriana; PEREIRA DA SILVA, Juraciara; PEREIRA DE MACEDO, Ronaldo; PONTES DE CARVALHO SILVA, Ayrton Pontes; PRADO, Ricarco; PRADO FALCATO, Aldmir; REIS, Sidney; RIBEIRO, Rosemary; ROCHA DE REZENDE, Bernardo; ROESE, Heloisa; SALGADO, Maria; SAMPAIO NETO, Maviael; SILVA, Fernanda; SILVA, Jacqueline; SILVA, Martha; SIMOES DE FREIRE, Marcos Vinicius; SUFFERT, Helga; TEBBE BORGES, Eric; TEIXEIRA, Rita; VAZ, Linai; VCHOA, Regina; VERISSIMO, Olga Maria; VOLPATO, Jose Mauricio; WARD MURTINHO, Eric;

Bulgaria

GUERCEV, Ilia; ILIEVA, Vanguelia; KAROUSHKOV, Aliosha; KASHANOV, Panayot; MATEEV, Nikolay; NENOV, Stanimir; PASKALEV, Anton; PENCHEV, Stanimir; TANEV, Ivan; VAMCJEV, Zaprian; VASSILEVA, Snejana; YANCHEV, Roumen; ZAPRIANOV, Antoni;

Canada

ABDO, Reema; ADAM, Marc; AGGISS, Sara; ALTWASSER, Garry; ANDERSON, John; ARMSTRONG, Alison Jean; AUDET, Marie Claude; BABITS, Laslo; BACON, Richard Mark; BANOS, Jean-Marie; BANOS, Jean-Paul; BARBER, George; BARIL, Claudine; BARRETT, John; BAUER, Heidi; BAUMANN, Alex; BENGSTON, Ric; BERGERON, Yvan; BERNIER, Sylvie; BETHUNE, Tim; BLACKWELL, Andrea Jill; BLAND, Nina; BOL, Rene; BORSHOLT, Lisa; BOTNEN, Anita; BOUTET, Michel; BRENNAN, Mike; BROTHERS, Tanya; BROWN, Geoff; BURTON, Dave; BUSH, Bev; CAMPBELL, Valerie Lynn; CAMU, Marie Helene; CAPPELLETTO, Ivana; CARDYN, Silvana Ines; CATALANO, Martino; CHAFE, Ross; CHAMBERS, Sandy; CHAMBUL, Luby; CHARTRAND, Celine; CHARTRAND, Phillipe; CHARTRAND, Valerie; CHOUINARD, Jean-Marc; CHURCHILL, David; CLARK, John; CLARKE, Sharon; COCHRAN, Beth Alice; COLLYER, Brian; COPP, Melinda; CORCORAN, Erin; COTE, Alain; COTE, Caroline Martine; COULTER, Allan Spencer; CROOKS, Charmaine; CURIK, Sharon; CYR, Claude; DAIGNEAULT, Julie; DANYLUK, Taras; DARLING, Barry; DE SERRES, Anne Marie; DESCHAMPS, Simon; DEWIS, Karen; DUCHARME, Isobelle; DUKESHIRE, Kelley; DUNTON, Susan Margaret; ENWEANI, Cyprian; FILLION, Denise; FITZPATRICK, Kenneth; FLEMONS, Wade; FRASER, Karen Lynn; GALLOWAY, Carol Elizabeth; GAMBLE, Susan; GARAPICK, Nancy; GARAY, Judy; GARNEAU, Louis; GAUDET, Daniel; GAUTHIER, Ginette; GIASSON, Benoit; GIBSON, Susan; GINGRAS, Natalie; GLASS, Jeffrey Laurence; GOODENOUGH, Terry; GRATTON, Paul Arthur Joseph; GRAY, Robert; GURUNLIAN, Varouj; GUSS, Lloyd; HARKNESS, Jack; HATCH, John; HAUCH, Rosemarie; HERBERT, Gordon Walter; HETHERINGTON, Jill; HINDS, Doug; HINDS, Sterling; HIRST, Jeff; HITCHCOCK, Dean Gary; HITCHCOCK, Monica Joan; HOAG, Glenn Arthur; HONOUR, Sandra; HOOGEWERF, Simon; HUBAND, Deborah; HUET, Sylvain; IWANCIN, Vernon; JAMES, Ian; JENKINS, Bill; JOHNSON, Ben; JONES, Thomas Donald; JOY, Greg; JUHASZ, Alexander; KAAY, John Adrian; KAMELI, Susan; KASTELIC, Donna; KAZANOWSKI, Gerald Francis; KELLY, Wayne; KELSEY, William Howard; KETRZYNSKI, Alexander T.; KILLINGBECK, Molly; KOKKOLA, Lorri Jean; KORDIC, Toni Angela; LACOULINE, Michel; LAHEURTE, Phillipe;

LAMBERT, Rory; LAPOINTE, Francois; LAROUCHE, Aline; LARSON, Ken; LEBLANC, Guillaume; LEBLANC, Louise Marie; LOCKHART, Paul; LONG, Warren; LUSSCHEN, Charlotte; MACDONALD, Roderick; MACDONALD, Stroud; MACKAY, Elizabeth; MAESSEN, Karin Maria; MARCIL, Claude; MARUBASHI, Naomi; MASSON, Alain; MASSON, Rob; MCARA, Tracie Lynn; MCCLOY, Paul; MCCLUSKEY, Michael; MCKAY, Beverly Dianne; MCKOY, Marc; MEAGHER, Danny Gerard; METULLUS, Alain; MEYER, Bill; MILLS, Jennifer Tracy; NEIL, Susie; NELSON, Karen; NEW, Maureen; NEWHOUSE, Ian; NUTZENBERGER, Frank; O'MALLEY, Jim; OLSEN, Marc; ONGARO, Alex; ORZEL, Mark; OTT, Peter; OTTEY, Milt; PAGE, Andrea; PASQUALE, Ilario Enrico; PAYNE, Marita; PENDERGAST, Anna Marie; PERREAULT, Daniel;

PAN, Shenghua; PENG, Yuanchun; PU, Xiaoxia; QIU, Shiyong; QU, Baowei; RONG, Ji; SHAO, Hong; SHEN, Lijuan; SHI, Meigin; SONG, Jin Wei; SONG, Weigang; SU, Lianfeng; SUN, Fengwu; SUN, Lunying; TAN, Liangde; TONG, Hui; WANG, Aiqin; WANG, Bin; WANG, Guili; WANG, Guiying; WANG, Hao; WANG, Jun; WANG, Libin; WANG, Meina; WANG, Minhui; WANG, Xiangping; WANG, Xiaotian; WANG, Yuping; WENG, Kangqiang; WENHONG, Xu; WOFU, Huang; WU, Jinhuang; WU, Qiuhua; WU, Yuezhen; XIAO, Qing Song; XU, Li; XU, Zhiqian; XUE, Cuilan; YAN, Jian Ming; YANG, Guiling; YANG, Li Gun; YANG, Rongxin; YANG, Wenqin; YE, Peisu; YE, Runcheng; YI, Liping; YIN, Qin; YU, Cuizhi; YU, Jue Min; YUN, Lou; ZHAI, Ji Xin; ZHANG, Bin; ZHANG, Liuru; ZHANG, Ren Jiang; ZHANG, Xingyan; ZHANG, Yanlong; ZHAO, Bilong; ZHIQIANG, Xu; ZHONG, Ni;

A rousing, standing ovation greeted the Canadian contingent which was last to march into the stadium for Opening Ceremonies July 1. Swimmer Alex Bauman of Laurentian University at Sudbury carried the flag for the host country.

PESCOD, Grant John; PETERS, Brad; PHILION, Madeleine; PITTER, Rob; POIRIER, Jacynthe, POLSON, Lynn Maxine; PONTING, Thomas; POPADICH, Milan; PULFER, Robert; RATNIK, Diane; REDDON, Allan; REID, Brigitte; REID, Cameron; REID, David; RICHARDSON, Jillian Cheryl; RICHARDSON, Kathy; RIDDLE, Jeffrey; ROBERTS, Katherine Marie; ROCHELEAU, Luc; ROOKS, Nancy; ROSS, Jill; SAGEMAN, Randy; SANDERS, Linda Jean; SAXTON, Donald S.; SCHLEGEL, Elfi; SCOTT, Debbie; SCOTT, Janet; SEALEY, Carole Jane; SENYK GAMBORG, Joyce Muriel; SEWARDS, Mike; SHARPE, Tony; SHEEHAN, Jeffrey; SHEMILT, David; SIMMS, Tony; SINCLARE, Kory; SLYTHE, Christine; SMITH, Suzette; SNIVELY, David Blake; SOKOLOWSKI, Michal; STEEN, David; STEINER, Shelley; STIEDA, Alex; SWEENEY, Sylvia; SZMIDT, Peter; TABOR, Beth; TAYLOR, Angela; TESKEY, Mary Jillian; THOMAS, Misty; TILLEMAN, Karl; TRIANO, Howard James; TURCOTTE, Serge; TURNEY-LOOS, Carol; TYSDALE, Jennifer; VANDYKE, Anita; VANTOL, Gordon; VERBEEK, Grace; VERRECCHIA, Wendy Ann; WAGNER, Randolph Thomas; WALL, Gwen; WALSH, Roderick Camillus; WATSON, Megan; WAY, Kelly Ann; WELBOURNE, Graham; WENNINGTON, William; WEST, Mike; WHITE, Julie; WILLIAMS, Andrea Ruth; WILLIAMS, Desai; WILLIAMS, Lynn; WILLIAMS, Paul; WILTJER, Gregory Hilko; WITTMEIR, Robin; WOODS, Fiona; WOSTENHOLME, Martin; WRIGHT, George; YOUNG, Daryl Glenn; ZAYONC, Richard; ZILKE, Laural;

ZHONGYI, Li; ZHOU, Jihong; ZHOU, Xiaolin; ZHOU, Zuohui; ZHU, Liping; ZHU, Qingyuan; ZONG, Yuming; ZUO, Xun;

Chile

MOLINA CIFUENTES, Cristian Eugenio; REGONESI MURANDA, Monica Patricia; SCHNEIDER ZUANICH, Luis Alberto; SQUELLA, Pablo;

Peoples Republic of China

BAO, Xi Sheng; CAI, Shengliu; CAI, Shu; CHEN, Chao; CHEN, Qin; CHEN, Xiao Qi; CHEN, Xiao Qi; CHEN, Yahui; CHEN, Ying; DENG, Jun; DING, Fenghua; FENG, Dawei; GAO, Shujun; GUAN, Shishi; GUAN, Yi Li; GUO, Yonglin; HAN, Pengshan; HAN, Quigling; HE, Ping; HUANG, Guangliang; HUANG, Guohua; HUANG, Long; HUANG, Xiuqin; HUANG, Ying; HUANG, Yunlong; JI, Yong Ping; JI, Zhaoguang; JIA, Wen; JIN, Fu; KUANG, Lubin; LI, Hongping; LI, Huahua; LI, Jianming; LI, Kongzehng; LI, Weinan; LI, Xinyi; LI, Yaguang; LIANG, Weifen; LIAO, Wenfen; LIMIN, Zou; LIN, Hui; LIU, Jianguo; LIU, Jianli; LIU, Meiling; LIU, Ruixia; LIU, Shu Hdia; LIU, Yongjun; LU, Jinqing; LU, Wei; LU, Yue; LUAN, Jujie; MA, Keqin; MA, Yaonan; MAI, Guoqiang; MULAT, O.;

Congo

BEMOU, Jean-Didace; KIAKOUAMA, Antoine; MANDONDA, Alphonse; MBOUALA, Mbouala; MOZENGUE, Joseph; NDINGA, Henri; NTSANA NKOUNKOU, Antoine; OBOUNGA, Gislain; RIZET, Ronald;

Cuba

ABREU ARCHER, Osvaldo Agustin; ABREU PASCUAL, Pedro; ALEMAN RODRIGUEZ, Francisco; ALFARO QUINONES, Jorge Luis; ALFONSO ARREU, Emilio; ALFONSO FREIRE, Clara; ALFONSO GARCIA, Noel; AMADOR GARCIA, Lazaro; ARTILES QUINTANA, Denis; AVEILLE UGARTE, Elida Maria; AVILA CRESPO, Alexis; BARRERAS BENITEZ, Juan Carlos; BELTRAN FERRER, Maria Antonia; BELTRAN RIZO, Lazaro; BENITEZ SUAREZ, Carlos; BICET CALZADO, Erasmo; BLAY GARCIA, Francisco; BORREGO VALDES, Jesus; CABRERA, Isreal; CABRERA ROSELL, Eduardo; CALDERON POZO, Raul; CAMPANIONI PASTRANA, Ruben; CASTRO MARTINEZ, Mario; CENTELLES AIZPURUA, Juan Francisco; CHACON ABREU, Ricardo; CHIVAS CLEGER, Elsa Lidia; CLEMENTE BARZAGA, Jose; COSTA ACOSTA, Silvia; COSTA MENDEZ, Lazard; CUESTA ZULUETA, Pablo Roger; DE VALLE GUTIERREZ, Jorge; DEGRASSE IBANEZ, Iris Elena; DEL RISCO RANDICH, Maria Mercedes; DELIS FOURNIER, Luis Mariano; DEROUVILLE DE AL CRUZ, Jesus; DIAZ BABIER, Tulio; DIAZ CERVANTES, Barbaro; DIAZ ESTUPINAN, Julian; DIAZ ESTUPINAN, Julian; DOMINGUES AVILA, Nelson; DOMINGUES AVILA, Juan; DUBOIS CUMBA, Raula; DURAN ZUNIGA, Carmen Luisa; DURRUTI WILSON, Mario Ismael; ECHEVARRIA TORRIENTE, Eloina Calixta; ESTRADA RAMOS, Caridad; FAVIEL SANDO, Efigenio; FERNANDEZ TORRES, Rosario; FRANKLIN LEYVA, Alberto; GALARRAGA ESQUIVEL, Julio; GARCIA GARCIA, Angel; GARCIA MARQUEZ, Robly; GONZALES, Odalis Moneno; GONZALES VASQUEZ, Rafael; GONZALEZ ACOSTA, Tania; GONZALES ALONSO, Sergio; GONZALEZ MOLINA, Milagros; GONZALEZ XIQUES, Herberto; GUERRA, Armando Perez; GUILLEN PEDROSO, Rodolfo; HECHEVARRIA DOMINGUEZ, Maira Caridad;

HENRY TORRIENTE, Wilfredo N.; HERNANDEZ-PEREZ, Antonio; HERNANDEZ, Enrique; HERNANDEZ ALBERNAZ, Pedro; HERRERA ORTIZ, Hector; HUNG SALAZAR, Roberto; ILISASTEGUI ARMAND, Alcibiades; INFANTE RUIZ, Argelio; ISALGUE CUMBA, Jose Luis; LAFERTE CHAVEZ, Ramon; LAVERDEZA MONTOYA, Jose; LEYVA BORRERO, Ricardo; LOWRY, Regina; LUACES RODRIGUEZ, Noangel; LUIS, Maria Rodriguez; MACHADO RUIZ, Grisel; MARCELINA, Rodriguez; MARCOS CRESPO, Dagoberto; MARQUÉZ RICHARDS, Edelmis Margot; MARTEN GARCIA, Maritza; MARTINEZ BENAVIDES, Drisel; MARTINEZ DESPAIGNE, Lazaro; MASSO RAMIREZ, Raul; MATURELL RAMOS, Alberto; MENESES, Lesula Artaga; MERENCIO GIRON, Pedro Roman; MOLA FUENTES, Walfrido Vidal; NEMAR ARMAS, Daniel; NOGUERA, Nelson Cruz; NUNEZ LEYVA, Miguel; NUSSA PENALVER, Agapito; OVIEDO BONILLA, Luis; PADRON HERNANDEZ, Eliecer; PADRON SANCHEZ, Juan Carlos; PAEZ ROJAS, Aguedo; PAGES, Guerra; PAVO SANTOS, Agustin; PERALTA CANDOCIA, Alberto; PEREZ ARMENTERO, Leonardo; PEREZ HERRERA, Roberto; PEREZ LEMUS, Enrique; PEREZ LOPEZ, Antonio Luis; PEREZ SUAREZ, Ileana; PORTELA AMEZAGA, Orlando; QUINTER BORGES, Antonio; RAMIREZ ONATE, Abel; RAMIREZ RODRIGUEZ, Juan Carlos; RAMOS HERNANDEZ, Auturo; RAMOS MANES, Hilda Elisa; RAMOS MONTALVO, Roberto Enrique; RAMOS SOLER, Jose A.; RIVERA GONZALEZ, Jesus Manuel; RUBIDO QUESADA, Anet Josefina; RUIZ LAGARGUE, Carlos Simon; RUIZ LORENZO, Fabio; SANCHEZ SALGADO, Ismael Isreal; SANTIESTEBAN ZAPATIN, Basilio; SARMIENTOS BIOS, Abel; SILIE TABARES, Leonardo; SIMON SALOMON, Roberto; SOLORZANO ALVAREZ, Israel; SUAREZ, Ma. Eugenia; SUAREZ AIMEE, Sergio Casimiro; TABLADA JIMENEZ, Carlos; TORRES BROCH, Felipe Herberto; TORRES TORRES, Gonzalo Manuel; TREJO BELEN, Jorge Luis; TRIANA ALMENARES, Adolfo N.; VIDAL, Walfrido; VILA MACHADO, Mayra; VILLAVERDE MARRERO, Lazaro; ZULUETA ARGUELLES, Juan.

Czechoslovakia

GAJDOSOVA, Jana; MARECKOVA, Eva; PITLOVICOVA, Iva; SARISSKA, Katarina;

Denmark

BERTELSEN, Henrik Bjorn;

Dominican Republic

SHILLINGFORD, Noella

Egypt

ABDEL HAMID, Essam; ABDEL MAGEID, Amr; ABO BAKR, Moustafa; ABOU EL ALA, Moustafa; ALY, Ashraf; ASKALANI, Ahmed; BALIGH, Khalid; BEKHEET, Khaled; BEKHEET, Nabeel; EL NAGGAR, Amr; EL SHAMOUTI, Ahmed; EL-ABDY, Ayman; EL-SHAMERLY, Sherif; FAHMI, Alaa; FARAG, M.; FARID, Tarek; FATHY, W; HAMDY, Ahmed Moataz; HASSAN, Adel; IBRAHIM, El-Sayed; MAOWAD, Essam; MORAD, Emad; MOUSTAFA, Ahmed; NADIM, A.; NOUR, Sherif; RAOOF, Hesham; SAID, Ahmed; SELIM, Khalid; SHABAN, Hesham; SHARAOUI, Mohamed; SHATTA, Ahmed; SOLIMAN, Mohamed; TAWFIK, Amr; TAWFIK, Ashraf; WALAA, Mohammed;

Finland

HEROLD, Roy Nicos; KAIVONEN, Pentti Olavi; KALLIO, Tapio Jaakko; KLINGA, Kari-Pekka; KOHO, Tarja Hannele; KULONEN, Kari Mauri; KUUSELA, Jari Petteri; LEHTONEN, Harri Tapio; PATTAKAINEN, Jouni; PENTTILA, Reijo Juhani; PURANEN, Kimmo; SAARELAINEN, Timo; SAJANTILA, Martti Tapio; SALMI, Mikael Olavi; SALMINEN, Mikko; SAMSTEN, Karl Tarani; VOUTILAINEN, Antti Petteri; WINTER, Lars;

France

ADAM; AMORIC, Carolle; ANIAUD, Francoise; ANTIBE, Viviane; BARBIERI, Lauren; BATAILLE, Dominique; BENINTENDI, Corinne; BENSIMON, Laurence; BERTHIER, Frank; BILY, Laurence; BOSERO, Catherine; BOUGNOL, Florence; BOUSSEMART, Jean-Jacques; BOUTARD, Michel; BOUVIER, Eric; BROTHIER, Gabriel; CABANE, Marie Christine; CALZOLARI, Sylvie; CANTI, Aldo; CERBONI, Marc; CHICHIGNOUD, Pascal; CLEZARDIN, Catherine; CLOAREC, Yvon; COLLET, Phillippe; DELAFOSSE, Patricia; DESERT, Isabelle; DEVOS, Lionel; ESCOBAR, Ine; ETIENNE, Nathalie; EWANGE-EPEE, Maryse; FABIANI, Alain; FALANDRY, Sophie; FAYROT; FRANCOIS; GARCIA, Andres; GOASDOUE, Dominique; GOUX, Richard; ISNARD, Guypaine; KACZMAREK, Christophe; LAGNEAUX, Sylvie; LAROCHE, Tierry; LAVIE, Andre; LEBLEU, Jaine Christine; LEMAIRE, Claire; LEMENAGE, Didier; LESAGE, Brigitte; LLASTER; LONGO, Jeannie; MALFOIS, Catherine; MAZZON, Herve; MEYGRET, Anne Christane Lucienne; MEYNARD, Michel; MOLLEX, Marie-France; MONTAGNON, Eric; MORTREUX, Karine; NICOLOSO, Isabelle; PAYS-LABROUSSE, Laurence; PHILIPPE, Francoise; PIQUEREAU, Anne; PRAWERMANN, Anabelle; QUENTREC, Yann; QUISTORFF, Agnes Francoise; RIBLET, Jean-Philippe; RIBOUD, Stefhane; ROSSARD, Philippe; ROUDET, Blandine; ROUILLAUX, J; SPEZZATTI, Robert; SRECKI, Eric; TABOURIN, Bruno; THIBERT, Anne-Marie; TILLIE, Laurent; TOUSSAINT, Jean-Francois; TRINQUET, Pascale; VATUONE, Philippe; VIGNERON, Thierry;

Gabon

MISTOUL, Odette; OLOLO, Jean David;

Federal Republic of Germany

ASZALOS, Anna; BAETJER, Autje; BARANSKI, Andreas; BECKER, Christine; BRINUMANN; BRUGGE, Jorg; BUEHLER, Beate; BUERKLE, Martin; CHRISTIANSEN, Udo; DECKER, Andrea-Freya; DRESSEL, Birgit; DRIES, Cornelia; EGGERT, Sven; EVERTS, Sabine; FAHRNER, Thomas; FEGERT, Vive; FELDLIN, Brigitte; FOEHRENBACH, ClausDieter; FRITZSCHE; FROBOESE, Jogo; GABRIEL, Marita; GAMBUE, Wolfram; GELHAUSEN, Udo Hermann; GEUYEN, Thomas; GOTZMANN, Andrea; GRIESE, Anne; UGESGEN, Stefan; HAAS, Kerstin; HASSENPFLUG, Peter; HEER, Fritz-Werner; HEIMERZHEIM, Ute; HEINRICH, Gerald Gustav; HELMS, Fritz; HERLE, Christoph: HERRLICH, Gabriele; HETZEL, E. Silvia; HIRSCH, Monika; HOLZHAUSEN, Ruth; HUDAK, Harald; KABLER, Klaus Werner; KARCK, Ulrich; KASS, Antonius; KELLER, Matthias; KEMPERDICK, Almut; KLEINBRAHM, Petra; KLOCKE, Gorg; KNIPPHALS, Geus Kare Willy; KNIPPING, Angelika; KOHLAT, Vico; KRAUS, Michael; KRIEG, Lothar; KRIPPNER, Gerhard; KRONBERGER, Renata; KROTT, Martina; KUCZMANN, Maria; LANG, Peter; LANGE, Hilmar; LIEBELT, Angela; LOSCH, Claudia; MACKERODT, Frank; MANECKE, Jugra; MICHELS, Joerg; NAGEL, Gerd; NEUMANN, Gabriele; OVERMANN, Audreas; PETER, Herbert; PETERS, Beate; PETRY, Kersten Pele; PLACE-BRANDEL, Terry; RADZEY, Michael; REY, Christiane; RIEK, Renate; ROEDDECKE, Andrea; RUEHMER, Brigitta; SALANDER, Axel; SANDER, Dirk; SARSKY, Klaus; SATTLER, Berno; SCHAUMANN, Alex; SCHENTEN, Dagmar; SCHEUFELE, Stefan; SCHMIDT, Andreas A.; SCHMITT, Uwe; SCHNEIDER, Andre; SCHOLZ, Peter; SCHOWTKA, Klaus Alexander; SCHREIBER, Helmut; SCHRODER, Anke; SCHUBERT, Christa; SCHULER, David; SCHULZE, Yens; SCHWARZ, Karin; SCHWARZ, Roman; SETTLEMAYER, Jochen; SEUSER, Axer; SPOTTEL, Michael; STADEN GELS MILOWIDOWO, Marina; STEINDOR; STOEWAHSE, Sabine; SUDE, Burkhard; TERSTEGGE, Sigrid; THRANHARDT, Carlo; THYSSEN, Yingrid; TILLER, Torsten Manhu; TRAPPE, Christoph; VANDER, BOSCH, Kai; VOLLMER, Elke; VOLMER, Peter; VOSS, Christian; VOSSEN, Regina; WATSCHUE, Corinna; WAYMENT, Heidi; WEGINER, Heinz Wilhelm; WIEGAND, Nicola; WILHELM, Angela; WILKING, Thomas; WITTE, Gudrun Gisela; WITTICH, Robert; ZASUE, Werner; ZIRNGIBL, Werner;

Ghana

DODOO, Francis; ISSAH, Stalin; KODUAH, Sam; MENSAH, Collins; OBENG, Ernest; OPOKU, Helena;

Great Britain

ARKWRIGHT, John; ASTBURY, Andrew; BARTLETT, Terence Joseph; BELL, Gwendoline Anne; BENT, Stephen; BERRY, Catherine; BETT, Michael; BLOWER, Joanne; BLOXHAM, Clifford; BONFIELD, Peter; BOOKER, Claire; BOTT, Julian; BUNYAN, Christopher Philip; BURRELL, Richard James; BUSWELL, Murray; BYNDE, Leon; CAMPBELL, Maureen; CARTWRIGHT, Paul; DAVIES, Simeon Evan Henry; DAVIS, Jonathon Simon; DEAR, Simon Wilfred; DONALDSON, Euan James; DONALDSON, Robert; DRANSFIELD, Andrew Simon; EDWARDS, Sadie Fiona; FARRELL, Peter; FIBBENS, Nicola; FORSTER, Kevin John; GREEN, Brian Neil; GRIFFITHS, Michael; HADWEN, Seymour; HARRIS, Stephen John; HARTLEY, Clive; HENRY, Norma; HERBERT, John; HOTTAGE, Kenneth; HUBBLE, Philip; JAMESON, Helen; JENNER, Sue; KENNISON, Robert; KILLINGLEY, Tracy Ann; KINCH, Beverley; KINSELL, Gregg; KLENERMAN, Paul; KOCHER, Kenneth; LANGLEY, Keith; LISTON, George David; LIVERMORE, Judith Beverley; LOUGHTON, Sally; MACMILLAN, Fraser; MCDERMOTT, Kirsty Margaret; MCGEORGE, Christopher Anthony; MCINTOSH, Fiona Jane; MCKENZIE, Neville James; MELLING, Duncan; MITCHELL, Ian; MORRISON, James; OBIKWU, Fidalias; PENNY, Kevin; POPE, Janice Irene; REID, Donald; ROLLO, Patricia; ROSS, Tamarin Elizabeth; ROWELL, Sarah; SCARBOROUGH, Madeleine; SCOTT, Joseph Guy; SMITH, Nicola; SPINK, Thomas Ian; STEWART, Neil Leighton; TACON, Joy; THOMAS, Allan John; THWAITES, Susan Lynn; TURNBULL, Geoffrey; VAUGHAN, Clyde; VESTY, Philip; WALDUCK, Vincent; WALLACE, Shaun; WEIR, Robert; WHITNELL, Tracey Jane; WILLIAMSON, Graham; WILSON, Craig;

Greece

DARA, Sofia; DELIFOTIS, Nikolaos; DELIPHOTIS, Dimitrios; GEORGAKOPOULOS, Konstantinos; GEORGE, Vamvakas; KOTSAMEASIS, Kostas; MICHAS, Demetrios; PANAGOS, Panayotis; STRATOS, Kosmas; TRIKALIARIS, Ioakim;

Guatamala

ALDANA PEREZ, David; ALVARADO PENADOS, Bruno; AGAGON, Lucrecia; ARAGON, Nora; ARAGON ORTIZ, Ana Lucrecia; ARAGON ORTIZ, Rafael Enrique; ARAGON ORTIZ DE ORELLANA, Nora Patricia; AREVALO TRIBOUILLIER, Ariana Akil; ASTURIAS, Jose Rodolfo: BLANCO GRAMAJO, Raul Eduardo; CANIVELL, Rocio; CARRILLE JUAREZ, Herbert Lionel; CENTENO, Marta; CENTENO, Mercedes; CENTENO, Mercedes: CENTENO, Silvia; CENTENO ORANTES, Hector Manuel; CHNCILLA SOLORZANO, Manuel Eduardo; CONDE ORELLANA, Manuel Eduardo; DIAZ GRANILLO, Angel Estuardo; GALINDO, Jose; GARCIA MOLINA, Hugo Allan; GUZMAN, Oscar Alfredo; HERERA, Norma; JORDAN, Astrid; KUHN MAZARIEGOS, Walter Estuardo; LEIVA, Reinaldo Arturo; LOPEZ DAVILA, Alberto; MARROQUIN, Edna; MARROQUIN MIYARES, Angel Roberto; MARTA, Centeno; MARTINEZ, Sonia; MEIGHAN, Dick; MENDOZA, Mayra; MENENDEZ DIAZ, Roberto; QUEVEDO, Carlos; QUINONES, Patricia; QUINONEZ LURSSEN, Werner Rene; QUINONEZ MAZARIEGOS, Dora Patricia; RECINOS TOBAR, Francisco; RODAS JUAREZ, Hector Gilberto; RUANO BARRIENTOS, Alicia; SAJCHE, Cesar; SAMAYOA OLIVA, Emilio Vladimir; SARAVIA, Zully; SCHUMANN, Christa; SOBALVARRO, Alfonso; VETTCRAZZI HERRERTE, Gerardo Alfonso; VILLAGRAN, Mario; ZULETA GUANCHE, Sergio Adolfo;

Hong Kong

CHAN, Betty; CHAN, Chor-Man Kevin; CHAN, Rainnie; CHAN, Shiu Hang; CHAN, Stella; CHAN, Wing Fat; CHENG, Wai Kwong; CHEUNG, Fan Sang; CHUNG, Vicky Wai Yin; KO, Tak Chuen; KWOK, Sai Lam; LAI, Pansy Wai Yee; LAU, Ting Ch; LEUNG, Wai Man; LI, Chi Kwong; LI, Yuk Keung;

LUI, Dat Shui; NG, Kit Wing; PUN, Chi Hoy; SHUM, Kam Wing Ivan; SUN, Man Fu; TANG, Po Loy; TONG, Anita; TONG, Kwok Keung; TSE, Chee Hung; TSE, Long Ming; TSE, Man Chuen; WONG, Daisy Ka Nar; WONG, Emily; WONG, Helen Pik Keun; WOO, Kar Wai Divid; YAU, Yi Kwong;

Holland

BLIKSLAGER, Hans Johann; BOEVE, Henk; DE BRUIN, Erik: DEGROOT, Maryke; DEMUTH; Daphne; DUCROT, Martinus Antonius; GEYSEN, Hansje; JAGER, Harm; JENNEN, Wilhelmus Hubertus Jozef; KOLKHUIS TANKE, Paschalis Radboud; KOREVAAR, Jan Japp; KRAUS, Annelies; LASSODY, Johannes Hendrikus; NIEUWENHUIZEN, Theodorus Anton; NONNEKES, Dick Arnold; STEENBRINK, Leonardus Hendrikus Lambertus; TE KULVE, Eric Paul; VAANHOLD, Johan Gerard; VAN BELKUM, Alexander Franciscus, VAN BELKUM, Stan; VAN DER HORST, Wouter; VAN NOORT, Roald Max Antione; VERVOORN, Cornelis; WAGENAAR, Rolf Jan Bastiaan; YSKES, Renier: ZIMMERMANN, Wessel; ZOONTJENS, Bernardus Theodorus Maria;

Indonesia

AFAAR, Julius; KARDIONO; MANDAGIE, Herman; PURNOMO; SOETOPO; Hawin; TINTUS WILBOWE, Azyanto; WALALANGI, Wailan

India

BASRA, Balbir Singh; BHARGAVA, Amit; BHARGAVA, Deepak; DATTA, Vijaya Mala; DODLA, Vivek Kuma Reddy; KURISHGAL ABRAHAM, Shiny; RAI, Amitab; SINGH, Jaspal; SINGH, Nirmal; SURATH, Narendranath; VASUDEVAN, S.;

Ivory Coast

ADAMA, Berte; AGNIMEL, Aristide; BODUIT, Polneau J. P.; BOGUI, Jean Claude Hubert; BONEBO, Michel; CHINTOH, Hondua Marc; DIE, Drissa; DIOMANDE, G.; DIOP, Abass; DJADJI, Clement; DJAKARIDJA, Sanogo; DJEDJEMEL, Meledje Rene; GOBEY, Theodore Camille; GUEYE, Bernard Gregoire; KAMARA, Djibril; KEIPO, Tetiali; KOFFI, Barthelemy; KOKO KOFFI, Alain; KONAN, Kouame Ferdinand; KOUADIO, Otokpa; LAGAZANE, Ovattara; LATH, Memel Alain; MAMADOU, Kone; MOUSSA, Traore; N'DA; Lucienne; SAKO, Blaise; SHOOTER, Samuel; TIACOH, Gabriel; TUO, Fozie;

Iceland

JAKOBSSON, Oskar; JONSSON, Ingi Thor; SIGURDSSON, Oddur; VILHJALMSSON, Einar;

Israel

BEN-ZVI, Sari; BLATT, David; BOGIN, Niv; DRORI, Nili; ELIMELECH, Israel; EYAL, Shlomo; GORENSTEIN, Michael; HANDELSMAN, Mark; KAUFMAN, Haim; LEVI, Yehuda; MACKLER, Yair; MOYAL, Johnny; NELSON, Korky; POYASTRO, Miguel; RIMON, Boaz; SACK, Mark; SHEFA, Doron; STRICHMAN, Ron-Hanan; ZISMAN, Shmuel; ZLOTIKMAN, Haim;

Italy

AMBONI, Rocco; ARMELLINI, Emanuele; ARZILLI, Anna; BAIARDO, Rosanna; BAUDINO, Stefano; BAVIERA, Michele; BELLONE, Stefano; BELLUCCI, Alessandro; BENELLI, Manuela; BERTINETTI, Marco; BERTOLI, Franco; BERTOLINI, G. Franco; BIANCHI, Gabriele; BIANCHINI, Orlando; BIGIARINI, Beatrice; BINAGHI, Angelo; BITTI, Raimondo, Ricci; BOFFI, Franco; BOLLATI, Lorenzo; BONAN, Giovanni Modesto; BONFIGLIOLI, Alessandra; BONGIORNI, GIOVANNI; BONO, Sandro; BORELLA, Andrea; BORMIDA, Gianni; BORTOLASO, Laura; BOZAN, Patrizia; BRUNATI, Aster; BUCCI, Marco; CALABRIA, Andrea; CANAPI, Antonella; CAPOTOSTI, Carlo; CASIMIRRI, Doriana; CAVALIERE, Massimo; CECCHINI, Stefano; CERRI, Fenina; CERVI, Federico; CHESINI, Agostino; CICCONETTE, Carola; CINA, Michele; CIPRESSA, Andrea; CIRULLI, Guiseppina; COLLODEL, Guila; COLOMBO, Grazia; COLOMBO, Marco; CORNELLA, Fulvia; COSTA, Luigi; CRAPIZ, Paolo; CUOMO, Alessandro; D'ALEO, Giovanni; DA VITO, Giovanni; DALLA BARBA, Gianfranco; DALLA VALLE, Manuela; DAMETTO, Giancarlo; DAMILANO, Giorgio; DAMILANO, Maurizio; DELL'VOMO, Marco; DESANTIS, Luigi; DI BERNARDO, Mauro; DIVANO, Maurizio; DORIO, Gabriella; DRECSHEL, Victor; ERRICHIELLO, Giovanni; FABIANI, Fabiana; FALCO, Fabrizio; FALCONE, Marco; FAUSTINI, Alessio; FERRIAN, Daniela; FIORELLA, Pierluigi; FLAMIGNI, Cinzia; FRANCESCHI, Raffaele; GALLUCCI, Gabriella; GIULIANI, Stefania; GOBBATU, Dianella; GRANDI, Stefano; GRAZIOLI, Giovanni; GUARDUCCI, Marcello; GUIDUCCI, Gloria; IACOCCA, Antonio; LACAVA, Luca; LANFRANCO, Giovanni; LAZZARICH, Diego; LAZZER, Franco; LAZZERONI, Alessandro; LUCCHETTA, Andrea; MANZI, Roberto; MARCHFRO, Alberto; MARIN, Marco; MARTINO, Marco; MASULLO, Marisa; MATERAZZI, Riccardo; MEGLIO, Ferdinando; MEI, Stefano; MENOZZI, Anna; MERCURIO, Carla; MINELLO, Ennio; MOCHI, Clara; MOLTRASIO, Emilio; MONETTI, Gabriella; NEGRI, Marco; NINFA, Maurizio; NUMA, Stefano; PAOLETTI, Roberto; PATRIGNANI, Claudio; PESCI, Fernando; PETTINI, Francesco; PEZZATINI, Alessandro; PIOCHI, Marco; QUADRI, Giorgio; QUINTARELLI, Cristina; QUINTAVALLA, Fausta; RASTELLO, Alessandro; REBAUDENGO, Piero; RECINE, Stefano; RECINE, Pietro; ROSSI, Erica; RUGGIERI, Vinicio; SACCHETTI, Gianluigi; SALADINI, Fabio; SAVI SCARPONI, Cinzia; SCAGLIA, Corrado; SCALZO, Giovanni; SCIACERO, Piertino; SCIAMANNA, Fabio; SCREMIN, Sergio; SCURI, Angelo: SECCHI, Piero; SPARACIARI, Annarita; SPIEZIA, Erminio; STERBINI, Sergio; TAMBERI, Marco; TEMPESTINI, Riccardo; TORNATORE, Marco; TOSTIGLIONE, Stephano; TRAPANESE, Paolo; TREVISAN, Riccardo; TRONCHINI, Rinaldo; VECCHI, Paolo; ZUCCHINI, D.;

Jamaica

BOWEN, Karen; BOYD, Andrew; DAVIS, Lee; HASTING, Charles ACKSON, Grace; LAING, Earl; LUKE, Courtney; MCDEAN, Hyacinth; SCOTT, Dorothy; SMITH, Karl; THOMAS, Elsia; VON DIGNALL, Yvonne; WRIGHT, Fredrica;

Japan

AIKYO, Shigeyuki; AKAZAWA, Koji; ANZAI, Kimihiro; ARAI, Hirohito; ARAI, Shinji; ARIKAWA, Hideyuki; ASABA, Kazundri; EBIHARA: Keizo; EHARA, Masaru; ENDOH, Rika; ENMOTE, Yoko; FUJII, Junko; FUJIMORI, Koshi; FUJIMOTO, Miyuki; FUJIMURA, Yukihiro;

Japan will host the 1985 Summer Universiade at Kobe.

FUJITA, Etsuji; FUKUI, Mikako; FUKUMOTO, Toshio; FURUKAWA, Yasushi; HIRATA, Mie; HIRO, Misato; HISHIKI, Etsuko; HOKI, Daisuke; HONMA, Daisuke; HORI, Masahiko; HORIKE, Nobuko; HORIUCHI, Shoichi; IDO, Yukari; IKEDA, Shigemasa; INOUE, Yoshihiro; ISE, Takemi; ISHIBASHI, Takako; ITO, Koji; IWASHIMA, Akihiro; IZUMI, Kenji; KABUTO, Yasuko; KAI, Shingo; KAMIYA, Ryusuke; KAMIYA, Teruhisa; KANAMARU, Satoshi; KANO, Yayoi; KARAKIDA, Tsukasa; KASAMA, Yuji; KATO, Kazutoyo; KATSUNO, Mariko; KAWAI, Shunichi; KAWAKITA, Rika; KIMURA, Junko; KIMURA, Nobuo; KIMURA, Yoshihiko; KIN, Michiyo; KOBAYASHI, Kazuya; KOIKE, Hirofumi; KOSAKA, Tadahiro; KOSHIMIZU, Hideka; KOYASU, Hidehachi; KUBO, Katsuyuki; KIJMADA, Yasundri; KIJME, Naoko; KURAHASHI, Naomi; KUSAKARI, Nobud; MUTSUI, Emi; MINETA, Takayuki; MISHIBA, Koichi; MITSUHASHI, Eizaburo; MIYAHARA, Mieko; MORIUCHI, Nobukazu; MURAKAWA, Hitomi; MURAMATSU, Akihiko; MURAMATSU, Toshiya; NAGAI, Masahiko; NAGATA, Hisayoshi; NAGAYAMA, Kazumi; NAKANO, Ikuko; NAKASHIMA, Masashi; NAKAYA, Taeko; NAKAYAMA, Kiyomi; NAKAZAKA, Kiyomi; NAKAZATO, Yoshikazu; NARIHITO, Taima; NUSHIMUTA, Akifumi; NOZAKI, Shuichi; OCHI, Shigeo; OGAWA, Yumi; OGIMA, Eiji; OHATA, Keiichi; OIKAWA, Azusa; OKADA, Keiko; OKADA, Taichi; OKAMOTO, Kumiko; OKUDE, Akemi; OKUNO, Hiroaki; OMORI, Shigenori; ONODA, Hiroyuki; OTSUKI, Yoko; OURA, Asami; OZAKI, Akiko; RIKUKAWA, Akira; SAITO, Shinichi; SAITO, Yoshifumi; SAKAI, Tatsuro; SAKAMOTO, Tsutomu; SARUDATE, Mitsugi; SASAKI, Tomoko; SATO, Ichiko; SATO, Toshimi; SAYAMA, Koichi; SHIBUTANI, Toshihiro; SHIMA, Keiko; SHIMIZU, Yoshihiro; SHIMOMURA: Eiji; SONOHARA, Takehiro; SUZUKI, Hitomi; SUZUKI, Yumiko; TACHIBANA, Kiyotaka; TAKAHASHI, Hidetoshi; TAKAHASHI, Shigehiro; TAKANO, Susumu; TAKANO: Yoko; TAKAO, Yuka; TAKEZAKI, Kunitoshi; TAKIKAWA, Kazuo; TAKIZAWA, Reiko; TANAKA, Koichi; TANAKA, Naoki; TANAKA, Ryuji; TATSUMI, Kimiko; TERANISHI, Takatsune; TERASHITA, Ikuhiro; TSUKAMOTO, Satoshi; TSUMURAYA, Yoshihiro; UEDA, Kiyomi; UMEZAWA, Shieru; WAKAYOSHI, Koji; WAKIYA, Toshihiro; WATANABE, Chieko; WATANABE, Ikuyo; YAMAMOTO, Yoko;, YAMAUCHI, Kenji; YONESHIGE, Shuichi; YOSHIDA, Miwako; YOSHIHARA, Kumi; YOSHIOKA, Noriko;

Jordan

ABDULLAH, Ali Mohamed; ABU HILAI, Khaled Awad; AL-MUSLEH, Zaid; ALAWNEH, Eisa Ali Eisa; HADDAD, Ammar Awad; JANHO, Butros Salim; JUNA, Esam; KALED, Rateb Kaled; MALOOF, Ibrahim Philip; MARDINI, Monther Hasham; MASRI, Ahmad; MATTAR, Osamh; MAWAJDEH, Aisham Mahammad; MORCOS, Samieer Fared; NASSER, Saleh Abdul Karim; QUIDDIS, Victor; QUNASH, Basel Mashour; RISHIK, Ismael Rohy; SARNI, Imad Sami; SHATTARAT, Ibrahim; SOUTARI, Said; SULEIMAN, Amjad; TABBALAT, Wael Ali;

Kenya

BITOK, Sosthenes; DEMELLO, Louisa Maria; KIPSANG, Jospeh; KOECH, Edwin;

Korea

CHO, Jin-Ah; CHO, Koon-Haeng; CHOI, Chul-Jueon; CHUN, In-Tae; EUHN, Heung-Ge; HAHN, Jang-Suck; HAN, Chung-Sik; HAN, Gi-Buem; HEO, Dae-Oh; HONG, Gie-Tack; JANG, Jae-Kuen; JANG, Tae-Eun; JANG, Yoon-Chang; JANG, Yun-Ho; JEON, Chang-Dae; JEON, Yeong-Dae; JUHNG, Euh-Tack; KIM, Bock-Ju; KIM, Bong-Man; KIM, Chong-Il; KIM, Dong-Fan; KIM, Gi-Poong; KIM, Hea-Jeong; KIM, Hyeon-Joon; KIM, In-Ok; KIM, Jin; KIM, Ju-Ook; KIM, Jung-Uk; KIM, Kwon-Jo; KIM, Sang-Bo; KIM, Sung-Moon; KIM, Yoon-Ho; KIM, You-Teag; KIM, Young-Soo; KO, Myung-Wha; LEE, Chae-Un; LEE, IlHee; LEE, Jeoung-Sik; LEE, Jin-Ok; LEE, Johng-Kyeong; LEE, Min-Hyun; LEE, SeungJun; LEE, Woo-Ryong; MOON, Yong-Kwan; NOH, Bum-Sik; OH, Sea-Woong; PARK, JongYong; PARK, Se-Yong; PARK, Yang-Ja; RA, Kwon; SHIN, Dea-Cheul; SONG, Dong-Wook; YANG, Jin-Oong; YOO, Jae-Haek; YOON, Nam-Jin; YU, Jung-Tack;

Kuwait

ABDULLAH, Anwar; ABDULLAH, Said Mabrouk S.; AL-SHARHAN, Anwar S.Y.Y.; ALASSAF, Khaled S.M.; AL-EID, Khaled Abdullah; AL-GHAITH, Adel Hamad; AL-HADHOUD, Samir; AL-HAMIDI, Khaled I.M.S.; AL-MOZUEL, Abdul-Munem N.H.; AL-ROOMI, Najem A.; AL-SAAD, Saad Y.Y.; AL-SALEM, Muhammad; AL-SALLAL, Faisal; AL-SALLAL, Adel Saud A.; AL-TAWEEL, Talal F.; AL-TELEAHI, Abdullah; AL-TELEAHI, Fadel; ATASH, Wae'l; MOHAMMAD, Anwar Khamees B.; NADOM, Yousuf GH. A.M.; SLIEMAN, Mohammad, A.E.;

Lebanon

ABOU CHEDIA, Doumith; ABOU SLEIHAN, Nayla; ABOU-HAIDAR, Wada; ABOUJAUDE, Elie; ALAMUDDINE, Leila; AMHAZ, Abdul-Fattah; AOUN, Antoine; BAUJI, Nazih; BEJJANI, Reine; BOUZER, Salem; CHACHDUB, Rina; DAGHER, Carole; EL CHARIF, Khaled; EL MOUDABBER, Jocelyne; EL-RIFAI, Bahi; ELSAYED, Sawsan; ESTEPHAN, Nawal; FADEL, Antoine; FADEL, Ninette; GUERBIDJIAN, Vahe; HADDAD, Boutros; HANA, Ziad; ISSA, Jamal; ISSA EL-KHURY, Gaby; ISTAFAN, Jean; JALABI, Mohamed Khaled; JAROUDI, Mounir; KANTARI, B.; KARKOUR, Naji; KASBAH, Mohamad Bakri; KOURJIAN, Sarkis; MAJDOUB, Fawzi; MANSOUR, Zakkia; MINA, Zeina; MOURAD, Chaya; MOUZAWAK, Abdo; NAJJAR, Jmad; SAAD, A.; SABA-AYUN, Amal; SABEH-AION, Nada; SAIF, Fawka; SALAME, Fady; SALAME, Jihad; SALIBA, Michel; SARDOUK, May; SARDOUK, May; SOOKENY, Adnan; TICAELIAN, Fadi; YASSINE, Ghina; YOUNIS, Walid;

Libya

ABDULHAMED, G.; ABOARGOB, Adel; ABOUSAOWEL, Mohamud; AMRONI, Ghieth; ASFAR, M.; DARDET, Fasel; ELAMARE, Jamal; ELASFER, M.; ELBEDE, Ali; ELBEDE, Salh; ELFAGI, Ahmed; ELKERIKCHE, Amad; ELMABROUK, Mohamad; ELTREKE, Mohsen; ERGAHNI, Mostfa; FATHI, Mohamad; MEHREZ, Abdalla; MEKAWA, K.; MILAD, Mohamad; MOHAMED, Khaled; MORTDE, Abo El Monhem; MUSBAH, Y.; NASSER, Omar; SHIBAN, Ali; SHILABE, El Moktar; SULEMAN, Yahia; TERAHIM, Aly Atieh; WERSHFANE, Nasser Edden; ZAKKA, Awad; ZARUHG, Jamal; ZOUBI, Abdel; ZOUBI, Ahmed;

Malta

CARVANA, Paul; ZAMMIT, Alan;

Mexico

ACEVES, Antonio; AGUILERA, Benjamin; ABUILERA: Jose; ALCALA, Gerardo; ARAGON, Danyra; ARCE, Martin; ARIAS, Justo; ARIAS, Pedro; AVALOS, Fernando; AVILA, Eduardo; BARRAZA, Elizabeth; CALIZ, Jorge; CARBONELL, Oscar; CASAR, Rodrigo; DEL VOLLE, Saul; DENNIS, Alan; DOMINGUEI, Genoveva; DORADOR, Lucrecia; ENRIQUEZ, Felipe; ESCOBAR, Karina; FLORES, Alexandra; GONZALES, Yolanda; J. SALVADOR: GONZALEZ, Jose M.; GONZDIEZ, Rafael; GUILLEN, Francisco; GUTIERREZ, Guillermo; HEREJON, Fernando; HERRERA, Susana; JIMENEZ, Martha; JIMENEZ, Meliton; LEAL, Carlos; LENK, Emilia; LOMEZ, Margarita; LOPEZ, Roberto; MALPICA, Laura; MUNOZ, Cuohujemoc; ORTEGA, Enrique; PACHECO, Mario; PREMIO, Sebastian; RETIZ, Carlos; REYES, Gerardo; RICO, Jose Luis; RODRIGUEZ, Luis; RUBACCAVA, Carmen; SANCHES, Carlos; SANCHEZ, Roberto; SILVA, Francisco; TREVINO, Julian; TRUJILLO, MAria; VEGA, Javier; VELAZQUEZ, Teresa;

Morocco

EL MOUTAOUAKKIL, Nawal; HOMADA, Hamid; LASBANE, Abdelali; LAHEI, Fadozi; LOTTAGUI, Mohamed; M'HAND, Said; MOUADDEN, Laroi; RGROUG, Khalid;

New Zealand

ASAKETTLE, Patrick; BOWDEN, John; BUIST, Michael; DAY, Murray; GRAHAM, Mark; KELL, Peter; DROON, Glenys; LOCKHART, Richard; MARSHALL, Johnathan; MOSSE, Anthony Robin; SEEMAN, Ruth;

Nigeria

AGBEBAKU, Ajayi; ALLI, Yussuf; ARINZE, T.C.; DANIEL, Victor; EGUNIKE, I.; IMOH, Chidi; NWAGUZXOR, P.; OGIDI, Daniel; OKON, Victor E.; OKOYE, J.N.; SADIC, A.; UTI, Sunday;

Paraguay

ALFONSO GONZALEZ, Galo Manuel Jose; BERGANZA BRUSQUETTEI, Luis; CANATA MARTINEZ, Nelson Bartolome; CARDOZO ESCOBAR, Oscar Martin; FIORIO AGUILLAR, Hordeio Robert; GOROSTIAGA, Ricardo Eugenio: HERMOSIALLA ALYARENGA, Jose Mario; KUSTER GUERREROS, Carlos Enrrigue; KUSTER RACHID, Carlos Gerardo; MARTI BENITEZ, Manuel; NAPOUT BARRETO, Oscar Emilio; ROJAS ORTIZ, Luis Gustabo; SANABRIA DUARTE, Carlos Alberto; TOMMASSI BENITEZ, Mario Jose; TORCIDA, Marcelo;

Peru

BOCANGEL, Patricia; BUSTIOS, Marita; BUTRON, Juan; CALDERON, Edgardo; DE LA PUENTE, Julio; DEL CASTILLO, Moises; GALDOS, Gonzalo; GAMERO, Carlos Luis; GAMERO, Javier; GONZALES, Alberto; GOYTIZOLO, Jose Luis; HERRERA, Marcela; MARCHANI, Henry; PAREDES, Arturo; RODRIGUEZ, Fernando; SALINAS, Luis Ernesto; SOLER SERAS, Roger; VELAZCO, Miguel;

Poland

BARON, Jan; BULKOWASKA, Danuta; CHRONOWSKI, Ludomir; CZOPEK, Agnieskz; DUBRAWSKA, Agnieszka, Tamara; DZIEDZIC, Grazyna; GIEGIEL, Romuald; GLODZ, Ewa; GORAK, Stanislaw; GORSKI, Leszek; JABLOKOWSKI, Piotr; JANUSZKIEWICZ, Zbigniew; JASKULKA, Stanislaw Wojciech; JUZYSZYN, Dariusk; KOLASA, Marian; KONIUSZ, Jaroslaw; KONIUSZ, Krzysztof; MAKOWKA, Wojciech; MALEC, Ryszard; NOWAK, Malgorzata Bozena; OSTROWSKI, Ryszard; PIASECKI, Mariusz; PODSIADLO, Mariusz; PODSIADLO, Wojoiech; PUZIANOWSKI, Krzysztof; ROBAK, Adam, Ryszard; RUTKOWSKI, Jacek; STRZALKA, Mariusz; SWORNOWSKI, Leszek; WODKE, Dariusz, Miroslaw; WOGDARCZYK, Miroslaw; WOJCIECH, Warchc; WOLNY, Dariusz; WOLOSZ PERKA, Danuta; WSZOLA, Jacek; ZIELKE, Dariusz;

Portugal

ABRANTES, Arnaldo; CUNHA, Carlos; FRICHKNECHT, Paulo Jose; HOPTA, Luis Gabriel; MATOS GOMES DE AZEVEDO, Paulo; NORA, Arvzo; OLIVEIRA, Ana Isabel; SOUSA, Vasco Nuno; YOKOCHI, Alexandre;

Puerto Rico

BATISTA, Carlos; BOCHETTE III, Liston Donneal; CARLO, Janice; DE JESUS, Madeline; DE JESUS, Margaret; LIND, Angelita; PEREZ SANTIAGO, Cesar;

Romania

ARDELEANU, Florin; BADINICI, Maria; BALAN, Liliana; BEDROSIAN, Bedros; BODOCZI, Miklos; BOSR, Stefania; BUCUR, Laurentiu; BUNACIU, Carmen; CARUTASU, Constantin; CIOBANIUC, Dorel; CIUBANCAN, Mandica; CONSTANTINESCU, Valentin; COSTRAS, Dorin; CRACIUNESCU, Florenta; CUSMIR, Anisoara; DAN, Aurora; DRAGOESCU, Petru; DUNCA, Rodica; EBERLE, Emilia; FEJER, Ivan; FILIP, Elena; GANCEA, Ionel; GEORGESCU, Aurelian; GORDAN, Cornel; GRIGORAS, Constanta; GUZGANU, Elisabeta; HATIU, Vlao; HINDA, Camelia; HOSSZU, Csilla; IONASIU, Octavian Mircea; IONESCU, Eugen; IONESCU, Valy; KISS, Gabriela; KUKI, Petru; LAUTARA, Gheorghe; MARCU, Adrian; ARKO, Sandor Gyorgy; MATEI, Sorin; MELINTE, Doina Dfelia; MITRACHE, Vasile; MOICEANU, Catalin; MOLNAR, Levente; NICOLAE, Felix; NICULA, Emilian; OLTEAN, Ioan; OROS, Rozalia; PALL, Maria Magdalena; PARASCHIV, Costica; PINTEA, Valentin; POPA, Mihai; POPA, Virginia; POPESCU, Serban; PROFIR, Nicoleta; RADU, Maria; MICIU, Mihaela; ROMANOV, Ludia; ROMANOV, Maria; RUPARCSICS, Csilla; SAITOC, Florin; SIMION, Dan Dumitru; SIMION, Mihai; STOCHITA, Cornelia; STOICA, Michaela; SZABO, Rudolf; TOCALA, Carmen; TUDOR, Mihai; UNGUREANU, Vasile; UNGUREANU, Vasile; VASILE, Nicultina; VISAN, Flavius; ZSAK, Marcela;

Romania, host country for the 1981 Summer Universiade

Rwanda

GATERA, Jean Marie Vianney; HABINEZA, Fausitin; KABAGABO, Lambert; KAMANZI, Abdul;
KARANGWA, Dismas; LYAMBABAJE, Alexandre; MAKUZA, Bernard; MUDAHERAWA, Jean Pierre;
MUHAWENIMANA, Alexandre; MURENGERANTWALI, Titien; NKUSI, SIphonse; NKUSI, Augustin;
NKUSI, Gerard; NTAWUKULILYAYO, Jean Damascene; NYARWYA, Aloys; NZIGAMASABO, Albert;
RUFANGURA, Florent; SEBALINDA, Antoine; SEBALINDA NGOGA, Dominique; SEMUTUTSI, Eugene;
SEZIKEYE, Jean Bosgo; UWANDAGAYE, Leonard;

Senegal

AHNE, Mouhamed Aly; BA, E.H. Amadou Dia; BATHILY, Moussa; CISSE, Tbrahima; DAFFE, Gora;
DIALLO, Boubacar; DIANE, Keletiqui; DOUMBIA, Ahmed Miloud; DOUMBIA, Yahiya; FALL, Moussa;
FALL, Moussa; FAYE, Boubou; GAYE, Moustapha; KONTE, Alpha; MBENGUE, Abdouaziz;
MBENGUE, Moussa; MBODJI, Papa Ndiack; NDIAYE, Adrame; NDIAYE, Amalah Amala;
NDIAYE, Moussa; NDOYE, Magatte; NDOYE, Moustapha; NIANG, Babacar; SENE, Souleymane;
WADE, Dusmane; WANE, Souleymane;

Somalia

ADEN, Jama M.; HUFANE, Ali, M.;

Spain

AZULAY; CALLEJA, M; CASABONA; EIZAGUIRRE, Ana; FERNANDEZ, B; FRAILE, Carmen;
GARCIA, Cecilia; GARCIA, J; GRAS, Elvira; HORMILLOS; JARCIS, Jorje; JIMENEZ, Rocio;
JIMENO, Raoul; JIMEUEZ, Concepcion; JUNYER, Ana; MAROTO, R;
MARTINEZ, Consuelo, MORENO, Elena; MOZUN, J; OGIS, Teresa; PRADO, J; ROLDAN, E;
SANCHEZ, A; SEOANE, Maluisa; TASCON, Pilar; VERA, A;

Swaziland

DLAMINI, Nelson; MAMBA, Cliffordd; MOTSA, Brian; MTHEMBU, Gideon; SHONGWE, Kim;
SWANE, Esau; SWANE, Sdi;

Sweden

HARSTROM, Ola; TIVENIUS, Jan; VAGGO, Bjorne; WAHLQVIST, Carina Margareta;

Switzerland

AGBISCHER, Daniel; BALTISBERGER, Kathrin; BEZINGE, Alex; BLOESCH, Daniel; BROSY, Urs;
CASSINA, Pablo; EGGER, Roland; EVEQUOZ, Gregoire; BLOCK, Felix; FORTER, Daniel; FURRER, Jim;
GUIDICETTI, Nicola; GREMINGER, Thomas; GUGLER, Chritian; HALSALL, Dano; HELBLING, Lisbeth;
HILBEBRAND, Phillip; HIRSCHY, Loraine; HUNGER, Beat; ISENSCHMID, Marianne; JACOT, Thierry;
JORAY, Vreni; KINDSCHI, Claudia; KOENIG, Eliane; KOENIG, Francis; KUHN, Andre;
LINFRNMSNN, Margaret; MADARASZ, Zsolt; MAYR, Marco; MODEL, Daniel; MONNET, Anne-Sylvie;
MORF, Felix; Mueller, Helena; NCALA, T.; NEIGER, Rolando; OTTO, Caroline; PFEFFERLE, Gerald;
PLUESS, Beatrice, RAPP, Marco; RETTIG, Yvonne; REYNARD, Toy; RUEGG, Annemarie;
SALVOLDI, Edith; SCHNEIDER, Corinne; SCHNEIDER, Roberto; SCHROETER, Pascal;
STAEUBLE, Marcel; STAUBLI, Thomas; STIERLI, Doris; UEBERSAX, Franzi; WILD, Thomas;
WILDHABER, Jennifer; WSCHIANSKY, Sebastien; ZIEROLD, Claudia;

Tanzania

AMO, Agapius; KYOMO, Nazel; MALEKWA, Zakayo;

Tunisia

ABAHNINI, Khemats; ACHOUR, Sami; ALOUINI, Mohamed; ANENE, Selma; BACCOUCHE, Rathi;
BACHAR, Hatem; BOUCHLEGHEM, Samir; BOUSSAA, Lassaad; CHEKIR, Abdellatif; GHATTAS, Faten;
MIRA, Habib; OUERDANI, Fethi; TOUIBI, Sarra; ZOGHLAMI, Abdelmajio;

Uganda

ABURA-OGWANG, David; NASIKE, Margaret; NYAMUGASIRA, Johnson; OJUKA, Edward;

U.S.S.R.

AGEEV, Vitaly B.; AIAPBERGENOV, Erlan; AKHREMENKO, Natalya; ALENINE, Sergei;
ANTONOVA, Olga; ARTAMONOV, Victor; ARTIEMOV, Vladimir; BELEVITCH, Sergei;
BELIAKOVA, Tatyana; BELOKON, Larisa U.; BERENDUGA, Victor; BESKROWNY, Alexander I.;
BIBOKOVA, Vera; BISEROVA, Elena; BLUDZUS, Aloizas; BORISOV, Vadim; BORISOVA, Loujdmila;
BUTCHA, Sergey; BUZELITE, Ishkute; KYKOVA, Tamara; CHAEV, Aleksandre; CHEN, Iolanda;
CHERNEVA, Svetlana; CHVETSOV, Alexei; DILLENBURG, Albert; DMITRIENKO, Oleg;
DOTSENKO, Alexey; DOUMCHEV, Youry; DROZHZHIN, Nikolay; FESENKO, Ekaterina;
FESENKO, Sergey; FILEV, Yuri; FILIPISHINA, Elena; FILONOV, Alexei; GAVRAS, Sergey;
GERASIMOVA, Irina; GIORGADZE, Mihail; GORCHAKOVA, Larisa; GORCHAKOVA, Z.;
GORCHANYUK, Yuri; GUELACHWILI, Emzar; GUICHIJANTS, Yelena; GVAHARIA, Davy;
IVANENKO, Gennady; IVANOV, Alexandr; JAKOVLEVA: Flora; KALACHIAN, Jiulietta;
KALININE, Andrei; KALINKIN, Viktor; KALUTSKYY, Anatoly, V.; KASHIRIN, Yury;
KHARLOV, Alexander; DIBARDINA, Nadegeda; KIBARDINA, Nadejdh; KIBARDINA, Nadegja;
KIRKWIDRE, Saida; KIS, Uriy; KITOVA, Svetlana; KLENIKOV, Oleg; KLIMOV, Viktor;
LKIOUCHINE, Andrei; KOBA, Tamara P.; KOLYADINA, Mila, N.; KONOVALOV, Ivan; KORBAN, Elena;
KORIAJKINE, Serguei; KOROLEV, Yuri; KOROLKOV, Evgeniy; KOROTAEV, Serguei G.;
KOULA, Dainis, E.; KOUTCHERIAVYI, Igor; KOUZNETSOV, Nicolay; KRASNOV, Alexandre;
KRASUK, Sergey; KRIVETS, Yuri; KRUPIN, Georgi; KRYLOVA, Iarysa; KURNIKOVA, Tattana;
KITSEBO, Serguei; KUZNETSOV, Victor; LARICHEVA, Irina; LISOVSKAYA, Natalya; LOGVINE, Vitali;
LOMTEV, Evgeny; LOUKIANOV, Jouzy; MAKAROVA, Ludmila; MALYCHINA, Elena; MANAKOV, Viktor;
MARKIN, Victor; MARKOVSKY, Alexei; MARTSINKIV, Stephan; MATVEEV, Nickolay I.;
MILOVANOVA, Larrissa; MINDIGRASSOV, Serguei; MOLOKOVA, Marina; MOROZOV, Sergey;
MOROZOVA, Lyudmila; MOUSIENKO, Nickolay K.; MURAVYEV, Vladimir; MUZHITSKY, Pavel;
NAUMOV, Sergey; NAVOLOKIN, Servei; OKOROKOV, Evgeny; OLHHOVNIKOVA, Irina;
ORAZALINOV, Askar; PAALIAKOVA, Tamara; PAITCHADZE, Evgueni; PAKLIN, Igor;
PANFILOV, Alexandre; PASTUKHOV, Yuri; PETROVA, Natalya; PETROVA, Tatiana;
PICHOUGIN, Serguei; PININGA, Maria; PODYALOVSKAYA, Irena; POGORELOV, Alexander;
POLAYKOV, Vladimir; POLEVAYA, Elena; POLIAKOVA, Tamara; PONOMARENKO, Elena;
POPTSOV, Nikolai, A.; POUGACH, Seruei; PROCOPCHUK, Pavel; PROKOFYEV, Andrei;
PUZANKOV, Oleg; RODIN, Sergei; ROMANOVA, Marina; RUSSKIKH, LKonstantin;
SALNIKOV, Vladimir; SALOMOUMEE, Erika; SALOUMIAEE, Erika; SAPEGA, Alexandr; SEDOV, Igor;
SEMENOV, Svyatoslal; SEMYKIN, Konstantin; SERGEEVA, Irina; SHALIGASHWILI, Sergej;
SHEMETOV, Vladimir; SHEVCHENKO, Yuri; SHKAROUPIN, Dmitry; SHUMOV, Eugeny;
SIDORENKO, Aleksandre; SIDOROV, Nickolay; SIDORVA, Irena; SIPATOVA, Elena; SISOEVA, Marina;
SKOPTSOVA, Evguenia; SLEPOKOUROVA, Lubov; SLEPOKOUROVA, Lubov; SMIRNOV, Sergei;
SMIRNOV, Vaycheslav, M.; SMIRNOVA, Ekaterina; SMIRYAGIN, Sergey; SOKOLOV, Vladimir;
SOMOV, Serguei; SOROKOLET, Alexandr; STARTIKOVA, Ekaterina; STOUKONIS, Donatas;
SUT, Pavel; TAMM, Yuri; TITOR, Anatoli; TKACHENKO, Vladimir; TOLSTIKOV, Yakov;
TROSCILO, Alexandre; TROSHIN, Viaecheslav; TSOTADZE, Liana; TSUKHLO, Yvegeny, A.;
TSYROULNIKOVA, Janna; URAKOVA, Lubov; UTENKOV, Gennadiy; VESELOVA, Elena;
VINNIK, Alexandre; VINOGRADOVA, Elena; VINOGRADOVA, Nadejhda; VOLKOV, Konstantin;
VOLKOV, Pavel; VORONIN, Sergei; ZABOLOTNOV, Sergey; ZAYTSEVA, Olga; SELCH-
LOTCHMELIS, Andris; ZHULPA, Robertas; ZOLOTAREV, Alexander, M.; ZORINA, Svetlana;
ZVEREV, Alexandr;

United States

ALSTON, Tanja; AMABILE, John; ANGELAKIS, Jana; ARAGON, Chuck; ARONS, Jeff Steven;
BABCOCK, Brian J.; BABERS, Alonzo; BACKUS, Jackie Joy; BAIR, Ann; BALDING, Peter Adams Jr.;
BARKER, Vera; BARKLEY, Charles Wade; BARKSDALE, Sharieffa; BARRINEAU, James;
BARRIOS, Roni Lynn; BAUER, Andrew; BEAUPREY, Jeanne; BERGESON, James; BILODEAUX, Caitlin;

163

BODNER, Darci; BODOR, R.; BOGACKI, Julia A.; BOLTON, Kelia; BOND, Marsha Ann; BOSWELL, Cathy; BRACKETT, Scott; BROWN, Judi; BROWN, Tanya; BUCKINGHAM, Jeff; BURKE, Douglas; CAMPBELL, Jeff; CAMPBELL, Peter; CAMPBELL, Robin; CAREY, Ed; CARR, Diane; CARTER, Mike; CAVANAUGH, Regina; CAVENER, Gregory Kent; CHADWICK, Bridget Anne; CHILDS, Jeanne; CLARK, Tracy Lynn; CLIETTE, Brenda; COLLINS, Dietre; COLLINS, Sheila; CONLEY, Mike; COONTZ, Janie; CRANDALL, Ellen; CREMENT, Bryan William; CULLINGAN, Maureen Catherine; CUTINO, Peter Jr.; DABNEY, Sharon; DAGGETT, Timothy P.; DASEE, Bonnie; DAWKINS, Johnny Early; DENNIS, Donna; DESANDO, Judeth; DIBARTOLO, Therese; DIVIDORFF, Lorrie; DIXON, Media; DONAGHUE, Ross; CORST, Chris; DRENTH, Jeff; DROST, Chris; DUBYOSKI, Paul; DURRANT, Devin George; EMERSON, Arlise; EMERY, Elizabeth; ERICSON, Eric; ETTUS, Heather; EVONIUK, Marco; EYESTONE, Ed; FERNANDEZ, Cecilia; FERNANDEZ, Edwin; FIGHTMASTER, Teresa; FITZGERALD, Benita; FOSTER, Sue; FOX, Chris; FRICKER, Mark; FRIEDBERG, John; FUREY, Eileen Mary; GABRIEL, Easter; GALLIEN, Richard Adam; GASSNER, Greg; GAULT, Willie; GAYLORD, Mitchell Jay; GENSEL, John; GERBER, Farley; GIBSON, Jayne M.; GIOVANAZZI, Leland Gregory; GIRKINS, Steven Clifford; GIVENS, Randy; GLOVER, Michelle; BOEWEY, Julie Bingham; GOLDIE, Daniel Clyde; GONZALEZ-RIVAS, George I.; GOODE, Andre L.; GOODLING, Jennifer; GORDON, Dave; GRADDY, Sam; GRANT, Margaret Roxanne; GREEN, Bill; GRESHAM, Alan; GRIER, Michael; GULNAC, Steven Walter; GUTOWSKY, Chris; HANLEY, John Minton; HANSEN, Joan; HARRIS, Janet; HARTUNG, James Nicholas; HAUSCHILD, Penny Lynn; HAYES, Kathy; KAYES, Lawrence; HEGG, Cristy Ingram; HENRY, Lea; HERING, Brad Vincent; HETLET, Brenda Lee; HIESLER, Randy; HIMMER, Toni Michelle; HUMPHRIES, John Jay; IDSTROM, John; ITTER, Randal Joseph; JACKSON, Alice; JACKSON, Bernard; JAGER, Thomas M.; JOHNSON, Alan Thorton (Charlie); JOHNSON, Jeffrey Richard; JOYNER, Al; KANE, Missy; KAPUT, Margie; KEANE, Brian G.; KEARNEY, Patty; KELLEMS, Suzy J.; KIMBALL, Bruce; KIRBY, Karolyn, M.; KONECNY, Hop; KRON, Peter; KYLE, Dallas Randolph; LACEY, Trudi; LAKES, Charles; LAMB, Monica Van Dora; LAUCHNER, Craig Edward; LAWRENCE, Ingrid; LEE, Deborah Ann; LEE, Keith; LETTIERI, David; LEWIS, Tim; LEWISON, Peter; LIDYOFF, Beverly Ann; LINZMEIER, Marybeth; LORSCHEIDER, Joerg; LOUGANIS, Gregory Efthimios; LOWN, Gwenn; LUYTIES, Ricci, J.; MACDONALD, Stuart; MAEGHER, Mary; MAJORS, B.; MALONE, Karl A.; MARX, Robert Gabriel; MASSIALAS, Gregory; MAYS, James; MCCORMICK, Kelly; MCCULLA, Pat; MCINTYRE, Sandra; MENKEN-SCHAUDT, Carol Jean; MERCER, Gray D.; MERCER, Julius; MERLO, Nancy Anne; MERRIOTT, Ron; METKUS, Andrew; MICHAELS, Charles; MONPLAISIR, Sharon Mary; MORMONDO, George; MOSS, Anita Louise; NEDD, Lashon; NEER, Penny; NEES, Lloyd; NEYER, Megan L.; NIX, Sunder; NONOMURA, George; OCHOWICZ, William Joseph; ODEN, Kim; OSTROWSKI, Mary Lynne; PARTIE, Robert Doug; PATRICK, Mark; PAUL, Julie Swain; PETERSON, Hans Christian; PETERSON, Orville; PICKNELL, Kathy; PIERCE, Jack; PINCKNEY, Edward; PITTMAN, Ricky; PUCCITTI, Perry; QUOW, Elliott; RATCLIFF, Pamela; RAY, Susie; REDWINE, Stanley; THODENBAUGH, Gregory Scott; RHODENBAUGH, Mark; RITCHBURG, Diana; ROBINSON, Beverly; ROBINSON, Cory Allen; ROBINSON, Edward; ROBINSON, Ken; ROCK, Angela Teresa; ROGERS, Taunia Rae; RUDDINS, Kimberly Grace; SAEGER, Richard; SAGELY, Michael Jerome; SALING, Amy; SAVRE, Dave; SCHIFRIN, Peter; SCHROEDER, Terry; SCHWARTZ, Karen; SCOTT, Lori Anne; SCOTT, Terry; SELTON, Sally Eckert; SEVELY, John Vincent; SHELLEY, Lee C.; SHIELDS, Laurence E.; SILVA, Christopher Lewis; SLACK, Jefferson Merlin; SLAUGHTER, Edwin paul; SMITH, Annette Marie; SMITH, Dana Rene; SMITH, Mark; SOMMER, Coleen; SPAULDING, Tresa Dawn; SPICER, Mike; SPRY, Ralph; STEVENS, Tom; STORK, Jeffrey; STORM, Shawn Fontaine; STUCK, Lisa M.; SULLIVAN, Michael E.; SUNAHARA, Reed Masashi; SUNDER, Nix; SWITZER, Veryl; TABRON, Elliott; TEMPLE, Deborah; THACKER, Angela; THOMAS, Malcom; THOMAS, Tammy; THOMPSON, Bernard Louis; THORTON, Audrey; TICHACEK, Jack; TIMMONS, Steve Dennis; TREVOR, Stephen S.; TURNER, Eric C.; VAN METER, John Marshall; VARGAS, John; VIDMAR, Peter Glen; VON JOUANNE, Roger; WAGSTAFF, Jennifer; WALKER, Joyce Denise; WALSH, Susay; WARD, Jeff; WASHINGTON, Jackie; WEINANTS, K.; WEISSMAN, Christopher; WESTFALL, Stacy; WHITE, Jackie; WILEY, Cliff; WILLIAMS, J.; WILLIAMS, Leo; WILLIS, Kevin Alvin; WILSON, David; WING, Andrew Nelson; WISSER, Maria Louise; WOLF, Augie; WOOLGER, Christy; WORTHAM, Blake; SYLAND, Wendy; YARDLEY, Bill Markham; YESKO, Jill Rachel; YOUNG, Candy; YOUNGBLOOD, Alan Curtis; ZEIS, Lisa; ZELLNER, Robin Jon; ZIMMERMAN, David; ZIMMERMAN, Lana; ZUMWALT, Betsy;

Venezuela

ARIAS, Roberto; AVIAS, Marcelo; CASTILLO, Jose; LEONARD, Adolfo; LIENTO, Marcos; MORENO, Alberto; PASTOR, Vicente; RAMOS, Andres; RODRIGUEZ, Henry; VALTEZ, Francis; ZALATAN, Jorge; ZALATAN, Jose; LUYEN, D.; PHU, T.; TRAN, Hung Manh; VO, Chau Ngoc; PALE, Harouna;

Viet-Nam

LUYEN, D.; PHU, T.; TRAN, Hung Manh; VO, Chau Ngoc;

Upper Volta

PALE, Harouna;

Yugoslavia

BOJOVIC, Biljana; BOZINOVIC, Snezana; BULJEVIC, Ivica; CANGALOVIC, OLIVERA; CANOVIC, Novica; CVJETICANIN, Danko; DEKLEVA, Cvetana; DORNIK, Polona; FIZOLET, Hrvoje; GOLIC, Sladjana; GRBOVIC, Goran; IVANOVIC, Markn; KNAPIC, Zeljko; KOMNENOVICH, Jelica; KRIVOKAPIC, Olivera; MAJSTOROVIC, Biljana; MUTAPCIC, Emir; PERASOVIC, Velimir; PERAZIC, Jasmina; PETKOVIC, Zoran; PETROVIC, Drazen; POKRAJCIC, Vinko; SARACEVIC, Zlatko; SAVOVIC, Milenko; SHUKA, Slavica; SUNARA, Ivan; UZELAC, Marija; VANGELOVSKA, Totjna; VUCUROVIC, Zarko; VUJACIC, Jadranko; ZDRAVKOVIC, Dragan; ZIZIC, Rajko; ZORKIC, Nebojsa;

Technical Officials

Athletics

ANDERSON, Aynsley; ANDREWS, Andy; ARNOLD, George; AUGER, Louis; BALCOM, James; BEARD, Keith; BEERLING, Dennis; BEERLING, Toni; BELL, Ronald; BLASCHUK, Lawrence; BLASCHUK, Alex; BLASCHUK, Ken; BODEN, Rod; BOYCHUK, Vic; BROWNE, Don; CALLAWAY, Barrie; CAMERON, E. Marie; CHAGNON, Richard; CHEVALIER, Irene; CONKLIN, Dorothy; COOP, Norman; CORMIER, Meddy; DARGIE, Elisabeth; DEAKIN, Barry; DELORME, Lorraine; FROST, Barclay; GAINER, Jerry; GAINER, Flo; GELINEAU, Jack; GRAPE, Jim; HEADLEY, Dr. Neville; HEDMAN, Ingvar; HEMSTREET, Gordon; HOGAN, Pauline; HOLM, Cathy; HOMER, Joan; HOMER, Gary; HUBBARD, Brook; HUME, Ian; HYSLOP, Ruth; HYSLOP, Craig; KEAY, Art; KRAEMER, Jurgen; KUBEK, Alice; KYLE, Carol; LACROIX, Michele M.; LAKE, Elaine; LAKE, Ken; LAKE, Peter; LANE, Stephen; LANGEN, Jim; LANGLEY, Brian; LANSDELL, Anne; LAPLANTE, Jean-Marc; LARSEN, Marion; LASSEN, Paula; LEITH, Jim; LEVESQUE, Claire; LISS, Sophia; LOAEWEN, Lowell; LORD, Tom; LUDVIGSEN, Del; MACDONALD, Bruce; MACDUFFE, Nicole; MARPLES, Justin; MARQUEZ DELA MORA, Alfonso; MARRONE, Nicola; MARRONE, Angela; MAVETY, George; MCCHATTIE, Olive; MCILRAITH, Doug; MCKAY, Barbara; MCKAY, Willie; MEVILLE, Louise; MICHAUD, Daniel; MITCHELL, Bryan; MITCHELMORE, Harold; MONROE, John; MONROE, Ian; MOORE, Joan; MOSBSACHER, Erwin; NEISSNER, Adam; NESDOLE, Evelyn; NEWELL, Keith; PEDDLE, Judy; PEZZARO, Theo; PORTER, Ken; RAYNSFORD, Anne; RAYNSFORD, Peter; RIVARD, Joan; RIVARD, Marcel; ROBERTS, John; ROWE, Jack; RUNG, Estella; SARTY, Amy; SARTY, David; SHEEHAN, Mark; SINGLETON, Harvey; SMITH, Bert; SMITH, Cecil; STAPLES, Bill; TEMPLE, Mary; TERPSTRA, Ron; TKACHUK, Sharon; TOSI, Jiuliano; TREMBLAY, Helene; WADE, Bob; WALKER, Douglas; WALL, Verna; WALSH, Ronald; WALTERS, George; WARICK, Judy; WASHBURN, Leroy; WISHART, Jacqueline; WITTENBERG, Eric; WITTENBERG, Jurgen; WOLFRAM, Olive; YOUNG, Virginia; YOUNG, Joe;

Basketball

ALLEN, Phil; BOETTGER, Tom; BOWIE, Gary; BROWN, Anthony; CAULFIELD, Roger; COLEMAN, Lynn; HUS, Harry; JENSEN, Kay; KARL, Francis; MANTHEY, Pamela; MCDONAUGH, John; MCFARLAND, Joan; MCHUGH, Francis; MOORE, Bill; MULLIGAN, Murray; NEILSON, Seward; OGDON, Bobby; PAYNE, Tony; PEUHKURINEN, Markku; PHIPPS, Peter; ROSS, Gilbert; STEEVES, Richard; STEPHENS, Kim; STEPONCHEV, Donald; STEWART, Grant; WALCOTT, Tedd; WOOD, James; ZANOLIN, Nar;

Cycling

BROOMFIELD, Jim; GAGNE, Pierre; RAUX, Roger; SINGFIELD, Dave; TYLER, Peter; WILD, William;

Diving

CUTHERT-MARKS, Linda; PETERSON, Gordon; TATHAM, Marnie;

Fencing

BERGENSTEIN, Karen; BICKELL, Marion; BICKELL, Darren; BOURDAGES, Helene; BOWLSBY, Craig; CARREA, Alexandra; CHAN, Steven; DUFOUR, Marie; DYCK, Walter; D'ASARO, Gay; FOURNIER, Denis; FRASER, Bruce; GARNER, Fran; GIRARD, Kirk; GIRARD, Katherine; GREEN, Cynthia; GREGOIRE, Louise; GRIFFITHS, Denyse; GUITTET, Manuel; HARRISON, Nigel; HARRISON, Christine; KENNY, Dave; KLUEPFEL, Mark; LACROIX, Jacques; LARIN, Lucie; LARIN-LACHAPELLE, Helene; LAVOIE, Marc; LEWIS, Lynn; LUI, Raphael; LUKAS, Arno; MAKOS, Terry; MALLON, Heather; MCCAUGHERTY, Dawn; MITCHELL, John; MOISON, Michelle; MOLAND, Kevin; MOULIN, Alan; NAGY, Imre; NELSON, Alan; OBST, Herbert; OFFEREINS, Calvin; PARKER, Cheryl; PEREVERZOFF, Paul; PERKINS, Jim; QUAN, Ho; REMPEL, Sterling; RICHTER, Coreen; SCHULTZ, Andrew; SEATON, Dorothy; SOFTLEY, Rick; STRATTEN, Douglas; TAM, Patrick; THIIFFAULT, Serge; VIDOSA, Christian; WETTERBERG, Donald; WETTERBERG, Donna; WIGNALL, James; WILSON, Wendy; WILSON, Russell; WORSFIELD, Gary; ZULKOSKEY, Anna-Beth;

Gymnastics

BECKER, Roger; BERNIER, Ginette; BRODERICK, Dree; CHOW, Olivia; COPELAND, Dave; CORN, Slava; DESCHENES, Raynald; DIPPONG, Albert; GALLE, Horst; GINGRAS, Andre; GOULD, Mary; HARRIS, Sue; HELD, Charlie; HO, Ralph; HOPKINS, Shelley; HUBBARD, Bill; JARRELL, Jean; LETHEREN, Carol-Anne; MASSICOTTE, Carolle; MCCHARLES, Doreen; MCLEOD, Robin; MIAZGA, Lynn; NICHOL, Mary; NICHOLL, Jackie; NOBLE, Ruth; PAQUIN, Robert;

SAMSON, Ronald; SMITH, Larry; STOESZ, Kathy; SZATHMARY, Lemke; THOMSON, Jeff; TYNDALL, Maria; VENNE, Michel;

Swimming

CLARKE, Robert; CUMMING, Mary; CUMMING, Thomas; CUPPAGE, Wendy; DEAN, Dave; DIGNEY, James; EWASHKO, Beverly; JACKSON, June; JACKSON, Bob; JORDHOY, John; LAZECKI, Larry; MCCUAIG, Ken; MUNRO, Joyce; NAGY, Michael; O'REILLY, Sandy; PONTING, Stu; PRICE, Glenda; SCHOFIELD, HENRY; SERVOS, Nick; SHEEHAN, Nancy; SLOAN, Betty Lou; THOMAS, Gerald; VAN TER MEY, Cornelius; WHYTE, Eleanor;

Tennis

BROWN, Jack; DAAL, Gus; FIELD, Gary; FREIWIRTH, Paul; JOSHUA, Ivor; LETARTE, Luc; MARTIN, Frances; MARTYN, Neville; MARTYN, Susan; MAYALL, Ita; POSNER, Walter; RUSSELL, James; SANTORO, Gretchen; STEWART, Stephen; ST. PIERRE, Daniel; VICKERS, Bryan; WOLFF, Dieter; YOUNG, John;

Volleyball

BRIDLE, Wezer; COTE, Raymond; STOCHANSKY, Walter;

Waterpolo

JONES, Kevin; MARSOLAIS, Jacques

Left: More than 1,000 technical officials and mission staff from 74 countries gave their expertise to Universiade '83. Here is one of those officials judging the swimming competition at Kinsmen Aquatic Centre.

165

Cultural Participants

Australia

Adolphus P.; Fletcher G.; Hinwood Rod; Hinwood R.; Pearce M.; Strachan A.

Brazil

Aceituno C.; Barnes J.; Broughton D.; Gomes C.; Guimaraes J.; Kelly C.; Lee M.; Lorenz J.; Williams S.

Canada

Adrian C.; Anderson, Mr. & Mrs.; Argue S.; Armitage; Armstrong; Arnold; Atkinson; Avila G.; Bacherman S.; Barrette; Barrett-Burgess J.; Bergeron Y.; Bevan M.; Blackstock T.; Blackwater B.; Blackwater H.; Bown B.; Brough; Brunet; Burgess N.; Burke; Cameron J.D.; Carss; Castonguay S.; Coleman D.; Coleman R.; Dallenbach C.; Danes M.; Davis H.; DeMarchais; Demmon; Desautels J.; Desautels L.; Dimitrov; Dubois P.; Eiserman D.; Erickson M.; Estabrooks; Ewer D.; Farch A.; Fladell E.; Fraser K.; Frechette; Gayfer; Gilbert; Gilfillan C.; Gillis W.; Graham K.; Hampson; Hannah A.; Hannah B.; Hannah K.; Hapwood; Harris M.; Harrison; Hawks; Henderson G.; Hendricks C.; Hiller D.; Hollis C.; Hopkins D.; Isles; Jasper; Jeffrey A.; Jeffrey M.; Jeffrey M.; Jensen D.; Johnson L.; Kankinen; Kerr J.; Le Flamme; Ledger; Lemonthe; Louge-Johnson M.; Lukaszek L.; MacCallum C.; MacLean C.; Malik K.; Malik M.; Malik M.; Marshall D.; McClinton; McGechey; McIntyre S.; McIntyre S.; McRae D.; McRae M.; McTavish; Mills F.; Milton D.; Moffat L.; Moore; Moore T.; Morgan T.; Morrison J.; Mowatt L.; Mowatt S.; Mowatt V.; Muldoe E.; Muldoe S.; Nemtin S.; Noster, Mr. & Mrs. & Child; Ouelette; Ouzounian A.; Ouzounian J.; Ouzounian M.; O'Brien F.; Page E.; Pennell; Piche; Pidcock C.; Pidcock T.; Pieschel S.; Plant J.J.; Pundy L.; Rae D.; Ramsay P.; Robichaud; Robinson L.; Romm G.; Ross L.; Roth E.; Robertson C.; Sampson F.; Sargent B.; Sargent P.; Schlenker E.; Schlenker J.; Scorah; Shanoss A.; Sheridan J.; Shields; Shier J.; Smith F.; Spriggs; Sullivan M.; Sutmoller R.; Sutmoller S.; Thomas; Thomasik L.; Tronsgard; Van Vlaaderen; Von Fersen L.; Watts E.; Weiss H.; Westin J.; Williams K.; Williams M.; Young.

China

Chen B.; Chen F.; Feng S.; Feng Y.; Guo S.; Guo Z.; Hong C.; Jiang N.; Kang W.; Liguang X.; Lin T.; Liu Y.; Liu Z.; Lu J.; Luan F.; Meng Q.; Shen W.; Tang F.; Tang W.; Wang Y.; Want Q.; Wu L.; Zhang B.; Zhang L.; Zhang X.; Zhang Y.; Zhao X.; Zhou Z.

Cook Islands

Ashin N.; Aue K.; Euna A.; Euna N.; George N.; Greig T.; Grieg A.; Iseraela M.; Mose P.; Ngapare S.; Ngateina G.; Ngateina N.; Ngatoko M.; Ngatoko T.; Papasua T.; Pita N.; Poina T.; Rakanui R.; Rua I.; Rua P.; Takai H.; Tararo N.; Tararo U.; Taruia M.; Tunni M.; Turu T.

Germany

Rhythmic Gymnasts

Ghana

Adeyeah G.; Adu-Kako W.; Agbenoheyi M.; Ahima J.; Ahima K.; Ahima L.; Amoakoatta J.; Antwi-Adjci G.; Asamoah S.; Asenso-Donkor S.; Aseidu-Mensah S.; Carl J.; Darko C.; Dzaneshie-Mensah L.; Effa-Sackey B.; Fiakpanu J.; Ganyo C.; Gathsma G.; Gyimah K.; Kanbi C.; Kanbi C.; Lurd-Kekey G.; Manu M.; Nyarkoaa-Mante V.M.; Offei C.; Offei J.; Opokuaa-Asare G.; Osei C.; Tettey-Mensah S.

Great Britain

Adams W.; Ahiagbede C.; Asafoatse R.; Ashley S.; Barford M.; Beagley L.; Cobboson F.; Cook K.; Fiawood D.; Foley R.; Hammond D.; Holoman R.; Hopkins D.; Hunter J.; Lamb A.; Lobb D.; Mason T.; Moody D.; Okai F.; Okine S.; Perrin A.; Pobee E.; Potts G.; Samuels J.; Skrzypiec M.; Tagoe E.; Tagoe E.; Tagoe I.; Togbe M.; Wagner M.; Wanzira B.; Wilson L.

Hong Kong

Chan K.; Cheng K.; Fung W.; Lueng S.; Luk C.; Shek K.; So Y.; Yu S.; Yu W.

India

Balasubramanium; Chandramouli B.M.; Mani T.A.S.; Nararaj M.A.; Ragavendra M.; Rajagopal R.A.; Ramamani R.A.; Ramesh T.M.; Ravi N.G.; Sampathlumar S.M.V.; Satyakumar R.; Shadagopal; Shashikumar T.M.; Sudarshan S.

Jamaica

Beckford L.; Bennett M.; Francis P.; Grant R.; Taylor-Bushay J.; Wilson D.; Wright B.

Japan

Kobe Dancers

Mali

Bouave F.

Mexico

Abrego O.; Gomez G.; Jordan T.; Lopez R.; Mancilla A.; Mancilla O.; Mancilla R.; Menchaca P.; Menchada C.; Menchada M.; Perez C.; Ramirez J.; Rayek J.; Roque M.; Soto C.; Tames M.; Urquidi A.

North West Territories

Angalik A.; Angalik M.; Angalik P.; Annanout S.; Arngnaanaaq M.; Dryneck J.; Klengenberg S.; Kowanak A.; Lafferty E.; Lennie H.; McKenzie M.; Nartok M.; Nitsiza C.; Nitsiza W.; Okpaga J.; Paraschak V.; Rabeska M.; Sallarina A.; Ugyuk C.; Ugyuk I.

Spain

Spain Performers

Sri Lanka

Amaradasa D.K.; Ariyapala A.K.D.; Attanayake D.; Galkotuwa R.S.; Nadasena Y.Y.G.; Podimahatthaya D.M.; Rodigo D.; Ukaasiri B.S.; Wickramage A.S.; Wijeratne D.

Sweden

Swahn L.

Trinidad

Clarke R.; DeFour S.; Dolabaille D.; Dolabaille E.; Dolabaille G.; Dolabaille K.; Evelyn L.; George W.; Husband A.; James M.; James R.; Marcelle T.; Marcelle T.; McLeish W.; Mohammed A.; Morris C.; Morson J.; Noel L.; Pierre S.; Salina C.; Salina S.; Salina T.; Springer C.; Walcott G.

Uganda

Acayam C.; Adolu; Ahimisibwe C.; Apisa; Birungi R.; Iwanga E.; Kasasa I.; Kiawuzisinga; Kiiza; Mbabikantana; Mikisa H.; Muhinga A.; Nannono F.; Nsimbe R.; Obbo; Okot G.; Okumu F.; Owiny; Rukanga A.; Serwada; Twinomugisha S.

United States of America

Abramowitz J.; Akaka K.; Bascon A.; Borgerhoft L.; Brisbane R.; Cassel D.; Casupang M.; Compton E.; Contemplo D.; Dillhauty R.; Engle B.; Fleming J.; Fo. P.; Herring T.; Hershey B.; Hilliard K.; Kaus B.; Knsdl J.; Kong E.; Lam G.; Lee K.; Lee R.; Maki J.; Mayo C.; Nakano S.; Philips G.; Punzal B.; Resgonia B.; Richardson K.; Sand G.; Semmons D.H.; Semmons T.; Shak L.; Sichel M.; Smith L.; Smith M.; Thorpe J.; Tom S.; Ward C.; Zimmerman W.

Upper Volta

Mathieu Z.; Rasmane D.

Venezuela

Fayat A.; Monlina J.

Yugoslavia

Aleksova T.; Cizbanovska S.; Dimitrova L.; Djurovska S.; Dzuklevski G.; Georgievski D.; Gerovski J.; Imeri D.; Ivanova V.; Jovanovski B.; Kazankovska M.; Kovancevski P.; Lalevska E.; Mirkovski M.; Misic J.; Mitrovic N.; Nancovska S.; Ognenova L.; Ognjanovski J.; Peovska M.; Seremetkovski M.; Slavkovska F.; Slavkovski I.; Slobodan I.; Stgilkovski I.; Stojanovski; Stojanovski D.; Tarbunov V.; Tasevska T.; Trajkcv M.; Zafirovski G.; Zankov M.; Zavkov D.; Zelkova A.; Zoran R.

Ambassadors

Jim Jones sold valve fittings throughout Alberta and Saskatchewan.

Cathy Shaw skipped Alberta's champion women's curling team.

Francine Kluak was a word processing operator and Sam Donaghey was in Peru today and China tomorrow promoting trade for the Government of Alberta.

They were presidents, bar tenders, politicans, world champions, businessmen and student athletes criss-crossing the world in search of a place on the national team. Eighteen others were members of a French Canadian club who sacrificed five successive weekends to dance on the streets, in shopping malls and church basements of thirty-five Alberta communities in support of Universiade '83.

There were eighty-three of them in number. In spirit and accomplishment, however, they were a virtual army spreading the word about the 1983 World University Games to all corners of the globe.

Their materials were 4,300 information kits, 27,000 souvenir pins, 220,000 decals, and 8,000 Games logo balloons. They addressed service clubs, sports banquets, executive meetings, church socials, trade conventions and small gatherings of athletes and media from Fort McMurray to Hong Kong.

These were our Ambassadors.

Al (Boomer) Adair – Minister, Tourism and Small Business, Province of Alberta;
Dr. A.C. Allard – President, Cathon Holdings
Debbie Bengston – Vancouver, Tennis Player
Ric Bengston – University Southern California, Tennis
Tor Bengston – Vancouver, President Canadian Tennis Association
David Boone – Edmonton Eskimos Defensive Captain
Debbie Brill – Vancouver, World-ranked High Jumper
Connie Broden – President, Molson's Alberta Brewery
Bev Bush – Edmonton Olympic Club
Iona Campagnolo – Vancouver, Former Minister Fitness and Amateur Sport, Canada
Chris Dallin – Edmonton Olympic Club
Terry Danyluk – Canadian Volleyball Team
Ivor Dent – Former Edmonton Mayor
Louis Desrosiers – Edmonton Lawyer
Sam Donaghey – Edmonton Travel Agent
Jack Donohue – Coach, Canadian Basketball Team
Jean Drapeau – Mayor, City of Montreal
Jack Gallagher – Past President, Dome Oil
Glen Gaudet – Manufacturer's Agent, Stanfields Ltd.
Eric Geddes – Past President, Edmonton Chamber of Commerce
Don Getty – President, D. Getty Investments Limited
Allison Godfrey – University of Alberta Diving Team

Don Gray – Director Public Relations, Molson's
Wayne Gretzky – Edmonton Oilers
Cam Henning – Edmonton, Canadian Swim Team
Dave Johnston – Edmonton, National Swim Coach
Jim Jones – Manager, A & G Tool and Die Company
Terry Jones – Edmonton Newspaper Columnist
Brian Kelly – Edmonton Eskimos Wide Receiver
Sandy Ketterer – Edmonton, National Junior Discus Champion
Egerton King – President, Canadian Utilities
Francine Kluak – Edmonton, Computor Company Executive
Diane Jones Konohowski – Saskatoon, World-ranked pentathlete
Mary LeMessurier – Minister, Culture, Province of Alberta
Peter Lougheed – Premier, Province of Alberta
Donald Love – Board Chairman Oxford Development Group Limited
Donald Lyons – President, Northwest Trust
Chuck MacDonald – Past President, Edmonton Chamber of Commerce
J.W. Grant MacEwan – MacEwan College President
Angus (Gus) MacFarlene
Carmen Madu – Owner, Hobbit's Fantasy Land, Edmonton
Bob McLean – CFRN Radio Talk Show Host
Jack McMahon – Edmonton, Accountant
Susan Nattrass – Edmonton, World Champion Trapshooter
Gary Nelson – Public Relations, Molson's
Ian Newhouse – Edmonton, World-ranked hurdler
Milt Ottey – University of Texas, No. 1 ranked world high jumper
Birgit Otto – University of Alberta, runner
Don Percy – CFRN Radio morning man
Bob Pierce – Executive Vice-President, NOVA Corporation
David Lee Pong – University of Alberta, Canadian Track and Field Team
Alan Reddon – Edmonton, Canadian Gymnastics Team
Dr. G.R.A. Rice – President, Sunwapta Broadcasting Limited
Mariane Richardson – Hostess, Molson's Alberta Breweries
Cathy Shaw – Edmonton, Skip Alberta Women's Curling Champions
John Short – Editor, Alberta Report Magazine
Adrian Shorter – Edmonton Olympic Club, runner
Bev Smith – Salmon Arm, B.C., Canadian Basketball Team
Graham Smith – University of Calgary Swim Coach
Sandra Smith – University of Saskatchewan Swim Coach
Jack Suggett – Edmonton Striders Track Club
Peter Szmidt – Edmonton, Canadian Swim Team
Peter Trynchy – Minister, Recreation and Parks, Province of Alberta
Billy Warwick – Publisher, Billy's Guide
Peter Wood – Manager, The Hat Hut

Volunteers

The Organizing Committee for Universiade '83 is profoundly grateful to the more than nineteen thousand volunteers and staff who dedicated their time, enthusiasm, and expertise to the success of the Games. One in every thirty-five citizens of Edmonton, along with hundreds of others from across Canada, played a role in the Games.... each of them a very important role.

We have attempted in The Pictorial Record to acknowledge these contributions but we are no less grateful to those who through inadvertent omission and sheer weight of numbers, have not been mentioned by name.

A

AAB, Donna Mae Christine; AARONS, Daniel; ABBAS, Mustafa Kamil; ABBASO, Naheed Naz;
ABBASI, Shahid; ABBOTT, Karen Joy; ABBOTT, Leslie Carlyle; ABBOTT, Stephen John;
ABDO, Abdulrahman; ABELL, Ginger; ABERDEEN, Beverly Rose; ABLITT, David Michael;
ABLITT, Scott Peter; ABOU-SHEHADEH, Houlio Dib; ABRAHAM, De Yang R.;
ABRAMS, Douglas Norman; ABRAMS, Vicky Lee; ABRAMYK, Patricia Denise; ABRAO, Maria;
ACEVEDO, Juan Ivan; ACHESON, Gary Robert; ACHILLES, Leslie Jean; ACKER, Leonard Andrew;
ACKERMAN, David Frank; ACKERMAN, Kathleen M.; ACKERMAN, Paul David;
ACORN, Glendyn Wallace; ACTEN, Janice Lee; ACTON, Cathy Lynn; ACTON, Donna Laurie;
ACTON, James Paul; ACTON, Jody James; ACTON, Kelly John; ACUNA, Richard Arturo;
ADAIR, Dorothy A.; ADAIR, Margaret Mary; ADAIR, Tom Rourke; ADAM, Beverley Anne;
ADAM, Garry Elwood; ADAM, Linda Anne; ADAM, Susan Jennifer; ADAMKIEWICZ, Richard;
ADAMS, Catherine Alison; ADAMS, Cyril; ADAMS, David C.; ADAMS, Evelyn Marie;
ADAMS, Georgina Ruth; ADAMS, Gwen; ADAMS, Helena E.; ADAMS, Janet Louise;
ADAMS, Joan L.; ADAMS, Joanne Lucille; ADAMS, Marilyn Denise; ADAMS, Marion;
ADAMS, Mary L.; ADAMS, Patricia Jean; ADAMSKI, Peter Michael; ADAMSKI, Valerie Jean;
ADAMSON, Kelly Sue; ADAMSON, Lance; ADAMYK, Drusilla; ADDINALL, Len; ADDORISIO, Rose;
ADILMAN, Audrey Gloria; ADLARD, David; ADIEM, Sarah, L.; ADIEM, Sean D.; ADLER, Marc David;
ADOLPH, Walter; ADRIAN, Bonnie; ADSHEAD, Margaret; AFAGANIS, Zoe; AFFELD, Marian Janet;
AGAR, Michelle Marie; AGATE, Keitha K.; AGBOGUN, Dr. Jacob; AGNES, Caron;
AGNEW, Genevieve Marie; AGRIOS, Jack N.; AGRIOS, Jack Nicholas; AGRIOS, Jean M.;
AGRIOS, John Andrew; AGRIOS, Ruth Coralie; AGRIOS, Susan K.; AGUIAR, George;
AGUILLON, Bernadette; AHAC, Alan Albert; AHMER, Heinz Ulrich; AHO, Kevin; AIDUN, Keikhosrow;
AIELLO, Leornardo Oscar; AIELLO, Marilyn; AIELLO, Susan Kestner De; AIELLO, Walter;
AIKENS, Janice Kathleen; AIME, Harry Alexander; AIME, Theodore Trent; AINSLIE, Dorothy Jane;
AINSLIE, Kathryn Margaret; AINSWORTH, Wendy; AIPPERSBACH, Sven; AIRTH, Tracey Layne;
AISTROPE, Edward Lionel; AISTROPE, Margaret E.; AISTROPE, Margaret E.A.;
AITKENHEAD, Diane M.; AITKIN, Judith; AITKIN, Judy; AKERLEY, Dennis Bruce; AKILI, Wanda;
AKINS, Ken Larry; AL-SALAM, Haithem; ALBERT, Fred Ray; ALBERTS, Patricia Janet;
ALBRECHT, Mark A.; AIBUS, Victoria; ALCOCK, Clive; ALCOCK, Karen Lynn; ALCOCK, Margaret;
ALDENRATH, Stefanie; ALDERMAN, Richard Brian; ALDERSON, Patricia L.; AIDI, Kim;
ALDRIDGE, Athelstan Arnold; ALEXANDER, Cheryl Evelyn; ALEXANDER, Colleen;
ALEXANDER, Colleen Edna; ALEXANDER, Michelle T.; ALEXANDER, Rick; ALEXANDER, Tara Michelle;
ALEXANDER, Trudy Joan; ALEXANDER, Wesley Armour; ALFONSI, Lorraine; ALFREY, Chris;
ALI, Suraiya; ALI, Usman; ALKASSAB, Jassam M.; ALLADIN, Mohammad I.;
ALLAIRE, Pauling Theresa; ALLAN, Catie; ALLAN, David K.; ALLAN, David Wright; ALLAN, Dorothy;
ALLAN, Dr. Donald Gordon; ALLAN, Edward Burritt; ALLAN, R. David; ALLARD, Dawn Irene;
ALLARD, Dr. Michael John; ALLARD, Elizabeth Mary; ALLEGRETTO, Leo; ALLEN, Bruce Alexander;
ALLEN, Catherine Elizabeth; ALLEN, Deborah Eve Isabel; ALLEN, Dr. Peter B.; ALLEN, Helen Gail;
ALLEN, Jeff; ALLEN, Judy Lorraine; ALLEN, Keith Alvord; ALLEN, Louis Lee; ALLEN, Michael Trent;
ALLEN, Hobert Lee; ALLEN, Sandy Lee; ALLEN, Susan; ALLEN, Susan Elizabeth; ALLER-STEAD, Frank Martin; ALLER-STEAD, Gail; ALLER-STEAD, Martin; ALLISON, Amy; ALLISON, Clay;
ALLISON, Stanley A.; ALLISON, Terrence Michael; ALLORE, Sonia; ALLSOPP, Blair; ALLSOPP, Ted;
ALMEDA, Jesus Quiambao; ALMOND, David; ALOISIO, Debbie Marleen; ALOISIO, Eliana;
ALPERN, Michael; ALPERN, Sylvia; ALTENBURG, John Theodore; ALTHER, Heidi;
ALTMANN, Eric Martin; ALTON, Bruce; ALTON, David Walter; ALTON, John D.; ALTON, Mary Jane;
ALVANOS, Steve; ALVAREZ, George Paul; AMBROSIE, Eli; AMELIO, Giuseppina;
AMENDT, Wes Peter; AMERONGEN, Denise; AMERONGEN, Robert Leo; AMERSHI, Farouk;
AMES, Barbara; AMES, Barbara Janet; AMES, Carol A.; AMICO, Linda; AMICO, Yolanda;
AMIANI, Hanie Badrudin; AMMANN, Darcy John; AMMAR, Claudia Marcela; AMODIO, Carlo;
ANCTIL, Edna Doris; ANDERSON-PESSOG, Halcyee; ANDERSON, Allan Wayne;
ANDERSON, Andrew M; ANDERSON, Arleigh; ANDERSON, Audrey; ANDERSON, Bryan Kent;
ANDERSON, Carolyn Joyce; ANDERSON, Cathy; ANDERSON, Dorothy G.; ANDERSON Dorothy Louise;
ANDERSON, Dougie Michael; ANDERSON, Douglas Lloyd; ANDERSON, Eileen Rose;
ANDERSON, Evelyn Marie; ANDERSON, Greg Dean; ANDERSON, Helene Marie;
ANDERSON, Helyn Arlene; ANDERSON: Hugh Lorne; ANDERSONK James E.;
ANDERSON, James R.B.; ANDERSON, Jamie Michael; ANDERSON, Janet Diane;
ANDERSON, Janet Yvonne, ANDERSON, Jean M., ANDERSON, Jim; ANDERSON, John Peter;
ANDERSON, Judy May; ANDERSON, Kandace Lee; ANDERSON, Karen Michelle;
ANDERSON, Keith Edward; ANDERSON, Kimberly L.; ANDERSON, Kyle Bennett; ANDERSON, Laura;
ANDERSON, Laura Lee; ANDERSON, Lori Jill; ANDERSON, Lorri Jane; ANDERSON, Margaret;
ANDERSON, Margaret A.; ANDERSON, Margaret K.; ANDERSON, Marina; ANDERSON, Patricia E.;
ANDERSON, Patricia K.; ANDERSON, Pirkko R.; ANDERSON, Sharon B. Bernice;
ANDERSON, William Bowden; ANDO, Kikomatsu; ANDRADE, Franklin A.; ANDRADE, Richard R.;
ANDRE, Susan Martha; ANDREAS, Dale M.; ANDREAS, Gladys; ANDREAS, Holly;
ANDREKSON, Alexander; ANDREKSON, Margaret; ANDREOU, Lena; ANDRESEN, Sandra;
ANDREW, Sylvia M.; ANDREWS, Bert; ANDREWS, Colleen; ANDREWS, David G.; ANDREWS, Diana;
ANDREWS, Donald J.; ANDREWS, Edmund W.; ANDREWS, Edna Mary; ANDREWS, Kent G.;
ANDREWS, Larry T.; ANDREWS, Shelley; ANDREWS, Shelley M.; ANDREWS, Therese E.;
ANDREYCHUK, Mary I.; ANDRIASHEK, Cheryl L.; ANDRIETZ, Tracey L.; ANDRIUK, Fay Marie;
ANDRUCHOW, Alex; ANDRUCHOW, Susan; ANDRUS, Jules Brian; ANDRUSHAK, Maxine;
ANGOH, Gaetan A.; ANGUS, Julia Ann; ANGUS, Nanna Maria; ANGUS, Richard J.; ANIA, Fernando;
ANNING, Patricia Fern; ANSLOW, Cheryl Lynn; ANTHONY, Brenda L., ANTHONY, Lorna Ruth;
ANTHONY, Stuart C.; ANTONELLO, Debbie; ANTONIO, Elizabeth; ANTONIUK, Andrew V.;
ANTONIUK, David N.; ANTONIUK, David W.; ANTONIUK, Joan J.; ANTONIUK, Trudy E.;
ANTONUCCI, Vincent; ANTOS, Tami Ellen; APEDAILE, Sarah E.; APON, Irene Stuart;
APPLBY, Nancy A.; APPS, Karen Sue; APPS, Michael John; APPS, Michelle Y.; ARABCHUK, Peter;
ARCAND, Suzanne F.; ARCH, Bonnie Lynn; ARCHAMBAULT, Owen; ARCH-DICK, Judith;
ARCHIBALD, Joanne M.; ARDELL, David Louis; ARENDS, John; ARENDS, Robert Lyle;
ARES, Louise Marie; ARGENTO, Karen Alice; ARGY, Melissa Louise; ARIASI, Daniel; ARIDI, Ridon F.;
ARIZA, Gordon I.; ARKESTEIJN, Conny T.; ARKESTEIJN, Shelley T.; ARKINSTALL, Peggy J.;
ARKLE, James; ARLIA, Rosetta; ARMENIAN, Atken; ARMITSTEAD, Barbara M.;
ARMITSTEAD, Barbara M.; ARMITSTEAD, Hazel; ARMITSTEAD, Jim M.; ARMITSTEAD, Laurie G.;
ARMITSTEAD, Maureen F.; ARMITSTEAD, Mearle C.; ARMSTRONG, Charles L.; ARMSTRONG, Darrel;
ARMSTRONG, Dorothy E.; ARMSTRONG, Douglas W.; ARMSTRONG, Elizabeth J.; ARMSTRONG, Ellen;
ARMSTRONG, Janice L.; ARMSTRONG, Johanna M.; ARMSTRONG, Kim S.;
ARMSTRONG, Kimberly H.; ARMSTRONG, Mary; ARMSTRONG, Mary-June; ARMSTRONG, Patty Lee;
ARMSTRONG, Sandra Lee; ARMSTRONG, Sandra-Lee Diane; ARNASON, Nancy Jane;
ARNDT, Sheryl Lynne; Arndt, Tara Lynn; ARNETT, Robert Blane; ARNIERI, Frances;
ARNIERI, Rita Maria; ARNOLD, Carol Anne; ARNOLD, Catherine E.; ARNOLD, David K.;
ARNOLD, Dr. Ian M.; ARNOLD, Susan H.; ARNOLD, Wendy; ARNOLD, William F.; ARNOTT, Arthur G.;
ARNOTT, Janet Joyce; ARNOTT, Paul T.; ARNOTT, William Kevin; ARONYK, Alan Stephen;
ARPS, Esther Gina; ARSENIAN, Elvira; ARTHURS, Darren J.; ARTHURS, Claudine S.;
ARTUSO, DonnaMarie; ARYCHUK, Agnes; ARYCHUK, Agnes; ARYCHUK, Melissa J.; ASANO, Hiroshi;
ASCHENBRENNER, Dawn; ASHCROFT, Richard M.; ASHE, Maureen Debra; ASHFORD, George B.;
ASHMORE, Rhonda B.; ASHTON, Anna Marie; ASHTON, Barbara P.; ASHTON, Diana;
ASHTON, Dr. Deidre; ASHTON, Marie; ASHTON, Rene Joseph; ASHTON, Robert Harry;
ASHWELL, Gen; ASQUITH, Keith; ASSALY, Karen; ASSALY, Perry W.; ASTLE-FLEMING, Linda Carol;
ASTLE, Dorothy K.; ASTLE, Michael P.; ASTLE, Thomas G.; ASTON, Glenn; ATHAIDE, Margaret;
ATHAIDE, Tina Marie; ATHIAS, Lee; ATIENZA, Chito; ATIENZA, Jay; ATKEY, Liz; ATKIN, Chrisopher;
ATKINS, Lloyd Edwin; ATKINS, Carolyn Marie; ATKINS, Ilene I.; ATKINS, Margaret;
ATKINS, Melanie G.; ATKINS, Tony; ATKINSON, Cecile Ellen; ATKINSON, Ethelene M.;
ATKINSON, Helen; ATKINSON, James T.; ATKINSON, Kerry E.; ATKINSON, Lindsay D.;
ATKINSON, Patricia P.; ATKINSON, William M.; ATMORE, Michael W.; ATWOOD, Don George;
AU, Connie LaiFong; AUBIN, Ronald; AUDY, Lorraine M.; AUGIS, Virginia; AUSTIN, David;
AUSTIN, Lillian A.; AUSTIN, Penny Jane; AUSTIN, Rosalind; AUTY, David Graham;
AVASTHI, Chander Kant; AVERY, Kenneth J.; AVES, Brenda Jean; AVIS, Pam; AVIS, Pamela;
AVRAMIDES, Anastasia; AVRAMIDES, Olga; AWID, Evelyn Audrey; AWID, Glenda Mari;
AWID, James; AWID, Jeffery Michael; AXANI, Patricia Jean; AXELSEN, Loretta;
AXELSON, Rawnald, W.; AXTELL, Donald F.; AXTELL, Glayne M.; AYER, Dorothy K.; AYER, Katherine;
AYERS, Betty Lou; AYERS, Daniel G.; AYERS, Larry Donald; AYLES, Susan Patricia; AYOTTE, Angela;
AYONG, Nicole Karen; AYOUNG, Wolston Peter Anthony; AYRE, Earl Wesley; AYRE, F. Connie;
AYRES, Mary; AYRES, Maureen S.; AZARKO, Debbie Lynn; AZOCAR, Sandra Ines;
AZZARONE, Antonio;

B

BABAD, Jacob William; BABB, Alice A.; BABB, Lila Elizabeth; BABBIK, Rose Vivian;
BABCHUK, Catherine M.; BABCHUK, Emil; BABIN, Denis Henri; BABIN, Sandra E.; BABIUK, Jean A.;
BABIUK, Michael W.; BABLITZ, Alice Maria; BACCHUS, Azam; BACCHUS, Rabena;
BACCUS, Roweena; BACCHUS, Sherine; BACH, Ryan Reginald; BACHAND, Corinne, L.;
BACHHAL, Upiwder Pal Singh; BACK, Carol; BACK, Ralph Maurice; BACKSTROM, Dr. Alvin;
BACOVSKY, Rosemary A.; BACULA, Sylvie Denise; BADGER, Brad L.; BADGER, Laurie;
BADGER, Tony David; BADRY, Denise C.; BADRY, Sharlene V.; BADURLA, Myrna;
BAECK, Marlynn Alice; BAER, Barbara Ann; BAER, James Dwight; BAER, Katherine Anne;
BAER, Kathy; BAER, Margaret Mary; BAERGEN, William G.; BAERT, Marcel; BAGGETT, Patricia;
BAGSHAW, Karen Fae; BAGWE, Anuradha; BAHNSEN, Glenna P; BAIER, Edna Ann;
BAIKLE, Carolyn G.; BAILER, Myron Ernest; BAILEY, Beverley J.; BAILEY, Charles; BAILEY, Gwyneth;
BAILEY, Wendy Elaine; BAIN, Darcy David; BAIN, Isabelle Jessie; BAIN, James Robert;
BAIRD, Christopher; BAIRD, Estella Merry; BAIRD, Howard Jeff; BAIRD, Peter Norman;
BAKER, David; BAKER, Duane John; BAKER, John Timothy; BAKER, Judi Anne; BAKER, Judith M.;
BAKER, Ken H.; BAKER, Ken Marvin; BAKER, Ken Todd; BAKER, Kimberley; BAKER, Laura Ellen;
BAKER, Margaret; BAKER, Michael Troy; BAKER, Nimer Ata; BAKER, Patricia;
BAKER, Robert George; BAKONYI, Tim S.; BAKOWCHUK, Mary; BALAN, Deborah Anne;
BALAY, Eugene Elmer; BALAY, Verna; BALCOM, Kenneth M.; BALDOCK, Donna Lynn;
BALDWIN, Cindy Vali; BALKO, Jody Lynn; BALL, Adeline; BALL, Barabara Jean;
BALL, Bradley Smith; BALL, Craig Douglas; BALL, Dawn Marie; BALLA, Robert Edward;
BALLUM, Chris Todd; BALOGH, Elaine; BALOGH, Jeno; BALOMBEN, Lil; BALOMBEN, Tim G.;
BALSDEN, Doug; BALTSIS, Konstadinos; BALTZER, Mavis Joy; BAMFORD, Elizabeth;
BANASCH, Cara Nicole; BANERIEE, Rajasree; BANH, Mai Back; BANKS, Barbara; BANKS, Carol;
BANKS, John Allenby; BANKS, Patrick; BANKS, Peter; BANNARD, Dawn L.; BANNER, Ken John;
BANTING, Tammie; BAPTIE, Gary A.; BAPTIE, Jan; BAPTIE, Jodi Lynn; BAPTIE, Lisa Jolane;
BARA, Claude M.; BARA, Gerald M.; BARA, Luczya; BARABASH, Elvira; BARBASH, Mary-Lou;
BARBER, Janet E.; BARBER, Linda; BARBER, Neil Edward; BARBOSO, Catarina; BARBUTZA, V. Keith;
BARCH, Debi Ann; BARD, Forrest Hugh; BARDSLEY, Barbara; BARER, Dr. Daniel J.; BARETTE, Janie;
BARIL, Armand G.; BARIL, Joanne Louise; BARIL, Leah; BARIL, Lucie Cecilia; BARIL, Raymond;
BARKER, Elsa Rebeca; BARKER, Greg; BARKER; Maureen; BARKER, Robert; BARKER, Susan;

BARKNOWITZ, Hellmut; BARLAGE, Gerald A.; BARLOW, Elsie; BARLOW, Karen Anna;
ARNARD, Dodi; BARNES, Elaine N.; BARNES, Jennifer; BARNES, Judith; BARNES Kathleen;
BARNES, Lorne R.; BARNES, Michael W.; BARNES, Neil Wilfred; BARNES, Peter Derek;
BARNES, Robert Stuart; BARNES, Sally M.; BARNES, Steve; BARNES, Sussan; BARNETT, Grace;
BARNETT, Sharon Mary; BARNHART, Ronald; BARNICOAT, Jill A.; BARON, Charlaine;
BARON, Elsa Sigrid; BARON, Glenn Richard; BARON, Laurette; BARON, Laurette Ann;
BARONE, Antonella; BARONE, Michael; BARONSFEATHER, William; BARR, Bonnie Carleen;
BARR, Dave; BARR, Gordon Edward; BARR, Kelly Elizabeth; BARR, William C.;
BARRANOIK, Curtis W.; BARRERA, Jaime G.; BARRETT, Jane Mary; BARRETT, Jennifer P.;
BARRETT, Mark; BARRETT, Robert; BARRETTE, Arlette-Suzanne; BARRIGAN, Charles;
BARRON, John Edward; BARRON, Marion; BARRON, Raymond; BARROS, Irvin Bruce;
BARROS, Sally R.; BARROS, Tony Esteves; BARROW, Josephine; BARRY, Anita Jean;
BARRY, Bruce Lorne; BARRY, Eva M.; BARRY, Joyce; BARSAM, Patricia; BARSNESS, Gail Diane;
BARSS, Patricia; BARTEL, Linda Ruth; BARTEL, William G.; BARTELUK, Janina; BARTH, C. Fred;
BARTH, Ingrid M.; BARTHOLOMEW, Everol; BARTI, Catherine M.; BARTI, Helena;
BARTLETT, Karen M. BARTLETT, Laura; BARTLEY, Joan; BARTLEY, Terri; BARTMAN, Marlene;
BARTON, Michael; BARTON, Thomas Wil; BARTOS, Darryl D.; BARY, Catherine Lois; BAS, Josef Leo;
BASARABA, Brad S.; BASARABA, Colleen; BASARABA, Elena; BASARABA, Lorraine;
BASARABA, Maria; BASARABA, Neil A.; BASARSKY, Karen A.; BASFORD, Linda C.;
BASKETT, Sandra; BASKETT, Tom H.; BASKEY, Beverly Lee; BASTIDAS, Narcisa: BASTIDAS, Rita P.;
BASTIDE, Victoria M.; BATEMAN, James; BATEMAN, Susanne; BATES, Anne Patricia;
BATES, Patricia; BATTISTELLA, Karen; BATTRYN, Ernestine; BAUCKMAN, Theresa;
BAUDER, Elaine M.; BAUDER, Paul Lou; BAUDERFIND, Boyd; BAUDERFIND, Jan;
BAUDIN, Joan Colleen; BAUER, Darrell N.; BAUER, Ed H.; BAULK, Tracey;
BAUMGAERTNER, Colleen Patricia; BAUMGARDNER, Brenda L.; BAUMGARTNER, Audra;
BAUMGARTNER, Thelma; BAVARO, Bruno; BAVATO, Dennis; BAVATO, Harry;
BAYANS, Toni Frances; BAYDALA, Stella; BAYDUZO, Christopher; BAYLEY, Doris C.; BAYLY, Jerry;
BAYNTON, Robert; BAYRAK, Catherine; BAZIN, Colette E.; BAZIN, Lawrence; BAZIW, Bradley;
BAZIW, Dean Allan; BAZYLEWICH, Leslie; BAZLEWICH, Selene; BEACH, Gordon; BEACH, Krista Kim;
BEACH, Shelley Ann; BEAKHOUSE, Catherine Doris; BEAKHOUSE, Phillip;
BEAKHOUSE, Vaughn Edward; BEALE, David Arthur; BEALE, Philip Walter; BEAMAN, Danny;
BEAMISH, Brenda; BEARD, Priscilla; BEARHEAD, Sherry; BEATON, Douglas; BEATON, Heather;
BEATTIE, D. Patricia; BEATTIE, Janet Noelle; BEATTIE, Joan; BEATTY, Kevin David;
BEAUCHAMP, Al Rene; BEAUCHEMIN, Marie; BEAUDETTE, Denise; BEAUDOIN, Danielle R.;
BEAUDOIN, Sherry; BEAUDRY, Richard; BEAUGARD, Sanda; BEAULIEU, Joey E.; BEAULIEU, Julie;
BEAULIEU, Maurice; BEAULNE, Suzanne; BEAUPRE, Lauren A.; BEBENSEE, Jane;
BECKER, Anne Leona; BECKER, David Kelsey; BECKER, Gregory Kim; BECKER, Nancy Lee;
BECKER, Thomas Otto; BECKETT, Karen; BECKINGHAM, Jean E.; BECKLEY; Derek J.;
BECKMAN, Monica; BEDARD, Cecile Marie; BEDARD, Doris Valerie; BEDARD, Lucie O.;
BEDARD, Ronda; BEDE, Suzy; BEDFORD, Cindy Lee; BEDNORZ, Mary-Anne; BEEKEN, Don;
BEEKEN, Richard Alan; BEERWART, Jeff; BEESON, Barbara M.; BELEGUIN, Lorraine; BEFUS, Albert;
BEFUS, Janice T.; BEGER, Joan A.; BEGG, Stuart G.; Begley, Marian; BEHIEL, Norman;
BEHM, Dawn-Marie; BEHM, Janice; BEHM, Kevin David; BEIER, Maurice A.; BELAIR, Isabelle T.;
BELANGER, Betty L.; BELANGER, Camille Marie; BELANGER, Douglas Anthony;
BELANGER, Janet Lea; BELANGER, Paul G.; BELANGER, Simone G.; BELCOURT, Penny-Laine;
BELDKAMP, Leona; BELHUMEUR, Louise; BELHUMEUR, Paulette; BELINGA-ARNOLD, Serge;
BELL, Gayle L.; BELL, Gordon; BELL, Jack Arthur; BELL, Jacqueline C.; BELL, Jean; BELL, Jill;
BELL, Joan M.; BELL, Kirk William; BELL, Leslie; BELL, Malcolm; BELL, Marjolaine;
BELL, Mary Ellena; BELL, Nancy-Jean; BELL, Nancy-Jean W.; BELL, Patricia F.; BELL, Peter James;
BELL, Peter Thomson; BELL, Shannon M.; BELL, Sharon Lynn; BELL, Stanley; BELL, Theresa;
BELLAMY, Elizabeth R.; BELLAMY, James; BELAN, Lester R.; BELLAN, Patricia Anne;
BELLAND, Dave; BALLAND, Lorraine; BELLAND, Nicole C.; BELLAND, Tracy; BELLEROSE, Randall;
BELLEY, Bernadette; BELLEY, Sonia Marie; BELLINGER, Jeffrey M.; BELLINGER, N. Colleen;
BELLINGROTH, Brian; BELLIVEAU, Elizabeth; BELLOW, Denise; BELLOW, Jean M.; BELMONT, John;
BELOPOLSKY, Dmitry; BELSHER, Ricky Kemis; BELTON, Donna V.; BELYEA, Frank; BELZIL, Collette T.;
BELZIL, Roxanne; BENAY, Stephanie; BENDER, Susan; BENDERS; Elizabeth; BENDICKSON, Pamela;
BENDZERA, Stella; BENEDET, Diane Lee; BENEDICT, Margaret; BENESOCKY, June; BENGTSON, Tor;
BENINCASA, Louis; BENKO, Lynda Ann; BENKO, Sharon Lynn; BENKO, Todd Anthony; BENNER;
James Dean; BENNETT, John; BENNETT, Alan Dean; BENNETT, Cheryl; BENNETT, Cheryl;
BENNETT, Elizabeth; BENNETT, Jane; BENNETT, Marion Irma; BENNETT, Shannon;
BENNETT, Stephen; BENNETT, Tennis M.; BENNIE, Chari Marie; BENOIT, Marieanne;
BENOIT, Romeo M.; BENOITAN, Rene David; BENSON, Debbie L.; BENSON, Doreen;
BENTLEY, Carolyn; BENTLEY, Lorraine; BENTT, Michelle K.; BENUSIC, Ken Michael;
BENVENUTO, Lawrence; BERCON, Ronald David; BERCOV, Ron; BERETON, James R.;
BERESFORD, Marg. B.; BERESKA, Tami Marie; BEREZAN, Joanne; BEREZAN, Orie M.;
BEREZAN, Richard V.; BEREZAN, Sharon Jane; BEREZANSKI, Albert; BEREZNICKI, Andrew;
BEREZNICKI, Annette; BEREZNICKI, Mark A.; BEREZOWSKI, Susan; BERG, Cindi Raelene;
BERG, June Marylyn; BERG, Nolan Kendal; BERG, Sharon; BERG, Sherrill; BERGE, Brian Edward;
BERGER, Joan Alison; BERGER, Marjorie; BERGER, Sandra C.; BERGET, Connie Rae;
BERGGREN, Heather; BERLIN, Kimberly J.; BERMEDO, Rembrandt; BERMATT, Brett Craig;
BERNAL, Victor; BERNEL, Ralph Jesus; BERNER, Bonnie-Fave; BERNER, Dr. Cecil A; BERNER, Susan;
BERNSTEIN, Ari Darryl; BERETTI, Antonella; BERETTI, Margaret; BERETTI, Massimiliano R.;
BERETTI, Simonetta; BERRIER, Darcy Warren; BERRINGER, Jo-Anne A.; BERRY, Brian William;
BERRY, Christine P.; BERRY, Darren; BERRY, Frances Joan; BERRY, Glenn Romain;
BERRY, Jerry Craig; BERRY, Patti Dawn; BERRY, Susan Joy; BERRY, Trevor; BERRY, Trudy E.;
BERRY, William; BERSON, Sonia; BERTHELSEN, Richard; BERTHOT, Jennifer; BERTOIA, Loretta;
BERTOLIN, Diana; BERTRAND; Paule; BERUBE, Bertrand H.; BERUBE, Joanne; BERUBE, Lorraine;
BERUBE, Martine; BERWICH, Cyril David; BERWICK, Ross David; BERZE, Maria Valeria;
BERZINS, Sandra Anne; BESSAI, Tom Haviland; BEST, Christina M.; BEST, Thomas Harold;
BESWICK, Naomi S.; BESWICK, Rhianon; BETCHINSKI, Elaine; BETHEL, Marnie Claire;
BETTGER, Dharma; BETTIOL, Nadia; BETTON, Carla; BETTS, Mary Norma; BEVERLEIN, Lavina;
BEUHLER, Roland; BEVAN, Jeffrey Scott; BEVAN, Richard E.; BEVILACQUA, Lino;
BEYER, Edythe Anne; BEYER, Valerie Jean; BHAGRATH, Raghbir Singh; BHAMBHANI, Jyoti;
BHAR, Amrita; BHARDWAJ, Saroj; BHARUCHA, Zarrin; BHATIA, Gurvinder Singh;
SHATIA, Nimirá Habib; BHATIA, Praveen Dev; BHATIA, Priti; BHATTACHARYA, Eileen;
BHUMGARA, Hushtasp; BIASONE, Peter; BIDDULPH, Delores; BIDNIAK, Martha Lily;
BIDWELL, Charles M.; BIEDERMAN, Brian; BIEDERMAN, Joan; BIELECH, Monique; BIELENY, Carol;
BIELENY, Lorraine; BIELENY, Patrick S.; BIELENY, Sharon; BIENSCH, Edna; BIGGS, Dr. David;
BIGGS, Leone Ruth; BIGLOW, Juanita Irene; BIGRAS, Sylvie; BILINSKI, Doug; BILLINSKI, Douglas;
BILLINSKI, John David; BILKO, Dora; BILKO, Mark Gregory; BILKO, William; BILLINGTON, Dave;
BILYK, Brian Orest; BINCE; Lorie J.; BINETTE, Claudette Therese; BING, Heddy;
BINNIE, Pamela Gwen; BIRCH, Valerie Janet; BIRD, Anne Louise; BIRD, Colleen Enid;
BIRD, Trevor C.; BIRDI, Deant Kaur; BIRDI, Sarbjeet Kaur; BIRKLAND, Fred Peter; BIRKLAND, John;
BIRKS, Wendy Margaret; BIRMINGHAM, Denis; BIRMINGHAM, Margaret; BISHOP, Audrey;
BISHOP, Elizabeth Anne; BISHOP, Larry James; BISHOP, Margaret Sharon; BISHOP, Ronald Peter;
BISHOP, Sara Elizabeth; BISHOP, Theresa Louise; BISHOP, Valerie; BISHOP, Valerie Frances;
BISHOP, Ward James; BISHOP, William Daniel; BISSON, Robert Claude;
BISSONNET, Allison Elizabeth; BISSONNETTE, Gerri; BITAMBA, Goretti; BITAR, Sonia;
BITTORF, Elizabeth Ann; BITTORF, Loa Rae; BIARNARSON, Marlene Francis; BIARNASON, Leona D.;
BIARNASON, Rick F.; BIERKE, Joyce S.; BIERKELUND, Leslie Jean Victoria; BLACK, Dana Bernard;
BLACK, Dr. William Robert; BLACK, Evelyn Marie; BLACK, Iris; BLACK, James Daren;
BLACK, James Douglas; BLACK, Leonard A.; BLACK, Patricia May; BLACK, Sharon Blanche;
BLACK, Steven Anthony; BLACK, Valerie; BLACKBURN, Jack Campbell; BLACKBURN, Jacquie A.;
BLACKFORD, Ann; BLACKFORD, Jason; BLACKLOCK, Carol Nedra; BLACKLOCK, Robert Harold;
BLACKMAN, Adam; BLACKMAN, Steven; BLACKWOOD, Mary Leone; BLADES, John William;
BLAHEY, Pauline; BLAIR, Carol; BLAIR, Dorothyanne Mae; BLAIR, Elizabeth; BLAIR, Leona Lynn;
BLAIR, Mervin Garth; BLAIR, Norman Robert; BLAIR, Susan Charlotte; BLAIS, Claude Joseph;
BLAIS, Elaine M.; BLAISE, Janine Marie; BLAKE, Edith Margaret; BLAKE, Kenneth A.;
BLAKELY, Tracey Lee; BLAKEMAN, Evelyn D.; BLANCHARD, Susan Joy; BLANCHETTE, Albert;
BLAND, Edward R.; BLANDCHETTE, Leanne Carol; BLANEY, Charlene Lynn; BLASCO, Marina Lynn;
BLATT, Martin; BLATZ, Maxine Anne; BLEAKLEY, Betty Ann; BLEAKLEY, Corinne May;
BLEAU, Dolores Janice; BLECHINGER, Gary Herman; BLEICH, Birdie Lyval Teresa;
BLEIER, Louise Marie A.; BLEIKEN, Kay Mary; BLEROT, Lorianne Marie; BLEVISS, Dr. Morley;
BLISCHAK, Kathy Lynn; BLOCK, Gordon Cecil; BLOCKA, Lori Anne; BLOXHAM, Toni Lynne;
BLUM, Elizabeth; BLUMENTHAL, Leonard; BLUMIE, Wyne; BLUMIE, Wyne B.; BLUNDELL, Elaine M.;
BLYTHE, E. Leslie; BOOKE, Dr. Rex Clark; BOBROSKE, Donna Arlene; BOBROSKE, Terry-Lee;
BOCHINSKI, Dr. Bruno; BOCHON, Linda Marie; BOCIAN, Debbie; BOCIAN, Geoff Ivan;
BOCKING, Kendall Ray; BOCOCK, Bruce William; BOCOCK, Gordon; BOCOCK, Linda F.;
BOCSKEI, Hope; BODDY, Walter L.; BODIE, Patricia; BODLACK, Ruby Anne;
BODNAR, Eugene James; BODNAR, Laureen Bertha; BODNARCHUK, Lisa Faye; BODNAR, Janie D.;
BOEHERS, Diane Ruth; BOEHM, Christine; BOEHRES, Frank Dieter; BOENDER, Adriana Wilhelmina;
BOER, Michael; BOETTCHER, Arnold Samuel; BOETTGER, Tom H.; BOGDEN, Shanna Marie;
BOGNER, Michael John; BOHAM, Heather Anne; BOHONOS, Gerald Randall; BOISIOLI, Anne Marie;
BOISSONNAULT, Antoinette Marie; BOISVER, Bob Omer; BOISVERT, Gloria Jean; BOISVERT, Guy P.;
BOK, Nick; BOKENFOHR, Kerry-Lynn; BOKENFOHR, Susan Maxine; BOLESKA, Peter;
BOLIVAR, John Henry; BOLOGNA, Sandy Anne; BOLSTAD, Jane; BOLTER, Susan Mary;
BOLTON, Garry; BONAVNI, Katherine; BOND, Dr. David William; BOND, Gaenor Jane;
BOND, Judith Joanna; BOND, Lawrence Alan; BOND, Pam; BONETTI, Marcio;
BONEVITCH, Carol Edith; BONEY, Rose; BONITZ, Max Albert; BONNEAU, Diane;
BONORA, Doris Celestina E.; BONVALET, Yuain Marc; BOODHAGEN, Michael Frederick;
BOODRAM, Karen Francia; BOOI, Jeffrey Trent; BOONSTRA, Cyndy Dawn; BOOS, Brian;
BOOS, Laurie Ann; BOOS, Paul John; BOOTH, Denise Alice; BOOTH, Lyndsey Ann;
BOOTH, Pam Elaine; BOOTSMAN, Kenneth Lloyd; BOOTSMAN, Marie; BORAS, Linda Jean;
BORCHUK, Shelley; BORDEN, Marie Jane; BORKENT, Dr. Herman Albert; BORLE, Doreen Edith;
BORLE, Joyce A.; BORLE, Sandra Gay; BORLOI, Helma; BORMAN, Andrea Gay; BORO, Virginia Lee;
BOROSS, Frank; BOROWICZ, John Michael; BORELLI, Angelo; BORELLI, Nick Matthew;
BORELLI, Rodolfo Rudy; BORRIS, Diane Marie; BORRIS, Louise Marie; BORROUGHS, Nel;
BORTOLON, Giancarlo; BORWICK, MArilyn Gail; BOSCH, Rita Rose; BOSCOE, Leonard Anthony;
BOSCOE, Patricia Alice; BOSE, Bijaya; BOSIAK, Janie Marina; BOSSERT, Brian Douglas;
BOSTRAM, Jane; BOSWORTH, Jean; BOSWORTH, Lori A.; BOSWORTH, Pamela Jean;
BOTNICK, Joshua; BOUCHARD, Jean; BOUCHARD, Leona Simone; BOUCHER, Bonnie;
BOUCHER, Michel; BOUEY, Robert Freeman; BOULANGER, Mario J.; BOULET, Jacqueline Sarah;
BOULET, Laurette; BOULT, Donald A.; BOURDON, Janine Marie; BOURGEAULT, Dale;
BOURGEAULT, Guy; BOURGEAULT, Jay; BOURGEAULT, Susan; BOURGEOIS, Maggie Gisele;
BOURGEOIS, Marie Christine; BOURKE, Maureen; BOURQUE, Joseph Lionel; BOURQUE, Paul;
BOUSLAMA, Syd; BOUTHILLIER, Etta Susan; BOUTHILLIER, James Gordon;
BOUTHILLIER, Marianne Josephina; BOUTIN, Agatha; BOUVIER, Robert Gerald Joseph;
BOUWMEESTER, Donna Lynne; BOWE, Jane A.; BOWEN, Betty; BOWEN, Betty Eileen;
BOWEN, George Johnston; BOWEN, Jo-Anne Carol; BOWEN, Marge; BOWEN, Robert William;
BOWEN, Susan Elizabeth; BOWERING, John; BOWERING, Kathryn; BOWERS, James Dorrance;
BOWERS, Laurie Eveline; BOWES, Dave Allan; BOWES, William E.; BOWIE, Daniel Richard;
BOWIE, Kim Lorrence; BOWKER, Hugh Neil; BOWKER, Valerie; BOWKER, Valerie A.; BOWLBY, Jeff;
BOWMAN, Graeme; BOWMAN, Kerry Kathleen; BOWN, Edward A.; BOWN, Rose V.;
BOX, Karen Antoinette; BOYACHEK Barry; BOYACHUK, Edward A.; BOYCHUK, Anne;
BOYCHUK, Catherine Karen; BOYCHUK, Diane Marie; BOYCHUK, Emily J.; BOYCHUK, Eugene A.;
BOYCHUK, John; BOYCHUK, Shirley Elizabeth; BOYD, Conrad Barkley; BOYD, Danny; BOYD, David S.;
BOYD, Deanne Jean; BOYD, Denise Beverly; BOYD, Eileen Sharon; BOYD, Helen Mary;
BOYD, James Jay; BOYD, Mildred Francis; BOYD, Robert Joseph; BOYD, Sheila; BOYD, Stephen;
BOYD, William Alexander; BOYER, Bridgette Anne; BOYES, Angela; BOYES, Robert Wayne;
BOYKO, Audrey Elva; BOYKO, Donna; BOYKO, Lydia; BOYKO, Michael Robert; BOYKO, Peter;
BOYKO, William; BOYLAN, Bruce; BOYLE, Christena Mary; BOYLE, John; BOYLE, Linda Lee;
BOYLE, Trevor Allan; BOYLES, Elvie Burton; BOYLES, Mary Ann; BOYSON, M. Gina;
BOZMAN, Gerard A.; BRAAM, Claerisse Simone; BRAB, Frank; BRABANT, Peter Van;
BRACEGIRDIE, Sharon Anne; BRACIO, Diana; BRACKO, Leonard; BRACUK, Linda Anne;
BRADEN, Debra Jean; BRADEY, Elsie Jean; BRADFORD, Terri-Lynn; BRADLEY, David Frederick;
BRADLEY, Ian; BRADLEY, Janice Lee; BRADLEY, Jay; BRADLEY, Karen; BRADLEY, Keith Richard;
BRADLEY, Michael Patrick; BRADLEY, Noreen; BRADLEY, Patricia; BRADLEY, Robbie;
BRADLEY, Robert Lloyd; BRADLEY, Tracy Ann; BRADLEY, Vivian L.; BRADSHAW, Diana Patrice;
BRADSHAW, Herbert Russell; BRADY, Darlene Ann; BRAEDLEY, Isabel Jane;
BRAIDWOOD, Nadeane Ann; BRAIDWOOD, T. John; BRAITHWAITE, Charlotte Ann;
BRAMBLEY, Bonnie Lynne; BRAMLEY, Lorna Gail; BRAND, I. Roy; BRAND, Peter; BRANDA, Barb;
BRANDER, Warren Alan; BRANDT, Donald R.; BRANDT, Elizabeth; BRANDT, Jose Roberto Thedim;
BRANNEN, Rosemary Betty; BRASS, Donna Lynn; BRASSARD, Janice Lynne; BRASSON, Paul;
BRAITON, Claudette Marilyn; BRATTON, Robert; BRAUN, Constance Marie; BRAUN, Doris;
BRAUNBERGER, Sheryl Nadine; BRAY, Ailsa Louise; BRECHT, Irma-Alexandra H.; BREEN, Debra D.;
BREEN, Richard Allen; BRRREITKREUZ, Janice Gail; BREKVELD, Keri-Lyn; BREMNER, Betty;
BREMNER, Bruce; BREMNESS, Joan; BRENDA, Denise Katherine; BRENNAN, Jim Samuel;
BRENNAND, Joanne M.; BRENNEIS, Carleen Marie; BRENNEIS, Dr. Fraser R.; BRES, Gonda;
BRESE, Anne Marie; BRETZER, Edwin; BREZINSKI, Linda Elaine; BRIDGEMAN, Valerie;
BRIDGES, Lucienne; BRIEN, Dr. William F.; BRIERE, Donald Lenard; BRIERLEY, Gail E.;
BRIGGS, Richard Frederick; BRIGGS, Wilfred James; BRIGHT, David Paul; BRIGHT, John David;
BRIGHT, Linda Jean; BRIGHTLEY, Garcia Alwyn; BRIGIDEAR, Lorraine M.; BRIGLEY, Linda Mae;
BRIKER, Arkady; BRIKER, Yevgenia; BRILL, Margaret Rose; BRITZ, Grant Stephen;
BRIMACOMBE, Elizabeth, Jane; BRIMACOMBE, Margaret Elle; BRIMACOMBE, Marwood G.;
BRINCKER, Roger; BRINER, Doug Michael; BRINKMANN, Bernhard Heinrich; BRINTNELL, E. Sharon;
BRIONGOS, Heliodoro; BRISTOW, Christine Agnes; BRITNER, Mark Francis;
BRITTAIN, Alice Elizabeth; BRITTON, Colleen Joy; BRITTON, Deanna Jo; BRITTON, Douglas Stephen;
BRITTON, Lynda; BRITTON, Peter Alexander; BRKIN, Zlatko; BRADLEY, Debora Lynn;
BROCKMAN, Diane Elaine; BROCKS, Guy L.; BRODA, Arlis Rosemarie; BRODDY, Craig;
BRODERICK, James Jason; BRODERICK, Kathy Alice; BRODEUR, Adrienne;
BRODEUR, Catherine Anne; BRODEUR, Emily; BRODEUR, Lawrence; BRODIE, Lydia Rosanne;
BRODIE, SHARON Lynn; BRODSKY, Boris; BRODSKY, Larisa; BROEN, Barb Jean; BROEN, Elizabeth;
BROERSON, Ingrid Anne; BROHMAN, George Andrew; BROKOP, Marvin K.;
BROMAN, Billie Jean Shelly; BROMLEY, Charlene Elizabeth; BROMLEY, Graham Glenwood;
BROMLEY, Patricia Anne; BROMMELAND, Laurel Jeanne; BRONSON, Robert Trent; BROOK, Ann;
BROOK, Peter Cutcliffe; BROOKER, Kyrsten Irene; BROOKER, Marion Irene; BROOKES, David Harold;

BROOKES, Kevin George; BROOKS, Audrey Margaret; BROOKS, George Allan; BROOKS, Georgiana; BROOKS, Laurie Kay; BROSNIKOFF, Kathie Debra May; BROSNIKOFF, Murray Randall; BROSSEAU, Lise Bernadette; BROTHERSTON, G. Lorne; BROTSCHI, Bernie; BROUWER-DENEEN, Elly J.; BROVERMAN, Janice Helen; BROWER, Yvonne Edith; BROWN, A. Doreen; BROWN, Alison Rosemary; BROWN, Angus Graham; BROWN, Betty Kathleen; BROWN, Bruce Lloyd; BROWN, Colette Elaine; BROWN, Corina Lea; BROWN, Daphne Maud; BROWN, David Fordyce; BROWN, David Grainger; BROWN, Donald Charles; BROWN, Doreen; BROWN, Doug; BROWN, Douglas Stephen; BROWN, Dr. Jack; BROWN, Dr. Jim J.; BROWN, Elizabeth; BROWN, Gail; BROWN, Geoffrey; BROWN, George A.; BROWN, Helen E.(Betty); BROWN, Jack; BROWN, James Ronald William; BROWN, Jeff Stewart; BROWN, John McKenzie; BROWN, Judith Anne; BROWN, Kenneth; BROWN, Kenneth Mcleod; BROWN, Kenneth Stephen; BROWN, Lorraine Marie; BROWN, Marion Karen; BROWN, Mavis A.; BROWN, Nicholas Oliver; BROWN, Robert; BROWN, Robert D.; BROWN, Terry D.; BROWN, Weldon; BROWN, Weldon Arthur Leigh; BROWN, William Gordon; BROWNE, Helen; BROWNLEE, Bettyanne; BROWNLEE, Gayle Jean; BROWNOFF, Rene; BROX, Dianne Elizabeth; BRUCE, Joan; BRUCE, Karen; BRUCE, Kim; BRUCE, Sharron E.; BRUDER, Ida Mary; BRUINSMA, Martina; BRULLOTT, June; BRUMLIK, Geoffrey Walter; BRUNAGA, Juan Rene; BRUNDIN, Rebecca; BRUNEL, Patricia; BRUNELLE, Loralie; BRUNELLE, Rawleigh Paul; BRUNI, Anna Maria; BRUNI, Franco; BRUNSCH, Doris H.; BRUSEKER, Marie Victoria; BRYAN, E. Joyce; BRYAN, John; BRYAN, John Alan; BRYAN, Peter Alan; BRYAN, Shelly Ann; BRYAN, Wendy Jane; BRYANT, Don Louis; BRYDEN, Janet Lynne; BRYDGES, Dean George; BRYENTON, E. Jack; BRYGADYR, Maryanne; BRYK JONES, Nadine; BRYKS, Douglas; BRYKS, Edward; BRYSHUN, Patti Lou; BRZEZOWSKI, Walter; BUCHAN, Donald Jerome; BUCHAN, Maurice E.; BUCHANAN, Brent Roy; BUCHANAN, Kathryn; ABUCHANAN, Lynn Maureen; BUCHKOWSKY, Brian; BUCHSDRUCKER, Karen Edith; BUCHWALD, Joyce; BUCHWALD, Julian David; BUCHYNSKI, Bruce; BUCHYNSKI, Susan; BUCK, Connie; BUCK, David John; BUCK, Elizabeth Anne; BUCK, Jeff Phillip; BUCK, Vera Ellen; BUCK Wendy Sue Pamela; BUCKO, Eugene George; BUDAY, Andrew Dalus; BUDAY, Roger Patrick; BUDGE, J. Kelly; BUDINSKI, Edward; BUDZAK, Michele Charlene Rose; BUECHNER, Helen Tracy Michelle; BUECHNER, Monica Elizabeth; BUERGER, Sharon Debbie; BUFFEL, Kristine Karen; BUFFIE, J. David; BUGIS, Dr. Joseph; BUGIS, Linda Rachelle; BUHLER, Conrad; BUHRMANN, Kristin Marie; BUIJS, Rosanne Marie; BUIST, David Methven; BUIST, Neal Patrick; BUKSA, Cindy G.; BULAT, Jennifer; BULLEN, Barry Robert; BULLER, Susan Marie; BULLOCK, Irene Mildred; BULMER, Sandy Grace; BUNDSCHUH, Otto; BUNKALL, Ruth Mary; BUNTEN, Dr. Earle Robert; BUNTING, Gilbert Spencer; BURBULEVICIUS, Rita; BURCH, Shirley Dawna; BURCHAK, Mary Anne; BURD, Daryl Raymond; BURD, Karen Lynn; BURDEN, Robert Earl; BURDETT, John William; BURDETT, Kevin Neil; BUREAUD, Henri; BURECHAILO, Ronalda Madeline; BUREGA, Richard; BURGER, Theresa; BURGERS, Lorraine Shirley; BURGERS, Peter John; BURGESS, Arthur C.; BURGESS, Brian; BURGESS, Dorothy; BURGESS, Jan; BURGESS, Lynda; BURGOYNE, Doug; BURKE, David Scott; BURKE, Dorothy Adelaide; BURKE, Gary Hudson; BURKE, Janice Anne; BURKE, Michael Joseph; BURKE, Patti; BURKE, Sonia Lynn; BURKE, Thomas Roy; BURMEY, Joan Eileen; BURN, Ian St. George; BURNASH, Helen Mary; BURNETT, Muriel Elizabeth; BURNHAM, Dr. Robert Scott; BURNS, Audrey Bella; BURNS, Bryan W.; BURNS, Donald Gordon; BURNS, Dr. Robert Anthony; BURNS, Felicity Ann; BURNS, Janet Mary; BURNS, John; BURNS, Karen Louise Jane; BURNS, Kenneth John; BURNS, Kevin James; BURNS, Margaret Emily; BURNS, Neil Stuart; BURNS, Peter; BURNS, Stephen Edward; BURNS, Terry Lyn; BURNS, W.A. Doug; BURRISON, Marlene Susan; BURRISON, Reginald Lloyd; BURROUGH, Sara Lynn; BURROWS, Clint Wayne; BURROWS, Colette Marie; BURROWS, Dorothy; BURROWS, Doug F.; BURROWS, Holly Anne; BURRY, Carol Lynn; BURT, Agnes Janette; BURT, David Robert; BURT, Jean E.; BURT, Karen M.; BURTON, Christine Diane; BURTON, Ewa J.; BURTON, Lawrence E.R.; BURTON, Raelynn; BURTON, Thomas; BURWELL, Carolyn Theresa; BURYN, Peter; BURZMINSKI, David Leo; BUSBY, Melanie; BUSCH, Robert Louis; BUSE, Carmen Frances; BUSH, Barbara; BUSH, Delphine Ann; BUSH, Laurie Jane; BUSH, Ralph Clair; BUSHOLZ, Joyce Lorraine; BUSS, Susan Ann; BUSSE, Douglas Alan; BUSSE, Leonard Wayne; BUSSE, Sandra Alice; BUSTOS, Lorenzo Ivan; BUTCHART, James Douglas; BUTLER, Rebecca Elizabeth; BUTLER, Susan Jean; BUTLIN, Robert; BUTT, Mary Lou; BUTZ, Y. Eleanor; BUXTON, Nona Charlotte; BUZAK, Ernest J.; BUZAK, Lawrence J.; BUZAK, Vera Mae; BYER, Jim; BYER, Mary-Lynn Irene; BYER, Marylynn Irene; BYERS, J. Calvin; BYKOWSKI, Gail Iris; BYRNE, Bonnie; BYRNE, Timothy Allan; BYRON, Margaret Jeanne;

C

CAAMANO, Claudio; CAAMANO, Jorge Leotardo; CABEL, J. Suzanne; CABOT, Karen; CABRAL, Maria; CABRERA, Wendy Sharyn; COFFREY, Jenny; COFFREY, Maria; CAFORIO, Sylvia T.E.; CAHOON, Tania Elizabeth; CAIN, Laurie Anne; CAINE, Peggy; CAINE, Peggy Sheila; CAIRNEY, Paul Andrew; CAIRNS, Cynthia Lou; CAIRNS, Mary Linda; CAIRNS, William; CAISSIE, Karen Marie; CALAMUNCE, Jim; CALDER, Hugh Arthur; CALDER, James; CALDER, John C.C.; CALDER, Lewis David; CALDERON, Jaime; CALENDA, Joseph A.; CALEY, Patricia Diane; CALHOUN, Dilys Audrey; CALHOUN, Laura; CALHOUN, Martie Lynne; CALKINS, Jack Cleveland; CALKINS, Karen Louise; CALKINS, Kelly Jack; CALKINS, Michael Cleveland; CALLAGHAN, Dr. John C.; CALLAGHAN, Linda T.; CALIHOO, Kim Monica; CALLOW, Olga Bernadette; CALVERT, Wendy A.; CAMARTA, Brian Victor; CAMENZIND, Werner; CAMERON, Alne Grant; CAMERON, Betty D.; CAMERON, Candy Lynn; CAMERON, Douglas Brian; CAMERON, Elaine; CAMERON, Eloise Gail; CAMERON, Etty Anna; CAMERON, Jane Louise; CAMERON, Lee Calvin; CAMERON, Nan; CAMERON, Shirley Yvonne; CAMERON, Tom; CAMMER, Sheila Marlene; CAMPBELLFOWLER, Sheila; CAMPBELL, Arden Eileen; CAMPBELL, Barbara Ann; CAMPBELL, Beth CAMPBELL, Beverley A.; CAMPBELL, Brenda Lynn; CAMPBELL, Carol Ann; CAMPBELL, Christopher John; CAMPBELL, David Watson; CAMPBELL, Derry Lee; CAMPBELL, Dianne C.; CAMPBELL, Doris Grace; CAMPBELL, Dr. Colin George; CAMPBELL, Dr. William Gordon; CAMPBELL, Elaine; CAMPBELL, Gary G.; CAMPBELL, Gordon; CAMPBELL, Grace A.; CAMPBELL, Hester Margaret; CAMPBELL, Ian; CAMPBELL, Iris; CAMPBELL, Jack Keith; CAMPBELL, James; CAMPBELL, Janine; CAMPBELL, Jean Edward; CAMPBELL, Jennifer; CAMPBELL, Joann; CAMPBELL, Joanne L.; CAMPBELL, John James; CAMPBELL, John Murray; CAMPBELL, John Wallace; CAMPBELL, Joyce Mary Ann; CAMPBELL, Judith Patricia; CAMPBELL, Karen Michelle; CAMPBELL, Ken; CAMPBELL, Laura Grace; CAMPBELL, Linda Ann; CAMPBELL, Marian Joan; CAMPBELL, Mary Elizabeth; CAMPBELL, Mary Lynne; CAMPBELL, Neil M.; CAMPBELL, Pamela Christie; CAMPBELL, Peter George; CAMPBELL, Phoebe Margaret; CAMPBELL, Raymond Thomas; CAMPBELL, Rhonda; CAMPBELL, Robert Lawrence; CAMPBELL, Sandra Gail; CAMPBELL, Sharon; CAMPBELL, Sheryl; CAMPBELL, Stuart Duncan; CAMPBELL, Susan Elizabeth; CAMPBELL, Theresa; CAMPBELL, Tracy Lynn; CAMPBELL, Violet G.; CAMPBELL, Wendy; CAMPBELL, Wendy Lynn; CAMPBELL, Wilfred B.; CAMPLIN, Patricia Audrey; CAMPLIN, Peggy Lynn; CANCIAN, Anita; CANCILLA, Ed; CANDLER, David Cameron; CANDLER, Ingrid Karen; CANDLER, Scott Wesley; CANDLER, Wesley M.; CANDY, Jeff Michael; CANN, Margaret Marion; CANN, Murray Grenville; CANNELL, Vivian Rae; CANNING, Jonathon Terry; CANNING, William; CANOLER, Bryan Wayne; CANTIN, Donna Lynn; CANTIE, Marie Lorraine;

CAOUETTE, Alyson; CAOUETTE, Dean Darcy; CAPIAN, Dr. Barry Leon; CAPOWSKI, Sherry Anne; CAPPELLETTO, Ivana Renza; CAPPELLETTO, Umberto Nino; CAPPON, Marcia; CARABOTT, Diane; VARBERT, Beverley Jean; CARBY, Michael Carl; CARDIN, B. Dianne; CARDINAL, Charles H.; CARDINAL, Dr. Jean Marc; CAREY, BetteAnne; CAREY, Diane Joy; CAREY, Gordon Stewart; COREY, Sheila Elizabeth; CARGO, Patricia Leath; CARINELLI, Assunta; CARIOU, Elly-Mae; CARLASCIO, Daniel; CARLISLE, Collette Verna; CARLOS, Hernan Alburquenque; CARLSEN, Barbara Ann; CARLSEN, Dagmar O.; CARLSEN, Kirstin Britt; CARLSON Carolyn Ann; CARLSON, Cheryl Lynne; CARLSON, Deanna Kathryn; CARLSON, Donald William; CARLSON, Karen Ann; CARLSON, Marianne; CARLSON, Richard John; CARLSON, Sharon Colleen; CARLSON, Sidney D.; CARMICHAEL, Betty Doreen; CARMICHAEL, Ernie; CARMICHAEL, Gina Beth; CARMICHAEL, John Fraser; CARMICHAEL, Margaret E.; CARMICHAEL, Murray Harold; CARMICHAEL, Robert Duncan; CARMICHAEL, Shelley Doris; CARMICHAEL, Susan; CARNAHAN, Ken; CARNAHAN, Ken William; CARNEGIE, Carolyn Corinne; CARNEY, Gordon H.; CARNEY, Sean Robert; CARO, Denis; CARON, Shirley; CARPENTER, Hazel; CARR, Donna Illana; CARR, Douglas Levison; CARR, Edward Gerard; CARR, Randy; CARREAU, Michael James; CARREAU, Michelle; CARREIRO, Martha; CARRERA-LOWE, Felicia; CARRIERE, Dolores; CARRIERE, Gwendolin Mary; CARRIERE, Lorette; CARROL, Lana Jean; CARROLL, Charles William; CARROLL, Lawrence John; CARROLL, Marjorie Ella; CARROZZA, Frank Vincent; CARRUCCIU, Piero; CARRUTHERS, Donald Lloyd; CARRUTHERS, Elizabeth; CARRUTHERS, Leigh-Ann; CARRUTHERS, Sandra Gail; CARSON, Donald Gordon; CARSON, Edward Francis; CARSON, Michael Rodney; CARSS, Gordon; CARSS, Greg; CARSS, Trudy; CARSTON, Walter; CARSWELL, K.I.; CARTEN, Linda Joy; CARTER, Christina Louise; CARTER, Dallas; CARTER, Deanna Doris; CARTER, Donna Mae; CARTER, Kelly Ann; CARTER, Kenneth Doug; CARTER, Paul Duane; CARTER, Peter; CARTER, Rawle; CARTER, Thomas John; CARTER, Will John R.; CARTIER, Rita Janette; CARTMELL, Joan Valerie; CARTMELL, Timothy John; CARVACHO, Luis Alejandro; CARVER, Jody Lynn; CARVER, Kipp; CASAULT, Jeni Lynn; CASHIONKALINOWSKI, Deborah A.; CASHMAN, Laurel; CASHMAN, Rose Mary; CASIMIR, Gemma; CASS, David D.; CASS, Jo Ann; CASSIE, Jacqueline; CASTANEDA, Eduardo; CASTELEIN, Richard Douglas; CASTELLI, Bruno Francesco; CASTER, May Lou; CASTER, Sandra Jane; CASTOR, Nellie; CASTRO, Fiordeliza Tolentino; CATEDRAL, Cecilia F.; CATHCART, Sean Christian; CATHREA, Linda; CATHRO, Kevin Bruce; CATHRO, Marlene Audrey; CAUNT, Calvin; CAUSGROVE, Janice Leslie; CAUTI, Cathy May; CAUTI, Piero; CAVANA, Kenneth Robert; CAVANAGH, Ellen; CAWKELL, Kenneth Anthony; CAYANGA, Isidro M.; CECHETTO, Mary Angela; CEKADA, Elizabeth; CENA, Josephine; CEREZKE, Jill Tanya; CERMINARA, Clara Mariolina; CESARIO, Kathie Ann; CHABA, Alex; CHAFE, Fons; CHAFE, Susan Maria Jacinta; CHAHLEY, Betty; CHAIPAYUNGPAN, Anna P.; CHAISSON, Phyllis Mae; CHALAN, Manual Bada; CHALCROFT, Margaret Marie; CHALDEZOS, Toni Lynn; CHALIFOUX, Edward Bernard; CHALLACOMBE, Stephen Laurence; CHALLIS, Dr. Edward Bruce; CHALMERS, Elizabeth; CHALMERS, Margaret F.; CHAMBERLAIN, David Theophilus; CHAMBERLAIN, Melinda; CHAMBERLAIN, Nancy Joy; CHAMBERLAIN, Nicole; CHAMBERLAIN, Robert; CHAMBERLIN, Chuck; CHAMBERLIN, Jane Elizabeth; CHAMBERLIN, Jeff Scott; CHAMBERLIN, Jill Ann; CHAMBERS, Donald; CHAMBERS, Dr. Steven W.; CHAMBERS, Margaret; CHAMBERS, Margaret Myfanwy; CHAMCHUK, Nick J.; CHAMCHUK, Perry Douglas; CHAMNEY, Jason David; CHAMPIGNY, Chrystal Denise; CHAMPION, Anne; CHAN, Angie Suisa; CHAN, Anthony Lloyd; CHAN, Barbara; CHAN, Eleanor Maria; CHAN, Grace; CHAN, Janice; CHAN, John Allum; CHAN, John Tak-Yan; CHAN, Ken James; CHAN, Lisa May Yee; CHAN, Monica N.; CHAN, Pandora Francis; CHAN, Paul Yu-Yan; CHAN, Pearlie; CHAN, Peter Shung Yan; CHAN, Ray K.Y.; CHAN, Vanessa; CHAN, Violet Yuk Lun; CHAN, Virginia Kit-Yee; CHANKASINGH, David A.; CHANNELL, Dorothy Ramana; CHANTER, Carol; CHAPELSKY, Duane Dee; CHAPELSKY, Walter M.; CHAPMAN, Darlene; CHAPMAN, Louise Z.; CHAPMAN, Nesta Diane; CHAPMAN, Peter George; CHARCHUK, Helen; CHARCHUK, Tamara Leigh; CHARCHUK, William; CHARCHUN, Sonya; CHARD, Elizabeth Ann; CHAREST, Gilbert Joseph; CHAREST, Lauraine Elaine; CHARLETTE, Ruth Ann; CHARLES, David Watson; CHARLES, John; CHARLESTON, Robyn; CHARRON, Benoit Roland; CHARTIER, Darren Michael; CHARTIER, Patricia Lynn; CHARTRAND, Michael Denis; CHARTRAND, Wilma H.; CHARUK, Cheryl Lynn; CHARUK, Donna Maureen; CHATEL, Christine Karen; CHATELAINE, Lise Alice; CHATWIN, John A.; CHOU, Andrew; CHAVAN, Deepak Daniel; CHAWDA, Rajendrakumar Mulji; CHAWNER, Brenda Lynne; CHECKWITCH, Kerry S.; CHEDZOY, Sandra Lee; CHEETHAM, Jessie Anne; CHEHAYEB, Imad Said; CHELEN, Lou; CHELICH, David Merron; CHELKOWSKI, Diane Marie; CHEMELLO, Sandra; CHEN, Alex, C.; CHEN, Grace, Y-C. CHENG, Fred Sekkin; CHENGZHU, Shen; CHEONG, Collette Margaret; CHEREWICK, Janice Marcia; CHERIAN, Joe; CHERNENKO, Diana Elizabeth; CHERNENKO, Susan Marie; CHERNESKI, Helen Sylvia; CHERNIAK, Janice; CHERNIAWSKI, Beth Helen; CHERNIAWSKI, Lorna; CHERNIAWSKY, Kenneth; CHERNIAWSKY, Rose; CHERNICHEN, Dennis Robert; CHERNICHEN, Doug; CHERNIK, Emilie Marie; CHERNIWCHAN, Judy Anne; CHERNIWCHAN, Sharon; CHERNIWCHAN, Wally; CHEROT, Monique Anselle; CHERRY, Muriel; CHERWENUK, Jennie; CHESNEY, John Lester; CHESSOR, David; CHESSOR, Valerie Jean; CHESTER, Bertha; CHESTON, Gladys Eileen; CHEUNG, Allan K.; CHEUNG, Bridget Suet Ngan; CHEUNG, C.H. William; CHEUNG, Dr. King; CHEUNG, Helen, K.Y.; CHEVRIER, E.L.; CHEYNE, Marguerite Leala; CHEYNE, Theresa; CHEZ, Irene; CHEZ, Mark; CHIASSON, Gisele Therese; CHICHAK, Andrei; CHICHAK, Judith P.; CHICHAK, Morris; CHICK, Richard Melville; CHIES, Mauro Anthony; CHIDERHOSE, Kelly Ann; CHILDS, Bonnie Jean; CHIKOWICH, Carol Lynn; CHIMERA, Elaine Margaret; CHIMKO, Philomena Mary; CHIN, Barry Fook; CHIN, Brian; CHIN, Deborah Ann; CHIN, Suzanne A.; CHING, Kam Wah; CHINN, Brenda Leanne; CHINN, Daniel Lewis; CHINNERY, Ann Helen; CHINNERY, Karen Elizabeth; CHINNERY, Susan Marion; CHIPERZAK, Sherry E.; CHIPMAN, June Elizabeth; CHIRAMETLI, Victor; CHISHOLM, Heather Jane; CHISHOLM, Lois Elaine; CHISWELL, Frances; CHISWELL, Geneva Bernice; CHITONDO, Fredrick; CHIU, Dr. John Francis; CHIU, Theary Lee; CHIU, Yvonne Shi-Wan; CHIEBAK, Clara Ann; CHIEBAK, Dr. Anna; CHMIELEWSKI, Grace; CHMIELOWIEC, Ted V.; CHMILAR, Ada E.; CHMILAR, Catherine Patricia; CHMILAR, Michael John; CHMILIAR, Cheryl Dianne; CHOI, Alastair; CHOI, John; CHAMA, Helen D.; CHAMA, Margaret Elsie; CHOMIAK, Cathie E.; CHOMIAK, John W.; CHOMIAK, Larysa V.M.; CHOMIAK, Michael David; CHOMIAK, Myroslava Alexandra; CHOMIK, Nestor L.; CHOMYC, Donald Dale; CHANG-TAI, Brandon Gerard; CHANG, Frederick Chai; CHANG, Penelope Suk-Ha; CHANKOLAY, Angus Chonkolay; CHOOT, Ewe Terry; CHOPIUK, Nola; CHOPIUK, Ray; CHOPRA, Anne; CHOPRA, Anne Bhanu; CHOPRA, Suneela; CHOPYK, Peter; CHORLEY, Ricky Dale; CHORNEY, Karen Joyce; CHORNEY, Maryann Katherine; CHORNEY, Michele Leanne; CHORNY, Olga; CHOW, Andrew Lee-Kong; CHOW, Dr. Ken; CHOW, Eugene Quon Limn; CHOW, Frank; CHOW, Janet Yee-Ming; CHOW, Lili; CHOW, Mae Lilly; CHOW, Chot Kwong; CHOY, Chris; CHRAPKO, William George; CHRISTENSON, Jon; CHRISTIANSEN, Cam Marty; CHRISTIANSEN, Carmi G.; CHRISTIANSEN, Gunner Lauge; CHRISTIANSEN, Karen; CHRISTIANSEN, Marie Margaret; CHRISTIANSEN, Peter Alan; CHRISTIANSEN, Trent W.; CHRISTIANSON, Jessie May; CHRISTIE, Charles R.; CHRISTIE, Marjorie Alice Garden; CHRISTODOULOU, Petros; CHRISTOFF, Jon Peter; CHRISTOPHER, Joyce; CHRISTOPHERS, Sandra Lynn; CHROMIK, Ben Norman; CHUCHMAN, Veronica Josephine; CHUCHMUCH, Norma; CHUCHMUCH, Wayne; CHUNG, Ai-June; CHUNG, Florence Chia Pei; CHUNG, Fredy Augusto; CHUNG, Henry Fine-Man; CHUNG, Nancy; CHUNG, Nancy Carvin; CHUNG, Thomas Kin-Kau; CHUPA, Charles Leslie; CHURA, Randal Wayne; CHURCHMAN, Robert William; CHYKERDA, Donna Marlene; CIANO, Aldo; CICHY, Carol J.; CIESLAK, Linda Susan; CIANA, Caroline; CIONA, Curtis John; CIONA, Jant Marie;

CIPIN, Caralyn Esther; CIPIN: Jennifer Leigh; CLAFFEY, Shirley Millinda; CLAIR, Edward J.; LANCY, Eva; CLANCY, Shannon Maureen; CLAPP, Bradley Randall; CLARK, Corinne Patricia; CLARK, Donald Ross; CLARK, Gary H.; CLARK, Hazel Elizabeth; CLARK, James C.L.: CLARK, Janet Margaret; CLARK, Karen Nanette; CLARK, Kenneth Wayne; CLAKR, Kevin James; CLARK, Larry A.; CLARK, Lorran Charles Duane; CLARK, Lynn; CLARK, Lynn Marie; CLARK, Mary Kathleen; CLARK, Penny J.; CLARK, Ronald James; CLARK, Stephen; CLARK, Susan A.; CLARK, William J.; CLARKE, Allan James; CLARKE, Anita Jean; CLARKE, Ann; CLARKE, Christine Alice; CLARKE, Colleen Dawn; CLARKE, Joanne; CLARKE, Margaret Verna; CLARKE, Robert Mason; CLARKE, Stella; CLARKES, John Gregory; CLARKSON, Laura May; CLARKSON, Margaret Elaine; CLAUGHTON, Kevin Michael; CLAVETTE, Martin Fernand; CLAYTON, Agnes Ann; CLAYTON, Margot Joanne; CLEAVE, Darrell Walter; CLEGG, Erina Eleanor; CLEGG, Susan Adrienne; CLEGG, Wendy; CLELAND, Brenda; CLELAND, Brian; CLELAND, Lauren; CLEMENT, Dawna Rae; CLEMENT, Eveline Raymonde; CLEMENT, Katherine Mary; CLEMENT, Kevin Michel; CLEMENTS, Carol Joan; CLEMENTS, Florence Marie; CLEMENTS, Jcqui; CLEMENTS, Julie Anne; CLEMENTS, Robert; CLENDENNING, Cory; CLERKSON, Margot; CLEVELAND, Shaunalee Janet; CLEVELEY, Debra Elaine; CLEVELEY, Maureen; CLEVERLEY, Pater R.; CLEVERLEY, Sharon Louise; CLIFFORD, Gavn; CLIFFORD, John Junt; CLIFFORD, Laurie D.; CLIFTON, Carrie Lee; CLIFTON, Joan Bernice; CLIMIE, Margaret Isabel; CLINE, H. Scott; CLINTON, Bert Arthur; CLINTON, Dennis; CLIPPERTON, Carrine Lynn; CLOSE, Diane Orise; CLOUGH, Arthur; CLOUTIER, Carmen Annette; CLUBB, Roni Laurel; LUGSTON, John; CLYNE, Wes; CO, Herbert; COAMBS, David; COATES, Penny Ann; COCAR, Desiree Pruedence; COCHRAN JR., Nelson; COCHRAN, Nelson Mccormick; COCHRAN, Pamela; COCHRANE, Robert Jack; COCKBURN, Diane Gil; COCKLE, Diane Lyn; COCKRALL, Barbara Anne; COCKS, Debbie R.; COCO, Anna Pia; CODE, Barbara Kathryn; CODE, Donna; CODERRE, Max; CODERRE, Shrri Lynn; COFFEY, Janet Eileen; COGHILL, William James; COGLON, Arlene Susan Marie; COHEN, Beverley; COHEN, Hoda; COHEN, Malcolm; COHEN, Mandy Sue; COKE, Jane Elizabeth; COLAK, Mat; COLBORNE, Cheryl Lynn; COLBURN, Dennis Mark; COLBURN, Dennis Wayne; COLE, Alberta W.; COLE, Curtis Dean; COLE, Gordon Arthur; COLES, Patricia Ann; COLEY, Lon Harold; COLEY, Marilyn; COLLETON, Michael James; COLLETON, Sylvia Ann; COLLEY, April Lynne; COLLEY, Tony; COLLIER, Christopher Thomas; COLLINGE, John Brison; COLLINGS, Adele; COLLINGS, Kerry-Lee Gladys; COLLINGWOOD, Tom; COLLINS-NAKAI, Dr. Ruth; COLLINS, Aileen J.; COLLINS, Alison Jean; COLLINS, Elaine; COLLINS, George; COLLINS, Mona Christine; COLLINS, Patricia Isobel; COLLINS: PATRICK Bruce; COLLINS, Simone; COLLINSON, Patrick Joseph; COLLISTER, Colin; COLLITON, Dr. Irene Elizabeth; COLOTELO, Douglas; COLOVOS, Alexander Diana; COLOVOS, Helen; COLWILL, Laura Dianne; COMEAU, Lynn; COMFORT, Elizabeth; COMFORT, Sheldon (Bob); COMPASSI, Paul; COMRIE, Theresea Margaret; COMRIE, William Harold; CONDON, Karen; CONDON, Margaret Mary; CONDON, Sandra; CONNELL, Terry Robert; CONNELLY, Margo A.; CONNERY, Connie; CONNERY, Richard I.; CONNIE, Donald G.; CONQUEST, Ralph Kendall; CONROD, Stephen Joseph; CONROY, Gregory Paul; CONSTANT, Brian Denis; CONSTANT, Christine Anne; CONSTANTIN, Michelle Lucie; CONSTANTINESCU, George; CONSTANTINESCU, Marie; CONSTANTINESCU, Vasile; CONTENTI, Marjorie; CONWAY, Hugh Alan; COOK, Dellis Audrey; COOK, Donna Marie; COOK, E. Marie; COOK, Howard; COOK, John H.; COOK, Judi Ann; COOK, Leila Dawn; COOK, Perry George; COOK, Shelby Noel; COOK, Trevor Edwin; COOKE, Alison; COOKE, Douglas Graham; COOKE, Edgar Douglas; COOKE, Francis Michael; COOKE, Geraldine Annette; COOKSHAW, James Brian; COOOKSLEY, Lucille Emillie; COOKSLEY, Ronald James; COOLEY, Pamela; COOMBS, Joan Elizabeth; COON, Gerald Arthur; COOPER, Barbara; COOPER, Jack Phillips; COOPER, Linda; COOPER, Michelle Dianna; COOPER, Monty James; COOPER, Patricia; COOPER, Renate; COOPER, Sheila M.; COPAN, Jean I.; COPELAND, Carol Jean; COPELAND, Dr. Catherine Mary; CORAZZO, Loretta; CORBEIL, Michel; CORBEIL, Sylvia; CORBETT, Christopher; CORBETT, Karen Rosalie; CORBETT, Nora Janet; CORBETT, Robert; CORBETT, Tracy G.; CORBETT, Trudi; CORCORAN, Marie Agnes; CORMACK, Cathy; CORMACK, George Graham; CORMACK, Moira; CORMIE, Donald Mercer; CORMIER, Guy; CORMIER, Jean-Claude; CORMIER, Laverne Adele; CORNACK, Margaret Evelyn; CORNEIL, Donna Dyelle; CORNEIL, Margaret Anne; CORNELL, Raylene Tracy; CORNESS, Donald Norman; CORNESS, Eloise Diane; CORNESS, Leslie Albert; CORNESS, Norman Frederick; corrado, Sylvia Lina; CORRIGAL, Linda; CORRIGAN, David James; CORRIGAN, Don Peter; CORRIGAN, Jean Geraldine; CORRIGAN, Rob Michael; CORRIGAN, Sheila Theresa; CORRINS, Leah Ann; CORRY, Beverly Grace; CORTES, Enrique R.; COSGROVE, Lesley May; COSSAR, Douglas Hugh; COSTIGAN, Douglas M.; COTE, Anne Marie; COTE, Gilles Wilfrid; COTE, Johanne; COTE, Keith John; COTE, Martine Andree; COTE, Monique Marie; COTE, Paul Charles; COTE, Paul Henry; COTECHINI, Marisa; COTT, Turlough; COTTR, Marcia Marion; COTTNAM, Elizabeth; COTTRELL, Joseph Glen; COTTRELL, Richard Noel; COUCH, Cindy; COULOMBE, Brenda Gail; COULOMBE, Danielle Rejane; COULOMBE, Gregory Joseph; COULOMBE, Monique; COULOMBE, Rachelle Louise; COULOMBE, Roland; COULOMBE, Ronald Andre; COULOMBE, Vivian Paulette; COULSON, John William; COULSON, R. Lanny; COULSON, Robina; COULTER, Geroge Alan; COULTER, Louise Katherine; COULTMAN, Sharon Jean; COUNTRYMEN, Brian; COUPLAND, Laurie E.; COUPRIE, K. James; COURT, Elaine; COURTEPATTE, Brian Henry; COURTNEY, Derrick; COURTNEY, Derick Richard; COURTNEY, James Stewart; COURTNEY, Lisa Ann; COUSINEAU, Gerald FGrank; COUSINAU, Lorraine Ann; COUTTS, Dr. Ronald T.; COUTTS, Kathryn Ann; COUTTS, Marion; COUTTS, Robert James; COUTTS, Sheenah Kirk; COUY, Anne; COUY, John; CXOVERT, Elizabeth Louise; COVERY, Debra Lee; COVLIN, Dianne Marie; COWAN, Arlene Lenore; COWRD, James Harold; COWARD, Patricia M.; COWIE, Heather A.; COWIE, Wendy Joan, COWLEY, Hugh F.R.; COWLEY, Martha Jane, COWLEY, Patricia Lillian; COWLING, Jane Christine; COWLING, Joan; COWLING, Nicole Leann; COWLING, Patricia Margaret; COWPER, Roger Charles; COX-BISHOP, Marlene Joan; COX, Ann Macpherson; COX, Carter Jay; COX, Cheryl Eva; COX, Corinne; COX, Darlene Francis; COX, Darlene Mae; COX, David Thomas; COX, Geroge Irvin; COX, Lynn Marie; COX, Martin David; COX, Peggy; COX, Sharon Diane; COX, Stanley Francix; COX, Susan Irene; COX, Suzanne Carolyn; COX, William; COYES, Greg; COYLE, Sharon L.; CRACKNELL, Sheila Mildred; CRAGG, Carolyn Louise; CRAGGS, John Newrick; CRAGGS, Tony; CRAIG, Charlie Allen; CRAIG, Colleen Marie; CRAIG, Joan D.; CRAIG, Michael Joseph; CRAIG, William Richard; CRAMER, Gisele A.; CRAMPTON, Colin; CRAMPTON, Jim; CRAMTON, M.J. Jim; CRAMTON, Michelle Dawn; RANE, Cheryl Ann; CRANE, James Matthew; CRANE, Rick; CRANE, Sharon Jean; CRANSTON, Shelley; CRAVEIRO, Paulo; CRAWFORD, Deborah Ellen; CRAWFORD, Leona Frances; CRAWFORD, Marilyn Joan; CRAWFORD, Neil; CRAWFORD, Shannon Dawn; CRAWLEY, Claudia; CRAWSHAW, Cheryl Lorraine; CRIBB, Lloyd A.; CRICK, Dorothy May; CRIGHTON, Tom; CRINKLAW, James Alexander; CRIPPS, Dolorse Blanche; CRISTALL, Robert; CRITCHLEY, Gail A.; CROCKER, Jennifer Ruth; CROCKER, Sheila; CROCKETT, Betty E.; CROCKETT, Bille G.; CROCKETT, Jay Miles; CROCKETT, John Kenneth; CROCKETT, Leigh Steven; CROCKETT, Marjorie Ann; CROCKETT, Sean Geoffrey; CROFT, Deborah Jane; CROMIE, Eleanor Jayne; CRONIN, Gertrude; CRONIN, John Ross; CRONIN, Stacey Lee; CROOKS, William F.; CROOKS, William George; CROSBY, Diane Josephine; CROSS, June Helen; CROSS, Shelley Anne; CROSSMAN, Gwynneth; CROSSMAN, John Eric; CROTEAU, Annette Marie-Cecile; CROUCH, Eileen Patricia; CROUSE, John; CROWDER, Angela Jane; GROWE, Gary Wayne; CROWE, Luxie C.E.; CROWE, Patrick; CROWELL, Randall Philip; CROWLEY, Sonny; CROWSTON, Wendy D.; CROZIER, Jean; CRUIKSHANK, Melville Leslie; CRUTHERS, Sharon Linette; CRUZ, Daniel Morasigan; CRUZ, Sergio Sidnei; CSILICS, Tony Joseph; CSOLLE, Leslie Csaba; CUDDINGTON, Leslie Ann; CUFFE, Clifford David; CUGLIETTA, Anne; CUGLIETTA, Francesca; CUGLIETTA, Joan; CUGIETTA, Luigi; CUIZON, Jocelyn D.; CULHAM, Rachel; CULYER, Helen Mary; CUMBY, Cathy Ann; CUMMING, Debbie Anne; CUMMING, Dwight; CUMMING, James Keith; CUMMING, Jarrod Earle; CUMMING, Murray Alexander; CUMMING, Teresa Marie; CUMMINGS, Dr. Garnet E.; CUNNINGHAM, David A.; CUNNINGHAM, Elisabeth Agnes; CUNNINGHAM, Grant A.; CUNNINGHAM, Jim; CUNNINGHAM, Katherine Anne; CUNNINGHAM, Lonna Gaye; CUNNINGHAM, Marietta E.; CUNNINGHAM, Paula Lynn; CUNNINGHAM, Rod Glen; CUNNINGHAM, Ronalee Joan; CUNNINGHAM, Roni Joan; CUNNINGHAM, Shelley Rae; CURR, Tom James; CURRAH, Willma Elizabeth; CURREY, Kevin Morris; CURRIE, Ed Blair; CURRIE, Ollie; CURRIE, Robin Bruce; CURRIE, Warren Roy; CURRY, Christine Ellen; CURRY, Jeffrey paul; CURRY, Sharon Louise; CURTIS, Connie Arden; CURTIS, Derek Allan; CURTIS, Evelyn May; CURTIS, Mary; CURTIS, Richard John; CURTIS, Sue; CUSACK, John Owen; CUSACK, Marie Louise; CUSH, Carolyn Ann; CUSH, Maureen Anne; CUSH, Mona Bernadette; CUSINE, Robrt; CUTTING, Ann-Marie; CUTTS, Herbert; CUTTS, Tricia Ann; CYCA, Patricia Alizabeth; CYGANEK, Ewa; CYR, Mark Steven; CYR, Natsuko; CYRE, George; CZAR, Dennis Michael; CZAR, Halia; CZEGLEDI, Arpad Charles; CZOBA, Lorie Kathleen; CZUCZMAN, Eugene John; CZUI, Ron Paul, CZUY, Karn; CZYZ, Terri;

D

D'AMUR, Patricia Anne; DASILVA, Francis; DABBS, Patricia; DABROWSKI, George Miroslaw; DACH, Edna; DACH, Shauna-Lee Anne; DACKIW, Ksenia Anna; KACKA, Jan; DACYSHYN, Anna Lorraine; DAELMAN, Gary Frank; DAFOE, Bruce M.; DAGOSTINI, Anna; DAHIBERG, Edward Jamon; DAHLQUIST, Carina; DAHLSTEDT, Diana Marie; DAIGLE, Nora; DAKERS, Geraldine L.; DAKIN, Joan Elizabeth; DALE, James Douglas; DALE, Kathryn Nellie; DALE, Lynn; DALEY, Karen; DALGLEISH, Phyllis Helen; DALLIE, Talal M.; DALLIN, Chrisopher; DALMER, Geoff; DALMER, Perry; DALPE, Sharon Anne; DALQUIST, Irene Una Thelma; DALZIEL, Diana Cheryl; DAME, Iris Mae; DAME, Joan M.; DAME, Joan Maxine; DAMGAARD, Jan; DAMGAARD, Janet; DAMMANN, Diane Laraine; DAMMANN, John Frederick; DAMMER, Monique Manon; DANAKE, Cindy Crystal; DANAKE, Stacey Leanne; DANBROOKE, Corinne Elise; DANCAUSE, Jocelyn; DANCER, Steven Timothy; DANCHAK, Tracee Lynn; DANCHUK, Max Michael; DANEYKO, Leanne; DANG, Chi Sieu; DANIEL, Demers; DANIEL, Graeme C.; DANIELS, Carol Anne; DANIELS, Dayna; DANIELS, Maria June; DANIELSON, Ruby; DANKOV, Marta; DANSEREAU, Donna; DANT, Noel; DANYLIUK, Donna; DANYLUIK, Judy Kathryn; DANYLUIK, Karen Lee; DANYLUK, Dana Leigh; DANYLUK, Dr. Joseph John; DANYLUK, John; DARBEY, Cheryl; DARIUS, Rolanda Christina; DARKE, M. Lorraine; DARRACH, Diane; DARRINGTON, Suzy Loree; DARWISH, Janet; DARY, Linda Helene; DAS, Kris; DAS, Sheela; DASCAVICH, Monica Rose; DAUB, William Donald; DAUS, Timothy Daniel; DAVID, Cheryl Anne; DAVID, Evelyn; DAVID, James Allen; DAVID, Tracy A.; DAVID, Walter Ellenton; DAVIDGE, Geoffrey Lawrence; DAVIDGE, Gillian Deanne; DAVIDIUK, Len; DAVIDSON, Blake Kenneth; DAVIDSON, C. Dianne; DAVIDSON, Chris; DAVIDSON, Donna; DAVIDSON, Donna Marie; DAVIDSON, Frank Albright; DAVIDSON, Grace; DAVIDSON, Heather Ann; DAVIDSON, Heather Elizabeth; DAVIDSON, Linda-Jean; DAVIDSON, Marion Ann; DAVIDSON, Nigel Anthony; DAVIDSON, Richard L.; DAVIDSON, Robert Geoffrey; DAVIDSON, Sheila Frances; DAVIDSON, Sheila Mary Marjorie; DAVIES, Caroline J.; DAVIES, Croline Jane; DAVIES, Diane Monika; DAVIES, Gwen; DAVIES, Joanne L.; DAVIES, Lorna Ellen; DAVIES, Lynn; DAVIES, Randall S.; DAVIES, Robert; DAVIES, Thomas Edward; DAVIS, Cindy L.; DAVIS, Connie Elleanor; DAVIS, Deborah Veronica; DAVIS, Dr. Lyle A.; DAVIS, Janet Elizabeth; DAVIS, Jennifer Susan; DAVIS, Jo-Anne; DAVIS, Joan Gwendolyn; DAVIS, Kelly; DAVIS, Linda Marie; DAVIS, Marie Kathleen; DAVIS, Marueen Alice; DAVIS, Michael Bruce; DAVIS, Stuart George; DAVIS, Suzanne Marlene; DAVIS, Wendy Marion; DAVISON, Linda; DAVISON, Norma Marjorie; DAVISON, Pamela Mary; DAVISON, Timothy A.; DAVISS, Sidney Richard; DAWDY, Angela Lorita; DAWE, Mary Elizabeth; DAWLEY, Dwayne; DAWRANT, Geoffrey; DAWSON, Brenda Lynne; DAWSON, David Lee; DAWSON, Janet; DAWSON, Janice Lynn; DAWSON, Shirley Elaine; DAWSON, Stewart Leonard; DAY, Brigham Grosvenor; DAY, Darlene Patricia; DAY, Derri Catherine; DAY, James Barrie; DAY, Laura Anne; DAY, Marilyn Jean; DAY, Maureen; DAY, Patricia Joan; DAY, Shannon E.; DAY, William Adam; DAYMAN, Marlee Deanne; DE ARMOND, Marischai; DE BEER, Darrol M.S.; DE CANGAS, Jose; DE LEEUW, Jacob; DE MELLO, Jay; DE SOUSA, Maria Teresa; DE HAAS, Pat; DE LEON, Leticia Isabel; DE MARCO, Margaret Anne; DE MILLIANO, Teresa Marie; DE MUNNIK, Betty Jean; DE SOUSA, Filomena; DEACON, John; DEAN, Celia; DEAN, Shannon S.G.; DEAN, Tammy St. George; DEAN, William Robert; DEANE, Robert; DEAR, David John; DEARBORN, John Robert; DEBEURS, Delia Elizabeth; DECECCO, Barbara; DECHENE, Paul Henry; DECKER, Douglas Pete; DECOINE, Lorna; DECORE, John Victor; DECORE, Karyn Raeschelle; DECORE, N. Maureen; DEDIEU, Michelle Lianne; DEDORA, Debbie J.; DEEB, Soraya; DEEHAN, Katherine Ann; DEERING, Arthur Michael; DEGAGNE, W.C.; DEGEER, Shelly; DEGELDER, Joyce Yvonne; DEGELMAN, Karen Louise Ann; DEGEN, Margarete Marie; DEGENSTEIN, Brenda; DEHAAN, Alex; DEINES, Leslie Claire; DEJONG, Terry Jane; DEJONGH, Elly C.; DEL DEGAN, Heather Mark; DEL ROSARIO, Fe; DELAGE, Leah M.; DELAMATER, Brian Roy; DELANO, Gemma Lucienne; DELCIOPPA, Leno Nicola; DELEON, Letecia; DELFOSSE, Arlene Yvonne; DELIA, Luis Alberto; DELLORTO, Emil Fred; DEMAN, Audrey Annette; DEMAN, Monique; DEMARCO, Dina Marie; DEMARCO, Louise Christine; DEMCHENKO, Elma; DEMCHUK, Joyce Margaret; DEMCO, Pat; DEMCO, Patricia Kim; DEMCO, Sandra Lynn; DEMERCHANT, Robert; DEMERS, Bernard Joseph; DEMERS, Chris; DEMERS, Diane; DEMERS Diane Lynne; DEMERS, Lisa S.; DEMERS, Lorraine Marie; DEMERS, Michelle Antoinette,; DEMERY, E. Doreen; DEMIR, Fethi; DEMUYNCH, Karen; DEMUYNCH, Sandra Elizabeth; DEN BOER, Pieternella Johanna; DEN-HAAN, David Albert; DENBOER, Ronald P.; DENIKE, Terry Lee; DENIS, Suzanne Gisele; DENISON, Donald Norman; DENISON, Samme; DENMAN, Debra Ann; DENNIS, Bradford John; DENNIS, Brenda; DENNIS, Karen; DENNIS, Lawrence H.; DENSMORE, Clarence Nelson; DENSMORE, Colleen Beatrice; DENSMORE, Larry; DENTON, Robin McConnell; DENYER, Leonard; DER, Esther; DER, Joseph Wing; DER, Ray Ronald; DER, Rose; DER, Sandra Jean; DERBAWKA, Barbara Mary; DERBAWKA, Dr. Allen John; DERBYSHIRE, Michele Marie; DERE, Dan; DEREE Shelley Ann; DERFLER, Carl Lawrence; DERIEU, Myrna; DERIEU, Perry Allan; DERK, Julie; DERKACH, Karen Lynn; DERKATCH, Cecile M; DERMOTT, Glenda Stacey; DERMOTT, Shauna Lee; DERWORIZ, Cheryl Ann; DERY, Thomas; DESAUINIERS, Jean-Paul; DESCHENE, Edna Marie; DESFOSSES, Dewis Norman; DESFOSSES, Suzanne; DESHAIES, Catherine Margaret; DESAYE, Audrey; DESHAYE, Mary; DESILETS-KOTOWICH, Simone; DESJARDINES, Pam; DESJARDINS, Ronald Arsene; DEJAURIERS, Evelyne Yvette; DESJAURIERS, Jeannette; DESOUSA, Estrela; DESOUZA, Marian Veronica; DESPINS, Elaine M.; DESROCHERS, Pierre Cyrille; DESWARTE, Sonia Jane; DETTLAFF, Rosemarie Katrin; DEUEL, Michele Roxanne; DEURLOO, Wouterina Catherina; DEUTSCH, Allan Henry; DEUTSCHER, Carol; DEVANEY, John E.; DEVIN, Geo James; DEVINE, Phyllis; DEVLIN, Leslie Anne; DEVLIN, Patrick Kevin; DEVOS, Bernhard J; DEVOS, Eunice Jean; DEVRIES, Carol Ann; DEVRIES, Geraldine Theresa;

DEVRIES, Patricia Elaine; DEW, George Edmund; DEWALD, Douglas Kenneth; DEWALD, Laverne R.;
DEWAN Teresanne; DEWAR, Jacqueline Edith; DEWAR, Margaret Nicol; DEWART, Krista Dawn;
DEWIT, Marietta C.; DEWITT, Jutta; DEXTROZE, Cathy Carol; DEZSE, Eval Helen; DEZSE, Gabor;
DHONT, Margaret; DI, Pietro, Lucy; DI, Vincenzo Adriana; DIACHUK, Teresa Lynn;
DIAMOND, Marlys; DIAZ, Ruben Augusto; DICK, Bernice Agnes; DICK, Cathy Ann; DICK, Charles;
DICK, Linda Jean; DICK, Wendy Lynn; DICKER, Kelly; DICKSON, Patrocia; DICKSON, Robert David;
DICKSON, Sybil Joyce; DICKSON, William; DIDLUCK, Ann Marie; DIEBERT, Lynn Marie;
DIEFENBACH, Christine; DIELEMAN, G. Carolyn; DIENO, Danielle Janine; DIENO, Joanne Lorraine;
DIENO, Linda Cheryl; DIEP, Kim; DIESING, Karen Krista; DIFILIPPO, Dino; DIGWEE, Shannon Marie;
DILKIE, Del; DILLON, Lee-Ann; DIMARCO, Mary Lee; DIMITROFF, Jane; DIMOCK, George R.B.;
DIMOCK, Patricia Lorraine; DING, Juliana Kit Wel; DINGMAN, Florence Louise;
DINGMAN, Garry Ralph; DINWOODIE, Dr. Alison Jean; DINWOODIE, E. Genevieve; DIRKSING, Joe A.;
DITOPPA, Dr. John C.; DITTY, Barbara May; DIVELL, Mark Leonard; DIXON, Duncan Edward;
DIXON, Herbert A.; DIXON, James Linley; DIXON, James Vernon Linley; DJURFORS, Sven Gunnar;
DLIN, Helen; DMITRUK, Karen; DMITRUK, Lorne Edward; DMYTRUK, Leslie Anita;
DMYTRUK, Orysia Irene; DOAN, J. Scott; DOAN, Lorna; DOBBE, Angela Mary;
DOBBINS, Carolyn Deborah; DOBELL, Michael; DOBIE, Donald James; DOBKO, Anne;
DOBKO, S. Mark; DOBLANKO, Brian Wayne; DOBLANKO, Elizabeth Anne;
DOBRESCU, Kendra Leanne; DOBSON, Carol; DOBSON, Darlene Margaret; DOBSON, Glenn Edward;
DOBSON, Patricia Rhodes; DOBSON, Roberta; DOBUSH, Doug; DOCHERTY, Betty Lou;
DOCHERTY, M. Margaret; DOCHUK, Don; DOCHUK, Daniel; DOCKERY, Craig Ronald;
DOCTOR, Howard; DODD, Barry Craig; DODD, John Buchanan; DODDS, Mavis Dorothy;
DODDS, Nora Elaine; DODGE, Cherry Delight; DODGE: Patrick Anthony; DOEDEL, Barbara Ellen;
DOERIG, Elisabeth; DOERING, Lillian Gwen; DOERKSEN, Carmen; DOERKSEN, Elmer Martin;
DOESBURG, John; DOESBURG, M. Rae; DOKIS, Laurie; DOLAN, Karen Edna;
DOLAN, Leonard Francis; DOLAN, Thomas Kevin; DOLFO, Mardi Janene;
DOLHA, Andrew John LINSKI, Audrey J; DOLINSKY, Marshall John; DOLL, Jacqueline Marie;
DOLL, Kathy; DOLLERY, Chris; DOLLEVOET, Grace; DOLPHINE, Bernie Ann; DOLPHIN, Patrick Robert;
DOLSKI, Barbara Ann; DOMBOWSKI, Carrie; DEMBRO, Lawrence Leif; DOMBROSKI, Emil Chester;
DOMECKI, Irene; DOMINGOS, Judith Natalie; DOMSHUE, M.C. Brenda; DONADT, Anita;
DONAGHEY, C.M. Sam; DONAHUE, Patrick James; DONALD, Dana Martin; DONALD, Groeme Rae;
DONALD, Sharon Phyllis Ann; DONALDSON, Lynda Marie; DONALDSON, Terry I.;
DONISON, Lillian Joy; DONIEVY, Lisa M.; DONLEVY, Sean; DONNALLY, Clare;
DONNELLY, Brian Micheal; DONNELLY, Jeanne; DONNELLY, Lauren Marie; DONNELLY, Thomas A.;
DONOHUE, Carol Marie; DONOHUE, Karen Lindsay; DONOVAN, Allan Patrick;
DONOVAN, Thomas Raymond; DONSELAAR, Ralph Von; DOOLITTLE, Douglas Ridley;
DOOLITTLE, Susan Lynn; DOORNBERG, Ann; DORAIS, Joanne M.; DORAN, Brian Dale;
DORAN, Jill Mary; DORAN; Julie Marie; DOREN, Patricia Doreen; DORIE, Amy Lynn;
DORIE, Peter Francis; DORIN, Murray William; DORION, Roe Donald James; DORLAND, Robert E.;
DORNAN, Kevin Patrick; DOROSH, Dale K.; DOROSHENKO, Linda; DOROSZ, Danusia;
DORSEY, Candas Jane; DORSEY, Sherry L.; DORT, Christopher Gary; DORTCH, Stephanie Jeanne;
DORVAL, Yvonne Alice; DOSMAN, Pat; DOUCETTE, Bill Anthony; DOUCETTE, Brian John;
DOUCETTE, Cathy A.; DOUCETTE, Dion Virgina; DOUCETTE, Dorine Louise; DOUGHERTY, Patricia;
DOUGLAS, Aloha Jeanne; DOUGLAS, Barbara Anne; DOUGLAS, Cindy; DOUGLAS, Derek Macbeth;
DOUGLAS, Doris Irene; DOUGLAS, James S.; DOUGLAS, Jean Florence; DOUGLAS, Joyce;
DOUGLAS, Joyce Eleanor; DOUGLAS, Laura; DOUGLAS, Patricia Dawn; DOUGLAS, Robert A.;
DOUGLAS, Susan Dorothy; DOUGLAS, Thomas Scott; DOUGLASS, Laura Dianne; DOURISH, Barbara;
DOURISH, Colin Trevor; DOUZIECH, Laurent Francis; DOVE, Richard Stanley;
DOWDIE, Thomas George; DOWELL, Douglas; DOWELL, Karen Diana; DOWELL, Suzanne;
DOWKER, Karen Lynn; DOWLER, Susan; DOWNES, Steve Lorne; DOWSWELL, Annette;
DOYLE, David; DOYLE, David Wayne; DOYLE, Michelle Colleen; DOYLE, Rose;
DRADER, Marilyn Barbara; DRAGER, Derek Campbell; DRAGINDA, Robert; DRAGISH, Helen;
DRAKE, Clare; DRAKE, Dolly Isabelle; DRAKE, Patricia Mary; DRAPER, Brenda; DRAPER, Brian;
DRAPER, Michael; DREDGE, Donnal; DREFS, Stacey William; DREGER, Ann Marie; DREHER, Karen;
DRESSIER, Judy; DREW, Clifford Thomas; DREW, Kevin; DREW, Tanya; DREWE, Daniel W.;
DREWE, Jean; DREWNIAK, Brent Joseph; DREWNIAK, Dale Thomas; DREWS, Marilyn Helen;
DROBOT, Vera Kassy; DROLET, Conrad; DRONYK, Eva; DRONYK, Suellen; DROUIN, Jean-Paul;
DROZDIAK, Nadia; DRUMMOND, David Thomas; DRUMMOND, James Milford;
DRUMMOND, Lisa Lorraine; DRUMMOND, Marg; DRUMMOND, R. Clare;
DRUMMOND, Wilma Margaret; DRURY, Peter; DRYDEN, Donna Marion: DRYSDALE, Margaret Lynn;
DRYSDALE, R. Bruce; DUBAS, Michael; DUBBELDAM, Yvonne Margaret; DUBE, Charles Paul;
DUBE, Leona Norma; DUBETA, Harry; DUBETZ, Evelyn Love; DUBETZ, Tommy Amber;
DUBOISE, Michelle; DUBULE, Celine A.; DUCE Christine Elizabeth; DUCHAK, Gary David;
DUDAS, Imre Zoltan; DUDDER, Leno B.; DUDOK VAN HEEL, Brian; DUDOK VAN HEELE, Shannon;
DUDZIC, Monika Maria; DUECK, Michele Joan; DUECK, Royce Lynn; DUFF, Joan: DUFF, W. Neil;
DUFFIELD, Hilda Florence E.; DUFFUS, Barbara; DUFFY, Barbara Jean; DUGGAN, Jeanne Marie;
DUGGAN, Kathleen Linda; DUGUAY, Maureen; DUHOLKE, Gordon Stanley;
DUHOLKE, Katheen Marguerite; DUHRO, Sukhi Singh; DUKE, Janice L.; DUKE, William Richard;
DUKELSKY, Jason Victor; DUKELSKY, Victor I.; DUKEWICH, Dee; DUMAINE, Michele Christine;
DUMONT, Donna; DUMONT, Francine; DUMONT, Guylaine, DUMONT, Lyle A.J.;
DUNBAR, Dr. Lawrence George; DUNBAR, Kathleen Rosemary; DUNBAR, Robert Lee;
DUNCAN, Alan Slater; DUNCAN, Dennis; DUNCAN, Gary; DUNCAN, Sarah Melinda;
DUNDAS, Minota Love; DUNDIN, James Christopher; DUNFORD, Doreen Elaine;
DUNFORD, Jennifer Mary; DUNGARWALLA, Rubjya; DUNLOP-O'BRIEN, Sheelagh; DUNLOP, Daniel J.;
DUNLOP, Grant Scott; DUNLOP, Heather Chrystal; DUNLOP, Holly Christine; DUNLOP, Marilyn L.;
DUNLOP, Mark Joseph; DUNN, Barry W.; DUNN, Charlene Rae; DUNN, R.A. Bob; DUNN, Sally;
DUNNE, Bernadette; DUNNE, Patricia Anne; DUNNIGAN, Colleen Beth; DUNNIGAN, Lawrence D.;
DUNNIGAN, Margaret M.; DUNNIGAN, Margaret, Mary; DUNNIGAN, Maureen Mary;
DUNNIGAN, Meghan Elizabeth; DUNPHY: Brian Alexander; DUNPHY, Julianna D.;
DUNPHY, Julianna D; DUNPHY, Mona Mary; DUNSTER, Theresa Lillian; DUONG, Hung Dai;
DUPONT, Gerry; DUPONT, Leona; DUPONT, Susan Louise; DUPUIS, Cheryl Fay; DUPUIS, Gisels;
DUPUIS, Sandra; DURANT, Christiane; DURANT, Sandra Elaine; DURNIN, Katherine Joanne;
DUROCHER, Jocelyne Odile; DURST, Lori; DURU, Tim; DUSHENSKI, Dave Gary;
DUSHENSKI, Margaret Joan; DUSHINSKI, Christopher Eric; DUSHINSKI, Dr. Leslie M.;
DUSHINSKI, Karen Mae; DUSHINSKI, Kenneth Leslie; DUSHINSKI, Myrna Carrie; DUSZO, Alice E.;
DUSZA, Christine; DUTKA, Lorina Rae; DUY. Y. Nguyen; DVORKIN, Stan; DWELSDORF, Eileen Joyce;
DWORKIN, Elisa Rhonda; DWORKOWSKI, Robert; DY-REYES, Antonette Santos; DY-
REYES, Rosalind Arabelle; DYBA, Walter Robert, DYCHKOWSKI, Emilio Anne; DYCK, Christopher;
DYCK, Danielle; DYCK, Jim; DYCK, Keith Brain; DYCK, Mary Belle; DYCK, Rory Jason;
DYCK, Terrance Brent; DYCK, Verline; DYCKERHOFF, Anina; DYCKERHOFF, Helga; DYER, Cindy Elaine;
DYER, Deborah; DYER, Sharon Grace; DYER, William Roberton; DYKES, Lilian;
DKYSTRA, James Allen; DYKSTRA, Yvonne Ann; DYKUN, Sherri; DYMIANIW, John Davie;
DYRVIK, Marilynn Margaret; DYSON, Charmaine Rita; DZENICK, Andrea Melanie;
DZENICK, Margaret Florence; DZIARMAGA, Zofia Maria; DZIDO, Joyce Rosalie; DZIERZECKI, Irene;
DZIERZECKI, Janine; DZIWENKA, Debbie Lea;

E

EADIE, Karen; EADY, Robert Harry; EAGAN, Patrick Joseph; EARL, Ida Marie; EARL, Maxine C.;
EARLE, Robin Kevin; EASON, Thomas McKitrick; EASSON, Karen; EASSON, Liane Dawn;
EASTMAN, Marvyn Norman; EASTON, Brenda Louise; EASTON, Douglas Gordon;
EASTWOOD, Shelley Ann; EATON, Dick; EATON, Jean Louise; EBY, June; ECCLESTON, Lorna Jean;
ECCLESTON, Roy; ECHINO, Linda Maye; EDDY, Cheryl Patricia; EDDY, William Cameron;
EDELMANN, Ruth; EDGAR, Donald James; EDGE, O. Dwayne; EDGE, Sheila Louise;
EDGELOW, M. Annette; EDINGA, Donna Louse; EDMONTON, Dan St. Clair; EDWARDS, Allan Manning;
EDWARDS, Allene; EDWARDS, Beth; EDWARDS, Donald Ernest; EDWARDS, Heather Frances;
EDWARD, Helena; EDWARDS, Ivar Keith; EDWARD, Jane Elizabeth; EDWARDS, John Charles;
EDWARD, Kathleen Allison; EDWARDS, Lisa Maria; EDWARDS, Marianne Catherine;
EDWARDS, Marne Ellen; EDWARDS, Mary Audrey; EDWARDS, Sandra Dean; EDWARDS, Sue Sophie;
EDWARDS, Susan Allison; EDWARDS, Tommy; EDWARDS, Thalia; EDWARDS, William;
EDWORTHY, A. Goldie; EEFTING, Yvonne Frances; EFFERTZ, Sigrid; EGAN, Colleen Marie;
EGAN, Meredith; EGBERT, Connie; EGGEN, Heather Jean; EGGEN, Jean Marion; EGGER, R. Todd;
EGGERTSON, Betty Mah; EGGERTSON, Thomas Edgar; EGGLESTON, Augustinal;
EGGLESTON, Augustine; EGLINSKI, Douglas W.V.; EHM, Hubert Franz; EIDEM, Patricia; EIDICK, Rita;
EIDSVIK, Kristine; EISNER, Dean C.; EKPAKOHAK, Robert; EL-ALAWA, Virginia; ELDARS, Farida; EL-
DORIEDY, Taha; EL-SHARKAWI, Hossam Khalil; EL-SHARKOWI, Wafa Abed; EL-SHEIKH, Amr; EL-
SHEIKH, Zak; ELABI, Abda; ELASCHUK, Ken H.; ELAVIA, Firoza Homi; ELAVIA, Sheroo;
ELBORNE, Craig Robert; ELCHUK, Stanley Carl; ELDER, Linda Karen; ELDER, Patricia;
ELDRIDGE, Burton Charles; ELDRIDGE, Margaret Janet; ELENIAK, Ronald Barry; ELENIAK, Val W.;
ELGERT, Frederick Sigfied; ELGERT, Les; ELHARD, Sharon Bernice; ELICKSEN, Lawrence;
SLING, Clarice Verona; ELING, Esline George; ELIUK, Olga; ELKE, Donna Lee; ELKOW, Dennis;
ELKOW, Lorne Allan; ELL, Elaine Rose; ELLARD, Denis Milne; ELLERBECK, Rick; ELLETT, Geoff John;
ELLINGER, John David; ELLINGHAM, Judy Ann; ELLIOT, Carey Blake; ELLIOT, Robert Andrew;
ELLIOT, William Ian; ELLIOT, Victoria; ELLIS, Barbara; ELLIS, David William; ELLIS, Dwayne Kenneth;
ELLIS, Earl Michel; ELLIS, Eleanor Phyllis; ELLIS, Judith A.; ELLIS, Kim Hamilton; ELLIS, Lora-
Mae Louise; ELLIS, Margaret; ELLIS, Margaret Mary; ELLIS, Roger; ELLIS, Roger Langrick;
ELLIS, Ronald William; ELLIS, Scott B.; Ellyin, Lise Christine; ELNISKI, Terry Russell;
ELNISKI, Thomas Stanley; ELSMORE, Angela Renee; ELZINGA, David John; EMBOO, Walter R.F.;
EMBREY, Ruth Diane; EMPEY, Myrna Jeanne; EMPSON, Sydney Claire; ENDO, Toshiro; ENGEL, Rick;
ENGELS, Robert Anthony; ENGEN, Raylene Andrea; ENGER, Donna; ENGER, Shannon Lee;
ENGER, Timothy Arnold; ENGLEHART, Betty Ruth; ENGLER, Roma; ENGLEY, Lloyd Ashley;
ENHAGEN, Ingrid Marguerite; ENNION, Robert; ENNIS, Alan L.; ENNIS, Jocelyn Elizabeth;
ENNIS, Valerie Lane; ENNIS, Christine Sheryl; ENNS, Janet May; ENNS, Louise Magdalene;
ENRIGHT, Jennifer Jean; ENRIGHT, Sarah Ann; ENS, Barbara Lynn; ENS, Christine Maria;
ENS, Marilyn June; ENSSIEN, Doris; EPP, Bella Velma; EPP, Elfriede; ER, Gong He;
ERASMUS, Anita Monique; ERBAS, Tulin; ERDEBIL, Ismail Husnu; ERDMAN, Elizabeth Jane;
ERDMAN, Kenneth Richard; EREISER, Evelyn; ERFANI, Aminollah; ERHARD, Angie Joan;
ERICHSEN, Robert Shelton; ERICKSEN, Lenore Mary B.; ERICKSON, Dale; ERICKSON, Dianna Lynn;
ERICKSON, Diane L.; ERICKSON, Sheila Lorraine; ERICKSON, Shelly Lee; ERIKSON, Lloyd Bernhardt;
ERKER, Dennis M.; ERKER, Doreen M.; ERLAM, Roselle; ERXIEBEN, Jurgen P.;
ESAK, Michaelene Joyce; ESAU, Marlene Edna; ESCH, Edythe; ESCH, Peter; ESHENKO, John;
ESHENKO, Luba Lang; ESHPETER, Cheryl; ESKELSON, Barbara Jeanne; ESLER, Maureen Kim;
ESPEIO, Aurora; ESPIRITU, Jr., Maximo; ESPIRITU, Aeleen Aseron; ESPIRITU, Cristina Ana;
ESPIRITU, Juana P.; ESSIER, Elaine Margaret; ESTEY, James M.; ETHERINGTON, David Hunter;
ETHERINGTON, Heather Lynn; ETHIER, C. Michel; ETHIER, Darlyne Mina; ETHIER, Gerard H.S.;
ETHIER, Irene M.; ETMANSKI, Merisa; ETTINGER, Nelson Murray; EVANS, Carolyn;
EVANS, Darrel Vern; EVANS, David James; EVANS, Debra Kathleen; EVANS, Elizabeth Henrietta;
EVANS, Gary Burn; EVANS, Janis Mae; EVANS, Lisa Ann Marie; EVANS, Lois;
EVANS, Lucio Elizabeth; EVANS, Marilyn Norma Ann;
EVANS, Robert Frank, EVANS, Rosita Seraphine Louisel EVANS, Sheryl; EVANS, Thomas John;
EVANS, Thomas Roy; EVANS, Wendy; EVENSON, Jacqueline Colleen; EVENSON, Richell Ann;
EVERALL, Robin Donne; EVERETT, April Lucy; EVERETT, Carol; EWANCHUK, Sharon Dee;
EWANCHUK, Shirley; EWANCHUK, Tom; EWASHKO, Tamara Melene Jan; EWASHKO, Tanya Marie;
EWASIUK, Brent Michael; EWASIUK, Jerry; EWASKOW, Jeannie M.; EWASYSHYN, Bonnie;
EWASYSHYN, Gerald; EWENSON, Linda; EWENSON, Pat; EWERT, Shirley Grace;
EWING, Anita Patrece; EWING, Stephen James; EWMETT, Anna; EWONIAK, Julie Jeanette;
EXELBY, Gail Marie; EYFORD, Thora; EYFORD, Vivian; EYKELBOSH, C.A. George;
EYKELBOSH, Rick George; EYSEL, Annika Lore Karin; EZEKOWITZ, Gavin; EZEKOWITZ, Justin;

F

FABRIZI, Anna M.; FABRO, Gerhart William; FACCHIN, Carlo; FACCIO, Susanna Annette;
FACEY, David Arnold; FAFARD, Florence Elizabeth; FAGAN, Terry Patricia;
FAGNAN, Poulette Suzanne; FAHLMAN, Lila; FAHMY, Sami Wassili; FAHRNI, Verena;
FAIR, David Robert, FAIR, Deana Isabell; FAIRALL, Margo; FAIBAIRN, Joanna Lynne;
FAIRBAIRN, Nicola; FAIRBAIRN, Nicola Justine; FAIRBAIRN, Robert James;
FAIRBROTHER, Diane Rae; FAIRBROTHER, Eileen; FAIRBURN, Sandra; FAIRLEY, Carolyn Genevieve;
FAIRLEY, Warner Grant; FALARDEAU, Edward Joseph; FALCONE, Jay; FALCONER, Isabelle;
FALCONER, John; FALCONER, Lynne Elizabeth; FALK, Anne; FALLIS, Kim Darlene; FALLON, Gerald;
FALLOW, Pamela Mae; FALLOW, R. Alex; FALTINSON, Brian William; FALTINSON, John Elwood;
FANNON, Terry A.; FARBRIDGE, Carmen Michelle; FARBRIDGE, Conrad Patrick;
FARELLA, Maria Donenico; FARGEY, Mary Joan; FARGHER, Lynda Job; FARHALL, Robert Frederick;
FARIES, Caroline; FARIES, Caroline Agnes; FARIES: Jerry Enoch; FARION, Tammy Lynn;
FARKAS, Gerald; FARLEY, Dr. Jack Franklin; FARLEY, Dr. John Dwight; FARLEY, Michele;
FARLEY, Sandra Jane; FARNELL, Charles Sean; FARNELL, George T.; FARNELL, Thomas A.;
FARNSWORTH, Elizabeth O.; FARQUHARSON, Barry James; FARQUHARSON, Rod;
FARQUHARSON, Tina; FARR, Michael; FARRAR, Crystal; FARRELL, Brian George; FARRELL, Curt;
FARRELL, Howard Roger; FARRELL, Neil Edmund; FARRELL, Terri Lynn Margaret;
FARRER, Siobhan Marie; FARRIS, Lorraine Rose; FARWELL, Margaret; FARYNA, Ronald David;
FARYNA, Rose; FARYON, Richard Rhodes; FAST, Larry Dennis; FAST, Malcolm Walter;
FAST, Sandra Joan; FATHY, Fohmy Nakhia; FAULDER, Elizabeth Jean; FAULDS, Robert Gordon;
FAULK, Joan Rosemarie; FAULKNER, David Graham; FAULKNER, Joanne Leslie;
FAULKNER, Paul Robert; FAULKNER, William Morrow; FAVRE, William Frederick;
FAWCETT, James Lindsay; FAWCETT, Lori; FAZIO, Aldo Joseph; FAZIO, Aldo Joseph;
FAZIO, Stephanie Heidi; FEAREY, Alan Edward; FECCIA, August C.; FECH, Rita Ann;
FECTEAU, William Kenneth; FEDCHUK, John; FEDECHKO, Douglas James; FEDECHKO, Marienne;
FEDERAU, Mary; FEDERWICK ,Yvonne D.; FEDEYKO, Sandra; FEDORATION, Cindy G.;
FEDORATION, jean; FEDORATION, Wilfred Edward; FEDORUK, Gwynne Rae; FEDORUK, Marie L.;
FEDORUK, Nestor; FEDROU, Don; FEDUN, Jacqueline S.; FEDUN, Michelle; FEDUNIW, Cindy;
FEDUNIW, Wendy Dawn; FEEHAN, Patrick John; FEENEY, Maureen Louise; FEGAN, John;
FEHLOU, Elsa Wally; FEHAUER, Beverly Ann; FEHLAUER, Ernie Norbert; FEHLER, Ellie Lisa;

FEIST, Brian Paul; FELBERBAUM, Moshe; FELEDICHUK, George james; FELIZARDO, Florentio;
FELLING, Jane; FELLING, John; FELTON, Sylvie; FENG, Martin; FENIUK, Andy;
FENN, Simon, FENNA, Neil; FENNEL, Carole Rae; FENNEL, Dr. Colin Wayne;
FENNEL, Lorianne Frances; FENRICH, Patricia Dianne; FENTON, David Nelson; FENTON, Mark Donald;
FENWICK, Jill; FERBEY, Bonnie; FERGUSON, Arthur Eric; FERGUSON, Bernice E.;
FERGUSON, Candace Donna; FERGUSON, Dianne Winifred; FERGUSON, Dr. David;
FERGUSON, Gary Alexander; FERGUSON, Irene June; FERGUSON, Joanne; FERGUSON, John T.;
FERGUSON, Laura D.; FERGUSON, Olga; FERGUSON, Sean Robert; FERGUSON, Sharon Alaine;
FERGUSON, Stewart; FERGUSON, Wendy Lea; FERFUSSON, Sidney John; FERNANDES, Maurice;
FERNANDEZ, Carlos Roberto; FERNER, Steven John; FERRA, Angela Jenny; FERRANTZ, Julio;
FERRERO, Flavia; FERRERO, Marcello FERIER, Nicola Joy; FERRIER, Rebecca Louise; FERRIS, R. Brian;
FESTER, Gordon Albert; FESTER, Martha Amy; FETH, Shelly; FEYGIN, Anna;
FIALKOW, Simen: FIDDES, Barbara Jane; FIDDES, Meg Jean; FIDLER, Carolyn, FIDLER, Colleen;
FIELD, Debbie; FIELD, Lois A.; FIELD, Peggy Anne; FIELHOBER, Kelly Joann; FIERRO, Fernando Fidel;
FIGOL, Donald; FIGUEROA, Angel Eduardo; FIGUEROA, Paul M.O.; FIGURA, Steve; FIKAR, Karl John;
FILON, Shelley Louis; FILER, Wendy Jane; FILEWICH, Kathy Marjorie; FILEWYCH, Cathy;
FILION, Andree; FILIPOWSKI, Maria Ewa; FILIPPELLI, Rino; FILIPS, Denis Frank;
FILIPS, Diane Elizabeth; FILIPS, Laverna; FILLION, Shannon C.; FILOMENO, Ada Angela;
FINCH, Morag; FINDLATER, Donna; FINDLATER, J. Barrie; FINDLAY, Bob; FINDLAY, Dave;
FINDLAY, Hilary; FINK, Rosemarie Renate; FINKEL, Eleonora; FINLAY, Barton Brett;
FINLAY, Irene Beatrice; FINLEY, Lori; FINNON, Patrick Plunket; FINNEGAN, Ken Norman;
FINNIGAN, Brendon; FINSTAD, Jacqueline L.; FINSTAD, John; FINSTAD, Leanne Grace;
FINSTAD, Roy N.; FIORINO, Dr. Michael; FIORINO, Maria Teresa Antiona; FISCHER, Brenda Marie;
FISCHER, Cheri Lynn; FISCHER, Della E.; FISCHER, Donna May; FISCHER, Patricia Ann;
FISH, Connie Grace; FISH, James Arthur; FISHER, Avrel Clare; FISHER, Darrin Kent;
FISHER, Elliot Hedley; FISHER, Gail Dorothy; FISHER, Harry Alexander; FISHER, Kathryn Alice;
FISHER, Keoma Lynn; FISHER, Marion A.; FISHER, Martin; FISHER, Stanley; FISHER, Warren;
FISHWICK, Birgitta Maria; FISK, Bob; FITES, Philip; FITI, Mary L.; FITZGERALD, Linda Anne;
FITZGERALD, Lynn Marie; FITZGERALD, Paul; FITZGIBBON, James Gerald; FITZNER, A.R. Jeffrey;
FITZNER, Garth N.H.; FITZNER, R. Timothy; FITZPATRICK, Beatrice Anne;
FITZPATRICK, James Joseph; FITZPATRICK, James Patrick; FITZPATRICK, Joy Carolyn;
FITZPATRICK, Marette E.; FITZPATRICK, Myrio Delio; FITZSIMMONS, Enid; FIX, Loree Ann;
FIERWOLD, Fernelle; FIERWOLD, Lisa Anne; FIERWOLD, Lisa Jo Anne; FLAMAN, Aura Lee Elaine;
FLAMAN, Elaine Betty Anne; FLAMAN, Janella; FLAMAN, Janelle, FLAMAN, Jerry J.; FLAMAN, Jo;
FLANNIGAN, Dan; FLANNIGAN, Terrance R.; FLASHA, Michelle Joan; FLATHERS, Colin Edward;
FLAVELLE, Tracy J.; FLECK, Dale Robert; FLECK, Dennis Wayne; FLECK, Phyllis; FLECK, Shelly Ann;
FLEGEL, Dalene Rose; FLEISHMAN, Ross James; FLEMING, Brenda Lee; FLEMING, C. Wayne;
FLEMING, Darlene Marjory; FLEMING, Ian; FLEMING, Margaret Grace; FLEMING, Robert Allan;
FLEMING, W. Gary; FLETCHER, Beth; FLETCHER, Douglas; FLETCHER, Frank H.;
FLETCHER, Linda Margaret; FLETCHER, Willian A.; FLINKFELT, Leif Tore; FLINT, Carol;
FLINT, Frances Ann; FLINT, Russell Arthur; FLOREANCIG, Cecilia; FLORES, Miguel Angel; FLORY, Jo-
Anne M.; FLOYD, Pamela Denise; FLOYD, Robert Bruce; FLOYD, Timothy Michael;
FLUET, Jean Andre; FLUKER, Antoinette Louise; FLYNN, Margaret; FLYNN, Margaret Joan;
FLYNNE, Dr. Paul; FLYNNE, Paul Rowland; FOBERT, Murray Edward B.; FODOR, Michael Dalzas;
FODOR, Ruth Ann; FOERGER, Linda Jean; FOERGER, Ralph Paul; FOERGER, Robert Harry;
FOGH, Liana; FOISY, Diane; FOISY, Renee Fernand; FOLEY, Roberta Cecile; FOLEY, Sue Ellen;
FOLKINGA, Hans; FOND, Mei Wah; FONG-WEYLAND, Betty Cainsen; FONG, Lisa; FONG, Mei Wah;
FONG, Robert James; FONG, Ying Lim; FONTAINE, David Paul; FONTAINE, Eric Paul;
FONTAINE, Lynn; FONTAINE, Nathalie Colette; FONTANA, Carla Tracey; FONTEYNE, Rhonda Joan;
FONTOURA, Sofia Gasparda; FOOTE, Robert Patrick; FOOTZ, Wally; FORBES, Eileen Georgina;
FORBES, Jane; FORBES, Kenneth Frederick; FORBES, Patricia Ann; FORCADE, Janice Lorraine;
FORCADE, Jean; FORD Elizabeth Frances; FORD, Gregory J.; FORD, Michael D.A.; FORD, Myrtle L.;
FORD, Sandra; FORD, Wes; FOREMAN, Douglas Raefield; FOREMAN, Drew Raefield;
FOREMAN, Joyce Jessie; FOREMAN, Pat L.; FOREMAN, Todd Andrew; FOREST, Adam;
FOREST, Betty Ann; FOREST, Cheryl; FOREST, Janet Laura; FOREST, Joanne; FOREST, Judy;
FOREST, Paulette Rose-Marie; FOREST, Phil Andre; FOREST, Richard Wayne;
FORESTIER, Debbie Pauline; FORGIE, Alexander; FORMANIUK, Scott Gerald; FORNER, Janette Rae;
FORNER, Kelly Jean; FORNER, Vivian Rae; FORRE, Cindy Annette; FORRE, Cynthia Annette;
FORREST, John; FORRESTER, David; FORRESTER, Janet Elizabeth; FORSCUTT, Donna;
FORSS, Bernice; FORSS, Elaine Catherine; FORSS, Karen Patricia; FORSS, Terence Douglas;
FORSTER, Dan Allan; FORSTER, Gilda; FORSTER, James Elliott; FORSTER, Molly Anne;
FORSTER, Sharon; FORSYTHE, Joyce; FORSYTHE, Wendy Maureen; FORTIER, Leo Albert;
FORTIER, Ruth Alberta; FORTIN, Daniel Eugene; FORTIN, Jean; FORTIN, Normand Gerard;
FORTIN, Serge Victor; FORTOWSKY, Lynne; FORTUNASO, Theresa May; FORTUNE, Dr. Robert Lloyd;
FORTUNE, Richard; FORYS, Lukasz; FOSDICK, Janice Beryl; FOSS, Lesley Kim; FOSSEY, Helen Diana;
FOSSEY, Norine Jill; FOSSEY, Richard Douglas; FOSTER, Blake Evert John; FOSTER, Deidre V.;
FOSTER, Dr. Brian Campbell; FOSTER, Elizabeth; FOSTER, Evelyn Jean; FOSTER, Ivor David;
FOSTER, Joseph S.; FOSTER, Joyce M.; FOSTER, Karen Ann; FOURNIER, Brenda Mary;
FOURNIER, Charlotte Anne; FOURNIER, Denis; FOURNIER, Francois Joseph; FOUTS, Kimberly Anne;
FOWLER, Brenda Gail; FOWLOW, Barbara Ann; FOX, Bonita Lynn; FOX, Heather; FOX, James;
FRAGOMENI, Claire; FRALICK, Robert Duane; FRANCESCUT, Mario; FRANCESCUT, Matthew John;
FRANCESCUT, Stefano Joseph; FRANCIC, Ksenia; FRANCIS, Dennis Frank; FRANCIS, Dori M.;
FRANCIS, Jack; FRANCIS, Robert Robertson; FRANCO, Sheldon; FRANDSEN, Gunhild;
FRANK, Suzanne Marie; FRANKE, Anthony Joseph; FRANKS, Lori Emily; FRANKS, Patricia J.;
FRANZ, Sylvia Anne; FRASCH, Norma Kathleen; FRASER, Bill Arthur; FRASER, Bruce Douglas;
FRASER, Catherine Anne; FRASER, Cedric Andrew; FRASER, D. Lorraine; FRASER, Dave;
FRASER, Douglas; FRASER, Douglas Michael; FRASER, Ian; FRASER, Ida Elinor; FRASER, Jean;
FRASER, Kent Donald; FRASER, Linda; FRASER, Lois Gertrude; FRASER, M. Jean; FRASER, Marjorie;
FRASER, Olga; FRASER, Scott Darrel; FRAER, Stu John; FRAUENFELD, Patrice Diane; FRAZER, Elsa-
Marie s.; FREDERICK Brian; FREDERICK, Debbie L.; FREDERICK, Yvonne D.; FREED, Irene Opal;
FREEDMAN, Dena Mariam; FREEDMAN, Herbert I.; FREEDMAN, Joseph Stuart; FREEMAN, Colleen;
FREEMAN, Deborah Rose; FREEMAN, Frederick A.; FREEMAN, Greg C.; FREEMAN, Iris Marie;
FREEMAN, Joan Martin; FREEMAN, Joy Dennis; FREEMAN, Susan Le; FREEMAN, Terry Dean;
FREMIT, Betty-Lynn; FRENCH, Derek Alan; FRENCH, Harry L.; FRENCH, Lois Olga;
FREUDENREIGH, Kathryn L.; FREYOLA, Catherine; FREY, Dora lydia; FREY, Roch John; FRIDEL, Robert;
FRIDEL, Stephina Anne; FRIDERICHSEN, Blanche; FRIDERICHSEN, M.G. Andreas; FRIEDEL, Sonia;
FRIEDMAN, David; FRIEDMAN, Elaine; FRIEDRICH, Charlene Ann; FRIEND, Larissa Joyce;
FRIESE, Douglas L.; FRIESE, Penny; FRIESEN, Abram Jaco; FRIESEN, Cheryl; FRIESEN, Janice Diane;
FRIESEN, Leonard: FRIESEN, Lynda Marie; FRIESEN, Peter Michael; FRIGON, Anthony J.;
FRIGON, Marianne P.; FRISKNEY, Karen; FRISS, Edward; FRITH, Timothy R.; FRITH, Tracey L.;
FRITZ, Bernadette; FRITZ, Glenn Ferguson; FRITZ, Ingeborg Hannelore; FRITZ, Lorrain;
FRITZ, Marianne Annemarie; FRITZ; Sandy Jo; FROEHLICH, Robert; FROELICH, Myrna;
FROESE, George; FROESE, Peggy; FROGGATT, Edwyn Scott; FROHLER, Dorothy Lynne;
FROM, Leslie Elwin; FROM, Rhonda Leanne; FROSE, Robert David; FROST, Aimee Louise;
FROST, Charles Edward; FROST, Frances Carol; FROST, Kenneth Raymond; FROST, Laura Susan;
FROUD, Linda D.; FRUNCHUK, Peggy Ann; FRUWCHAK, Darcy; FRY, Bertha; FRY, Kelly Anne;
FRY, Sandra Dawn; FRYER, Sharon; FUCHS, Kay; FUCHS, Ralph George; FUHR, Joanna Lynn;
FUHR, Robin John; FUJII, Juanita Wynne; FUJIOKA, Shigeru Kenneth; FULKERTH, Margaret Anne;
FULLER, June; FULLER, Wayne Roland; FULLERTON, Georgia Ann Lucine; FULLERTON, Joan L.;
FULLET, Pamela; FULMORE, Marian Avis; FULTON, Chris Peter; FULTON, Ernie Leonard;
FUNDYTUS, Edward J.; FUNG, Larry Siu-Kuen; FUNK Dawn; FUNK, Dawn Renee;
FUNK, Joan Marlene; FUNK, Joan May; FUNK, Jocelyn Elaine; FUNK, Shane; FURBER, Darrold;
FURMANEK, Linda Maryann: FURMANEK, Regina; FURNEAUX, Keith Allan;

G

GABEREAU, Morgan Patrick; GABIE, Adine; GABLE, Guy Grant; GABRE, Girmaye;
GADD, Dylan Thomas; GADD, William; GAETZ; Lynne E.; GATIUK, Donna Marie; GAGNE, Irene A.;
GAGNE, Louis Carter Joseph; GAGNE, Marie Claude; GAGNE, Paul Leo; GAGNON, Brigitte;
GAGNON, Shirley Denise; GAGO-ESTEVES, Natalie Maria; GAHIR, Malvinder Singh;
GAHR, Waldemar Alfred; GAJECKI, Theresa Lois; GALASSO, Robert Stephen; GALBRAITH, Meredith;
GALBRAITH, William David; GALE, Doreen Joan; GALE, Janet M.; GALENZA, Shirley;
GALET, Yvonne A.M.; GALL, Nancy Nina; GALL, Nancy Rae; GALL, Ray; GALLAGHER, James Patrick;
GALLAGHER, Marvey June; GALLAGHER, Robert Brian; GALLANT, Catherine; GALLANT, Lori Diane;
GALLANT, Mary Ann; GALLANT, Murray Gerard; GALLANT, Tellex W.; GALLEN, Beth; GALLEN, Larry;
GALLER, Sabine Renate; GALLINGER, Jody Ann; GALLINGER, Theresa; GALLIS, Cathy;
GALLOWAY, Deborah J.T.; GALLOWAY, Esther Helen; GALLOWAY, Melanie Edith;
GALLOWAY, Susan Carol; GALLOWAY, Susan May; GALWAY, Carol Joan; GAMMEL, Annette Dolores;
GAMMIE, Stella; GANIE, Edward Anton; GANS, Wendi Colleen; GARANIS, D.J.;
GARBE, James Daniel; GARBUTT, Emerson; GARCIA, Lucia Maria; GARDENER, Jane Elizabeth;
GARDNER, Alexander Richard; GARDNER, Dr. Ken; GAREAU, Rita Marie J.; GARLAND, Jim;
GARLAND, Leslie Allison; GARNEAU, Janet; GARNEAU, Janet Mary; GARNEAU, Lorraine Alice Marie;
GARNEAU, Robert; GARNER, Glen James; GAROFALO, Pina; GARROWAY, Naisan Robert;
GARRIOCK, Margaret E.; GARRISON, Linda Ann; GARRISON, Sandra Lynn; GARROW, Juliette;
GARTEN, Warren; GARTNER, Jaime Richard; GARTNER, Michelle Lynn; GARTNER, Rita E.;
GARTRELL, John Wood; GARVIE, Jennifer Leigh; GARVIN, Catherine Anne; GARVIN, Cathy Sharon;
GARWASIUK, Kathi; GATES, Cara; GATES, Donald James; GATES, Glenn Court; GATES, Janet Gail;
GATES, Nancy; GATES, Philip Anthony; GATIEN, Angele Suzanne; GATIEN, Ronald Joseph;
GATT, Carmel; GATT, Jane; GOU, Maureen Anne; GAU, Patricia Anne; GAUCHER, Sylvia;
GAUDET, Michael Joseph; GAUDET, Terry Marie; GAUDREAULT, Denis; GAUF, Barbara Ann;
GAUF, Joan; GAUK, Natalia; GAUL, Geoffrey Robert; GAUNT, Jennifer Beth;
GOUTHIER, Brian Gaston; GOUTHIER, Isabel; GOUTHIER, Leanne Lucienne;
GAVINCHUK, Alice Patricia; GAVIRIA, Sussana; GAWRZYJAL, Eva Mary; GAYLARD, Dolores;
GAYLARD, Douglas Lyle; GAYLER, Liane Elizabeth; GAYO, Thelma; GAZZOLA, Rosanne;
GEDDESD, Eric; GEDDES, Geoffrey Robert; GEE, Gilbert; GEE, Herman; GEE, Margaret; GEE, Nyna;
GEE, Yankui; GEEFS, Jody Lynn; GEEKIE, Anne Marie; GEERS, Susan; GEHRING, Randall Earl;
GEISIER, Renetta; GEIST, Michael; GELDART, Patricia Ann; GELDART, Thomas Reid;
GELDSETZER, Torsten; GELETA, Dorothy M.; GELFAND, Dr. Elliot T.; GELLATELY, Wendy Theresa;
GELLENY, Susan; GEMER, Tara Yvette; GEMI, Marion Ester; GEMMELL, Dan William;
GENDALL, Marguerite Amela; GENDRON, Andre Gilles; GENDRON, N. Heather;
GENEREAUX, Michele Carla; GENEREAUX, Roland R.; GENSIER, Lisa; GENT, Kelly Margaret;
GEORGE, Brenda Mary; GEORGE, Cynthia Joy; GEORGE, Dianne; GEORGE, Jacqueline Anne;
GEORGE, Jenny; GEORGE, Julie Heather; GEORGLADIS, Leonard Stelyanes;
GERALDI, KIM, Catherine Louise; GERBITZ, Armgard; GERENCSER, Andrea Lldiko;
GERENCSER, Mary M.; GERES, Gina Lorene; GERLACH, Cherry Josephine;
GERLACH, Jacqueline Francis; GERLACH, Lois Ade; GERLACH, Nancy Ann; GERLING, Anita Laurette;
GERMAIN, Joanne Mary; GERMAIN, Kenneth; GERMAIN, Cecilia; CERMAINE, Olinda Elsie;
GERMAINE, Ron J.; GERMAINE, Theodore Alfred; GERMAN, Margaret; GERMAINIUK, Debbie Karen;
GEROCHI, Rosy J.; GEROLAMY, Barbara Jo; GEROW, Jean; GERRITSEN, Maria; GERVAIS, Anne-
Marie Suzanne; GERYLO, Donald M.; GESS, Douglas Melvin; GESSESSE, Meron Mengesha;
GESSESSE, Retta Mengesha; GWEETH, Angela Rose; GHAFFAR, Akram; GHIZ, Mona;
GIACOBBO, Marisa Virginia; GIAP, Hoang; GIBB, Alexis Jean; GIBB, Donna Jean; GIBB, Duane D.;
GIBB, Gilbert Girard; GIBB, Kent hildon; GIBB, Marlene Francis; GIBB, Scott Allan;
GIBB, Stacey Lorraine; GIBB, Tracy Elizabeth; GIBB, Wendy Solveig; GIBBARD, Beverly Joyce;
GIBBENS, Iris Elaine; GIBBON, Patricia Lynne; GIBBON, Ronald James; GIBBON, Dawn B.;
GIBBONS, Jenny; GIBLIN, Cathy Lynne; GIBNEY, Noel; GIBSON, Amanda Ruth;
GIBSON, Aurelie Lynn; GIBSON, Cheryl Anne; GIBSON, Donald Lawrence; GIBSON, Donald N.;
GIBSON, Dorothy Joyce; GIBSON, Frank Gregory; GIBSON, Maryanne; GIBSON, Pat Anita;
GIBSON, Rod; GIES, Deborah Julianne; GIESBRECHT, Lorne Gavin; GIESBRECHT, Margaret Joan;
GIESINGER, Jill Suzanne; GIETZ, Cathy Theresa; GIETZ, Marnie Susan; GIEZEN, Chris Gerdine;
GIFFEN, Norman Barry; GIFFORD, Shirley Irene; GIGNAC, Denis Jean-Pierre; GILBERT, Andrew Noble;
GILBERT, James; GILBERT, Judity Jane; GILBERTSON, Ronald; GILCHRIST, A. Joan;
GILCHRIST, Anne Georgina; GILCHRIST, Elaine; GILCHRIST, Kelly; GILES, Mervin Dale;
GILFILLAN, Darcy; GILFILLAN, Lisa Dawn; GILFILLAN, Scott James; GILGILLAN, Lisa Dawn;
GILHAM, Roy; GILHAM, Susan Faye; GILHESPY, Mari; GILHOLME, Judith Helen;
GILHOLME, Maragery Anne; GILHOOLY, Lee; GILKER, Terry June; GILL, Florence; GILL, Mary;
GILLANDERS, Brian; GILLARD, John Douglas; GILLEN, Leslie-Ann; GILLESPIE, Ann R.;
GILLESPIE, Carolyn Leigh; GILLESPIE, Jane; GILLESPIE, Lilias M;. GILLESPIE, Margaret Jean;
GILLESPIE, Muriel; GILLESPIE, Myrna Lorraine; GILLESPIE, Stephanie Mary; GILLESPIE, William A.;
GILLETT, Sandra Gail; GILLIAM, Mat; GILLIES, Sheila; GILLILAND, Alastair Gardiner;
GILLIS, Janis Lee; GILLIS, Jeffrey William; GILLIS, Kenneth George; GILLMOR, Ed;
GILMOUR, Diana Belle; GILMOUR, Jeannie; GILMOUR, Kathy Lynn; GILMOUR, Sandra Lynne;
GILROY, Douglas Reid; GILVERSON, Pam; GINN, Mary Susan; GINTER, Debby; GINTHER, Lois Jean;
GIRARD, Albert Alfred; GIRARD, Brenda Gayle; GIRARD, Cindy K.; GIRARD, Jacqueline Suzanne,
FIRARDIN, Denis Louis Joseph; GIRGULIS, Annie Pik-Yu; GIRGULIS, Mary Beth;
GIRVAN, Robert Mclean; GISLASON, Corinne Alma; GISLASON, Toni Marie; GIVENS, Bessie Louise;
GIVENS, Celine M.; GIVENS, Celine Marcia; GIVENS, Christine Anne; GIVENS, Louise Elizabeth;
GIZOSKI, Cathy Lynn; GLASS, Gosette Jacqueline; GLASS, John; GLAS, Neil James;
GLASSFORD, Alice Marie; GLASSFORD, Robert Gerald; GLAZIER, Irene A.; GLEASON-
GRAHAM, Helen Gwen; GLEAVE, Frank Gregory; GLEAVE, Ruth Sandra; GLEGLOFF, James Kenneth;
GLEN, Louise; GLEN, William Airston; GLENN, Angela Darlene; GLENN, Maria Rubilie;
GLIENER, Grace Esther; GLIENER, Isidor; GLOECKLER, Wally; GLOSSOP, Michael;
GLOVER, Ronald Fearon; GLOVER, Susan Eileen; GLUNZ, Beverley Joan; GNENZ, Mabel Marie;
GNIDA, Blair Frederick; GOBEIL, Brigitte Helene; GOBEIL, Michelle Renee;
GODBOUT, Suzanne Estelle; GODDARD, David Charles; GODDARD, Joanne L.; GODEAU, Sylvia;
GODFREY, Eldon Charles; GODFREY, Joan Elizabeth; GODWIN, Ellen Beatrice; GODZIUK, Donna-Rae;
GOEBEL, Gail A.; GOEDBLOED, Adrian Joos; GOEDBLOED, Jose; GOERRES, Brigitta;
GOERTZ, Catherine; GOERTZ, Catherine (Kay); GOERTZ, Harvey; GOERTZ, Kay;
GOERTZEN, Brent Irwin; GOERTZEN, Brian Larry; GOETZ, Mona; GOH, Dr. Keng-Eok;
GOHEEN, Kelly Dale; GOLD, Bernard Edward; GOLD, Shawn Morgan; GOLDBECK, Linda Elizabeth;
GOLDBECK, Robert; GOLDEN, Tom Preston, GOLDENBERG, John David; GOLDING, Dawn Clare;
GOLDSTEIN, Leanelle; GOLDSTICK, Bessie; GOLDSTONE, Leslie; GOMES, Carlos Alberto;
GOMEZ, Ernest; GONCALVES, Maria Luisa; GONZALES, Luis;

GONZALEZ, Enrique Pablo, GOOD, Cheryl Dawn; GOOD, Greg William; GOOD, Judith;
GOODALE, Janet Lynn; GOODE, Gretchen J.; GOODMAN, Sherry Lee; GOODRICH, Ada Mary;
GOODRICH, Clive Millar; GOODRICH, Gordon; GOODWIN, Jeanette Karen; GOODY, Linda;
GOOREVITCH, P. Michael; GORCAK, Carmen; GORCHYNSKI, Sylvia Anne; GORDEY, Anita Noel;
GORDEYKO, Bernice; GORDICHUK, Christie Lee; GORDICHUK, Susan;
GORDON, Alexander Main Duggie; GORDON, Danny James; GORDON, Dr. Kenneth M.; GORDON, Ian;
GORDON, Inez Agnes; GORDON, Lawrence David, GORDON, Linda; GORDON, Margaret Elizabeth;
GORDON, Phyllis D.; GORDON, Ross D.; GORDON, Winsome; GORE, Jean; GORGICHUK, Fred Daniel;
GORGICHUK, Janice; GORMAN, Dr. Robert John; GORMAN, Mariette; GORODETSKY, Oleg;
GORZNY, Sonja Maria; GOSINET, Bit; GOSS, Kenneth; GOSSE, Charlene; GOSSELIN, Joe Jack;
GOSSELIN, Renee Marie; GOTH, Jeffery William; GOUDREAU, Dora Helen;
GOUDREAU, Roxanne M.A.; GOUIN, Carol; GOUIN, J.Y. Ivan; GOUIN, Theresa Maria;
GOULET, Barbara Anne; GOULET, Charles Odias; GOULET, Dorothy Elaine; GOULET, Marie;
GOULET, Michelle D.; GOURINE, Joanne Marie; GOURLEY, David Eric; GOURLAY, Kimberly Dawn;
GOURLEY, Neil; GOVENDER, Pragashini; GOW, Danny; GOY, Wendy Lee; GOYEAU, Pier Jan;
GOYETE, Marjan Frances; GRABIA, Mel; GRACA, Marian Ted; GRADY, Paul Nicholas;
GRAFF, Barbara Lynn; GRAHAM, Cameron J.; GRAHAM, Charles David; GRAHAM, Christopher Scott;
GRAHAM, Greta; GRAHAM, Jacolyn Dianne; GRAHAM, Karen; GRAHAM, Margaret Christina;
GRAHAM, Marguerite Irene; GRAHAM, Maryse Bibiane; GRAHAM, Michelle;
GRAHAM, Noella Winnifred; GRAHAM, P. Donald D.; GRAHAM Shauna; GRAHAM, Shirley;
GRAHAM, Susan Kathleen; GRAHAM, Tom Andrew; GRAMLICH, Ivan James; GRAMLICH, Paulette A.;
GRAMS, Doreen Margaret; GRANDE, Carmelo; GRANDISH, Anna Marie; GRANDY, Karen Elizabeth;
GRANGER, Luce; GRANHOLM, Hans; GRANSTROM, Kathy; GRANT, April Melody;
GRANT, Brenda Michele; GRANT, Carol Ann; GRANT, Carol Ann; GRANT, David M.;
GRANT, Gayle Adeline; GRANT, Jacquie; GRANT, James MacKay; GRANT, Jamie Fraser;
GRANT, Joan Margaret; GRANT, Lynn Dee; GRANT, Patrick Neal; GRANT, Sandra Jessie;
GRANT, Sean Francis; GRANT, Sheilah Elizabeth; GRANT, Stacy Kent; GRANT, Teena Deanne;
GRAS, Neil Patronella; GRASCHUK, Maryjane; GRASLEY, Paulette Joan; GRASSICK, Anne M.;
GRASSICK, Geo Al; GRATTIDGE, Kim Lorna; GRATTON, Dave Reynold; FRATTON, Diana Lynne;
GRATTON, Doreen Irene; GRATTON, Jr. James; GRATTON, Lisa Maire; GRAVELLE, Sheila;
GRAVES, Deborah Jill; GRAVES, James Thomas; GRAY, Audrey Francis; GRAY, Bonnie Lynnmarie;
GRAY, Devin Bruce; GRAY, Donald S.K.; GRAY, Georgina Louise; GRAY, Karen Louise;
GRAY, Kelly Scott; GRAY, Kendra Elan; GRAY, Myrtle Etta; GRAY, Patsy Ellen; GRAY, Taina Helina;
GRAY, Vicki L.; GRAY, Victoria Winifred; GRAY, William; GRAY, William George;
GREAVES, Frederick Louis; GREAVES, Helen Ruth; GREEN, Amanda; GREEN, Caroline;
GREEN, Dawn Lorraine; GREEN, Heather; GREEN, Mary-Jean; GREEN, Peter Brian;
GREENE, Geoffrey Peter; GREENE, Ronald Allen; GREENHAM, Donald Wayne Scott;
GREENHILL, Dr. Brian John; GREENIDGE, Dr. Arthur; GREENING, Leslie Carrol;
GREENOUGH, Audrey Marie; GREENOUGH, James Gregory; GREENOUGH, Jean;
GREENWAY, Allan Wesley; GREENWAY, Allana Gay; GREENWAY, Tata; GREENWOOD, Paul Geoffrey;
GREER, John Charles; GREFFARD, Lucie Noreen; GREGG, David Andrew; GREGG, Pamela Anne;
GREGG, Randy John; GREGORY, Elaine Karen; GREGORY, Joy Leanne; GREGORY, Paul Godfrey;
GREGORY, Paul Wilson; GREGORY, Ron C.; GREIBROK, Terry; GREIDANUS, Dr. Thomas H.;
GREIDANUS, Nelson Victor; GREIDANUS, Robet Ian; GREIDANUS, Tom Glenn; GREIG, Cornelia;
GREIG, Donald; GREIG, Helen June Allyson; GREKUL, Helen; GREKUL, Kelly Lorraine;
GRENIER, Antoinette; GRESCHUK, Loreen Carol; GRETSINGER, Gail; GREY, Newton Rowan;
GREYEYES, Roberta Mae; GRIBBLE, Cynthia Margaret; GRICE, Diane; GRIERSON, Willa May;
GRIEVE, Lisa Ann; GRIFFIN, John Edward; GRIFFIN, Paula Louise; GRIFFITH, Catherine Grace;
GRIFFITH, Lori-Anne; GRIFFITHS, Becky Leigh; GRIFFITHS, Karen D.; GRIFFITHS, Kim Annette;
GRIMES, Mary-Beth Elizabeth; GRIMMELT, Ben Frederick; GRIST, Caroline A.; GRIWKOWSKY, Anne;
GROBEL, Laurie Anne; GROBERMAN, Ruth; GROENEWEG, Johanna; GRONNESTAD, Wendy Jane;
GROOME, Barbara Laureen; GROSS, David Irwin Paul; GROSS, Mark M.A.;
GROUIX, Lucien Gean Joseph; GROVE, Maike Marie; GROVER, Phyllis Jay; GROVER, Shelly;
GROVER, Wendae Dianne; GROVES, Marie Louise; GROVES, Thomas Albert;
GROVES, Tracey Johanne; GRUBISICH, Laura Mae; GRUNDBERG, Glenys Elaine;
GRUNDMANIS, Peter; GRUNDY, Ruth Ellen; GRUNSKY, Al; GRUNSKY, Shirley; GRYBA, Connie;
GRYSCHUK, Treena Irene; GUAY, Kathlyn; GUENETTE, Dana Lee; GUENETTE, Darin Kenneth;
GUENETTE, Denise Lauren; GUENETTE, Mark Alan; GUERIN, Danielle; GUERLUK, Corine;
GUERREIRO, Fern M.; GUEST, Laurie Kathleen; GUEST, Laurie Kathleen; GUEST, Richard Wayne;
GUGLISH, Wendy Jane; GUIGNION, Diane; GUIGNION, Kimberley Ellen Mae; GUILD, Alice;
GUILD, Barbara Janet; GUILFOYLE, Marian Elizabethe; GUILLOTTE, Yvon A.;
GUIMOND, Francine Marie; GUINDON, Suzanne Irne; GUINHAWA, Dante Roxas; GULAYETS, Kevin;
GULAYETS, Mary Anne; GULBRANDSEN, Penny; GULLIFORD, Debra; GULSTENE, Sheila Marie;
GUMAS, Dorreen Sharron; GUMMESNEN, Donald Lane; GUNN, Anne Kelly; GUNN, Doris Roberta;
GUNN, John Robert; GUNN, Tim; GUNN, William; GUNSON, Martin; GUPTA, Hem Lata;
GUPTA, Ingra; GUPTA, Joti; GUPTA, Narendra; GUPTA, Narendra Kumar; GUPTA, Ved Prakash;
GUPTA, Vijay; GURBA, David; GURBA, Karen; GURBA, Patrick Craig; GURBA, Rose-Marie;
GURLEY, Debbie Elizabeth; GURNEY, Cindy Elizebeth; GURPREET, Johal GURTEK, Poonia;
GUSSO, Nadia; GUST, Bill A.; GUST, Doreen Alice; GUST, Joanne Louise; GUSTKE, Richard Eberhard;
GUTHER, Aileen Joanne; GUTHRIE, Bradley Thomas; GUUPTA, Ashok; GUY, Donald Johnson;
GUZZO, Carmela; GWARTNEY, Jim Franklin; GWARTNEY, Pat; GYLANDER, Donald Gary;
GYSELINCK, Margaret Ottellia;

H

HAAS, Marion J.; HAAS, Michelle Katherine; HAAS, Terrance Daniel; HABERMAN, Edward William;
HABERMAN, Theresia Florence; HABIB, Rozmina A.; HACHE, Gail Elizabeth; HADLEY, Ronald Thomas;
HADLEY, Sharon Marie; HADZIYEV, Dr. Dimitri; HAFNER, Betty Lynn; HAGAN, Wendy-Mae Belle;
HAGEN; John C.A.; HAGENDORN, Bruce Charles, HAGERMAN, Laurie Joan;
HAGERMAN, Thomas Jeffery; HAGERTY, Patricia A.; HAGEY, Patrick Harold; HAGG, Daniel William;
HAGSTROM, Christine Amanda; HAHN, Adibi; HAHN, Barbara Karen; HAHN, Heather Marie;
HAIG, Brenda; HAIGH, Cathrine; HAIGHT, Gloria; HAILES, Jacqueline; HAINES, Mariette Denise;
HAIRE, Sheila; HAJAR, Ray M.; HAJEK, Milos Dimitri; HAJEN, Ingrid Rosemarie; HALABI, Kamal Joe;
HALEY, Carol Agnes; HALEY, David Glen; HALEY, Dr. Frank Cecil; HALIBURTON, Myra Alexis;
HALICKI, Darla Jean; HALL, A. Ann; HALL, Beverley Ellen; HALL, Brenda Claire; HALL, David Alan;
HALL, Dr. William Francis; HALL, F. Faye; HALL, Jack; HALL, Josephine; HALL, Lovena Ellen;
HALL, Lynda Ruth; HALL, Shirley Ann; HALLAM, Donald Robert; HALLETT, Blair William;
HALLETT, Randolph; HALLEY, Colin Thomas; HALLIDAY, GORDON William; HALLIDAY, Steve Gough;
HALLIS, Beatrice Mary; HALLIWELL, Albert Alexander; HALMERS, Shaun Avery;
HOLOWSKI, Mathew P.; HALOWSKI, Norma M.; HALWA, Verda; HALYK, Jeanette M.;
HAMBLETT, Michael W.; HAMBLIN, Vickie Jane; HAMDON, Faye; HAMDON, Lorrine;
HAMDON, Patricia; HAMEED, Syheda; HAMEISTER, Lois Caroline; HAMEL, Michelle Rannou;
HAMILTON, Clyde Reynold; HAMILTON, Don Richard; HAMILTON, Gary; HAMILTON, Ian Russell;
HAMILTON, Mai Brittann; HAMILTON, Maureen; HAMILTON, Vera J.; HAMLIN, John Robert;
HAMLIN, Phyllis; HAMM, Bert John; HAMM, Daniel; HAMMAN, Bryan Roderick;
HAMMINK, Ellen Marieka; HAMMOND, Kathryn M.A.; HAMMOND, Kim; HAMMOND, Kim R.E.;
HAMMOND, Sabrina K.; HAMMOND, Wayne Scott; HAMPTON, Corinne Rae;
HAMPTON, DOROTHY Rose; HAMPTON, Evelyn Ellen; HAMPTON, Kellie Suzanne;
HAMPTON, Marcia; HAMPTON, Raymond Grant; HAMPTON, Valerie; HAMRAN, Aurel;
HAMRAN, Zsuzsanna Katalin; HAMULA, Linda Freda; HAMULA, M. Clayton;
HAMULA, Raymond William; HAMZA, Amro Hassan; HANAS, Karen; HANASYK, Max J.;
HANCHARD, Roslyn; HANDFORD, Douglas Ralph; HANDLEY, William; HANDS, Thomas Christopher;
HANEY, Catherine Ann; HANEY, Linda Marie; HANIK, Wenzel; HANNA, Jean Arlene;
HANNA, John Ashley; HANNAMANN, Michele; HANNAS, Maryanne; HANNON, Eveline Ann;
HANRATTY, Gladys Mary; HANSEN, Cathy Louise, HANSEN, Clarice Marie; HANSEN, Henning;
HANSEN, Jeannie Dawn; HANSEN, Karen Freda; HANSEN, Knud Erik; HANSEN, Patricia;
HANSEN, Shirley Anne; HANSEN, Steven; HANSEN, Walter Ray; HANSON, Edna; HANSON, Gerrard;
HANSON, Ken Grant; HANSON, Loreen Marie; HANSON, Mary Anne; HANSON, Richard Burpee;
HARAPNIUK, Katharine; HARASYMCHUK, Cathy Lynn; HARBIN, Jennifer Joy; HARCOURT, Dan;
HARCOURT, Judy M.; HARCOURT, Sandra; HARDEN, Dawna; HARDER, Henry; HARDER, Louise;
HARDER, Molly Lillian; HARDER, Nola; HARDER, Nola June; HARDING, Christine Shirley;
HARDING, Ed; HARDING, Patrick John Ronald; HARDMAN, Lee Murray; HARDY, Albert Mark;
HARDY, Brenda Diane; HARDY, David A.; HARDY, Evelyn; HARDY, Norman Scott;
HAREL, Robin Christine; HARGREAVES, David; HARGREAVES, Laura Cheryl; HARIPERSAD, Ishana;
HARKE, Sheila Lydia; HARLE, Craig David; HARLE, Sarah Eileen; HARLEY, Richard C.T.;
HARLIN, Linda Laverne; HARMER, Allen Fraser; HARMON, George; HARNETT, Faith Elizabeth;
HARPER, Brian George; HARPER, Evelyn Lorraine; HARPER, James E.; HARPER, Lin Jean;
HARPREET, Sara; HARRADINE, Amanda; HARRINGTON, Karen; HARRIS, C. Peter;
HARRIS, Cardinal Athelstan; HARRIS, Geoffrey Lee; HARRIS, Glenda Ann; HARRIS, Gordon Edward;
HARRIS, Jeffrey Richard; HARRIS, Karen Lee; HARRIS, Laura Ellen; HARRIS, Lorraine Viola;
HARRIS Ross Edward; HARRIS, Sharon; HARRIS, Ula A. I.; HARRISON, Donald W.;
HARRISON, Dorothy Ann, HARRISON, Emly; HARRISON, Evelyn Kim; HARRISON, Kenneth Darryl;
HARRISON, Linda Marie; HARRISON, Marilyn; HARRISON, Mark Kenneth; HARRISON, Mary Anne;
HARRISON, Shirley Jane; HARRISON, Timothy Henry; HARROP, Joyce Edith; HART, Barbara Elaine;
HART, Lorna I.; HARTEL, Colleen Louise; HARTEL, Larry John; HARTENBERGER, Larry;
HARTLEY, Carole; HARTLING, Lois Pauline; HARTLOPER, Derek Alexander; HARTMANN, Christa;
HARTMANN, Randy K.;, HARTOG, Dr. Robert Lodewijk; HARTSELL, Heather; HARTT, Marjorie Louise;
HARTY, Colleen Rae; HARVEY, Donald Robertson; HARVEY, Doreen Mary; HARVEY, Dr. Janice;
HARVEY, Dr. John Harold; HARVEY, Martha Louise; HARVEY, Maureen; HARWARDT, Cheryl D.;
HARYSH, John; HASELGRUBER, Roxane Peggy; HASHIMOTO, Kenji; HASIMOTO, Atsumi;
HASIN, Farida; HASINOFF, Frances Alexander; HASSAN, Bev Natalie; HASSAN, Jack Kenneth;
HASSAY, Wendy Claire; HASSELGREN, Katherine Mary; HASWELL, Philip; HATCH, Stacey Carmen;
HATFIELD, Barbara; HATFIELD, Robert Vernon; HATLEN, Paul Thomas; HATLEN, Teresa;
HATT, Andrew Donald; HATTIE, Gary Wayne; HAUCA, Harold Ernest; HAUCH, Colin David;
HAUCH, Adam Mathew; HAUGEN, Judith Mae; HAUGEN, Tina; HAUGH, Rodney Dale;
HAUGHEY, Jean Marie; HAUGHEY, Mark; HAUGHIAN, Maureen Louise; HAUGHIAN, Patricia Joan;
HAUGLUM, Arvid Palmer; HAUGRAD, Rose Edith; HAUGRUG, Ruth Gail; HAULT, Esther Margaret;
HAULT, Robert; HAUSCH, Karen Evelyn; HAUSCH, Martin; HAUSE, Eileen Helen;
HAUSER, Lois Marlene; HOUTZINGER, Addy; HAUTZINGER, Danette Mary; HAVILL, Kathryn Mary;
HAVINGA, Dorothy Christine; HAWIRKO, Timothy Wayne; HAWKER, Dawn Laurel;
HAWKES, Helen Beatrice; HAWKESWOOD, Barry; HAWKINS, Sheryl Louise; HAWKSWELL, Judith;
HAWRELAK, Stephen William; HAWRYLUK, Zonia E.; HAWRYSCHUK, Wally M.; HAWRYSH, Kate;
HAY, Douglas Charles; HAY, Glenn Alan; HAY, Susan; HAY, Trudy; HAYASHI, Allen;
HAYASHI, Katherine Anne; HAYASHI, Lynda Mae; HAYDEN, Frank; HAYDEN, Matthew Scott;
HAYDEN, Mitch K.; HAYDUK, Anthony Peter; HAYES, Frances Merrill; HAYES, James;
HAYE, Leuana E.; HAYES, Mary Lou; HAYES, Rick Dale; HAYLOCK, John Brent;
HAYMAN, Richard David; HAYNES, Harold Guy; HAYNES, Helen; HAYNES, Lawrence John;
HAYS, Peter; HAYSOM, Catherine; HAYSOM, Tim John; HAYWOOD, John William;
HAZELWOOD, Mary Elizabeth; HAZLEDEN, Margaret Ann; HEACOCK, Edward Kenneth;
HEACOCK, Mary Elizabeth; HEALY, John Barry; HEALY, Laurance Gerald; HEALY, Richard;
HEANEY, Brian Patrick; HEATH, Gillian; HEATH, Kenneth Barry; HEATH, Robert Fraser;
HEATHERINGTON, Laura; HEATHERINGTON, M. Patricia; HEATON, Gordon Robert;
HEBER, Linda Catherine; HEBERT, Kenneth R.; HECK, Donna Marie; HECK, Jean; HECK, John J.;
HECK, John Jacob; HECKER, James Patrick; HECKER, John Sheridan; HEDINGER, Jerzy;
HEDLUND, Jodi Lorraine; HEEKS, James Dale; HEERAMAN, Danny; HEERAMAN, Ramkaran Danny;
HEFFEL, Brian Robert; HEFFEL, Gordon C.; HEGSTROM, Kenneth Hilmer; HEIDLER, Eileen Sharon;
HEIDT, Julie Ann; HEILAND, Laura Jean; HEILAND, Peter; HEIMSOTH, Kathleen Victoria;
HEIN, Dale Richard; HEIN, Joyce Alison; HEINE, Gary Lee; HEINE, Karol Jane; HEINLEIN, Elizabeth;
HENIZ Jr., Heinrich; HEINZ, Ursula Springmann; HEISLER, Cindy Lee; HEISLER, Tamie Jean;
HELLINGS, Patricia; HELLQUIST, Wayne A.; HELLWEG, Beccy Kathleen; HELM, Robert W.;
HELMAK, Mark Peter; HELMAN, Mike Daniel; HELMKAY, Christine Tracy; HEMING, Peter Ogilvie;
HEMPHILL, Kathleen Janette; HEMSTOCK, Diane Marilyn; HEMSTOCK, Heather Lee;
HENDERSON, Brad A.; HENDERSON, Brian Donald; HENDERSON, Brian John;
HENDERSON Dennis Gordon; HENDERSON, Donald H.; HENDERSON, Dr. John E.S.;
HENDERSON, Grahame; HENDERSON, Hamish James D.; HENDERSON, Jill G.;
HENDERSON, Joyce Wilma; HENDERSON, Lynne; HENDERSON, Ronald Brian;
HENDIN, Stephanie Patrice; HENDRICKSON, Grace Elizabeth; HENDRICKSON, William;
HENDRIE, Ann; HENDRIKS, Andrea; HENDRIKS, Michals B.; HENELY, Margot Lucia;
HENKELMAN, Maureen; HENKELMAN, Richard Neil; HENLEY, Marleen; HENLEY, Melinda Anne;
HENNESSEY, Christine T.; HENNIG, Kelsey W.; HENNIG, Wendy Jean; HENNING, Joan Marie;
HENNING, Mark Carl; HENNING, Mervin Dewayne; HENNING, Patti Lynne; HENNING, Robert W.;
HENNINGSON, Carina Margareta; HENRIQUEZ, Carlos; HENRIQUEZ, Lorena;
HENRIQUEZ, Sandra Elizabeth; HENRY, Doris Frances; HENRY, Mark Allan; HENRY, Philip;
HENRY, Ross Allen; HENRY, Stephen Brent; HENSLEY, Marion; HERB, Richard;
HERBERT, David Craig; HERBERT, John Duncan; HERBERT, Tania Anne; HERBISON, James R.T.;
HERBRIK, Tim Florian; HERCHEN, Brich; HERCHEN, Leonard; HERCHUK, Theresa;
HERGERT, Catherine Mary; HERGOTT, Glenn William; HERGOTT, Neil J.; HERMANUTZ, Sandra Marie;
HERMES, Martine Baudot; HERNANDEZ, David; HERNANDEZ, Manuel; HERON, Donald James;
HERON, Randy Andy; HEROUT, Sharon Patricia; HERRING, Sandi; HERRMANN, Helmut;
HERRMANN, Lorraine Diane; HERRON, Bobby R.; HERSACK, Patricia Dion; HERZOG, Greg Paul;
HESHKA, Jonathan W.; HESIEDAL, Evelyn; HESLIP, Dr. Patrick Guy; HESSE, Sherry;
HESSON, Nancy Carol; HESTON, Dee; HESTON, Maurice; HETHERINGTON, Valerie G.;
HEWLETT, Douglas Allan; HEYDEN, Uwe; HIBBARD, Jeanette Ann; HIBBARD, Judy P.;
HIBBARD, Karyn Joy; HIBBARD, Linda Marjorie; HIBBARD, William Ross; HIBBEIN, Paul;
HIBBERD, Judith; HEBBERD, Patricia Ruth; HIBBERT, J. Elaine; HICKEY, Delores;
HICKEY, Jane Elizabeth; HICKEY, Maryann; HICKINBOTTOM, Patrick David;
HICKMAN, Sandy Thomas A.; HICKS, David Russell; HICKS, James; HICKS, Ron; HIDE, Mary Angela;
HIEMSTRA, Yvonne M.; HIERLECHY, Marg; HIERLIHY, Judith Carol; HIERLIHY, Margaret Ellen;
HIGGINS, Maxine Anetta; HIGGINS, Paul Douglas; HIGGS, Sandra Carolynn;
HIGNELL, Lawrence Gordon; HILBIG, Margie; HILBRECHT, Ginter; HILDEBRAND, Sandi L.;
HILDEBRANDT, Alexandra S.; HILDEBRANDT, Gus John; HILDEBRANDT, Kate;
HILDEBRANDT, L. Sharon; HILDEBRANDT, Waldemar E.; HILDERMAN, Inez; HILL, Cheryl;
HILL, Donna Lorraine; HILL, Edward G.; HILL, Frank Stanners; HILL, Helena M.; HILL, Judith Cassie;
HILL, Maryann; HILL, Maureen A.; HILL, Patricia Irene; HILL, Sherry Ann; HILL, Thomas James;

HILL, Trudy Anne; HILLARY, Jacqueline; HILLARY, John Edward; HILLARY, Judith Susan;
HILLERUD, Ruth Adele; HILLIS, Michael Thomas; HILLMAN, Donald Edward;
HILTS, Linda J. HIMMEL, Barbara Heidi; HIMSCHOOT, Shirley Denise; HINCZ, Chester Karol;
HINDLE, Nicholas; HINDLEY, David Allen; HINDMAN, Dorren H.; HINDMARCH, Marilyn Louise;
HINECKER, Ann Marie; HINES, Judith Patricia; HINES, Phoebe Violet; HINKELMAN, Kimberly Sue;
HINKS, Denise E.; HINMAN, Beverly Lawrence; HINTERLEITNER, Sandy Doris;
HINTERSCHUSTER, Elvira; HIOB, Daniela; HIPKIN, Anne Elizabeth; HIRATSUKA, Yasuyuki;
HIRONAKA, Gaye Koko; HIRSEKORN, Brenda; HIRST, Barbara Maud; HIRUKI, Lisa Machiko;
HIRUKI, Yasuko; HISCOCK, Barb; HISLOP, George R.; HISLOP, Jessie Eloise Janice;
HITCHCOCK, Barbara Rae; HITCHINGS, Jack; HITE, Brent William; HITE, William L.;
HIERTAAS, Dr. Kenneth Randall; HLECK, Lisa Anne; HLUS, Joseph Harold; HLUS, Teresa J.;
HLUS, Theresa Bernadette Marie; HNYBIDA, Marianne Doreen; HO, Christopher Anthony;
HO, Francis C.; HOARE, Marjorie Williamson; HOBAL, Jacqueline; HOBAL, Wayne Stephen;
HOBBS, H. Pauline; HOBBS, Muriel E.; HOBLER, Susan Gale; HOCHREUTHER, Linda Marie;
HOCKLEY, James S.; HODA, Lorraine Marie; HODA, Mary K.; HODGE, Janice Louise;
HODGES, Ronald William; HODGINS, James; HODGINS, Michael; HODGKINSON, Leanne Mae;
HODGSON-WARD, Audrey Anne; HODGSON, Ellen Eileen; HODGSON, Karen Lynn;
HODGSON, Lisa Carol; HODGSON, Lucy Shelly J.; HODGSON, Lynn A.; HODGSON, Marion;
HODGSON, Marion Louise; HODKINSON, Roger Grant; HOFF, Mike Arthur; HOFFMAN, Doug Ray;
HOFFMAN, Karen Louise; HOFFMAN, Linda; HOFFMAN, Mathew Ross; HOFFMAN, Samantha;
HOFFMANN, Karen Janette; HOFNER, Betty; HOFS, Gail Anne; HOFSTEDE, Conrad;
HOFSTEDE, Diane Brenda; HOGAN, Candace Paula; HOGAN, Christine; HOGAN, Gerard Terrance;
HOGAN, Michael Donal; HOGAN, Thelma Lorna; HOGARTH, Gail Joan; HOGARTH, Kenneth B.;
HOGARTH, Teresa Lyn; HOGER, Harold Herbert; HOGG, John; HOGG, Lynette Elaine;
HOHN, William Bruce Scott; HOHOL, Harry James; HOITINGH, Angela Alexandria;
HOLBEN, Maureen Lynne; HOLDEN, Carol Ann; HOLE, James Douglas; HOLE, James Frederick;
HOLE, June Pamela; HOLE, Karen Anne; HOLGERSEN, Lene; HOLINSKI, Patricia Ann;
HOLLAND, Mary Lou; HOLLANDS, Henrietta; HOLLANDS, Lucille Margaret; HOLLAS, Sandy;
HOLLINGSWORTH, Clare Miller; HOLLINSHEAD, Tom; HOLLISTON, Allen; HOLLO, Lanna Yael;
HOLLOWAY, Hope; HOLLOWAY, Hope; HOLLOWAY, Lillian Catherine; HOLM, Allan David;
HOLM, Dorothy Ruth; HOLM, Sheila Marleine; HOLMAN, Nancy Eileen; HOLMES, Bob;
HOLMES, Ian G.; HOLMES, Jennifer; HOLMES, Margaret E.; HOLMES, Marilyn Ann;
HOLMES, Randy James; HOLMES, Thomas Frederick; HOLMES, William Ray;
HOLMSTROM, Joan Mary; HOLOSH, Martha; HOLOSH, Ruth Maria; HOLOSH, Vera Lucia;
HOLOWACH, Heather Yvonne; HOLROYD, Donald Brian; HOLROYD, Gary Ray;
HOLROYD, Kimberly Christine; HOLROYD, Pamela Michele; HOLROYD, Violet Olive;
HOLT, Larry Kenneth; HOLTORF, Elizabeth Ann; HOLVICK, Hidred Leone; HOLZER, Donald;
HOMENIUK, Roderick Scott; HOMYNYK, Jill; HONDERICH, Maxine; HONEY, George F.;
HANEY, Janis Roberta; HANSAKER, Leni; HOOD, Jenny; HOOD, Jo Anne Evelyn; HOOD, Julie E.N.;
HOOD, Kathleen Lynn; HOOD, Shirley Lynda; HOOK, John Arthur; HOOKS, Arthur;
HOOKS, Carol Elaine, HOOPER, Helen Marie; HOOPER, Kenneth G.; HOPE, Adair Mary;
HOPE, Douglas John; HOPE, Greg; HOPE, Marlene; HOPE, Tracey Lynn; HOPEWELL, Esther;
HOPKINS, Linda Louise; HOPKINS, Lucille; HOPKINS, Patricia Margaret; HOPKINS, Sherri Lynne;
HOPKINSON, Shirley Averille; HOPKYNS, Andrew; HOPMAN, Hetty G.; HOPPER, Suzanne Jeannette;
HOPPINS, Robert William Ryan; HORBASENKO, Jodi Shannon-Lee; HORBAY, Andrew Adrian;
HORE, Deborah Louise; HORE, Diane Margaret; HORLACHER, Everett Edison;
HORMAZABAL, Claudia Loreto; HORNBECK, Harold Richard; HORNBECK, Hugh William Doug;
HORNBECK, Robert Marshall; HORNBY, Frances; HORNBY, Michael Robert; HORNBY, Valerie Anne;
HORNE, Christopher Eric; HORNE, Geoffrey; HORNE, Jon J.; HORNE, Neil Alistair;
HORNE, Robert Grahame; HORNER, Betty Anne; HARNJATKEVYC, Andrij; HORNLAND, Glen Carl;
HOROWITZ, Barbara; HOROWTIZ, Myer; HORRICKS, Ross; HORRICKS, Wendy Lynn;
HORROCKS, Kathryn Joanne; HORVATH, Josee Lucie; HOSCHKA, Paula Marie;
HOSELTON, Gordon Craig; HOSHKO, Olga Maria; HOSHOWSKI, Rhonda M.;
HOSHOWSKI, Stephen Jan; HOSTLAND, Robert Dean; HOTRA, Diane Tracey; HOTRA, Rose Anne;
HOUG, Lorraine Caroline; HOUG, Trent Ronald; HOULE, Anita Marie;
HOULE, Laurie, HOULE, Leanne May, HOULE, Real, HOULE, Victor George; HOULIHAN, Carmen;
HOULIHAN, Nell; HOULIHAN, Tim Joseph; HOUNCAREN, Margaret Marie; HOUSTON, Christine;
HOUSTON, Gordon; HOUSTON, Luana Marguerite; HOVEDSKOV, Betia; HOVIND, Karey;
HOW, Rachel; HOW, Wanda; HOWARD, Edmund John; HOWARD, Jodi Lynne; HOWARD, Jodi-Lynne;
HOWARD, Kenny Ernest; HOWARD, Marla Dawn; HOWARD, Mary Louise; HOWARD, Richard;
HOWARD, Robert; HOWARD, Tony; HOWDEN, Patrick Wayne; HOWE, Arlene Joy;
HOWE, Grace Ellen; HOWE, Sharon; HOWELL, David Francis; HOWELL, Edna May; HOWELL, James;
HOWELL, Lanny; HOWEY, Margaret; HOWIE, Laurie Lynn; HOWIE, Sharon A.;
HOWRISH, Sharon Theresa; HOY, David C.; HOY, Diane; HOYER, Ellen Cornelie; HOYLE, Heather Ann;
HOYLE, Victor Gordon; HOYLES, Hugh; HOYT, Allison Louise; HRABI, David James; HRABI, James S.;
HRABI, Lydia Marie; HRITZUK, Daisy L.; HROMOTA, Gloria Lillian; HRSAK, Robert John;
HRUSHOWY, Francis Irene; HRYCAK, Josephine Lorraine; HYRCHUK, Beth Irene;
HRYCHUK, Susan Elaine; HRYCYK, Andy; HRYNCHUK, Judy Lynn; HRYNCHYSHYN, Cathy Anne;
HRYNCHYSHYN, Michael John; HRYNEW, Lori Sean; HRYNEW, Marion George;
HRYNYK, Helen Theodora; HSU, Liang; HSUNG, Ju Har; HSUNG, Yew Har; HSUNG, Yew-Har;
HUANG, Cheng-Yah Robert; HUBBARD, Gayle; HUBBARD, Linda Dawn; HUBER, Leonard R.;
HUBER, Lori Ann; HUBER, Margaret L.; HUBER, Sheila Dale; HUBER, Vera Georgena;
HUBINEK: Lucie; HUCKELL, John Richmond; HUCKELL, Truda Marion; HUCULAK, Bonita Mildred;
HUCULAK, Brian Michael-John; HUCULAK, Lee-Ann Christine; HUCULAK, Maurena Gail;
HUCULAK, Nestor William; HUDSON, Derek Rodeny; HUDSON, Diane Kim;
HUDSON, Gwendolyn Anne; HUDSON, Joseph A.; HUDSON, Margaret Hannah;
HUDSON, Robert Brian; HUDSON, Sheila; HUGHES, Brendan Thomas; HUGHES, Dr. Sheila Lynn;
HUGHES, Ellen Patricia; HUGHES, Joan Louise; HUGHES, Karen Lynn; HUGHES, Keith Douglas;
HUGHES, Kim; HUGHES, Kim Marie; HUGHES, Laura Hildaguard; HUGHES, Mark Christopher;
HUGHIS, Tina; HUGHTON, Anna A.; HUI, Donald; HUI, Ernie; HUI, James; HUI, John C.; HUK, Irene;
HULLEY, Jayne; HULS, Kathy; HULZENGA, Elly; HUMBERT, Joan Margaret; HUMBLE, Aine Marie;
HUMBLE, David G. Mackenzie; HUMMEL, Gloria Irene; HUMMEL, Keith Christian; HUMPHREYS, Ian;
HUMPHRIES, Sam; HUMPHRIES, Sharon; HUNCHAK, Linda Lou; HUNG, Kim; HUNG, William;
HUNGAR, Wendy Li; HUNKA, Carmelle Dee; HUNKA, Egar; HUNKA, Larry E.; HUNT, Bill Andrew;
HUNT, Brian Geoffrey; HUNT, David Thurston; HUNT, Fay L.; HUNT, Harlen H.; HUNT, Hugh Walter;
HUNT, Jody Anne; HUNT, Laurie Emily; HUNT, Murray; HUNTER, Barbara; HUNTER, Beatrice Elsie;
HUNTER, George Howard; HUNTER, James Stewart; HUNTER, Joanne Marie; HUNTER, Joseph N.;
HUNTER, Lisa Charlayne; HUNTER, Lisa Margaret; HUNTER, Michele T.;
HUNTER, Sheila Dale Elizabeth; HUNTER, Shelly A.; HUNTER, Wayne Alan;
HUNTINGFORD, Robert Walter; HUNTINGTON, Doreen; HUOT, Suzanne Marie;
HURLBURT, Danial Mark; HURLBUT, Nancy Lillian; HURREL, Karen Patricia; HURST, Cameron Lindsay;
HURST, Don Douglas; HURT, Fred; HUSBAND, Andrew M.; HUSER, Glen Anton; HUSHAGEN, Judy;
HUSSAIN-ALI, Sami Abbas; HUSSAIN, Syed Qutubuddin; HUSSEIN, Gulshan; HUSZAK, Judith Helen;
HUSZTI, Audrianna Gayle; HUTCHINGS, Charles; HUTCHINGS, Colleen June;
HUTCHINGS, Norma May; HUTCHINGS, Theodore Kevin; HUTCHINSON, Jane Elizabeth;
HUTCHINSON, Jill; HUTCHINSON, Norma; HUTCHINSON, Theresa A.; HUTNAN, Sharon Lynn-Patricia; HUTTON, Colin G.; HUYBENS, Barry Julian; HUYER, Jonathan; HYCHA, Denise Lynn;
HYDE, Dr. Harry; HYDE, Marion Webster; HYDE, Nancy Eleanor; HYDE, Patricia Lynne;
HYDER, Janice Celeste R.; HYNDMAN, Alexander William; HYNDMAN, Harriet Louise;
HYRACHUK, Dan; HYRL, Mary Ann; HYSTAD, Brian David;

I

IANSON, Douglas; IBRAHIM, Sadiyeh; IDICULA, Anna Dawn; IFTODY, Delima;
IGGULDEN, Elizabeth Janet; IGGULDEN, Lee Brian; IGNACIO, Cecilia Maria; IGNATOV, Nickolas;
IKEMURA, Hirami; ILER, R.J.; ILEY, Grant; ILICA, Petru; ILL, Ron Joseph; IMRIE, Sandra Margaret;
INCH, Eric Leslie; INCH, Yvonne Mary; INGALL, Mary Pauline; INGERSOLL, Douglas K.;
INGERSOLL, Elizabeth Chown; INGHAM, Gail Rachelle; INGHAM, Jerrold Frances;
INGHAM, Sakoe Florence; INGHAM, Violet Ann; INGIBERGSSON, Asgeir; INGLEE, William Kenneth;
INGLIS, Albert Colin; INGLIS, Colleen; INGLIS, Gordon W.; INGLIS, Linda Ino;
INGOLDSBY, Maureen A.; INGRAM, Heather Anne; INGRAM, Joyce; INGRAM, Stuart Owen;
INGRAM, Susan Valerie; INGROSSO, Dolores; INNES, Jim Donald; INNES, Susan E.; IOFFE, Zahar;
IONESCU, Christina; IORIO, Lucia R.; IOZZO, Jean Vincent; IP, Maureen; EPSEN, Kield Johansen;
IRELAND, Cathy Jean; IRELAND, Dave Sidney; IRELAND, Patricia; IRVINE-GOULET, Fiona Ann;
IRVINE, Vicki Lynn; IRVING, Hazal Agnes; IRVING, Jean Isobel; IRVING, Reginald P.; IRVING, Wendy;
IRWIN, Donald Bennett; IRWIN, Hilda Helene; IRWIN, Mark Cameron;
IRWIN, Robert Roycroft, IRWIN, Robert Wayne; IRWIN, William Christopher; ISBISTER, Robert James;
ITO, Catherine Naomi; ITO, Daniel Narushi; ITTERMAN, Nicoe Rayanne; IVES, Betty;
IVES, Eleanor Louise; IVES, William C.; IVITY, Beverly Candis Marie; IVITY, Dennis Bert;
IWANICKA, Jeanette Marie; IWASCHUK, June J.; IZUMI, Masanami; IZZORD, Pauline Anne;

J

JABIONOWSKI, Uwe Ewald; JACK, Lancelot Athelstan; JACKMAN, Karen Anne;
JACKNICKE, Catherine; JACKSON, Allen Andrew; JACKSON, Arthur Lyle; JACKSON, Brenda;
JACKSON, Chris; JACKSON, Colleen Donna; JACKSON, Dianne; JACKSON, E. Kathleen;
JACKSON, Elizabeth Agnes; JACKSON, Frank; JACKSON, Freda Carol; JACKSON, Freeman Joseph;
JACKSON, Harry George; JACKSON, Jill Cassilda; JACKSON, Joanne Louise;
JACKSON, Joyce Clewer; JACKSON, Larry; Jackson, Laura Ann; JACKSON, Linda Gail;
JACKSON, Patricia; JACKSON, Renate Christina; JACKSON, Richard Patrick; JACOBS, Darren Henry;
JACOBS, Deborah; JACOBSEN, Claire Rosemary; JACOBSEN, Fritz H.; JACOBSEN, Mary;
JACOBSEN, Terrena Mari; JACOBSON, Nan Elizabeth; JACOBSON, Robert;
JACQUES, Lynda Christine; JACQUES, Norman; JACULA, Sophia Lillian;
JAEGER, Andreas, JAEGER, Brigitte; JAEGER, Edna; JAFFER, Nick Mansoor; JAFFER, Zack Mohamed;
JAFFIR, Shanif; JAGGARNAUT, Dianne Veronica; JAGIELLO, Gerald Albin; JAGOE, Byran Arthur;
JAGAE, Karen Beverly; JAHN, Johanne; JOHNS, Kristin Amy; JAICZAY, Fred; JAICZAY, Fred L.;
JAICZAY, Victoria; JAKEWAY, Dr. George William; JAMAL, Samina; JAMES, Angeline V.;
JAMES, Carol R.; JAMES, Colleen Ethel; JAMES, Daniele; JAMES, Kenneth Wynn;
JAMHA, Darrell Robert; JAMHA, Elizabeth Mary; JAMHA, Glenn D.; JAMIESON, Don;
JAMIESON, Susan; JAMISON, Alan Clifford, JAMISON, George Spence; JAMISON, John Douglas;
JAMNIK, Carla Susan; JAMPOLSKY, Fia Judith; JAMPOLSKY, Noel Arran; JAMPOLSKY, Sonya;
JANDEWERTH, Betty Erika; JAMES, Tracy Diana; JANIK, Maria; JANOSKO, Joe; JANSE, Eric Ray;
JANSEN, Marco Godifridus; JANSON, Don; JANSSEN, Christian T.L.; JANUSZ, Krystyna;
JANUSZ, Miet; JANZ, Carol Anne; JANZ, Laurie; JANZEN, Avaleen Paulette;
JANZEN, Kimerie Julene; JANZEN, Paulette, JAP, Paul; JAQUES, Sheila Margaret;
JARDINE, Lynne Anne; JARDINE, Paula Frances; JARMOLICZ, Linda Regina; JARRAH, Carmen;
JARRAH, Majed Anwar; JARRAH, Mohamad A.; JARRON, Heather Dell; JARRON, Margo Louise;
JARRON, Ronald Bruce, JARVIS, Barbara Alice; JARVIS, Catherine Florence;
JARVIS, Cathy, JARVIS, Madeleine Jo-Ann; JARVIS, Patricia Linda; JASINOSKI, Deborah Colleen;
JAVORSKI, Ellen Jane; JAVORSKY, Sharon Anne; JAYCOCKS, Barbara; JEAN-LOUIS, Maxim;
JEAN, Doris Jeanette; JEAN, Lucie A.; JEDE, Barbara; JEDE, Lorrie Debbie;
JEDRASIK, Ursula Loretta; JEFFERIES, Lisa Mary; JEFFERIES, Scott; JEFFERIES, Roy David;
JEFFERY, Linda Selina; JEFFREY, Edward Charles; JEFFREY, Robert Douglas; JEFFREY, Roy Lonny;
JEFFREY, Verona Marie; JEHLE, Karen; JELEN, Blanka; JELEN, Pavel; JELEN, Sarka;
JELINSKI, Daniel Patrick; JELINSKI, Patricia Elaine; JENKINS, Anita; JENKINS, Marian Nancy;
JENKINS, Robert F.; JENKINS, Sandra; JENNER, Caroline; JENNER, Michael; JENNER, Peter M.;
JENNER, Susan Aleen; JENNINGS, Gail Kathryn; JENNINGS, John Allen; JENNINGS, Kerry;
JENNINGS, Kevin Francis; JENNINGS, Shirley Kathryn; JENSEN, Holm Annette; JENSEN, Noreen;
JEONG, Julie Shinja; JERIA, Manuel J.; JERKE, Keith Alexander; JERKE, Wendy;
JERMANIA, Manjeet Singh; JERRETT, Chuck; JERRETT, Kevin Roy; JESKE, Maureen; JESKE, Ron;
JESKE, Ronald Gordon; JESKE, Wolfgang Dieter; JESS, Allen L.; JESSOP, Bruce Charles;
JETTE, Diane Claudette; JETTE, Nancy M.; JEVNING, Margaret Andrea; JEWELL, Joan M.;
JEWETT, Hilary; JEWETT, Ronal Theron; JEWSEN, Shirley; JICKLING, Barbara; JICKLING, Robert;
JIM, Carolyn Gail; JIM, Cheryl Lynn; JIMENEZ, Jaime; JIMENEZ, Maria Socorro R.; JIN, Pearl Jean;
JINTES, Haus; JO, Francis; JOBERG, Leslie; JOBIN, Maryse; JOBIN, Nicole;
JODOIN, Paul, JOFRE, Monica; JOHANNESEN, Donna Marie; JOHANNESSON, Edward Brian;
JOHANNSSON, Gerald William; JOHANSSON, Valerie A.; JOHN, Christina Margaret; JOHN, Daisy;
JOHNS, David Frank; JOHNS, Kathryn; JOHNS, Robert Harold; JOHNSON, Alison Dawn;
JOHNSON, Barbara Helen; JOHNSON, Beverley Anne; JOHNSON, Carolyn Esther;
JOHNSON, Cheryl Anne; JOHNSON, Dan Alexander; JOHNSON, Darrel Eugene; JOHNSON, Dave;
JOHNSON, Dennis Vernon; JOHNSON, Don H.; JOHNSON, Donald; JOHNSON, Donald Andrew;
JOHNSON, Douglas Jack; JOHNSON, Emma; JOHNSON, Gail Marion; JOHNSON, Gwon T.;
JOHNSON, Harold K.; JOHNSON, Herbert Warren; JOHNSON, Hubert Charles;
JOHNSON, Irma Kathleen; JOHNSON, Jacqueline Helen; JOHNSON, James Alexander;
JOHNSON, Jason; JOHNSON, John Carl; JOHNSON, John H.; JOHNSON, John J.;
JOHNSON, Karen Lisa, JOHNSON, Kathleen Margaret; JOHNSON, Keith; JOHNSON, Keith David;
JOHNSON, Keith Gerald; JOHNSON, Kelly; JOHNSON, Kenneth Albert; JOHNSON, Lana Marie;
JOHNSON, Leah Louise; JOHNSON, Lorne Welburn; JOHNSON, Lorraine; JOHNSON, Lorrie Jean;
JOHNSON, Lyn; JOHNSON, Margaret; JOHNSON, Margaret Joan; JOHNSON, Marvin P.;
JOHNSON, Mary; JOHNSON, Phyllis Lois; JOHNSON, Randall Scott; JOHNSON, Robin Adele;
JOHNSON, Robyn Adele; JOHNSON, Rose; JOHNSON, Sallie Dunsmore; JOHNSON, Sandra Louise;
JOHNSON, Sean Matthew; JOHNSTON, Carolyn Jane; JOHNSTON, Cecilia I.; JOHNSTON, Dave T.;
JOHNSTON, Dennis Robert; JOHNSTON, Dianne Lee; JOHNSTON, Douglas Percy; JOHNSTON, Fran;
JOHNSTON, Frank Alexander; JOHNSTON, Keith; JOHNSTON, Kenneth R.;
JOHNSTON, Leanne Gayle; JOHNSTON, Linda Diane; JOHNSTON, Pamela Booth;
JOHNSTON, Paul D.; JOHNSTON, Peter; JOHNSTON, Robert Wayne; JOHNSTON, Stefan;
JOHNSTON, Stuart John; JOHNSTONE, Barbara Ann; JOHNSTONE, Beryl Rose;
JOHNSTONE, Charles Vernon; JOHNSTONE, Linda Joy Rita; JOHNSTONE, Magdalene Marie;
JOHNSTONE, Sandra; JOLY, Charles, JOLY, Claire Yvonne, JOLY, Germaine M.C.; JOLY, Lise Ann;
JOLY, Maurice Rene; JOLY, Monique Michelle; JONAT, Dr. Lorne Vernon; JONAT, Jean V.;
JONAT, Lorne Vernon; JONES, Allan Earl; JONES, Armande; JONES, Carole Dawn;

JONES, David Robert; JONES, David Sharron; JONES, Dennis; JONES, Dr. Graham R.;
JONES, Frank Richard; JONES, George Robert; JONES, Georgia Susanne JONES, Glenn R.;
JONES, Heather Lynne; JONES, Ian William; JONES, James Douglas; JONES, Jeanne W.;
JONES, Jennifer Jeri; JONES, John Brian; JONES, Karen B.R.; JONES, Kathryn;
JONES, Kristine Elaine; JONES, Laurie; JONES, Lawrence Harvey; JONES, Leslie Colleen;
JONES, Linda Kathleen; JONES, Lindsay E.; JONES, Margaret Ruth; JONES, Marie Antoinette;
JONES, Mary Isobel; JONES, Mary Yardley; JONES, Michelle; JONES, Penny Rita; JONES, Rene F.;
JONES, Rick D.; JONES, Ron; JONES, Shelley; JONES, Wendy; JONES, William R.; JONG, Allen De;
JANSON, Sheila Ann; JANZAN, Sheron; JORDAAN, Bernard; JORDAAN, Bernard John;
JORDAN, Carolyn Geraldine; JORDAN, F. Elsie; JORDAN, Juliette Anne; JORDAN, Susan Elizabeth;
JORDE, Greg Trevor; JORDHEIM, Andrew Raymond; JORGENSEN, Donald Harold;
JORGENSEN, Joyce Lee; JORGENSEN, Peggy Ann; JORGENSEN, Ray; JORGENSEN, Shelley Anne;
JOSEPH, Steven; JOSEY, Dianne Marie; JOSEY, Kenneth Edward; JOSH, Lucien; JOSHEE, Krishan;
JOSHEE, Rashmi; JOSHEE, Reva; JOSSY, Kathleen Anne; JOURNAULT, Lucille; JOURNOUD, Maryse;
JOY, Darrell; JOY, Deborah Mary; JOY, Linda Mae; JOYCE, Augustina; JOYCE, Derek William;
JOYCE, Robert Anthony; JOYES, Gayle Estelle; JR., Roy Kenneth Gilham; JUBINVILLE, Brian E.;
JUCHLI, Douglas William; JUCHLI, Josephine Ann; JUCHLI, Linda Beth; MUCHLI, Margaret Elaine;
JUCHLI, Richard James; JUCHLI, Shelley Jane; JUDGE, Mary; JUDY, Weiss; JULE, Clark Laurier;
JUNDKIND, Nancy; JUNG, Bai; JUNGKIND, Brigit; JUNK, Darlene Janet; JURLIEW, Daniel Paul;
JURNEY, Sylva Carol; JYOTI, Ashwani K.;

<h1 style="text-align:center">K</h1>

KAASA, Dr. Roderick Bruce; KAASA, Walter Henry; KABAN, Sharon Lee; KACHKAR, Fouad;
KOCHKAR, Jack Fred; KACHKAR, John Hana; KACHKAR, Randa; KACHKOWSKI, Allan;
KACHMAR, Lesley Ann; KACHUK, Emilia; KACHUR, Anne; KACHUR, Carolyn Margaret;
KODATZ, Lyle Wayne; KODERLE, Diana Lynn; KAFTAN, Janice R.; KAGANOVSKAYA, Sophia;
KAHLINA, Mark Marijan; KAINZ, Sheryl Ann; KAISER, Dianne J.; KAISER, Rolf Peter;
KOLDESTAD, Wayne D; KALIAN, Judith Carol; KALIAN, Steven Ron; KALINOWSKI, D. Cheryl;
KALINOWSKI, Dianne Sheryl; KALINOWSKI, Heidy Susan; KALINOWSKI, Katherine;
KALIS, Jacqueline Dawn; KALKE, Catherine Lynn; KALKE, Jacqueline; KALLAL, Susan Margaret;
KALLECHY, Randy Ellis; KALMACOFF, James F.; KALMACOFF, Naida;
KAIMANOVITCH, Michael John R.; KALNITZKY, Leo Lou; KAIRA, Yash Pal;
KALVERIA, Dirk Friedrich Gerard; KALVERIA, Ellen; KALWAITYS, Margaret V.;
KALYNCHUK, Dennis Edwin; KALYNCHUK, Gary Robert; KAM, Sandy; KAM, Sharon Lo;
KAMDAR, Dr. Lalit; KAMENETZKI, Elizabeth; KAMENETZKI, Peter; KAMINSKI, Maurice Leslie;
KAMINSKI, Stan; KAMRA, Ardis Daphne; KAMSTRA, Fran; KANE, Daniel Noel; KANE, John J.;
KANEHL, Susan; KANG, Wing Kiong; KANO, Marshall John; KANTERS, Alberta A.; KANTOR, Paul;
KANTYPOWICZ, Carol Marie; KANTYPOWICZ, Denise; KANTYPOWICZ, Janice;
KANTYPOWICZ, Lisa Diane; KANUNGO, Dipak; KAPATCH, Jeanette R.; KAPLAN, Owen Michael;
KAPLANSKY, Anna; KAPLANSKY, Grigory; KAPLANSKY, Mikhail; KAPLER, Lloyd James;
KAPLER, Marna Carmen; KAPOOR, Jean Cecilia; KAPUSCINSKI, Frank; KARAIM, Cynthia Elizabeth;
KARAS, Wilfred Allen; KARBONIK, Colin Neil; KARBONIK, Par; KARBONIK, Sheryl;
KARIMIAN, Jacqueline; KARN, Diane Christina; KARN, Murray David; KARN, Susan Margaret;

KARNER, Brent Vincent; KARNER, Christiane; KAROL, Donna Marie; KAROLES, Lorena;
KARP, Terri Lynn; KARPETZ, Heather Mary; KARPOFF, Carolyn Anne; KARPOFF, Lillian;
KARR, John Ian; KARST, Terrance; KASHUBA, Dr. Steven C.; KASIANIUK, Elaine Joan;
KASOWSKI, Michael Edward; KASPER, Dr. Richard Charles; KASPER, Helen; KASPER, Leslie;
KASPER, Mary Marianne; KASSAM, Parviz; KASSIAN, Carol; KASSIAN, Darlene Carol;
KASSIS, Elias George; KASSIS, Rima; KASTELIC, Ellen Doris; KASTENDIECK, Karen;
KASTENDIECK, Uta; KATERYNYCH, Donelda Natalie; KAUK, Brian; KAUK, Brian J.;
KAVANAGH, Jim Gerard; KAWALILAK, Katherine Rose; KAWASHIMA, June; KAWASHIMA, Ken;
KAWERAU, Sigurd; KAWULCH, Bradley; KAWULYCH, Elana Adele; KAWALYCH, Elsie;
KAWALYCH, Margaret Louise; KAWULYCH, Maria; KAY, John Michael; KAY, Keri Lynn;
KAY, Kevin Wynne; KAY, Margaret Ellen; KAY, Raymond; KAY, William C.; KAYAND, Siddhi J.;
KAYANDE, Jivan A.; KAYNE, Elaine Marie; KAYNE, Gary George Edward; KAYNE, Jeanine Anne;
KAZEIL, Michael Royce; KEARNS, John J.; KEARNS, John Robert; KEATS, Kathy Mary;
KEBARIE, Paula; KECK, Fern Marie; KEDDY, Gail T.; KEELER, Rick Wayne; KEELEY, Susan;
KEEN, Leslie Lynn; KEENAN, Elizabeth; KEENAN, Gail Marie; KEENE, Angela Kathleen;
KEHLER, Edwin G.; KEHOE, Dennis M.; KEIL, Howard Lucian; KEITH, Bonnie; KEITH, Trisha;
KELBA, Lena Janet; KEICHER, Sheila; KELEHER, Roberto E.; KELEMEN, Lorraine Cynthia;
KELEMAN, Thomas Stephen; KELL, Audrey Jean; KELL, William; KELLAM, Shelley Leah;
KELLAM, Wendy Deneen; KELLAR, Gordon Edward; KELLER, Brian J.; KELLER, Joseph;
KELLER, Kenneth Donald; KELLMAN, Ethan; KELLMAN, Kathleen; KELLOCK, Jane Elizabeth;
KELLOWAY, Karen; KELLS, Patricia Mary; KELLY, Colin Geoffrey; KELLY, Corinne Dallas;
KELLY, Craig Edward; KELLY, Deanna Jane; KELLY, Frances; KELLY, Gloria Susan;
KELLY, Jean Audrey; KELLY, John G.; KELLY, John Robert; KELLY, Lawrence Macdonald;
KELLY, Michael Dean; KELLY, Nicole; KELLY, Pat; KELLY, Raymond; KELLY, Sarah;
KELLY, Sharon Elizabeth; KELLY, Sharon Louise; KELLY, Sheila Marjorie; KELLY, Shirley Jean;
KELLY, Tracy Karan; KELM, Bonnie Lynne; KELM, Brenda; KELM, Charlene May;
KEMP, Carolyn Patricia; KEMP, Marie Esther; KEMP, Richard Alfred; KENDALL, Debra May;
KENDALL, John Reginald; KENDALL, L. Hazel; KENNEDEE, Rhonda; KENNEDY, Adrian;
KENNEDY, Anne; KENNEDY, Barry K.; KENNEDY, Brenda; KENNEDY, Carolyn Edith;
KENNEDY, Debra Anne; KENNEDY, Grant Hugh; KENNEDY, James Kenneth; KENNEDY, Jocelyn Leigh;
KENNEDY, Kathleen; KENNEDY, Kay; KENNEDY, Kevin Hugh; KENNEDY, Marg Christina;
KENNEDY, Marjorie Rose; KENNEDY, Mary Alice; KENNEDY, Mike Robert; KENNEDY, Paul;
KENNEDY, Richard; KENNEDY, Robert George; KENNEDY, Robina Jane; KENNEDY, Sharon;
KENNEDY, Terry Ingrid; KENNEDY, William Francis; KENNEDY, William Ian; KENNERD, Forrest;
KENNY, Joseph Patrick; KENNY, Karen Leah; KENNY, Shawn Kevin; KENT, Georgina Dorothy;
KENT, Joanne Ada; KENT, Robert G.; KENWELL, Maria; KEOGH, Eileen Siobhan;
KEOGH, Joseph Wayne; KEOHAN, Yvonne Johanna; KERELIUK, Darlene Patrice; KERELIUK, Sonia;
KERN, David; KERNOGHAN, Marianne J.; KERNOGHAN, Robert Clifford; KEROACK, Albert Arthur;
KEROACK, Jacqueline Marie; KERR, Allison Joanne; KERR, Astley George; KERR, David Wayne;
KERR, Gisele Marie; KERR, Jeremy Leroy; KERR, Joan Agnes; KERR, Margaret Joan;
KERR, Sharon Emily; KERR, Sheila Augustine; KERR, Tracie Lynn; KERSCHER, Marguerite;
KERVIN, Michael Richard W.; KERVIN, Virginia Mary; KESSELS, Martina Kathaleen;
KETCHESON, Linda; KETTERER, Candace Charlotte; KETTERER, Fred; KETTERER, Sandra Gay;
KETTLE, Wilfrid John; KEWLEY, Claude T.; KEY, John William; KEYLOR, Elaine; KEYS, Judy L.;
KEYS, Kerrie L.; KHALIQ, Abdul; KHAN, Anium; KHAN, Bianca; KHAN, Nadeem; KHAN, Steven;
KHARROUBI, Mohamed; KHEHRA, Mona; KHEHRA, Nina; KHULLAR, Ritu; KICH, Larry Michael;

More than 19,000 volunteers gave freely of their time and expertise in support of the World University Games at Edmonton. A few of them enjoy a rare respite from their work during the Closing Ceremonies

KICHTON, Vera; KICKS, David Russell; KIDD, Beatrice Lewis; KIEFER, Dominique Colette;
KIEL, Herbert; KIEL, Lori; KIELLER, Bev E.; KIELLER, Brenda Lynn; KIENITZ, Silke;
KIERAN, Daniel Michael; KIEREN, Thomas Ervin; KIERSTEAD, Sharon; KIERSTEAD, Sharon Elizabeth;
KILEK, Gordon Gunther Ernst; KILEWSKI, Denise Leanne; KIKUCHI, Dennis Kazuo; KILB, Brad;
KILLEEN, Raymond E.; KILLEEN, Valerie June; KILLIPS, Roberta Maxine; KILPATRICK, Donna-Jean;
KILPATRICK, Robert James; KILPATRICK, Shirley Anne; KILVERT, David; KIM, Chang Hyun;
KIM, Connie; KIM, Duksan; KIM, Henry S.; KIM, Jay; KIM, Mary Meéae; KIM, Muncha;
KIM, Peter Dongjung; KIM, Seung Kwan; KIM, Yong; KIMBER, June Catherine; KIMENIUS, Dwayne;
KIMENIUS, Judy; KIMMIS, Richard Clark; KINCADE, Teresa Joan; KINCH, Renee;
KINDLEMAN, Betty-Lou; KING-COLLIER: Margaret E.; KING, Albert Benjamin; KING, Anne Elizabeth;
KING, Bill Stevenson; KING, Christine; KING, Christine Patricia; KING, David James;
KING, Geoffrey Cameron; KING, Herbert G.; KING, Irene Elizabeth; KING, Janice Helen;
KING, Jean Helen; KING, Joan; KING, John W.; KING, June B.; KING, Kathy; KING, Paul;
KING, Richard Alfred; KING, Sarajane; KING, Winnifred; KINGAN, Elizabeth;
KINGSBURY, Gordon Henry; KINGSMILL, Brenda Mae; KINNEAR, Maureen Lynn; KINEE, Glen James;
KINNELL, Vicki; KINOSHITA, Daniel Eitaro; KINSELLA, Wendy Diane;
KINSMAN, Jacqueline Marie: KINSMAN, Marilyn Marie; KINZEL, Matthew; KINZEL, Ria;
KIRBY, Sandra; KIRCHMEIR, Katheryn Erika; KIRIAKA, Karen Lynn; KIRK, David Johnstone;
KIRK, Donald Archibald; KIRK, Dorothy Anne; KIRK, Elma Elaine; KIRK, James Robert;
KIRK, Lucile Anne; KIRK, Micheal Nevin; KIRK, Paul J.; KIRK, Sheila Geraldine; KIRK, Timothy David;
KIRKLAND, Bruce H.; KIRKPATRICK, Herbert; KIRSTEIN, Jill Marie; KISH, Douglas Howard;
KISH, Gaile Lillian; KISILEVICH, Cindy Kimberley; KISILEVICH, Lavern C.; KISPAL, Bonnie Lynn;
KISS, Gillian; KISS, Laszlo Kalman; KISS, Linnet Fern; KISS, Peter Morgan; KISSAM, William A.;
KITT, Michelle Jeness; KITTLE, Donna Marie Edith; KITTLE, Grace; KIZAN, Linda Fern;
KIEARSGAARD, Larry Andrew; KLAASSEN, Jewel Fae; KLANN Patricia Dorann; KLAPAUSZAK, Ruth;
KLAPSTEIN, Carol; KLAR, Leslie S.; KLAR, Steven Ferencz; KLASS, Charles; KLASSEN, Gail Sandra;
KLASSEN, Garth George; KLASSEN, Roxanne Cheryl; KLATT, Tara; KLAVER, Odetta; KLEIN, Arlene;
KLEIN, Cindy Lee; KLEIN, Lina Lenore; KLEIN, Stephen Ross; KLEMEN, Vincent John;
KLEMKA, Dr. Philip James; KLEMMER, Dean Allan; KLEMMER, Joyce Lorraine;
KLEMMER, William John; KLESS, Loraine Carol; KLETTER, Anita Ellen; KLIMO, Antal;
KLINGBEIL, Adolf; KLINGZAHN, Debbie; KLINKE, Dr. W. Peter; KLOOS, B. Norma;
KLUSHIN, Donna Marie; KLUTHE, Carrol Irene; KLUTHE, Norman Joseph; KLYMKOWYCH, Lydia;
KLYMOK, Carol Mary; KMECH, Faye Monica; KMECH, Lori Abnne; KMECH, Monica Faye;
KMECH, Peter Vincent Gregory; KNAFF, Patricia; KNAUER, Gerold Leopold;
KNEBEL, Steven Alexander; KNEBEL, Valerie A.; KNEBEL, Valerie Annette; KNEELAND, Robin;
KNICHEL, Linda; KNIGHT, David Gordon; KNIGHT, Kit; KNIGHT, Lois; KNIGHT, Margaret H.;
KNISELY, Dale M.; KNODEL, Benno; KNODEL, Louise M.; KNOLL, Carolyn Louise;
KNOLL, Duncan Adam; KNOLL, Karen Marilyn; KNOPP, Carolyn Kim; KNOPP, Delores;
KNOPPERS, Linda Sue; KNOWLES, James Murray; KNOWLES, Jessie McGregor;
KNOWLTON, Edna Elizabeth; KNOX, Karen; KNUDSEN, Garth Robert; KNUDSEN, Hope;
KNUDSLIEN, Denise Annette; KNUDSON, Gail Ann; KNUDTSON, Terry James; KNULL, Cheryl Dianne;
KNUTSON, Andrea; KNUTSON, Andrea Lynn; KNUTSVIG, Sherry Ann; KOBAYASHI, Junko;
KOBELUCK, Gloria Linda; KOBES, Darlene Alma; KOBYLANSKI, Debbie Jean;
KOBYLANSKI, Diane Michelle; KOBYIKA, Deborah Leah; KOCH, Howard Alexander;
KOCHAN, Karen Lynn Maria; KOCHAN, Louise Evelyn; KOCIOLEK, Adam; KOEHLI, Allen T.;
KOENIG, Kenneth E., KIFIN, Tom; KOH, Gene Alain; KOH, Yong Khoon; KOHAR, Gregory Vernon;
KOHL, Patty Lynn; KOHLER, Trudy E.; KOHLI, Santosh; KOHUT, Christina Martha Sophia;
KOHUT, Myroslaw Basil; KOHUT, Phyllis Joyce; KOKOTILO, Joanne Lori; KOLACH, Karen Lynn;
KOLASKI, Beverly Anne; KOLBA, Anna Ida; KOLBA, Lynda Lee; KOLIDO, Stan Paul;
KOLISNIAK, Craig Walter; KOLISNIAK, Kathryn; KOLODZIEI, Danuta Veronica;
KOLOSETTI, Blanka Clara; KOLOT, Jana Carice; KOLSKOG, Maynard; KOLTHAMMER, Helen Rae C.;
KOMARNISKY, R. Evelyn; KONANZ, Leo; KONARZEWSKI, Kathleen V.A.; KONARZEWSKI, Mariette;
KONWLSKY, Shauna; KONG, Edmond; KONG, Margaret; KONOPACKI, Rob William Blaine;
KONOPADA, Christine Ann; KONOPASEK, Peter; KONSKI, Christopher; KONTIO, Vyrki Tapeo;
KONWICKI, Michael Lawrence; KOO, Jarley; KOOLLOOS, Robin; KOOTNAY, Karen K.;
KOPECKY, Janice Diane; KOPIAK, Janette Eileen; KORBUT, Colleen Mary-Joan; KORBY, Kim Noell;
KORBY, Laurel Joy; KORBY, Margaret; KORCHINOS, Mervin John; KORDIC, Lilia; KORENIC, Ann;
KORN, Lane John; KORN, Michele Yvonne; KORNBERGER, Rae; KORNELSEN, Mari;
KORNELSON, Daryl Neil; KOROBANIK, Lynne Louise; KOROL, Janina; KOROL, Jennifer Liz;
KOROLUK, Darin William; KOROLUK, Janet Fay; KOROLUK, Mary Ruth; KORP, Michael;
KORPLEINSKY, Douglas Paul; KORTBEEK, Lloyd Anthony; KORTENBACH, Lidy Christina;
KORTES, Mariena Patricia; KORTHUIS, Patricia Ann; KORZENOSKI, Brenda Louise;
KORZENOWSKI, Mary Jo; KOSACK, Terry; KOSAK, Cheryl Maureen; KOSAK, Glenn Robert;
KOSCH, Rudy; KOSCIUK, Bozenna Zdzislawa; KOSCIUK, George John; KOSCIUK, Nicola Michelle;
KOSHKA, Jean Marie; KOSHKA, Ray E.; KOSHMAN, Brian Tom; KOSHMAN, Roberta;
KOSHUTA, Margaret A.; KOSKINAS-KOUTSOUKI, Demetro; KOSKINEN-DODGSON, Ellen Anita;
KOSKINEN, Paivi; KOSALOWSKI, John; KOSSMAN, Katherine Marie; KOSSOWAN, Millie;
KOSSOWAN, Peter; KOSTASH, Mary; KOSTASH, Robert Allan; KOSTEK, Keith; KOSTEK, Theresa;
KOSTENUK, Marrion Lynn; KOSTER, Emlyn Howard; KOSTER, Maryse; KOSTIUCK, Joan Lucille;
KOSTIUK, Maureen Gale; KOSTIUK, Neil Edward; KOSTURA, Rose; KOSTYNA-ALLEN, Marilyne;
KOSZEC, Eva; KOTASH, Caroline Andrea; KOTHARI, Zabina; KOTOMKINA, Elena;
KOUDIJS, Robert N.; KOVACS, Jean; KOWAL, Elizabeth Jean; KOWALCHUK, Auriana Leah;
KOWALCHUK, Barbara Anne; KOWALCHUK, Darlene Zina; KOWALCHUK, John S.;
KOWALENKO, Michael Gregory; KOWALSKI, Mickaline; KOWAND, Maureen Ruth; KOYANAGI, Allan;
KOZAK, Gregory Nicholas; KOZAKAVICH, Shelaine; KOZAR, Kenneth Robert;
KOZIKOWSKI, Margaret Stacha; KOZORIZ, Marie Barbara; KRAHN, Elfriede;
KRAHN, Marcio Evangeline; KRAMCHYNSKY, Eileen Lois; KRAMER, John; KRAMER, Lorna Ardelle;
KRAMERS, H. Joanne; KRAMERS, Roger Dean; KRAMPL, Joan; KRAMPS, Deborah Ann;
KRANENBURG, Konnie; KRASNIC, Elisabeth; KRASNOW, Shelley D.; KRATKO, Mary Ann;
KRATOCHVIL, John; KRATSCHMAR, Connie; KRAUS, Kathie Dawn; KRAUS, Michael,
KRAUS, Richard; KRAUSKOPF, Adele; KRAUSKOPF, Judi; KRAVITZX, Sari; KRAWCHUK, Shelli;
KRAWEC, Ron Allen; KREBES, Ron Anthony; KREISER, John Wayne; KREISER, Roberta M.;
KRELL, Kari; KREMPIEN, Connie; KRENZ, Laura Margaret; KREPAKEVICH, Jerry David;
KREPFUL, Dennis Wayne; KRESNYAK, Margaret Ellen; KRESNYAK, Robert James;
KRESS, Bertha Katrina; KRETZEL, Gerald R.; KREYENHOP, Frido; KRIKLER, Dr. Samuel Howard;
KIRKUN, Mike; KRILL, Charlene; KRISHKE, Gregory David; KRISPIN, Gisela; KIRSTA, Marie Daley;
KRISTOPOVICH, Deborah; KRISTENSEN, Jacqueline Leah; KRISTENSEN, Leah Jacqueline;
KROEGER, Angelika Victoria; KROENING, Leslie L.; KROETSCH, Deanna May;
KROETSCH, Veronica Caroline; KROGH, Sylvia Anne; KROLL, V. Marlene; KROOK, Gwen;
KROOK, Gwen Arlene; KROPP, Bernard Wayne; KROPP, Brenda Joy; KROWCHYNSKI, Paula Anne;
KRPAN, Maggie; KRUEGER, Bernhard; KRUGER, Carol Jayne; KRUHLAK, Dmytro;
KRUKEWICH, Patricia Ann; KRUMM, Joan Irene; KRUPA, Daryl M.; KRUPA, Glory Cynthia;
KRUPNIK, Arkady; KRUPNIK, Pesya; KRUPP, Judy; KRUSE, Keith; KRUSHEL, Brian;
KRUYER, Yolanda; Krysik, Ursula Elizabeth; KRYSKO, James Lyle; KRYSTOFIAK, Asifa;
KRYZANOWSKI, Karen Jane; KRYZANOWSKI, Leonard Mitchel; KU, Kam Hong; KUBAC, Dr. George;
KUBALIK, Dale Lee; KUBROK, Shirley May; KUCHERAWAY, Cindy Lou; KUCHISON, Sandy A.;
KUCHMA, William John; KUCHTA, Nadia Elizabeth; KUDRYK, Dr. William H.;
KUDRYNESKY, Carey George; KUEHN, Ashley Arthur; KUEHN, Cheryl; KUEHN, Violet Gabrielle;
KUERSCHNER, Dirk Carsten; KUHN, Marilyn D.; KUHRT, Claudia Maria; KUIPERS, Penny Anne;
KULAK, Anice; KULAK, Francine Catherin; KULAK, Nancy Doris; KULAK, Stephen Clifford;
KULAY, Sandy Lee; KULIK, Wanda Stella; KULY, Chris Lynn; KULY, Delis; KUMAR, Anil;
KUMISH, Brad John; KUMISH, Edward; KUMISH, Karen Lynn; KUMISH, Lillian Ann;
KUMOREK, Rosina Amry; KUMPF, L. Bella; KUNG, Allen; KUNISKI, Carol; KUNIK, Valentin;
KUNITZ, Dwane Peter, KUNITZ, Kim Christopher; KUNTZ, Marjorie Ellen; KUNY, Michael Anthony;
KUNY, Penny; KUNZ, Erica Lydia; KUPPEVELD, Cornel Johan Van; KURANY, Susan; KURIE, Joyce B.;
KURYLO, Stella; KUSHNER, Martha; KUSHNER, Shirley F.; KUSHNIRUK, Lori Lyn;
KUSHNIRUK, Maureen; KUSHNIRUK, Vicki; KUSMIERZ, John D.; KUTARNA, Elizabeth Ann;
KUTARNA, Marian Therese; KUTASH, Anola; KUTASH, Caroline Andrea; KUTASH, Kay Sophie;
KUTERA, Anna Julia; KUTSCHERO, Kurt; KUYSTERMANS, Gail Mary Ann; KUZEL, Paul;
KUZIKOWSKI, Sharline Kim; KUZYK, Richard; KWAN, Harvey Kee; KWAN, Keith Fee;
KWAN, Marlene Jean, KWAN, Marvin Jim; KWAN, Stephen Fee; KWOK, Kun-Yu; KWONG, Jackson;
KWONG, Regina; KWONG, Shelley Sue-Ling; KYLE, Edgar; KYLE, Warren; KYNE, Alana Jay;
KYSELYTZIA, Alex Paul; KYSELYTZIA, Steffany Katherine;

L

LAFRANCE, Marc A.; LAMARRE, Barbara Ann; LAPOINTE, Diane; LATOUCHE, Lloyd;
LABBE, Annette Bernadette; LABBE, Roland E.; LABBE, Simone Germaine; LABBY, Bryan David;
LABELLE, Andre; LABELLE, Margaret Catherine; LABERGE, Anna; LABONTE, Roy;
LABOUCANE, Jeanine Marie; LABRECQUE, Rita Louise; LABRENTZ, Graham Gerald;
LABRENTZ, Mark Lane; LABRIE, Rita Louise; LABRIE, Therese; LABUICK, Darryl Douglas;
LACH, Joan; LACHOWICH, Gary Fredric Ray; LACIKA, Livia; LACOMBE, Oscar John;
LACOURSIERE, Carol; LACOURSIERE, Michelle Marie; LACROIX, Alan Francis;
LACROIX, Barbara Joan; LACROIX, Monica Patricia; LACROIZ, Barbara Joan;
LADEROUTE, Andre Roger; LADEROUTE, Michael Roger; LADEROUTE, Victor R.;
LAFONTAINE, Robert Earl; LAFOREST, Bernard; LAFORTUNE, Michele; LAFRAMBOISE, Joseph;
LAGACE, Helen Florence; LAGROIX, Rodney Lawrence; LAHEY, Gail; LAHAFER, Loretta J.;
LAHOLA, Lida; LAI, Caroline Y.L.; LAI, Shek Chung; LAIDLOW, William Roy; LAIDLEY, Inger Conradi;
LAIDLEY, Wendell Holdane; LAIN, Cindy B.; LAIN, Richard John; LAING, Darryl John;
LAING, Don William Joseph; LAING, Elaine Pearl; LAING, Pamela Mary; LAING, R. Stephanie;
LAING, Robert John; LAING, Robert Kevin; LAIPNIEKS, Emma Concetta; LAIPNIEKS, Peter John;
LAISS, Debbie; LAISS, James; LAISS, Lillian; LAISS, William; LAJEUNESSE, Jeanne Marie;
LAJOIE, Daniel Ralph; LAKE, Dr. Dave; LAKEY, Dr. William Hall; LAKEY, Jonathan Robert Todd;
LAKEY, Shirley Ann; LAKEY, Steven Kenneth; LAKUSTA, Christine; LAKUSTA, Tracy Claire;
LALANI, Zulfikarali H.; LALIBERTE, Betty Mae; LALIBERTE, Dianne; LALONDE, Louise;
LALONDE, Robert Glen; LALONDE, Susan Lynn; LALOR, Wayne R.; LAM, Eva; LAM, Phi Trieu;
LAM, Winnie Fung Kwan; LAMARCHE, Carol P.; LAMARRE, Marie Lynn Joan; LAMB, Brian Henry;
LAMB, Brian Neil; LAMB, Cindy; LAMB, Gerard, LAMB, Janice Christopher; LAMB, Linda Carol;
LAMB, Robert W.; LAMB, Travis Wellesley; LAMERS, Jacqueline; LAMMERS, Shirley Edna;
LAMOND, Lance; LAMONT, Rose; LAMONTAGNE, Mona; LAMOTHE, Louise Mary;
LAMOUREUX, Gerald Stephen; LAMOUREUX, Monique Lee; LAMOUREUX, Stephen Joseph;
LANDO, Luis; LANDRY, Chris; LANDRY, Francine C.; LANDRY, Mary; LANDRY, Vincent Jeffrey;
LANDVATTER, Kenneth Clarence; LANDVATTER, Maureen; LANE, Rhoda;
LANES, Alice E., LANG, Frances; LANG, Kathleen Theresa; LANG, Michael J.; LANG, Valeta Karen;
Lange, Brenda Mary; LANGE, Bruce Francis; LANGE, Irma; LANGEVIN, Louise Gracia;
LANGEVIN, Roger I.; LANGFORD, Marilyn; LANGFORD, Michael Terrance;
LANGHANS, Linda Kathleen; LANGLANDS, Dave William; LANGLEY, Alice Marie;
LANGLEY, Helen Audrey Claire; LANGLEY, Linda C.; LANGLOIS, Claudia Diane;
LANGLOIS, Helen Leone; LONGMAN, James Alberta; LANGMAN, Loralie Jeanette;
LANGRIDGE, Shari; LANGVAND, Aaron Dexter; LANIGAN, Brent; LANK, Petronella Francisco;
LAPERLE, John Eugene; LAPLANTE, Daniel; LAPOINTE, Adele Marie Rolande;
LAPOOLE, Michelle Ellaine; LAQUERRE, Gilles; LARAMEE, Therese; LARIO, Anne Margaret;
LARIVIERE, Arthur Melvill; LARKE, Dr. R.P. Bryce; LAROCHE, Cindy Sue; LAROCHE, Jerry H.;
LAROCQUE, Bonnie; LAROCQUE, Claudette Marie; LAROCQUE, Stephane; LARSEN, Janice Marie;
LARSEN, Lesley Maureen; LARSEN, Sheilagh; LARSEN, Werner Soholm; LARSON, Gerold Lee;
LARSON, Glen; LARSON, Jordon Alan; LARSON, Lorraine Marie; LARSON, Monica;
LARSON, Susan Patricia; LASHMAR, Corene Gay; LASKIN, Monty; LASKIWSKI, Orest John;
LASKOWKY, Bryan Victor; LASNIBAT, Juan Danilo; LATOSKI, Betty Anne; LATOSKI, Robert Peter;
LATOSZEK, Karen Lynn; LATREILLE, Mark D.; LATTA, Helen; LAU, Stephen Y.M.; LAU, Tim;
LAUDER, Leanne Marie; LAUDER, Wallace; LAUF, Ulrich; LAURELL, Gunilla Christine;
LAURITZEN, Osa; LAUTEN, Jean; LAUTT, Ray Sheldon; LAUSON, Dennis; LAVALEE, Janine Carmelle;
LAVALEE, Tim Allyn; LAVANDER, Carol-Anne; LAVER, Laura; LAVERGNE, Sharyn Ann;
LAVERS, Howard Charles S.; LAVERS, James Fredrick; LAVERS, Mark; LAVERY, Patricia Eilish;
LAVOIE, Daniel; LAVOIE, Dr. Michel Victor; LAVOY, Donald Alfred, LAW, John Duer;
LAW, John Michael; LAW, Karen; LAWEC, Mary; LAWRENCE, Georgina Lynn;
LAWRENCE, Joyce Mary; LAWRENCE, Mark Ashley; LAWRENCE, Peter Gordon;
LAWRENCE, Samantha; LAWRENCE, Sharolyn J.; LAWRENCE, Veronica;
LAWRENCE, Wendell Robert; LAWTON, Daniel W.; LAY, Colin Michael Robert; LAYETZKE, Maureen;
LAZAR, Curtis George; LAZARENKO, Joseph M.; LAZARUK, Dr. D. Ivan; LAZENBY, Robyn Lynn;
LEBLANC, Marie Josee; LE, Kim Son; LEADLAY, Dawn; LEADLAY, Myrtle Bernice; LEAHY, Frances C.;
LEAKE, Anthony K.; LEAKER, Catherine Joan; LEAKER, Shirley; LEARMONTH, Barbara Elaine;
LEASON, Kenneth William; LEASON, Mark Patrick; LEBLANC-DEMGOAARD, Janet A.;
LEBLANC, David Alphonse; LEBLANC, Deborah Anne; LEBLANC, Grace Ann;
LEBLANC, Jean Paul Joseph; LEBLANC, Terrance Leo; LEBRAY, Colin;
LEBUKE, Dawn Marie Elizabeth; LEBUKE, Elaine Mary; LEBUKE, Marilyn Elaine;
LEBUKE, Scott William; LECHELT, Alice Rita Marie; LECKELT, Jennifer Diane, LECKY, Bruce Mckinnon;
LECLAIR, Giselle; LECLERC, Ernest Aime; LECLERC, Kathie Jeanne; LEDDA, Belinda Corpuz;
LEDE, Herbert Eric; LEDE, Jennifer Jean; LEDERER, Robert Hugo; LEDGER, Betty; LEDGERWOOD, Jo-Anne; LEDIG, Bradley Michael; LEE, Alison Sinduk; LEE, Brenda Kaye; LEE, Brian William;
LEE, Calvin Everett; LEE, Chang-Ho; LEE, David James; LEE, De-Lei; LEE, Din-Chun Peter;
LEE, Dr. Bernard; LEE, Gabriel Seung; LEE, Jessie Marguerite; LEE, Jong Bae; LEE, Judith Jane;
LEE, Karen Grace; LEE, Kelly James; LEE, Marilyn; LEE, Marilyn Ann; LEE, Marlene Foon-Lan;
LEE, Maureen Joy; LEE, Ralph; LEE, Sandra; LEE, Shirley Yee; LEE, Slow Fong; LEE, Wan Fung;
LEE, William Arnold; LEECK, Ernie Emil; LEECK, Irene Iris, LEEDER, Brenda Gail; LEETI, Johanna Rose;
LEFEBURE, Dr. Rober Ellear; LEFEBURE, Marie J.; LEFEBURE, Rollande; LEFEBVRE, Gail Andrea;
LEFFLER, Darren James; LEFFLER, Lowell Stuart; LEFKO, Russell Kalman; LEFLAR, Cory William;
LEGGRE, Marc Charles; LEGATT, Dr. Donald; LEGATT, Roberta Denise; LEGERE, Wayne J.;
LEGGE, Gerald Dwayne; LEGGO, Christopher Andrew; LEHMAN, John; LEHMANN, Goldie;
LEHN, Flor Marina; LEHODEY, Colette M.; LEIER, Maureen; LEIGHTON, Sue Anne;
LEIMAN, Fredda Isabelle; LEIMAN, Len; LEINWEBER, Conrad; LEITCH, Carol Anne;
LEITCH, Gillian Irene; LEITCH, Hugh Corley; LEITCH, Kenneth Garry; LEITCH, Robert Bruce;
LELACHEUR, Carol Rose; LEMA, Frances Elizabeth; LEMA, Kathryn Elizabeth; LEMA, Tracy Lee;
LEMAY, Charles; LEMERMEYER, Linda Ann; LEMIEUX, Suzane; LEMISKI, Kathleen Anne;
LEMISKI, Linda; LEMISKI, Terrance, LEMKE, Dieter; LEMKE, Markus; LEMOAL, Clifford Allan;

LENEY, Bev; LENNIE, Carol Eleanor; LENNIE, Linda Marie; LENOS, Margo Lynne; LENT, Frank Irving; LENTZ, Lorna Janice; LENTZE, Jacqueline Janny; LEONARD, Dennis Arthur; LEONARD, Jennifer M.; LEONARD, Mary Elizabeth; LEPAGE, Andre; LEPAGE, Carolyn; LEPAGE, Michelle Marie; LEPARD, Ross Heath; LEPINE, Janice Julia; LEPINE, Ralph W.; LEPPARD, Catherine Jean; LEPPARD, John Emerson; LEPPARD, Pamela Joan; LEPPARD, Susan Elizabeth; LEPPART, Mark; LEPPS, Devin; LEPPS, Elizabeth Anthoinetta; LEPPS, Jacqueline Iona; LERNER, Sol Robert; LERNER, Tyrone William; LEROHL, Adeline Mildred; LEROHL, Karen Kristine; LEROUX, Lance Wayne; LESHER, Penny Joe; LESHER, Shelley G.; LESHURES, Judith B.; LESLIE, Gary William; LESNIK, Alberta; LESPERANCE, Danial; LETAIN, Marjorie Annette; LETAWSKY, Joannie Marie; LETAWSKY, Juliet Marie; LETAWSKY, Marlene; LETCH, Albert George; LETCHER, Rachelle Marie; LETELIER, Roberta Belmar; LETENDRE, Jason; LETENDRE, Roxanne Melanie; LETKI, Thomas Donald; LETOURNEAU, Rene Joseph; LETTY, Ducusin; LETWIN, Cheryl Lynn; LETWIN, George William; LETWIN, Gloria Darlene; LETWIN, Margaret Rose; LETWIN, Pat Jean; LEUNG, Andrew; LEUNG, Carol; LEUNG, Christina; LEUNG, David; LEUNG, Dominic Man-Sun; LEUNG, Kai Yuen; LEUNG, Paul; LEUNG, Po Ling; LEUNG, Simone Se-Min; LEVANG, Chris Lynn; LEVANG, Donna Marguerite; LEVANG, Gordon Leroy; LEVENTAL, Egar; LEVESQUE, Adele; LEVESQUE, Darcy Lloyd; LEVINE-FULLER, Cheryl Lynn; LEVITES, Eduard; Levitess, Edvard; Levitt, Margaret; LEVITT, Maureen Ellen; LEVY, Maurice Lloyd; LEW, Leely; LEW, Sidney; LEWAK, John Donald; LEWAK, Marguerite Elsa; LEWIS, Carolyn Mary; LEWIS, Catherine Anne; LEWIS, Christopher; LEWIS, Darcy Charles; LEWIS, Laura Eva; LEWIS, Maureen Cynthia; LEWIS, Peter; LEWIS, Shirley; LEWIS, Susanne Elizabeth LEWIS, William John; LEWKE, Dr. Bogle Liesl; LEWONIUK, Maryann; LEWYCKY, Alec Raymond; LEY, Leona Mae; LEY, Patti J.; L'HIRONDELLE, Maxine Dolly; LI, Ivy; LI, Joseph; LI, Min-Chun; LI, Tillotson Pak-Chuk; LIAN, Maroun; LIAO, Janice; LIAZ, Joselino Compillo; LICIS, Brian Allen; LIDSTONE, David; LIEM, Ruby Maria; LIEN, Barbara Joyce; LIEN, Patricia Ann; LIEN, Vernice Lila; LIEW, Irene; LIEW, Mimi; LIGHTBODY, Lynn Margaret; LIGHFOOT, Helen N.; LIIMATAINEN, Arvi John; LILGE, Charlene; LILGE, Chris Gayle; LILLEY, Dr. John Thomas; LILLEY, John William; LILLEY, Judith Anne; LIM, Anatasia Ming-Yee; LIM, Lee-Ling; LIM, Mouy; LIM, Sieu; LIMONOV, Charlotte; LINARES, Edgar Alfonso; LINARES, Luis Ernesto; LIND, Susan; LINDAL, Karen Lynn; LINDBERG, Dr. Ronald Charles; LINDBERG, Frederick Algot; LINDBERG, Janis Marie; LINDBERG, Jennifer Jo; LINDBERG, Robert James; LINDBERG, Robin Leigh; LINDBERG, Wally L.; LINDENLAUB, Martin John; LINDENMAN, Edito Annali; LINDHOLM, Larry Gregory; LINDQUIST, Florence; LINDSAY, Anne; LINDSAY, Barb J.; LINDSAY, David; LINDSAY, David G.; LINDSAY, Kandis Valintine; LINDSAY, Peter L.; LINDSAY, William David; LINDSTROM, Eric Aime; LINEKER, Donna Mae; LINEKER, Ruth Elaine; LINES, Daniel James; LINEXER, Robert Frank; LING, Henry Albert; LING, Moses Hwee-Leong; LINGLEY, Janice Miriam; LINHART, Angela Mary; LINK, Rita; LINK, Rita Erika; LINKS, Dr. Harold; LINNELL, Annette Darllen; LINTON, Natalie Deanne; LINTZ, Moira Anne; LIPOVELSKY, Mike Yosif; LIPOVSKI, Henry Joe; LIPPE, Bob; LIPPOLT, Gordon Bryan; LISCHEWSKI, Karin; LISTER, Adeline; LISTER, June; LITHGROW, Christine; LITKE, Dee; LITTLE, Catherine Anne; LITTLE, Jack Lorne; LITTLEFAIR, David Michael; LITTLEFAIR, Scott Michael; LITVEN, Brian Andrew; LITVEN, Donald; LITVEN, Liane; LITVINCHUK, Michelle C.; LIVINGSTONE, Connie B.; LIVINGSTONE, David William; LIZOTTE, Carole Nicole; LLEWELLYN, Kristine Inez; LLOYD, Dale Patrick; LLOYD, Dorothy E.; LLOYD, Leah Denise; LLOYD, Robert Victor; LO, Allan; LO, Hune Kei Alex; LO, Siuto Raymond; LOADES, Adrian Alan; LOBAY, Dr. Gary William; LOBAY, Mary; LOBE, Corrinne; LOBLICK, Patricia; LOBO, Audra; LOBO, Michelle; LOBO, William Cyril; LOBREAU, Michael T.; LOCKERT, Kim K.; LOCKLIN, Karen Ann; KOCKREM, Hazel Ray; LOCKWOOD, Don F.; LOCKWOOD, Sally Nora; LACONTE, Anthony Nicholas; LACONTE, Marie; LACONTE, Vito Franco; LODER, Charles Ralph; LODER, Evelyn Bonnie; LODER, Patricia; LOEFFLER, Douglas E.; LOEFFLER, Marguerite; LOESCH, Dianne Patricia; LOGA, Julie Charlotte; LOGAN, Carol Ann; LOGAN, Donald N.; LOGAN, Phyllis E.; LOGAN, Velma Jean; LOHRENGEL, Mariel Cecilia; LOISEAU, Denise Sheila; LOITZ, Michael John; LOMAS, Gino; LOMAX, Joyce Alma; LOMBERG, Denise Michelle; LONEY, Karen; LONG, Alan Wayne; LONG, Kelly Lynn; LONG, Maureen; LONG, Patricia Jeanne; LONGENECKER, Nadine; LONGSON, Ginger Marie; LONGSON, Lucille Evangeline; LONNEBERG, Ann; LOO, Susan; LOOSEMORE, Dale; LOOSEMORE, James Harold; LOOSEMORE, Sawn Elin; LOOV, Valerie Edith; LOPATKA, Laurel; LOPES, John Joseph; LOPEZ, Mauricio Leopoldo; LOPUSHINSKY, Barbara; LOPUSHINSKY, Heather Halina; LOPUSHINSKY, Sonia Lovie; LORD, Dr. Chris; LORD, Gladys; LORD, Hugh Christopher; LORD, Nancy Lees; LORD, Shannon; LORE, David James; LORE, Lida Marie; LORE, Maryiane; LORENCZ, Mabel Irene; LORENSON, Troy Adair; LORENTZ, Joann Elaine; LORENZ, Hans Jeurgen; LORENZ, Norbert Neil; LORIEAU, Pierre; LORINCZI, Judith; LOSERT, Radana; LOSHNY, Irene; LOSHNY, Walter; LOSIE, Barbara Jeanne; LOSIE, Doreen Elinor; LOSIE, John Philip; LOSING, Marie Wilma; LOSIO, Garth Edward; LOTH, Jane; LOTNICK, Patricia Wanda; LOTOSKI, George F.; LOTZER, Terry Marie; LOUGH Kerry Joseph; LOUGHEED, Lila M.; LOUIE, Anthony; LOUKO, Margaret; LOVATT, Olga mary; LOVE, DAVID: LOVE, Donald Lawrence; LOVE, Kathleen Ann Marie; LOVE, Kenneth Andrew; LOVE Warren Dean; LOVEJOY, Laura Gail; LOVELL, Catherine Louise; LOVELL, June Gwendoline; LOVELL, Mavis Elsie; LOVELL, Sharon Virginia; LOVELL, Sheldon George; LOVERIDGE, Edna; LOVERIDGE, Paul James; LOVETT, Angela Helen; LOW, June Lorraine; LOW Larry; LOW, Tracey Dawn; LOWE Eleanor; LOWE, Frances Lillian; LOWE, Mary Nancy; LOWRY, Malcolm Byran; LOXTERKAMP, Patricia Agnes; LOYER, Angela Maria; LOYER, Evelyn; LOYER, Kenneth Bruce; LOZINSKI, David Carl; LOZON, Donna Doherty; LOZON, Jeffery C. LUBCHYNSKI, Louise; LUBERT, Renie Naomie; LUBIANTORO, Sutedio; LUBOVAC, Brenda; LUCAS Doug O.; LUCAS, Katherine Diane; LUCAS, Tracy Darlene; LUCHAK, Sue; LUCHKOW, Ken; LUCKI, Patrik John; LUCO, Thelma Jean LUCHSHUN, Ray Frank; LUCESCHER, Hanna; LUDU, Amita; LUECK, Karen Patricia; LUEDERS, Audrey Jane; LUELOFF, Dieter U.; LUELOFF, Loretta; LUETHE, Helga; LUI, Albert; LUI, Kin Yue; LUK, Anna; LUK, Tung-Chuen Simon; LUKACH, Jo-Ann; LUKASEWICH Laura; LUKASIEWICH, Sandra Lee; LUKAWESKY, Ressell James; LUKAWY, Thomas; LUM Mae-Mah; LUMBY, Donald; LUMMIS, John; LUMSDEN, Margaret; LUMSDON, Theresa; LUNAN, Carolanne Marie; LUND, Beverly A.; LUND, Birgitte; LUND, Faue; LUND, Galan Thomas; LUNDEEN, Dr. Richard Clarence; LUNDELL, David; LUNDELL, David Allan; LUNDID Brenda; LUNDID, Victor S.: LUNDQUIST, Elizabeth; LUNDQUIST, Marion; LUNG, Kevin Ernest; LUNG, Margaret Ruth; LUNTY, Carmen Gwen; LUNTY, Karen Pearl; LUNTY, Wallace; LUONG, Victor; LUPSOR, Corrine M.; LUPTON, Nancy P.; LUPUL, Maria Fernanda; LUPUL, Terrance Geroge; LUSCOMBE, Karen Lynn; LUSCOMBE, Pamela Gweneth; LUSCOMBE, Patricia Anne; LUST, Albert; LUTIC, Leslie; LUTOMSKY, Holly Dawn; LUTZ, Karen Lee; LUTZ, Linda Ann; LUU, Dieu Phu; LUX, Derek Warren; LUX, Donna Mary; LUX, Warren Rodney; LY, Minh Phuoc; LYNCH-STAUNTON, M. Kim; LYNCH, Agnes Marie; LYNCH, Donna E.A.; LYNCH, Frederic Clifford; LYNCH, Karen A.; LYNCH, Niall; LYNCH, Norman; LYNCH, Sharon Kelly; LYNCH, Terrence F.; LYNN, Helen Amillia; LYONS, Cheryl Cathy; LYONS, Gary Lawrence; LYONS, Sharon Patricia; LYSACK, Janie; LYSAY, Dave Allan; LYTVIAK, Dr. Margaret Anne;

M

MA, Antonieta Liamas Parada; MA, Daniel Chung-Ming; MA, Nancy Kam; MABBOTT, Jane Elizabeth; MABBOTT, Leslie Donald; MABBOTT, Linda Arleen; MABON, Nick Andrew; MACDONELL, Patricia Anne; MACADAM, Michael Joseph; MACAFEE, Lisa Marie; MACALLISTER, Allen Stewart; MACALLISTER, Menzies Alexander; MACALLISTER, Stewart Gault; MACANDREW, Iris Lynn; MACANDREW, Janet Lynne; MACARTHUR, Catherine Ann; MACARTHUR, Max George; MACARTHUR, Patrick Francis; MACARTHUR, Shauna Lynne; MACARTHUR, Shirley Ann; MACASKILL, Willian Arthur; MACAULAY, Linda Dianne; MACAULEY, Nancy; MACBEATH, Sandra Elizabeth; MACALUM, Liliane B.; MACCALLUM, William Ormond; MACCRIMMON, Linda; MACDONALD, Andrew H.; MACDONALD, Ann Maureen; MACDONALD, Barbara Gray; MACDONALD, Brian Harper; MACDONALD, Bryan Alexander; MACDONALD, Carole Anne; MACDONALD, Catherine Marie; MACDONALD, Cathy; MACDONALD, Charles Robert; MACDONALD, Dawn; MACDONALD, Denis; MACDONALD, Douglas Haig; MACDONALD, Dr. Giles Fredrick; MACDONALD, Elizabeth E.; MACDONALD, Ester Maud; MACDONALD, Gail Merydith; MACDONALD, Janet; MACDONALD, Jayme Paul; MACDONALD, Jill Wynne; MACDONALD, Jillian; MACDONALD, Joyce E.; MACDONALD, Kenneth E.; MACDONALD, Laurel Anne; MACDONALD, Letta Theresa; MACDONALD, Lloyd Ramsey; MACDONALD, M. Karen; MACDONALD, Mark Stephen; MACDONALD, Mary Catharine; MACDONALD, Melanie Irene; MACDONALD, Neil; MACDONALD, Pamela Kathy; MACDONALD, Robert; MACDONALD, Teresa Catherine; MACDONELL: Ronald Gorden; MACDOUGALL, Bruce; MACDOUGALL, Donald Hebert; MACDOUGALL, Julie Marie; MACEACHERN Tara Jane; MACEK Bozena; MACEWKO, Luba Melania; MACFADYEN, Lois Fay; MACFARLANE, Angus; MACGILLIVRAY, Elmer Benedict; MACGREGOR, Bruce Grant; MACGREGOR, Cathrine Irene; MACGREGOR, Fiona Margaret; MACGREGOR, Heather Lynn; MACGREGOR, Janet Ann; MACH, Helmut; MACHAN, Deborah Lynn; MACHNEY, Gary David; MACIE, Mary; MACIEYOWSKI, Mary; MACINNIS, Linda Louise; MACINNIS, Sharolyn F.C.; MACINTOSH, Edward Kenneth; MACINTOSH, Rita Rose; MACINTYRE, Shawn Heather; MACIVER, Karen Anne; MACK, Benjamin J.; MACK, Donna; MACK, Linda; MACK, Lisa Marie; MACK Roland Norbert; MACK, Rolinda Duen; MACKAY, A. Douglas; MACKAY, Anne; MACKAY, Arthur Ian; MACKAY, Eleanor; MACKAY, F. Archie; MACKAY, Margery A.; MACKAY, Maureen Elizabeth; MACKAY, Stuart; MACKAY, Susan Aurena; MACKAY, Veronica Agnes; MACKAY, William Dawson; MACKEL, Dr. John Vincent; MACKENZIE, Cameron Stephen; MACKENZIE, David Donald; MACKENZIE, Debora Elizabeth; MACKENZIE, Jeanne Lucienne; MACKENZIE, Joyce Margaret; MACKENZIE, Kathleen; MACKENZIE, Lisa Marie; MACKENZIE, Sharon; MACKENZIE, Terri Andree; MACKENZIE, Maureen Florence MACKI, Mia; MACKIE, Carol Ann; MACKIE, Dr. John William; MACKIE, Gordon C.B.; MACKIE, Richard Gerald; MACKIE, William Frederick; MACKINLAY, Helen C.; MACKINLAY, Margaret Jean; MACKINNON, Alic Ruth; MACKINNON, Bernice Ann; MACKINNON, Elizabeth Mary; MACKINNON, John D.; MACKINNON Margaret Joan; MACKINNON, Margo Ann; MACKINNON, Robert Paul; MACKLEM, Brent F.; MACKLIN, Jacob Melvin; MACKOWETZKY, Loran Douglas; MACKRILL, Barbara Gail; MACLACHLAN, Dorothy Eileen; MACLACHLAN, J. Howard; MACLACHLAN, Mary E.; MACLAUCHLAN, Julie Anne; MACLEAN, Babe; MACLEAN, Babe Noella; MACLEAN, Carmen Marguerite; MACLEAN, Colette Marie; MACLEAN, Dale Alexander; MACLEAN, Denise Michele; MACLEAN, Elizabeth Jean; MACLEAN, G. Richard; MACLEAN, Leah Mae; MACLEAN, Robert A.B.; MACLEAN, Shane; MACLELLAN, Anne Marie; MACLELLAN, John; MACLELLAN, Natalie; MACLENNAN, Jacqui May; MACLEOD, Ian Donald; MACLEOD, Maureen Amber; MACLEOD, Norman Pentiand; MACLEOD, Roslyn Jane; MACLEOD, Sandra Lynn; MACLEOD, Wayne; MACMILLAN, Donald John; MACMILLAN, Hayley; MACMILLAN, Ian; MACMILLAN, Jeannette Marie; MACMILLAN, Katherine I.B.; MACMILLAN, Laurie Anne; MACMILLAD Lesley; MACMILLAN, Ralph Baldwin; MACMULLIN, Bernadette; MACNAB, Bruce; MACNAMARA, Anne Natalie; MACNAMARA, Julia Margaret; MACNEIL, James Roy; MACOLOR, Jose P.: MACPHAIL, Milfred Douglas; MACPHEE, Jayne Christine; MACPHERSON, Brian Edward; MACPHERSON, Sharon Lynn: MACPHERSON, Sharon Patricia; MACQUEEN, David John; MACQUEEN, Douglas Alexander; MACQUISTEN, Carol; MACRAE, Barb Lynn; MACRAE, Bonnie Jane; MACRAE, Brian; MACRAE, Elizabeth Louise; MACRAE, Melissa Ann; MACRAE, Pamela Joan; MACRAE, Susan Diane; MACRAE, Wendy Leigh; MACTOGGART, Fiona Osborn; MACTOGGART, Sandy A.; MACWILLIAM, Lourin Alice; MADAY, Ange; MADAY, Charicia Rose; MADDEN, John Francis; MADILL, Andrew John R.; MADILL, Helen M. MADRO, Anthony Mathew; MADSEN, B. Joyce; MADSEN, Joy Ellen; MADU, Bruce Eldon; MADU, Gail; MADU, Kenneth Andrew; MAEDA, Yoshihiro; MAERTENS-POOLE, Beverly; MAERTENS-POOLE, Bill; MAERTENS-POOLE, Vernell Jay; MAGARRELL, James N.; MAGEAU, Dennis Pierre; MAGEE, David James; MAGEE, Dr. David James; MAGEE Evelyn; MAGEE, Evelyn Irene; MAGEE, Ione Elizabeth; MAGEE, Mamuel Allan; MAGEE, Thomas Paul; MAGEE, Timothy Ian; MAGILL, Joyce Elaine; MAGILL, Mance Laurette; MAGNAN, Denise Lise; MAGNAN, Rosceline Marie; MAGNAN, Susan Norah; MAGUIRE, Dr. Terry Michael; MAGUIRE, Kathleen Mary; MAGUIRE, Lesley M.; MAGYAR, Alex; MAH-JONES, Dianna; MAH, Barbara Ann; MAH, Donald Sang; MAH, Esther; MAH, Gee; MAH, Gloria Ruby; MAH,Hazel Pui Yee; MAH, Helen Joan; MAH, James; MAH, James King; MAH, Janet; MAH, Jean; MAH, Jim; MAH, Kelly Fat; MAH, Kim Bill; MAH, Lily; MAH, Linda G.; MAH, Melanie; MAH, Monica Li Ping; MAH, Sally; MAH, Sandra; MAH, Sharon; MAH, Stan; MAH, Susanna; MAH, Vic; MAH, Virginia Gwen; MAHADY, Anne Elizabeth; MAHAFFEY, Barbara J.; MAHE, Jocelyn Paulette; MAHER, David William; MAHEUX, Todd; MAHOOD, Kerry Johanna; MAIDMAN, David William; MAIER, Bradley John; MAILO, William Raymond; MAINES, Glen Mcbride; MAIORANA, Filippo Gianni; MAIR, Lindy; MAISONNEUVE, Dolores M.; MAISONNEUVE, Greg J.; MAISONNEUVE, Susan Lee; MAITLAND, Alan Williams; MAITLAND, Craig John; MAITLAND, Gary Adam; MAITLAND, Karen Margaret; MAITLAND, Katherine; MAITLAND, Liane; mMAITLAND, Michael; MATLAND, Robin Leigh; MAICHER, Bernice; MAIDPOUR, Abdi; MAIEAU, Tammy Marie; MAIEED, George R.; MAIESKI, Kevin Dale; MAIOR, Alice; MAJOR, Cathy Anne; MAJOR, Janet; MAJOR, Pearl J.; MAK, Anthony Kwong; MAKAR, Dr. Donald John; MAKARENKO, Janet E. MARAROWSKI, Barbara Frances; MAKAROWSKI, Lani Marie; MAKAVITA, Dona Cynthia; MAKI, Marilyn Francine; MAKINSON, Zoe Flora; MAKOHONIUK, Daniel George; MARKORTOFF, Rose; MAKOWECKI, Susan; MAKSYMIC, CoriL-A; MAKSYMIC, Debbie Lynn; MAKSYMNUK, Carmen; MALARYK, Jean Ann; MALASHUK, Cliff Walter; MALASHUK, Jeannette Marie; MALCOLM, Carol Joanne; MALCOLM, Laura Lynn; MALDONADO, Herman; MALDONADO: Mirta; MALESZEWSKA, Jadwiga; MALESZEWSKI, Lester; MALICK, Douglas Gordon; MALINOWSKI, Albert; MALINOWSKI, Dr. Ben Andrew; MALINOWSKI, Devin Shane; MALINSKI, Barbara; MALINSKI, John; MALKINSON, Brenda; MALKINSON, Elaine Annie; MALLETT, Debra Jean; MALLOY, Linda Caroline; MALONE, Evelyn Grace; MALONE, Evelyne Grace; MALONE, Maureen Catherine; MALONE, Shannon; MALONEY Dan; MALONEY, Diane; MALOWANY, Mark Christopher; MALOWANY, Mike David; molthouco, Richard Charles; MAITIN, Ronald Rockmel; MALYCHUK, Carlene; MANCHAK, Leonard William; MANCINI, Gina Marie; MANDAU, Roland Horst; MANDIUK, Heidi Caroling; MANDRUSIAK, Deila Loreen; MANDZIUK, Steven Nicholas; MANGAT, Harjinder Paul; MANGAT, Jyoti Pran; MANN, Bonnie P.; MANN, Dave Aaron Charles; MANN, Debra; MANN, William A.; MANNILA, Michele; MANILLA, Michele Anneli; MANNING, Annette Marian; MANNING, Sarah Ellen; MANNING, Wendy Gaye; MANOLESCU, Raylene; MANSELL, Natalie; MANSELL, Robert Beverly; MANSELL, Shelley Christine; MANSKE, Thomas; MANT, Kristen E.; MANTIA, Donna Laverne; MANTON, Peggy Lee; MANUEL, Paul; MANUEL, Shirley Edith; MANUEL, Shirley Edith; MANULAK, Clarence Walter; MANY, Lucille; MANYIUK, Stan H.; MANZIE, Alan A.; MAPLETHORPE, Ian; MAPPLEBECK, Elizabeth Lynn; MAR, Betty; MAR, Divid Chao-Chi; MAR, Serena Gay;

MAR, Vincent Chiun Shan; MARATOVIC, Victor Vladimir; MARBERG, Erna; MARCH, Patricia Ann;
MARCHAK, Marilyn Joan; MARCHAK, Susan Carol; MARCHAND, Bradley Derek;
MARCHANT, Richard Edward; MARCHE, Janet; MARCHEIL, Victor Edward;
MARCHESIN, Silvia Matilde; MARCHIEL, Peter Paul; MARCIAK, Margaret Rosalind;
MARCUK, Leslie Ann; MARCUSHAMER, Samuel; MAREAN, Margaret D.; MARECHAUX, Johannes W.;
MARGOLUS, Mona Ester; MARGULIS, Eugene; MARIAN, Jeannie; MARIASH, Dona Gayle;
MARIASH, Kenneth William; MARIER, Jacqueline; MARIKA, Margaret; MARION, Alexander Ross;
MARION, Cheryl Anne; MARION, Dolores Dee; MARION, John George; MARION, John Grey;
MARK, Diane; MARK, Hazel; MARK Kenneth Welbourne; MARKATTI, Micheline Bibine;
MARKE, Douglas Andre Elliot; MARKEVYCH, Doria; MARKLAND, Alice Elizabeth; MARKO, Kathy Jane;
MARKO, Peggy Marie; MARKOWICH, Barbara Isabel; MARKOWICH, Margaret Anne;
MARKOWICH, Penny Lynn; MARKOWSKI, Michael Peter; MARKS, Lynn Patricia; MARKS, Trevor;
MARLATT, Christy M.; MARLER, Leslie Janet; MARLER, Ralph Douglas; MARLES, John Donald;
MARPLES, Kelly John; MARPLES, Susan Lynne; MARROZZO, Mario Tony; MARRELLO, Lou D.;
MARSH, Barbara Joan; MARSH, Howard Glenson; MARSH, Jody Kathryn; MARSH, John R.;
MARSHALL, Beverly Ann; MARSHALL, Carol Louise; MARSHALL, Carol-Lee;
MARSHALL, Charles Grant; MARSHALL, Clayton Ronald; MARSHALL, Cyril;
MARSHALL, Gaston Alejandro; MARSHALL, Janice Erica; MARSHALL, John Ralph;
MARSHALL, Kirsten; MARSHALL, Ralph John; MARSHALL, Richard Franklin;
MARSHALL, Sharon Joanne; MARSHALL, Shelley; MARSHALL, Sherrill Jean;
MARSHALL, Wilma Margaret; MARSLAND, Margaret Elizabeth; MARSTIO, Tuija;
MARTA, Daniel Robert; MARTEL, Jessie Louise; MARTELL, Kenneth Delano;
MARTELL, Maureen Dolores; MARTELL, Robert Clyde; MARTELLS, Blossom; MARTENS, Sid;
MARTIN, Barbara Ann; MARTIN, Bryan W.; MARTIN, Cindy Lee; MARTIN, Cornelia;
MARTIN, Denise Iva; MARTIN Denise Marie; MARTIN, Eric roland; MARTIN, Fran;
MARTIN, H. Milton; MARTIN, J. Jeanette; MARTIN, Jacqueline Ann; MARTIN John Bain;
MARTIN, John Robert; MARTIN, Lea; MARTIN, Lisa Cheryl; MARTIN, Lois Naomi;
MARTIN, Margaret Susan; MARTIN, Mary Jayne; MARTIN, Michael Alexander;
MARTIN, Michael Peter; MARTIN, Mona; MARTIN: Paula Kathleen; MARTIN, Richard L.;
MARTIN, Ronald Steve; MARTIN Sandra Alison; MARTIN, Sharon L.; MARTIN, Susan Elizabeth;
MARTIN, Trudy Lynn; MARTIN, Vivienne Geraldine; MARTIN, Wendy Patricia; MARTYN, John;
MARTYNUIK, Charlotte Ann; MARTZ, Sheryl A.; MARUSIN, Wendy Diane; MARUSYK, Paula M.;
MARVIN, David Edward; MARVIN, Donna Margaret; MARVIN, Jau-Ruey Lynne;
MARVIN, Linda Marie; MARVIN, Tara; MARVIN, William Robert; MARXHEIMER, Sue;
MARXHEIMER, Suzette; MAXCIUCH, Irene; MASCIUCH, Leo R.D.; MASER, Kim Kerry;
MASH, Patricia Lynn; MASHINTER, Laura-Dawn; MASKELL, Donald; MASKELL, Frances Mary;
MASLIC, Nadina; MASON, Anthony Roberts; MASON, Brian Withers; MASON, Daniel Stewart;
MASON, Doug Fredrick; MASON, Sandra Laura; MASON, Shawna Lea; MASSNER, Shirley Marlene;
MASSON, Brenda Lee; MASSON, Jane; MASSON John; MAST, Denise Marie-Anne;
MASTERSON, Bernie; MASTERSON, Patricia Ann; MASTRONARDI, Annette;
MASTRONARDI, Silvana; MATACHE, Vasile C.; MATEJICEK, Leona Anna; MATHER, D. Iris;
MATHER, Dick J.W.; MATHER, Joan; MATHER, Spencer John David; MATHER, Weslyn Melva;
MATHES, Ruth I.; MATHESON, Alan Bruce; MATHESON, Danald Kenneth;
MATHESON, Dr. Gordon Omar; MATHESON, James Parker; MATHESON, N. Philip;
MATHESON, Nancy Margaret; MATHEWSON, Bruce W.; MATHEWSON, William Wallace;
MATHIESON, Margaret Jean; MATHIEU, Jennifer Joanne; MATIASZOW, Peter John;
MATILAINEN, Peter; MATISHAK, Andrea Marie; MATLOCK, Ken John; MATOSEVIC, Ana;
MAOVINOVIC, Anna; MATSON, Donna Joan; MATSUBA, Eiko; MATSUBA, Greg Alan;
MATTHEW, Tina; MATTHEWS, Debora Candace; MATTHEWS, Rodney Robert; MATTIA, Vince Andre;
MATTIELLO, Louise Maria; MATTISON, Ronald Ralph; MATTISON, Ronald Thomas; MATTON, Lea;
MATTSON, Daisy Mae; MATWICHUK, Emily Mary; MATWIE, Betty M.; MAURER, Alfred Bert;
MAWHINNEY, Diane Lynn; MAXIMO, Espiritu; MAXNER-MACKENZIE, Susan L.; MAXWELL, Hugh;
MAXWELL, Theresa Helen; MAY, Carole Patricia; MAY, Karen Jo-Ann; MAY, Marianne Elizabeth;
MAYBANK, Pat; MAYBEE, Mary-Ellen Noverre; MAYBEE, Patrick Harrison; MAYER, Beate Anita;
MAYER, Max; MAYFIELD, Marian Elaine; MAYHEW, Dennis S.; MAYHEW, Joan Suzanne;
MAYKO, Bill; MAYNER, Dean Paul; MAYSKY, Sylvia; MAZAR, Barbara Lynn; MAZE, Larry Fredrick;
MAZEPPA, Daniel; MAZEPPA, Mavis E.; MAZER, Candice Lou; MAZUR, John;
MAZUREK, Cathleen Anne; MAZUREK, Martin Anthony; MAZUREK, Pauline Mary;
MCADAM, Arthur P.; MCADIE, Richare; MCAFEE, Heather Anne; MCAFFER, Patrick;
MCAFFER, Verda; MCALEAR, Beverly A.; MCALEAR, Cathy L.; MCANNALY, Frances D.;
MCANDLESS, William Scott; MCANULTY, Dorothy Valerie; MCARA, Janiec;
MACARA, Winnifred Grace; MCARTHUR, Duncan R.B.; MCARTHUR, Duncan Robert Baly;
MCARTHUR, Jerelyn Carol; MCARTHUR, Peter G.; MCATEER, David Anthony; MCATEER, Patty Helen;
MCATEER, Peggy Anne; MCAULEY, Gloria Lynn; MCAULLY, Sarah Anne; MCAVOY, Doug;
MCAVOY, Marily Ann; MCBAIN, A. Ross; MCBAIN, Donna Lee; MCBAIN, Joan; MCBAIN, R.W. Allen;
MCBAIN, Susan Jean; MCBEAN, Karen Gail; MCBLAIN, Elizabeth; MCBRIDE, Elizabeth;
MCBRIDE, William Robert; MCBURNEY, Monica Dorothy; MCCABE, Judy Anne;
MCCAFFREY, Janice Leslie; MCCAFFREY, Mark Raymond; MCCAFFREY, William Joseph;
MCCAGHERTY, Judy; MCCALL, Dr. John Gerald; MCCALLA, Jane Muriel; MCCALLA, Peter Douglas;
MCCALLISTER, D.W.; MCCALLUM, Colleen; MCCALLUM, Donald George; MCCALLUM, Myles Corey;
MCCALLUM Norma Elizabeth; MCCAMMON, Carol Duicie; MCCANN, Mitchell Gregory;
MCCANN, Paul; MCCANN, Sharon Elaine; mccann, Shauna louise; MCCARTHEY, Devid William;
MCCARTHY, Jeff Edward; MCCARTHY, John Michael; MCCARTHY Margo Helen;
MCCARTHY, Maura Kathleen; MCCARTHY, Pam Beverley; MACCARTNEY, Barbara Lynn;
MCCARTNEY, Bernice Jean; MCCARTY, Maureen Grace; MCCAUGHEY, GERALD Sheldon;
MCCAUGHNEY, Rosemary C.; MCCAUGHNEY, Sean; MCCAULEY, Dr. Graeme D.;
MCCAULEY, Patricia Lynn; MCCLARTY, Darren W.; MCCLARTY, Hazel G.; MCCLEAN, Bonnie Corrine;
MCCLEARY, Christine; MCCLEARY, John E.; MCCLEARY, Katherine Patricia;
MCCLEARY, Philip Andrew; MCCLELLAND, Ian Grant; MCCLOSKEY, Helen Mary Louise;
MCCLOY, Lisa Michelle; MCCLUNG, Suzanne Mary; MCCLURE, Doris; MCCLURE, Jane;
MCCLUER, Margaret Jane; MCCLURE, Rae; MCCLYMONT, Ethel Doreen; MCCOMBIE, Dolly Lee;
MCCONNELL, Dianne W.; MCCONNELL, Douglas John; MCCONNELL, Edward Walter;
MCCONNELL, Gail Ann; MCCONNELL, Gordon Gibson; MCCONNELL, Roy J.; MCCONNELL, T. Mark;
MCCOOEYE, Shauna Leigh; MCCOOL, James Francis Patrick; MCCORMACK, Joyce;
MCCORMACK, Sherri Dianne; MCCORMICK, D.A. Rebecca; MCCORMICK, Dale Allan;
MCCORMICK, Rita Corinne; MCCORMICK, Sharon Hope; MCCORMICK, Stuart; MCCORRISTER, Bruce;
MCCORRISTER, Gail Charlene; MCCOY, Diane J.; MCCOY, Kathleen; MCCRACKEN, Anne;
MCCRACKEN, Gerald; MCCRACKEN, Jack; MCCREATH, Margrit S.; MCCREATH, Margrit Susanne;
MCCREATH, R. Scott; MCCROY, Sharleen Bridget; MCCUAIG, Dorothy Grace;
MCCUAIG, John Clifford; MCCUBBING, Margaret Elizabeth; MCCUE, Garry James;
MCCULLOGH, Lorraine Joan; MCCULLOCH, Margaret-Anne; MCCULLOCH, Tom;
MCCULLOUGH, Brian Douglas; MCCULLY, Robert Allan; MCCULLY, Rosemary Lee;
MCCUMBER, Svellen Mary; MCCUNE, William; MCCURDY, Don Valyere; MCCURDY, Kathleen Grace;
MCCURDY, Robert Dean; MCCUSKER, David Bruce; MCCUTCHEON, Debra Joy;
MCCUTCHEON, Wayne Scott; MCDANIEL, Linda Marie; MCDERMID, Danny, Lloyd;
MCDERMOTT, Patrick; MCDONALD-ADAM, Janette; MCDONALD, Brian John;
MCDONALD, Catherine Marie; MCDONALD, David R.; MCDONALD, Dorothy;
MCDONALD, Dr. Norman Angus; MCDONALD, Eileen; MCDONALD Gerald Paul;
MCDONALD, Heather Joan; MCDONALD, Heather Lynne; MCDONALD, Julie A.;
MCDONALD, Kathleen W.; MCDONALD, Kahtleen W.; MCDONALD, Margaret C.;
MCDONALD, Margaret Eileen; MCDONALD, Mary Penelope; MCDONALD, Nancy Claire;
MCDONALD, Penny; MCDONALD, Sandra Jane; MCDONALD, Sharon Gay; MCDONALD, Sheila;
MCDONALD, Sylvia; MCDONALD, William; MCDONNELL, Karen Rae; MCKONOUGH, Betty Verneta;
MCDONOUGH, James Edward; MCDONOUGH, Mary; MCDOUGALL, Deena Joelle;
MCDOWELL, K. Patricia; MCDOWELL, Robert Jospeh; MCDOWELL, Vickie Lynn;
MCEACHERN, Alexander Duncan; MCELGUNN, Dr. Dennis M.; MCELWAIN, Lester C.;
MCEWEN, Bonnie May; MCEWEN, Lilian; MCFADDEN, Nancy; MCFADDEN, Pamela Jane;
MCFALL, Patricia; MCFALL, Tom Earl; MCFALLON, Andrew Greig; MCFARLAND, Kathleen Monica;
MCFARLAND, Lynn Margaret; MCFARLANE, Debbie Anne; MCFARLANE, Irene;
MCFARLANE, Suzanne Faye; MCGARRY, Caroline; MCGARVEY, Anne; MCGARVEY, William John;
MCGAW, Kenneth John; MCGEACHY, David Alan; MCGEACHY, Leanne Carol;
MCGEACHY, Patricia Jean; MCGEE, John Ernest; MCGHEE, Heather; MCGILLIS, James Kenneth;
MCGILLIVRAY, Daniel Robert; MCGILLIVRAY, Susan Martha; MCGINN, Heather Maureen;
MCGINNIS, Irvin Dwain; MCGINNIS, Jacqueline Louise; MCGINNIS, James Francis;
MCGINNIS, Linda Gail; MCGOVERN, Donnamarie; MCGOVERN, Mary Therese;
MCGOWAN, William Robert; MCGREGOR, Robert; MCGREGOR, Robert Duncan;
MCGUINNESS, Sean Snthony; MCGUIRE, Patrick; MCGUIRE, Sharon Monica; MCGUIRE, Tom;
MCGUIRE Yvonne Mary; MCGURK, Margaret Anne; MCGALE, Mia; MCHARDY, Carole Ann;
MCHARG, Shauna Lynn; MCIIHARGEY, Patricia Marne; MCIIVEEN, Gerald Brian; MCIIVEEN, Ken G.P.;
MCIIWAIN, Joyce Marie; MCIIWAINE, Stephen Edward; MCINALL, Margaret Ann;
MCINERNEY, Elvira; MCINERNEY, Georgeann Maureen; MCINNES, Tammy Lyn;
MCINNIS Jayne Leola; MCINROY, Lesley Ann; MCINTOSH, Anne; MCINTOSH, Diane;
MCINTOSH, Dr. Donald M.; MCINTOSH, George HI; MCINTOSH, maureen Margaret;
MCINTOSH, Valerie Pamela; MCINTYRE, Diane C.; MCINTYRE, Donna Ann;
MCINTYRE, Helen Marjorie; MCINTYRE, John Patrick; MCINTYRE, Karen Anne; MCINTYRE, Ken N.;
MCISAAC, Colin Francis; MCISAAC, Patricial Marie; MCKAGUE, Elwood Lawson;
MCKAGUE, Ruby Kathleen; MCKAY, Belinda Isabel; MCKAY, Cathy Anne; MCKAY, Corinne Margaret;
MCKAY, Davie; MCKAY, Mavis Margaret Louise; MCKAY, Peggy Mae; MCKEE, Brent Arnold;
MCKEE, Heather Joan; MCKEE, Irvine Wm; MCKEE Robert Bruce; MCKEE, Ronald Clinton Emerson;
MCKEEN, Edith Elizabeth: MCKEEN, Roberta Ann; MCKELLAR, Douglas; MCKELLAR, Laurel;
MCKELLAR, Loreen; MCKENDRY, Kevin John; MCKENDRY, Thomas; MCKENNA, Paul Martin Joseph;
MCKENZIE, Dr. Alvin H.; MCKENZIE, Edward William; MCKENZIE, John Alexander;
MCKENZIE, Margaret Valerie; MCKENZIE, Patricia Anne; MCKENZIE, Shirley;
MCKENZIE, Susan Joan; MCKERNAN, Barbara J.; MCKERNAN, Tamara Dawn;
MCKERRALL, Scott Doug; MCKIGNEY, Randy William; MCKIM, Bruce Peter; MCKIM, Harry Robert;
MCKINLEY, Dan; MCKINNEY, Sheila Rose; MCKINNON, Graham Hugh;
MCKINNON, Margaret Sydney; MCKINNON, Sara Ann; MCKNIGHT, Jean R.; MCLACHLAN, Brian M.;
MCLACHLIN, Aletha Margaret; MCLACHLIN, Douglas Edward; MCLACHLIN, Dr. Herb;
MCLAREN, Brenda Ann; MCLAREN, Christine R. MCLAREN, Florence Heather;
MCLAREN, Josephine Ann; MCLAREN, June Violet; MCLAREN, Laura Jane; MCLAREN, Linda S.;
MCLAREN, Shirley May; MCLAUCHLAN, Alix Catherine; MCLAUCHLIN, Barbara Joan Meale;
MCLAUCHLIN, Jodie Kim; MCLAUGHLEN, E. Allan; MCLAUGHLIN, Fawn Victoria;
MCLAUGHLIN, Jodie Kim; MCLAUGHLIN, Ken; MCLAUGHLIN, Pauline Mary; MCLEAN, Cheryl;
MCLEAN, Judith; MCLEAN, Linda Marie; MCLEAN, Marie Anne; MCLEAN, Roberta Dawn;
MCLELLAN, Claudia; MCLELLAN, Jacqueline; MCLENNAN, John Duncan; MCLENNAN, Laura Marie;
MCLENNAN, Mary MCLENNAN, Rose F.; MCLEOD, Elizabeth Anne; MCLEOD, Gordon George;
MCLEOD, Harry D.; MCLEOD, Karen Jeanne; MCLEOD, Lorne Douglas; MCLEOD, Patricia E.;
MCLEOD, Ronald Norman; MCLEOD, Shila Marie; MCLUHAN, Betty; MCMAHON, Janelle Susan;
MCMAHON, Neil James Hastings; MCMAHON, Roderick William; MCMANN, Neil D.,
MCMANUS, Beryl Eileen; MCMANUS, Maureen Elizabeth; MCMANUS, Sandra Jane;
MCMARTIN, Eleanor; MCMATH, Anne Douglas; MCMILLAN, A.G.; MCMILLAN, Adelaide Elaine;
MCMILLAN, Barbara Jean; MCMILLAN, Barbara Joan; MCMILLAN, Bonnie L.; MCMILLAN, Carol T.;
MCMILLAN, Connie Lynn; MCMILLAN, Dr. Jim F.; MCMILLAN, Grace; MCMILLAN, Joanne Elaine;
MCMILLAN, Robert; MCMILLAN, Trish M.; MCMAW, Les Lloyd; MCMULLIN, Tamaris Marilynne;
MCMURDO, Leslie Carol; MCMURDO, Trudy Heather; MCMURPHY, margaret; MCMURPHY, Pauline;
MCMURRAY, Donna Lynne; MCMURRAY, Wendy Jean; MCNAB, Christine Lynne;
MCNAB, Gladys Carol; MCNABB, Wyatt; MCNALLY, Robert; MCNAMARA, Daniel Peter;
MCNAMARA, Francis G.: MCNAMARA, Jim Arthur; MCNEELY, Janet Lynn; MCNEIL, Sharon Marlene;
MCNEIL, Wilfred John David; MCNEILL, B. Yardley; MCNEILL, Barb Ellen; MCNEILL, Beryl;
MCNEILL, Gordon Henry; MCNEILL, Karen; MCNEILL, Vicki Jane; MCNISH, Brian William;
MCNISH, Valerie Margaret; MCNULTY, Kathleen Thresa; MCPHAIL, Cheryl Lynne;
MCPHAIL, Daneda Marjorie; MCPHEE, Edward A.; MCPHEE, Edward Brent; MCPHEE, Kent Andrew;
MCPHEE, Melville Anthony; MCPHERSON, Carol Rhona; MCPHERSON, Don Scot;
MCPHERSON, Donna; MCPHERSON, Gary William W.; MCPHERSON, Randal Terry;
MCPHERSON, Robert Scott; MCPHERSON, Roby Francais John; MCQUARRIE, Jill Alison;
MCQUARRIE, Stephen Andrew; MCQUEEN, Dr. J. Craig; MCQUILLEN, Jill; MCRAE, Ann Elizabeth;
MCSHANE, Donna Joan; MCTAVISH, Allan Douglas; MCTAVISH, Barbara Louise;
MCTAVISH, Donald Robert; MCTAVISH, June Helen; MCTAVISH, Karen; MCTAVISH, Karen Lynn;
MCVEAN, Donald Christopher; MCVEIGH, Jeffery James; MCVEIGH, L. Isabel; MCVEIGH, Laurel;
MCVITTIE, Reginald Joseph F.; MCWHORTER, Joan; MEAD, Alette Catherina; MEADOWS, Ken Neil;
MEADOWS, Neil C.; MEAGHER, Mary; MEARNS, Lenore Jeanette; MECELE, Pam Marie;
MEDDINGS, Karen; MEDLAND, M. Noreen; MEDYNSKI, Sheri Lynn; MEEK, Ross Lee;
MEEKISON, Robert; MEERLOO, Ashely Ian; MEEWISSEN, Adri Johan; MEHERIUK, Teresa Roseann;
MEHTA, Fred B.; MEHTA, Mona Mahendro; MEHTA, Nirmal; MEIERHOFER, Karen Marie;
MEIGHAN, Helen Elaine; MEIKLE, Bruce A.; MEIKLE, Janet A.; MEIKLE, Janet Anne;
MEIKLEJOHN, Andrea Joy; MEIKLEJOHN, Dorothy G.; MEILICKE, Jackie Elizabeth;
MEILICKE, Michelle Ann; MEILLEUR, Jean Claude; MEIR, Avi Yoav;
MEIR, Gili MEJICANOS, Gasser Solina; MEKKINOSSON, Johann; MELAMED, Assir; MELAX, Stanley;
MELDRUM, Arlene Elizabeth; MELE, Francesco; MELECH, Bradley David; MELECH, Victor;
MELENCHUK, Dalton Joseph; MELENKA, George; MELENKA, Rosalie; MELESKIE, Mike;
MELIK, Susan; MELIN, Randy Philip; MELIN, Ronda kae; MELIN, Trevor John;
MELLAN, Jacqueline Mary; MELLON, Mary Winifred; MELLORS, Varerie Anne;
MELMOCK, Peggy Joyce; MELMOCK, Peggy Margaret; MELNYCHUK, Kenneth Stephan;
MELNYCHUK, Linda; MELNYCHUK, Ralph Mitchell; MELNYK, Al; MELNYK, Alex Gary;
MELNYK, Elizabeth Anne; MELNYK, Kaulin; MELNYK, Marie; MELNYK, Patricia Gwen;
MELNYK, Susanne Nadia; MELNYK, Vivian; MELOCHE, J. Pierre; MELTON, Cheryl Lynn;
MELTON, Mary-Beth; MELTON, Timothy Charles; MELVILLE, Kenneth George;
MELVIN, Richard James; MENDES, Larry; MENDES, Vivian Bernice; MENSINK, Naomi Margaret;
MERAW, Deborah; MERAW, Douglas Eugene; MERAW, Kelly Lynne; MERCADO, Edwin;
MERCER, Donna Maryann; MERCHANT, Bernard John; MERCIER, David George;
MEREDITH, Carol Lorraine; MERENIUK, Terry; MERGAERT, Cindy Ann; MERGI, Peter;
MERKLER, Barbara; MERKOSKY, Karen; MERLE, Agnes Vanaistyne; MERMELSHTAIN, Ernest;
MERMELSHTAIN, Raya; MERONYK, George; MERONYK, Henry Joseph; MERRETT, Janet;
MERRICK, Dianne Lynne; MERRIFIELD, Peggy; MERRILLS, Daniel Thomas; MERRISON, Willard Curtis;
MERRITT, Beverley Margaret; MERRITT, Elaine Annette; MERRITT, Jerry Louis; MERRIT, Leigh Ann;
MERRITT, Roy W.; MERTENS, Patricia Katharina; MERTH, Erin Isabel; MESS, Janet Shedden;

MESS, Norman Anderson; MESSIER, Theresa Anne; MESSMER, Joe; MESSUM, Lucie Mary;
MESTER, Fran; MESTER Louis Thomas; MESTON, Debbie Lynn; METCALF, Deborah Ann;
METCALFE, Brenda; METCALFE, Nancy Dianne; METERS, Leanne Marie; METHVEN, Jeannie;
METSELOAR, Angela; MEYER, Ann M.; MEYER, Brigitte; MEYER, Denis; MEYER, Jim M.;
MEYER, Wilfried; MICHAEL, Karlynne J.; MICHAEL, Phillip; MICHAEL, Samantha E.;
MICHAEL Violet Geraldine; MICHALES, Craig Richard; MICHAELS, Frank; MICHAELS, Jean Imelda;
MICHAL, Donna M.; MICHAUD, Lucie; MICHAUD, Renee Laure; MICHEL, Nathalie Hugette;
MICHELL, Dorothy Jane; MICHELL, Robert Douglas; MICIAK, Cheryl May; MICIAK, Kathleen Ann;
MICIAK, Quentin Joseph; MICKELSON, Aileen H.; MICKELSON, Margaret; MICKO, Margaret;
MICKO, Michael; MICKO, Michelle; MIDBO, Sandy; MIDDELTON, Doreen Evelyn; MIDEGS, Viola;
MIDGLEY, Hazel; MIDGLEY, Paul; MIEDZINSKI, Lilly J.; MIGADEL, Linda louise;
MIGHALI, Ugo Salvatore; MIHLI, Violet I.; Mikulic, Voya; MILANOVICH, Elizabeth;
MILANOVICH, Steve; MILDENBERGER, Douglas R.; MILDER, Susan; MILES, Ann Laverne;
MILES, Daniel Douglas; MILES, Murray Paul B.; MILES, S. Kathleen; MILL, Leanne Helen;
MILLAR, Brenda Jeanne; MILLAR, Don; MILLAR, Donald E.; MILLAR, Jenny Jean; MILLAR, Judy I.;
MILLAR, Kelly Rae; MILLAR, Melinda; MILLAR, Nancy; MILLAR, Robert W.; MILLARD, Beth L.;
MILLARD, James Glenn; MILLAS, Margaret C.; MILLER, Arliss June; MILLER, Arthur Roger;
MILLER, Barbara; MILLER, Bruce William; MILLER, Catherine Dawn; MILLER, David James;
MILLER, Debbie; MILLER, Donald O.; MILLER, Dori; MILLER, Dr. Elizabeth Weir;
MILLER, Dr. Jack David; MILLER, Eileen Denise; MILLER, Elaine Louise; MILLER, Elizabeth Joyce;
MILLER, Errol; MILLER Gerda; MILLER, Gordon Matthew; MILLER, Holly; MILLER, Irving;
MILLER, Isabel; MILLER, James; MILLER, James Leigh; MILLER Joan Anne; MILLER, Jon;
MILLER, Leigh Paul James; MILLER, Marvin; MILLER, Mary; MILLER, Matthew Charles;
MILLER, Maureen Louise; MILLER, Michelle L.; MILLER, Myrtle Kathleen; MILLER, Peter John;
MILLER, Robert Gordon; MILLER, Robert John; MILLER, Rosalie Marion; MILLER, Tevie Harold;
MILLER, William John; MILLERS, Iness; MILLIGAN, Brian Craig; MILLIGAN, John Alexander;
MILLIGAN, Nikoi; MILLIGAN, Verna Bernice; MILLIGAN, William Alenander; MILLS, Audrey G.;
MILLS, Deborah; MILLS, Harry N.; MILLS, Iris Grace; MILLS, John; MILLS, Lisa Maren;
MILLS, Richard John; MILNE, Bruce Hunter; MILNE, Carolyn Elizabeth; MILNE, Donald Rae;
MILNE, Heather; MILNE, Lillian; MILNE, Patrick Dennis; MILNE, Peggy; MILNE, Phil;
MILNE, Shauna Leanne; MILNE, Tracy Margaret; MILNER, Theodore Edgar; MILOBAR, Theresa Mary;
MILROY, William P.; MILTON, Dwight Charles; MILTON, Judy Alma; MILTON, Rick Ronald;
MIN, Hyung Keun; MINAKER Anne Marie; MINDLIN, Joan; MINDLIN, Stan; MINER, Alexis Jane;
MINER, B.A. Brand; MINER, Fay Marie; MINER, Jill Jeanette; MINERVINI, Virginia; MIGZHANG, Sui;
MINIACI, Dominick; MINIACI, Valerie Hope; MINNIKIN, Tracey Wadsworth;
MINSOS, Jennifer Rebecca; MINTO, Judith may; MINTO, Richard Walter; MIREAULT, Joseph Robert;
MIRTH, Diane Mary; MIRZA, Najeb; MIS, Christopher G.; MISCHUK, Jennie; MISKI, Beverly G.;
MISKIW, Debbie; MISKO, Dr. Glen Joseph; MISKO, Marianne; MISKULIN, Mary H.;
MISTAL, Clarence Joseph; MISTRY, Balvant Dajibhai; MITCHELL, A. Jenell; MITCHELL, Bob;
MITCHELL, Brenda; MITCHELL, Donna Louise; MITCHELL, Conna Mae; MITCHELL, Douglas Bruce;
MITCHELL, Dr. Marvin; MITCHELL, Jill; MITCHELL, John Bowser; MITCHELL, Kenneth;
MITCHELL, Kristie; MITCHELL Margaret Mary; MITCHELL, Marion M. MITCHELL, Melanie;
MITCHELL, Michael John; MITCHELL, Nancy Lynn; MITCHELL, Renel Denise; MITCHELL, Robert John;
MITCHELL, Ross A.; MITCHELL, Russell Gordon; MITCHELL, Shauna Lee; MITCHELL, Tammy Louise;
MITCHELL, Thelma Gwendolyn; MITCHELL, Warren Dale; MITCHELL, Wayne Michael;
MITCHELL, Wendy Lee; MITTELSTADT, Charlotte E.; MIX, Lawrence Kendall Wayne;
MIX, Lawrence Wayne; MIYAGISHIMA, Joy Louise; MICUCH, Bronislava; MLINARIC, Margita;
MLYNARCZYK, Joan Helen; MOAD, Patricia Marguerite; MOAN, Cindy; MODIN, Kelly Jo;
MODIN, Shelley Rae; MOE, Loyal Oliver; MOELIGOU, Martine Le; MOEN, Lynda J.;
MOEN, Lynda June; MOEN, Wayne James; MOEN, Wendy Marie; MOERTH, Sylvia;
MOFFAT, Mary Ann; MOFFATT, Evaughn Mary; MOFFATT, Janice Elaine; MOFFATT, Russell Patrick;
MOFFITT, David Graham; MOHAMED, Yassin Farah; MOHAMEDBHAI, Bashir; MOHAMMED, Rhoda;
MOHLER, Janice Lynn; MOHR, Eldeen Gayle; MOHS, Judy Marie; MOISAN, Marcel Henry;
MOISAN, Miriam Lise; MOIELLA, Nick; MOLESWORTH, Katherine Patricia; MOLINA, Jaime H.;
MOLINARI, Mario; MOLLOT, Claude Guy; MALLOY, Carmen Charlotte;
MOLNAR, Constance Maureen T.; MOLNAR, Robert John; MOLSTAD, Janie; MOLSTAD, Tara;
MONAGHAN, Eileen Karen; MONCK, Barbara Nevada; MONCK, Jesse Adam;
MONCK, Vincent Walker; MONCRIEFF, Hugh G.; MONCRIEFF, Paula Mary; MONDOR, Albert Jacques;
MANNINGTON-PRYCE, Frances; MONROE, Diane; MONSMA, Gayle J.; MONSON, Gayle Louise;
MONTFORD, Gordon Hugh; MONTGOMERY, Donna Jane; MONTGOMERY, Donna Lynn;
MONTGOMERY, Edward; MONTGOMERY, Lorraine; MONTGOMERY, Peggy;
MONTPETIT, Marcel Herve; MOON, Barry; MOONEY, Richard James; MOONEY, William Patrick;
MOONIE, Doris; MOONIE, Janet Louise; MOORE, Aileen Ruth; MORRE, Deborah Ann; MOORE, Denis;
MOORE, Diane Louise; MOORE, James Russell; MOORE, Janice Louise; MOORE, Katharine Elizabeth;
MOORE Kenneth Gordon; MOORE, Laurie Marion; MOORE, Loretta Kay; MOORE, Robert Edward;
MOORE, Ron William; MOORE, Sandra; MOORE, Waivo Gay; MOORHOUSE, Jermy;
MOORS, Janet Josephine; MOORS, Josephine Bernice; MORALES, Pedro J.;
MORDEN, Margaret Fairley; MORE, Robert Brian; MOREAU, Dr. Paul G.; MOREAU, Marc Joseph;
MORELL, Tatiana Silvia; MORENO, Luis Carlso; MORGAN, Angela; MORGAN, Barbara Joanne;
MORGAN, Mary; MORGAN, Melanie Jane; MORGAN, Michael Glyn; MORGAN, Robert Charles;
MORGAN, William John; MORGULIS, Anton Anatolevich; MORGULIS, Victor Analtolevich;
MORI, Harold; MORIARITY, Casey Kim; MORIC, Patrick Mathew; MORIE, Jeffery Marshall;
MORIN, Holly Ann; MORIN, Louis Charles; MORIN, Marguerite; MORIN, Marie B.A.; MORIN, Mark;
MORIN, Marlene Jacqueline; MORIN, Rhonda Kelly; MORIN, Susan Elizabeth;
MORISSETTE, Henri Andre; MORISSETTE, Odette Noella; MORISSETTE, Rosanne Lynne;
MARITZ, Kathryn Lynn; MARITZ, Lloyd Wayne Edward; MORLEY, Brian James;
MORLEY, Devin Charels; MOROKHOVICH, Mikhail; MOROZ, Irene; MOROZ, Terry Roman;
MORRICE, Helen P.; MORIS, Camille B.; MORRIS, Christine Elizabeth; MORRIS, Ellen;
MORRIS, Ellen M.; MORRIS, F. Alvin; MORRIS, Kelly Edward; MORRIS, Kevin Lee;
MORRIS, Linda Gay; MORRIS, Lorie; MORRIS, Reginald Clifford; MORRIS, Ronald B.; MORRIS, Sue-Ann; MORRISON, Donald; MORRISON, Donald J.; MORRISON, Elizabeth Ann;
MORRISON, Jennifer Lynn; MORRISON, Kathryn Grace; MORRISON, Sheila Jean Mary;
MORRISON, Valerie Anne; MORRISSEY, Clifford; MORRISSEY, Teri Lee;
MORROW, Christopher Ronald; MORROW, Dianne Lynn; MORROW, John Martin; MORSE, Eric Steen;
MORSE, James Norman; MORSE, Nancy Lynn; MORSON, Donald Maurice; MORSTAD, Cal;
MORSTAD, Dawn Michelle; MORSTAD, Marion Verna; MORSTAD, Todd Merrill; MORTEMORE, Jim;
MORTER, M. Jean; MORTIMER, Michael Anthony; MORTIMER, Ruth Allison; MORTON, Neil M.;
MOSCARDELLI, Gino; MOSCATELLI, Yvon; MOSELE, Robert; MOSES, Rick; MOSHER, Merv;
MOSKALYK, Jerry; MOSS, Armano J.; MOSS, Bradley David; MOSS, Donna Lee; MOSS Dr. Martie G.;
MOSS Leslie; MOSS Leslie Roger; MOSS, Valerie Ann; MOSTOWICH, Sandra Faye;
MOTKOSKI, Lyn Ann; MOTTRAM, Branda June; MOUNFFORD, Michael William; MOUNZER, Stan;
MOUSSEAU, Malcolm Richard; MOWAT, Robert Allen; MOWAT, Thomas Fredreck; MOXLEY, Tim Ian;
MOYER, Janice Lynn; MOYLES, R. Gordon; MOYLES, Robert Gordon; MOZAFARI, V. Michele;
MOZAK, Marie; MOZILE, Fannie; MRAZEK, Margaret; MRKONJIC, Frank; MRKONJIC, Linda Antonija;
MRKONJIC, Mary; MUCCIARONE, Tony Doug; MUCHA, Barbara; MUCHA, Mary;
MUDALIER, Ram Krishna; MUDIE, Corinne Louise; MUELLER, Joan W. MUELLER, Rita Alys;
MUENCH, Sandra Carol; MUERTH, Karin Helen; MUHLBIER, Cindy; MULLAN, Jacqueline Lioy;
MULLEN, Adrienne Marie; MULLEN, Bill Michael MULLEN, Donna Marie; MULLEN, Kathleen Anne;
MULLEN, Morraine; MULLEN, Robert Donald; MULLER, Arlene Aliseman; MULLER, Beryl Merle;
MULLER, Ellen Joy; MULLER, James Richard; MULLER, Peter; MULLIGAN, David Michael;
MULLIGAN, Linda Marie; MULLINS, Barry Alexander; MULLINS, Harold Noel; MULOIN, Dana Scott;
MULYK, Andrea Rose; MUMBY, Verna; MUMERT, Martha Gwen; MUNAWICH, Bernard Alexander;
MUNDY, Brian Thomas; MUNDY, Diana Faye; MUNGALL, Joanne J.; MUNGALL, Robert Cameron;
MUNK, Margaret Elizabeth; MUNOZ, Angelica Viviana; MUNOZ, Christina; MUNRO, Aileen;
MUNRO, Albert G.; MUNRO, Alison Jill; MUNRO, Bengiman Arnold; MUNRO, Debbie Louise;
MUNRO, Douglas Ian; MUNRO, Enid Vivienne; MUNRO, Lori Lynn; MUNRO, Stanley; MUNROE, Carol;
MUNROE, Carol Ann: MUNSEY, James Fraser; MUNSTERMANN, Ernie; MURAKAMI, Allison Chiemi;
MURCH, Halia N.; MURCH, Marijo; MURCHIE, Donald Gordon; MURDOCK, Carolyn Ruth;
MURPHY, Barbara; MURPHY, Enid Martha; MURPHY, Joann Kristin; MURPHY, Joe; MURPHY, Joyce;
MURPHY, Pauline Theresa; MURPHY, Rita Marie; MURRAY, Bonnie May; MURRAY, Carol Gay;
MURRAY, Catherine; MURRAY, Charles Donald; MURRAY, Colin John; MURRAY, Dr. Allen Roger;
MURRAY, Eva; MURRAY, Irene B.; MURRAY, Jacqueline Elizabeth; MURRAY, James Michael Philip;
MURRAY Kathleen Lynn; MURRAY, Kathleen Marie; MURRAY Laura; MURRAY, Lori Jane;
MURRAY, Marion; MURRAY, Moreen Elizabeth; MURRAY, Pearl; MURTI, Reshma Bai;
MUSGRAVE, Sandra G.; MUSIC, Glen Edward; MUSSCHE, Franklin Henri; MUSTAPHA, Majeed;
MUSTARD, Fiona; MUSTARD, Joyce B.; MUSTARD, Marion Allison; MUSTO, Allan James;
MUSURICHAN, Leonard Paul; MUZICHUK, Nickolas; MVUNGI, Ignace Rajabu; MYASKOVSKY, Oleg;
MYERS, Lorinda Sue; MYERS, Violet; MYHR, Candace Jayne; MYRITYSCUN, Dale;
MYLES, Terry James; MYLOD, Jaina Ann; MYLYMAK, Pamela Marie; MYRDEN, Blair David;
MYRONIUK, Lynn Tracy; MYRONIUK, Sharon E.; MYRONIUK,Shirley M. MYSHCHYSHYN, Irena;
MYTRUK, Helen; MYTRUNEC, Christine Margaret;

N

NABOULSI, Hazem; NABOULSI, Nafez; NACHFIGALL, Dieter; NADON, Sandra;
NADRATOWSKI, Romvald; NAGY, Fay Loretta; NAHAYOWSKI, Arthur Lawrence;
NAHIRNIAK, Deborah Rose; NAHMMACHER, Jochen; NAHORNIAK, Carol Sandra;
NAHREBESKI, James Donald; NAIDOO, Hemla Devi; NAJIM, Ali Farman; NAKAMURA, Danny S.;
NAKAMURA, Emiko; NAKAMURA, George K.; NAKAMURA, Terumi Edward; NAKAONO, Yuka;
NAKHLA, Hoda; NAKONECZNY, Al Joseph; NANDA, Madhu Bala; NAROIN, Latchman;
NARGAL, Mohd Sadiq; NASH, Fredrick; NASH, John Franklin; NATHANAIL, Melina Maria;
NATRON, Steve; NATRON, Susan; NATSUYAMA, Kozuko; NAWAS, Nodima; NAY, Len W.;
NAYLOR, Anthea H.; NAZARAL, Adil Jafferali; NEAL, Dr. Carolyn Sarah; NEARY, Joyce A.;
NEATE, Anna; NEATE, Harold Maurice; NECHEFF, Olga; NEESER: Glen; NEGI, Jayanti;
NEIFER, Roy A.; NEIGEL, Ivy May; NEIGEL, John; NEIL, Barbara; NEIL, Barbara Joan;
NEIL, Daneil Robert; NEIL, R. Stewart; NEILL, Bonita; NEILL, Brian William; NEILL, John;
NEILSON, Frances Lorraine; NEILSON, John; NEILSON, John Douglas; NEILSON, Kim Stephanie;
NEIS, Nadine Zephie; NEITFCH, Feter; NELSEN, Margaret Cecile; NELSON, Arley;
NELSON, Carol Kay; NELSON, Claudine Brenda; NELSON, Daniel Robert; NELSON, Edna Beatrice;
NELSON, J. David; NELSON, Ken R.; NELSON, Kim Deanna; NELSON, Leslie W.;
NELSON, Patricia Ann; NELSON, Sheila Faye; NELSON, Stewart William; NELSON, Wendy Lynn;
NESDOLE, James Lionel; NESDOLE, Lorna Carolyn; NESS, Arnold Edward; NESS, Dr. Andrew;
NESSEL, Allan Eugene; NESSEL Donald Alfred; NESSEL, Sharon Arlene; NESTER, Phyllis Ann;
NETT, Arnold B.; NETT, Mary K.; NETTER, Brenda M.B.; NEUBAUER, Frank Allen; NEUFELD, Doug;
NEUFELD, Gayle Yvonne; NEUFELD,Herta; NEUFELD, Norma; NEUMAN, Carolyn Deanne;
NEUMAN, Darrel; NEUMAN, Sheryl; NEUMANN, Gesa; NEUMANN, Isabelle Irene;
NEUMANN, Jean; NEUMEYER, Arthur Lawrence; NEUSCHAEFER, Peter; NEVEU, Thomas Edward;
NEW, Ronald James; NEWBOLD, Freddy Arnold; NEWBOLD, Maxine Belva;
NEWCOMBE, Barry James; NEWCOMBE, Merry-Lee Ann; NEWEL, James Douglas;
NEWELL, Christine; NEWHOUSE, Charles Graham; NEWMAN, Anoush; NEWMAN, Barbara;
NEWMAN, Betty; NEWMAN, Brian; NEWMAN, David C.; NEWMAN, David Gordon;
NEWMAN, Heather Kim; NEWMAN, Kenny Diane; NEWMAN, Kerry Diane;
NEWMAN, Stanley K. NEWNHAM, P. Diane; NEWSOME, Marvin Lee; NEWTON, George Fredrick;
NEWTON, Joanne Ruth; NEWTON, Leslie Susan; NEWTON, Liz Marguerite; NG, Irene;
NG, Mary Toni; NG, Shana Shun; NG, Siu Mei Irene; NG, Tai Keung Bill; NGAI, Alberta;
NGAI, Helen Mee Lan; NGAN, Helen; NGATIA, Peter; NIAWCHUK, Pauline; NIAWCHUK, Ron;
NIBLETT, Jessie Alice; NICHOLAS, Brian J.; NICHOLL, Robert Gunn; NICHOLLS, Doug;
NICHOLLS, Ernest Alfred; NICHOLLS, Marie Ann; NICHOLS, Jennifer; NICHOLS, John Edward;
NICHOLSON, Ginny; NICHOLSON, Gregory Orland; NICHOLSON, Keith Lloyd; NICHOLSON, Rea Jane;
NICHOLSON, Ruth Iona; NICKERSON, Jack; NICKERSON, Richard;
NICKERSON, Trudy S. NICKOLCHUK, Larry Alvin; NICKOLCHUK, Maureen Patricia;
NICOL, Joy e. NICOLL, Christopher Robert; NICOLOSI, Milton; NIEGEL, Brenda Dawn;
NIEGEL, Mark Andrew; NIEISEN, Keith Ray; NIELSEN, Kristene Olive-Irean; NIELSON, Maggie Anne;
NIEMAN, Ellen: NIEMANN, Gerda Frieda; NIEMANTSVERDRIET, J.C.; NIGHTINGALE, Joan;
NIKICEVIC, Susan; NIKICEVIC, Maya; NIKIFORUK, Phyllis; NIKOLAI, Alfred;
NIKOLAI, Yvonne Margaret; NILES, Doreen Eleanor; NILSEN, Johanne; NISBET, Myrna Dale;
NISHIKAZE, Kimberly Louise; NISHIWAKI, Yoshihiro; NISHIZAKE, Catherine Atsumi;
NIVEN, David Cecil; NIXON, Donna Lynne; NNABUO, Peter Matthew; NOCENTE, Norma Mary;
MOCHOMOVITZ, Heather; NOCHOMOVITZ, Michael; NOEL, Carmen; NOEL, Georgina Marie;
NOEL, Kathy; NOEL, Peter A.; NOKLEBY, Dawn M.; NOLAN, Kerry Marie; NOLAN, Shauna Lee;
NOOITGEDAGT, William Anthony; NOON, Bud Roger; NOON, Elmer Eugene Donald;
NOONAN, Barbara Jean; NOPPERS, Fred; NORDSTROM, Janet Marie; NORDSTROM, Linda S.;
NORDSTROM Ronald James; NOREN, Elaine Rosalyn; NORLIN, A. Grant; NORMAN, Bev Ann;
NORMAN, Terrance James; NORMAND, John Albert; NORRIE, Karen B.; NORRIS, Celia G.;
NORTH, Joanne Lorene; NORTH, Pamela Lea; NORTH, William Joseph; NORTON, Glen Ernest;
NORTON, Trevor Dean; NORWOOD, David C. NORWOOD, Nancy Wynn; NOSELSKI, Peter;
NOTDORFT, Erwin; NOTDORFT, Gary; NOTT, Kathy Lorraine; NOVACK, Yvonne Marie;
NOVAK, Antonia; NOVODVORSKY, Lada Marie; NOVOSEL, Erica; NOVOSIWSKY, S. Joyce;
NOVOTNY, Rosmarie Eliesabeth; NOWAK, Larry Walter; NOWAK, Ryszard; NOWICKI, Harriet;
NOWICKI, Julian; NOWICKI, Theresa; NURSALL, Mary; NUTHACK, Judith Ray;
NUTTALL, Joanne Lesley; NUTTALL, Robert Stephen; NUTTER, Sandra; NUTTER, T. Suzanne;
NYBAKKEN, Ralph William; NYBERG, Janet Christine; NYCHOLAT, Alice; NYCHOLAT, Douglas-James;
NYCZ, Avaleen: NYENHUIS, Ronalda Edita; NYHUS Bernice; NYHUS, Glen Eldon; NYKOLYN, Linda;
NYKOLYN, Patricia T. NYLAND, Barbara; NYTCHAY, Barry;

O

OAKLEY, John Anthony Ronald; OATES, Candice Lee; OATWAY, Mavis; OATWAY, Rick;
OBACZ, Derek William; OBALL, Eloise; OBERFELD, Alexander A.; OBERFELD, Arkady;
OBERFELD, Sveteana; OBERIE, Elise Ann: OBERLE, Keith Ernest; OBLAK, Caroline Josephine;
O'BOYLE, Sharon Joan; OBREGON, Madeline; O'BRIEN, Desiree Angela; O'BRIEN, George;
O'BRIEN, Gilbert Bruce; O'BRIEN, Linda; O'BRIEN, Mark Gregory; O'BRIEN, Maureen P.;
O'BRIEN, Nancy Lynne; O'BRIEN, Ron F.; O'BRIEN, Sandy Jean; O'BRIEN, Sheila Ann; O'BRIEN, Tim;
OBST, Elisabeth; O'BYRNE, Dawn Melanie; O'BYRNE, Dean, Michael; O'BYRNE, Gillian Denise;

O'BYRNE, Jeanne Elizabeth; O'BYRNE, Kevin Thomas; O'CALLAHAN, Patricia; OCHOA, Carmen M.;
OCHOTTA, David; O'CONNELL, Mary Christine; O'CONNOR, Brian Peter;
O'CONNOR, Dr. Gregory John; O'CONNOR, Len M.; O'DOHERTY, Shawn Rodney;
O'DONNELL, Darren Ken; O'DONNELL, Dennis Anthony; O'DONNELL,Fiona;
O'DONNELL, Fiona Farquharson; O'DONNELL, Peter Stephen; O'DONNELL, Troy Kevin; ODURO, Enock;
O'DWYER, Eileen A.; O'DWYER, Peggy; ODYNSKI, Darlene G.; ODYNSKI, Troy; O'FARRELL, Dr. Terry;
O'FLANAGAN, John Joseph Mark; OGG, Anthony; OGILVIE, Heather Julia; OGILVIE, Jessie Adella;
OGILVIE, Mora Jeannine; OGINSKI, Clifford Edward; OGRODNICK, Chantal;
OGRODNICK, Charlene Grace; OGSTON, Anne Marie; OGSTON, Brian Jack; O'HARA, Marie;
OHASHI, Bonnie; OHAYON, Simon; OHKI, Takashi; OHKI, Yasushi; OHLHAUSER, Tory;
OHMAN, Dale; OHMENZETTER, Lori; OHERN Jocelyn; OHTA, Haruko Hirabe; OHUCHI, Tomiko;
OHUCHI, Toshio; OISHI, Rose Yureko; OKE, Cindy Lou; O'KEEFE, Kevin Michael;
O'KELLY, Sheila Patricia; OKO, Darren Stewart; OLANDRIA, Deogenes; OLASZ, Edith;
OLEARCZYK, Jerry Allen; O'LEARY, Caitlin Katherine; OLEITSCHUK, Rose Marie; OLEKSIW, Grace L.;
OLEKSMY, Val; OLEKSUIK, Jackie Marie; OLESKY, Brian Orest; OLESKY, Lynn Susan;
OLESKY, Orest Steve; OLEXIN, Donna Ann; OLGUIN, Roberto; OLGUIN, Susan Patricia;
OLIJNIK, Helen; OLIJNYK, Bohdan Volodymyr; OLINYK, Cheryl; OLIVER, Hugh; OLIVER, Jean Elaine;
OLIVER, Particia Ann; OLMSTEAD, Lyle Vernon; OLMSTEAD, Paula Charlene; OLNEY, Karen Michele;
OLSEN, G. Gane; OLSEN, Ivan; OLSEN, Kelly John; OLSEN, Miles Clarence; OLSEN, Wayne;
OLSEN, Wendy Myrene; OLSON, Allan Stuart; OLSON, Candy Kelly;
OLSON, Carol Ann OLSON, Colleen Joan; OLSON, Corrie; OLSON, Frances Ruth; OLSON, Heath;
OLSON, Judy Jean; OLSON, Mark Harrison; OLSON, Maria Dawn; OLSON, Michael Allan;
OLSON,Michael Francis; OLSON, Pauline Louise; OLSON, Tim Allan; OLSON, Trudy Lavern;
OLSON, Venus Antoinette; OLSON, Warren Todd; OLSSON, Sheila Mary; OMAN, John Charles;
OMELCHUK, Dr. Alex; OMNESS, Dianne Mauree; OMSTED, Cecilie; ONCIUL, Evelyn Kauss;
O'NEIL, Audrey Catherine; O'NEILL, Daniel C.; O'NEILL, Peggy Ann: ONG, Mui Chin Christina;
ONGARO, Alex Anthone; ONGARO, Anne Marie; ONGARO, Claudio; ONGARO, Rino; ONGARO, Rudy;
ONGMUILIN, Andelina; ONSKO, Boris R.; ONUFERKO, Irene Luba; ONUSHKO, Emily;
OORAIKUL, Buncha; OOSTERHUIS, Thomas Jacob; OPALINSKI, Jane Elizabeth;
OPAZO, Anabella Marjorie; OPAZO, Aurora Marisol; OPAZO, Jaime; OPAZO, Marcelo;
ORAM, Wynne Darlene; ORCHARD, Brent Hebert Eric; ORCHARD, Debra Anne; ORCHARD, Maureen;
ORCHARD, Phyllis Marion; ORCHESKI, Charlene Gail; ORCHIN, Jaime; ORCHIK, Marylyn Geneva;
OREILLY, Daniel timothy; ORKUSZ, Darlene; ORKUSZ, Darlene Renee; ORLANDO, Karen Anne;
ORLESKI, Georgina; ORR, Jennifer; ORR, Kenneth Gordon; ORR, Nony Jean; ORR, Shirley Elizabeth;
ORTLIEB, Orvill E.; OSADCHUK, Dick; OSADETZ, Carl; OSADETZ, Elsie; OSAKA, Joann Kazuko;
OSATCHUK, Karen Lee; OSBORN, Thelma Faye; OSBORNE, Charles James; OSBORNE, Daniel Jay;
OSBORNE, Greg Lee; OSBORNE, Karen Brenda; OSBORNE, T. Faye; OSELIES, Allan Hermann;
OSELIES, Vivian; O'SHEA, Darleen Lynne; O'SHEA, Jenny; O'SHEA, Joan Mary; O'SHEA, Vincent;
OSHRY, Felicia; OSHUST, Lucy Mae; OSINCHIK, Ilona Jane; OSKIN, Emily; OSLAND, Petra Angelika;
OSLAND, Patrick Joseph; OSMOND, Julie Ann; OSS-CECH, Fran; OSS-CECH, Maurizio;
OSTAFICHUK, Peter; OSTAPIUK, Joan Elizabeth; OSTAPIUK, Kelly Lynn; OSTAPIUK, Larry Edward;
OSTASHEK, Colleen; OSTASHEK, Coleen Gail; OSTASHENSKY, Theresa Christine;
OSTASHEWSKY, Takas Andrew; OSTERWOLDT, Renata; OSTFIELD, Arnold; OSTIAK, Lynn Denise;
OSTRY, Elaine; O'SULLIVAN, Donald Stacey; O'SULLIVAN, Kathryn; O'SULLIVAN, Michael Augustin;
OSWALD, Caren Louise; OSWALD, Colton; OSWALD, Gillian; OSWALD, Helga; OSWALD, Linda May;
OSWALD, Tania; OSZUST, Vera M.; O'TOOLE, Mary Elizabeth; OTTERDAHL, Karen Ann;
OTTERY, John; OTTLEY, Verna Geraldine; OTTO, Joanne Helen; OUASSA, Kouakou; OUDEL-
SMITH, Brenda M.A.; OUELLET, Marie Anne; OUELLET, Mylene; OUELLETTE, Adele Cecile;
OUELLETTE, Anna Marie; OUELLETTE, Julie Danielle; OUELLETTE, Louis Albert;
OUELLETTE, Stacy Lynn; OUGH, Lois Janet; OUIMET, Bernard; OUWERKERK, Cor;
OUYANG, Chou Wei; OUZGANE, Lahoucine; OVENS, John Christopher; OWEN, Seka Helen;
OWEN, Tom; OWENS, Colleen B.; OWENS, Monica Lynn; OWENS, Sean Patrick;
OWENT, William Patrick; OWRE, Lester; OZANO, Douglas Francis; OZBEY, Hasan Riza;
OZBEY, Necla; Ozinchuk, Iiona Jane; OZIPKO, Craig; OZORIO, Rene; OZUBKO, Peter;

P

PACKER, Donald; PADFIELD, Clive A.F.; PADGET, Donald Bradford; PADGET, Elizabeth J.E.;
PAETZ, LESLIE Christine; PAEZ, Natalia Victoria; PAGACZ, Sylvia; PAGANINI, Deborah Ann;
PAGE, Brian; PAGE, Elaine Roberta; PAGE, Lester John; PAGE, Murray N.; PAGE, Phyllis Eileen;
PAGE, Shayne Alexander; PAGE, Shayne Hazen; PAGEE, Bernice M.; PAGET, Anne Charlotte;
PAGOLA, Celia Lajarca; PAISLEY, James Ross; PALAMARCHUK, Catherine Anne;
PALAMAREK, Cheryl; PALAMAREK, Ella; PALAMAREK, Janice O.; PALAMAREK, Michael;
PALAMAREK, Theodor; PALCZA, Annette Dianne; PALEOLOGOPOULOS, Nick; PALEY, Audrey Orissa;
PALEY, Mona Leonora; PALKOWSKI, John Michael; PALLARD, Reginald;
PALMER, Elizabeth Winnetta; PALMER, James; PALMER, Patricia Mildred; PALMER, Roberta Joy;
PALTZAT, Bernadette Ann; PALUDET, Paul Peter; PALUMBI, Tony; PANASIUK, Donna;
PANCHBAYA, Dr. Ismail; PANCHISHIN, Elaine Janice; PANCHYSHYN, Dale John;
PANCHYSHYN, Derek M.; PANCHYSHYN, Joyce; PANCIUK, Mircea; PANESAR, Davinder Jit;
PANGRASS, Carl: PANGRASS, Catherine Isabel; PANGRASS, Donna; PANTEL, Daryl; PANTEL, Heinz;
PANTEL, Ute; PANYLYK, Adrian Harold; PANYLYK, David Michael; PAOLINI, Domonic;
PAPADOGONAS, Perry; PAPAGEORGE, Donald; PAPAPIRNIK, Tim J.; PAPAY, George Ondrei;
PAPINEAU, Brian; PAPINEAU, Phyllis; PAPIRNIK, Michael Adrian; PAPIRNIK, Nicola;
PAPPES, Val Cyneath; PAPINIAN, Fredrick; PAPROSKI, Luanne Marie; PAPROTKA, Dean;
PAPUGA, Marija; PAQUETTE, Alphonse E. PAQUETTE, Danielle Jeanne; PAQUIN, Sharon Ilene;
PARADIS, Cathleen Marie; PARADIS, Elizabeth Jane; PARADIS, Michelle Marie; PARANCHYCH, Fred;
PARANICH, Darrell Edward; PARAS, Dwight; PARDO, D. Fernando; PARDOEL, Henk William;
PARENT, Micheal James; PARENTEAU, Julie; PARFETT, Betty Heloise; PARFETT, James Gordon;
PARHAM, Edward William; PARHAM, Permeila; PARIS, David L.; PARIS, Louise; PARISEAU, Benoit;
PARK, Alastair Cooper; PARK, Betty M.; PARK, Debra; PARK, Diane; PARK, Eleanora; PARK, Ian D.;
PARK, Jack Leroy; PARK, K. Darwin; PARK, Kenneth; PARK, Luica H.J.; PARK, Michael John;
PARK, Roxi; PARK, Ryan Gene; PARK, Sheila Margaret; PARK, Susan; PARKER, Christopher John;
PARKER, David James; PARKER, Dianne; PARKER, Douglas Vernon; PARKER, Ellen Lorna Preuss;
PARKER, Gordon William; PARKER, Helen; PARKER, Imrie Elizabeth: PARKER, Joan Alana;
PARKER, Malcolm Neil; PARKER, Ronald James; PARKER, Shannon Lee; PARKER, William Mills;
PARKES, Cheryl Dawn; PARLIAMENT, Andrea Lynn; PARLIN, Debra Lynn; PARMELEE, Gail;
PARR, Gavin Nicholos; PARR, Katherine; PARR, Richard Ernest; PARR, Valerie;
PARRAGUEZ, C. Benjamin; PARAGUEZ, M. Louise; PARROTTA, Peter; PARSLOW, Robert Frederick;
PARSONS, Dr. Ralph Duncan; PARSONS, Joan; PARSONS, Sheila; PARSS, Ann Doris;
PART, Kathleen; PART, Mike; PARTINGTON, Fred; PASEMKO, Peter J.; PASHNIAK, Lisa;
PASHNIAK, Sandra; PASMORE, Evelyn; PASQUA, Rose Maria; PASQUAL, Anastasio;
PASQUAL, Arcadio; PASQUAL, Lucio Gidone; PASS, Diane Christine; PASTAZYK, Rick L.;
PASTUSZENKO, Vera Nadia; PASTYZYK, Carol Lynn; PASULA, J. Elaine; PASULA, Linda Ann;
PASUTTO, Franco Mario; PASZEK, David Anton; PASZEK, Ted Anton; PATAWARAN, Manny;
PATCHES, Darren Randall; PATEL, Aradhana; PATEL, Arun; PATERSON, Barb;
PATERSON, Barbara Lynn; PATERSON, Daryl; PATERSON, Dorothy Eldora; PATERSON, Edna;
PATERSON, J. Duncan; PATERSON, James Harley; PATERSON, Judith Anne;
PATERSON, Scott John Gordon; PATERSON, Shirley; PATRIC, Andrew Grahame;
PATRICK, Granton Alexander; PATRICK, Joan Ellen; PATRICK, Karen Maureen; PARICK, Lynn Allen;
PATRICK, Melody Ann-Marie; PATRICK, Roberta; PATRICK, Roberta Colleen; PATT, Thomas Raymond;
PATTERSON, Frederick, PATTERSON, Jan; PATTERSON, Jo-Ann Lee; PATTERSON, Leonora Jean;
PATTERSON, Linda Elaine; PATTERSON, Sanantha Joy; PATISON, Janet; PATTON, Anne Rose;
PATTON, David Alan; PATUELLI, Paola; PAU, Frank Chungyuen; PAUL, Barry Jerome;
PAUL, Binder K.; PAUL, Darren C.: PAUL, Dawn E.; PAUL, Gary Craig; PAUL, Kathy A.;
PAUL, Randall Joseph; PAUL, Rose; PAULENCU, Donald James; PAULSEN, John;
PAULSEN, Mary Ruth; PAULUTH, Ingrid; PAVELICH, Katherine Anne;
PAVLIC, Walter John, PAVLIN, Joseph Paul; PAWLIUK, R. Anne; PAWLIUK, Robert James;
PAWLIW, Teresa Ann; PAWLOWSKI, Ron; PAWLYK, Eugenia; PAWLYK, Vera;
PAXTON, Terri Elizabeth; PAYNE, Bonnie Grace; PAYNE, Darrel Clare; PAYNE, Laura Danielle;
PAYNE, Maureen Helen; PAYNE, Shaun Michael; PAYTEN, Mark; PAYTEN, Mark James;
PEABODY, Janice Rae; PEACOCK, Georgine Geraldine; PEACOCK, Kimberly Ann; PEACOCK, Sara, L.;
PEACOCK, Sonja; PEARCE, Frank N.; PEARCE, Vivian Marlyne; PEARMAN, Gelaine;
PEARS, Douglas Grant; PEARSON, Debra; PEARSON, Drusilla Cluley; PEARSON, Gary;
PEARSON, Gerald Edward; PEARSON, Keir Gordon; PEARSON, Margaret Irene; PEARSON, Lea;
PECHTOL, Yoshiko; PECKHAM, Jeanne; PECOVER, Jack Ferris; PEDDIE, Janet J.;
PEDDLE, Dawn Lynn; PEDERSEN, Heidi Marie; PEDERSON, William Darrell; PEDRICK, Marjorie;
PEDRONI, Grigitte; PEEL, Gwyneth Violet; PEEL, Patricia Ann; PEERS, Jami Anthony;
PEERS, Jay James; PEERS, Marc Gerard; PEETS, Kristin; PEGRUM, Margaret Rene; PEGRUM, Rene;
PEI, Winston; PEINOVIC, Josip Branko; PELECH, Fiona; PELKIE, Norma Gail; PELLAND, Brenda Joan;
PELLAND, Shirley Ann; PELLEGRINI, Janis Lea; PELLERIN, Elizabeth K.; PELLERIN, Keith Robert;
PELLETIER, Norman Dean; PELLRINE, Jacqueline Edna; PELOQUIN, Marie-Claude;
PELSTER, Sylvia Irene; PEMBERTON, Ken George; PENA-RODRIGUES, Luis Manuel;
PANAFLOR, Edgar Caspillo; PENFOLD, Alice Edith; PENFORD, Margaret; PENGELLY, William A. S.;
PENMAN, Colin Douglas; PENN, George Henry John; PENN, Vicky; PENNER, Clark;
PENNER, Dr. Darrell; PENNER, H. Jean; PENNER, Joanne Catherine; PENNER, Leona M.;
PENNER, Marjorie; PENNEY, Wendy Elaine; PENNIE, Tom Douglas; PENNINGS, Linda;
PENNINGTON, Dexter H.; PENNOCK, Andrew Louis; PENNOCK, D. Bruce; PENNOCK, Evelyn Hope;
PENNOCK, Steven Louis; PENNY, Dr. Heather F.; PENNY, James D.; PENNY, Jennifer Mary;
PENNYFEATHER, Michael Sydney; PENTLETON, Damien; PENTLETON, Marc James;
PERARCE, Martin, Clifford; PERCHINSKY, Michael John; PERDUE, Nola, Marlene;
PERERA, Mukundadura T.; PEREZ, Claudio Esteban; PEREZ, Marcela Beatriz; PERFREMENT, Eileen J.;
PERFREMENT, Richard L.; PERKINS, Bradley John; PERKINS, Louise; PERKINS: Louise;
PERKINS, Martha; PERKINS, Richard Kim; PERKINS, Sylvia; PERKINS, Thomas Edmund;
PERL, John Charles; PERRA, Marie Lillian A.; PERRAS, Raymond Robert; PERIN, David Clarence;
PERRIN, David William; PERRIS, Audie; PERRON, Maurice; PERRON, Patricia E.;
PERRON, Terry Lawrence; PERROT, Michael David; PERROTTA, Bruno Aniello; PERRY, Beth Anne;
PERRY, Dr. Douglas Cameron; PERRY, Gordon; PERRY, Sheelagh Anne; PERT, David Allan;
PERTSCHY, Elizabeth; PESKE, Yolande Velma; PESKETT, Danny Ronald; PETA, June;
PETCH, Christopher Joel; PETER, John; PETER, Karen; PETERS, Alex John; PETERS, Brian K.;
PETERS, Claire; PETERS, Donald; PETERS, Dorren; PETERS, Helen Marie B.; PETERS, John Lyle;
PETERS, Juergen; PETERS, Katherine; PETERS, Marlene Alice; PETERS, Michael Kerry;
PETERS, Richard Kerry; PETERS, William Bernard; PETERSEN, Fred; PETERSEN, Gary;
PETERSEN, Sheila Louise; PETERSEN, Thomas Alfred; PETERSON, D. Janine;
PETERSON, Deborah Lynne; PETERSON, Don Edward; PETERSON, Davin; PETERSON, Jan Peter;
PETERSON, Joyce; PETERSON, Kathleen Freda; PETERSON, Patricia; PETRAS, Eva;
PETRIN, Diane Marie; PETROSKEY, Craig Michael; PETRUIC, Darcy Lynette; PETRUK, Larry Denis;
PETRUK, Margaret-Anne; PETRUSZCZAK, Ann; PETRYK, Sharon; PETTEN, Rachelle E.;
PETTEN, William; PETTIGREW, Cecile; PETTIGREW, Edythe Jarrett; PETTIGREW, John Keith;
PETTS, Herb A.; PETZOLDT, Doug Oscar; PEYTO, David; PFEFFER, Russell Clare;
PFRIMMER, Dawn Marion; PFRIMMER, Gail Louise; PFRIMMER, Ione; PFRIMMER, Karen Elaine;
PFRIMMER, Keith; PHALEMPIN, Kathleen Ann; PHAN, Trung Binh; PHARE, Laura Catherine;
PHELAN, John Mitchell; PHLAN, Sean Thomas; PHILIPPSON, Susan Yvonne; PHILLIPS, Anne Marie;
PHILLIPS, Cheryl Julie; PHILLIPS, Cindy; PHILLIPS, Clifford H.P.; PHILLIPS, David William;
PHILLIPS, Dr. Harold James; PHILLIPS, Garth; PHILLIPS, Janice L.; PHILLIPS, Margaret Wilson;
PHILLIPS, Patti Anne; PILLIPS, Rae-Lynne Gayle; PHILLIPS, Goss Keith; PHILLIPS, Sylvia Enid;
PHILLPOTTS, Re. Joshua H.; PHINNEY, Jenniver Joan; PHINNEY Joan Meredith;
PHINNEY, Margaret Marlene; PHIPPS-MARTA, Valeska; PHIPPS, Raymond Browning;
PHOTINOPOULOS, Tasia Nancy; PIASTA, Maria Christine; PIAUMIER, Oliver Fabien;
PIBROVEC, G.R. Jolantha; PICARD, Norman; PICHE, Paul Raymond; PICHECA, Julio;
PICHONSKY, Yvonne Cerise; PICKETT, Sandra Lynn; PICKETT, Sharon; PICKLES, Dorothy Elaine;
PIDDE, Paul Jeffery; PIDNER, Anne; PIDNER, Frank; PIDRUCHNEY, Florence P.;
PIDRUCHNEY, Marina Florence; PIDWERBESKY, Lisa Rosalee; PIDZARKO, Lyle Scott;
PIEDMONT, Betty J.; PIERCE, Catherine Irene; PIERCE, John David; PIERCE, William David;
PIERRE, Margaret R.; PIERRE, Margaret Renton; PIETRUSIK, Donna; PIIRONEN, Patricia Clark;
PILARSKI, Mark M.; PILIP, Michael Wolodymyr; PILIP, Myron John; PILIP, Vicki Ann; PILLAI, Thara;
PILLING, Ann Cheryl; PILMEIER, Ursula M.; PILQUIL, Carlos; PINCHBECK, Brian;
PINCHBECK, Lara Jean; PINCHBECK, Yvonne; PINCHIN, Doris Pearl; PINCHIN, James Henry;
PINNICK, Alexander Ofeoritse; PINO, Fran; PINO, Harry; PINSENT, John Harold Charles;
PINSENT, John Leonard; PINSKY, Max; PINTO, Cathy Jean; PINTO, Ludo; PINTO, Marina Consuelo;
PINTO, Rossetti Shalini; PIPER, Douglas; PIPER, Suzanne; IPRPYAPOKSOMBUT, Pattra; PIRO, Gerry;
PIRO, Nan Forbes; PIRZEK, Zoria Violet; PISACTKY, John Henry; PISARCHUK, Berth Juliana;
PISESKY, Irene; PISESKY, Joe; PISESKY, Katherine Gay-Anne; PISKA, Norma Helen; PISKO-
DUBIENSKI, Glenda A.; PISKO-DUBIENSKI, Ralph P.; PISTAWKA, Angela Sandra;
PISTAWKA, Coleen Janet; PITRE, Diane Shirley; PITRE, Rosemary; PITT, Christopher Michael;
PITT, Heather Ann; PITTS, Rodney; PITZEL, Joseph; PIWOWAREK, Adam; PIXLEY, Richard Stanley;
PIZANIAS, Caterina; PLACE, Janice; PLAIZIER, Corrie: PLAIZIER, Peter C. PLASKITT, Lilian Pamela;
PLASKITT, Pamela; PLANTHAN, Peggy Karin; PLATO, Nancy Louise; PLATTS, Shirley Elizabeth;
PLATZER, Brenda Ann; PLATZER, Krista; PLATZER, Krista Jayne; PLAYDON, Clofford E.;
PLECASH, Barbara Amina; PLECASH, James Miles; PLEHWE, Sylvia; PLETCHER, Grace Margaret;
PLOC, Gretel; PLOSKINA, Yelena; PLOTKINA, Zhermena; PLOTS, Yevgeny; PLOUFFE, Mark Timothy;
PLUECKEN, Angelika Maueia; PLUECKEN, Silvia Claudio; PLUMB, Donna Roberta;
PLUMB, John (Jack); PLUMMER, Athalinda Louise; PLUMMER, Deborah Lynn;
PLUMMER, Olwen Gwladys; PLYTKA, Anne; PODDAR, Taruna; PODEMSKI, Cheryl Linda;
PODGURNY, Amelia; PODIVINSKY, Thomas Joseph; PODLOSKY, Linda Rose;
POSLUBNY, Kenneth Dale; PODLUBNY, Louis; PODLUBNY, Robert Dale; PODLUBNY, Vera;
PODLUZNY, Max; PODOLSKY, Erlinda; POHL, Jake G.; POHL, Joyce Elise; POINTE, Joanne;
POINTE, Reginald; POIRIER, Nancy Lynn: POIRIER, Paulette Dorothy;
POIRIER, Ron F. PORIER, Sister Marion W.; POISSANT, Angeline Rose; OPITRA, Denis Jean Robert;
POITRAS, Marcel Bernard; POITRAS, Michael Paul; POLES, Sererino; POLES, Silvio Sante;
POLIAK, Evelyn; POLISCHYUK, Kevin Richard; POLLOCK, Linda; POLLOK, Roger E.;
POLOWAY, Janete; POLOWAY, Marlene Larose; POLOWY, Jacqueline; POLZIN, Kevin Larry;
POMEDLI, Beryl Ruth; POMERLEAU, Pierre Florien; PON, Daisie; PON, Daisie W.; PON, Gerry;

PON, Ronald Arthur; PON, Tui-Ling Hester; PONCE, Waldo Washington; PONICH, Diana Kathleen; PONICH, Nicholas Matthew; PONIEWAZIK, Adolf; PONIEWOZIK, Dennis Marie; PONIEWOZIK, James Joseph; PONIEWOKIK, Marilyn Magdelin; PONOPAREV, Sofia; PONTING, Edna May; POOHKAY, Peter; POOLE, Barbara Caroline; POOLE, Gerry Kevin; POOLE, John Edward; POOLE, Nora Warner; POOLE, Rick Cameron; POOLE, Robert William; POON, Albert K.; POON, Cecilia; POON, Dale Richard; POON, Donna Mae; POON, Eva R.; POON, Gary; POON, Judy S.; POON, Larry; POON, Linda Jade; POON, Roger Edward; POON, Simon; POPAL, Marguerite Edith; POPAL, Marlayne Georgette; POPE, Ian Douglas; POPE, Leslie Corine; POPE, Melanie Dawn; POPOWICH, Janet Kim; POPOWICH, Lorraine Claudia; POPOWICH, Sandra Lynn; POPOWIXZ, Tersa Regina; POPP, Carol Ann; POPP, Christina Tracy; PORETTI, Grazia; PORETTI, Marc; PORISKY, Elaine Lois; POROZNI, Natalie; PORSNUK, Peggy Joy; PORTEDUS, Richard; PORTER, Darlene; PORTER, George Wade; PORTER, Gilaine A.; PORTER, Lorri Margaret; PORTER, Scott Graham; PORTER, Steve Francis; PORTERFIELD, Mary Kathleen; PORTIS, Andrew John; PORTLOCK, Peter; POST, Caroline E.; POSTERARO, Margaret Susan; POSTON, Gail Patricia; POT, Jerry; POTTAGE, marilyn Margaret; POTTER, Helen; POULIN, Johanne Josee; POULIN, Wendy Adelaide; POULSEN, Ann Hjordis; POULSEN, Deanna Michelle; POULSEN, Mathilde; POULSEN, Timothy Kurt; POUNDER, Veronica Lucille; POUNTNEY, Edward Ernest; POUNTNEY, Kathryn Elizabeth; POW, Laurie; POW, Randall F.; POWELL, Anthony James; POWELL, E. Patrick; POWELL, Edwin James; POWELL, Frank; POWELL, Ian; POWELL, Marilyn; POWELL, Robert Antonio; POWELL, Shirley Louisa; POWELL, Wallace Kenneth; POWELSON, Barbara Jean; POWER, Nancy C.; POWER, Sandra Kristine; POWERS, Douglas Bryan; POWER, Kenneth Allan; POWLEY, Joyce; POWOROZNIK, Melanie; POWOROZNIK, Tamara; POWYS-LYBBE, Kathryn Lynn; POZZOBAN, Robert; PRODELLA, Geoffrey Michael; PRAJZ, Nikola; PRASAD, Sindula; PRATLEY, Mary-Jean; PRATT, Barbara Ethel; PRATT, Beverly Ann; PRATT, James Henry; PRATT, Joan Alice; PRATT, Lucy; PRATT, Marna Lee; PRATT, Sam Mcnicoll; PRATT, Vera N.; PRATT, William Edward; PRECHT, Paul L.; PREFONTAINE, Guy Joseph; PRELORENTZOS, Salvos; PRENDERGAST, Angela Fay; PRENT, Marwina; PRESHING, William A.; PRESLEY, Violet Olga; PRESTON, Alexander H.; PRESTON, Arnold Wayne; PRESTON, Carol Anne; PRESTON, Karen Lynn; PRESTON, Lillian V.; PRESTON, Mary Sue; PRESTON, Michael Stephen; PRETZLAFF, Chris; PREVEY, W. Douglas; PREVILLE, Doreen Ruth; PREVILLE, Philip; PREVISH, Terri; PREVOST, Maria; PREVOST, Thena; PRICE, Barry Donald; PRICE, Joyce Eileen; PRICE, Leslie G.; PRICE, Linda; PRICE, Lloy Marie; PRICE, Michele Alice; PRICE, Paul Gregory; PRICE, T. Sylvia PRIDDLE, Lorna M.; PRIEMAZA, Maryanna Janet; PRIEST, Robert John; PRIESTLY, Christopher James; PRIESTLY, Robert Huw; PRIESTLY, Tom Michael S.; PRIESTNALL, Jackie; PRIESTNALL, Lawrence Harold; PRIME, Dennis Gordon; PRIMEAU, Cyla Anne Catherine; PRIMEAU, Kevin Lawrence, PRIMEAU, Marie Louise; PRIMEAU, Therresa Jane; PRIMOSCH, Richard Frederick; PRIMROSE, Helen Judy; PRIMROSE, John Martin; PRIMROSE, Kim Marie; PRINCE, Kristi Diane; PRINGLE, Edward Neil; PRINGLE, Frederick Thomas; PRIOR, Neila Diane; PRITCHARD, Dereil Wynne; PRITCHARD, John A.; PRITCHARD, Susan Linda; PRITCHARD, Vivian; PROCHNAU, Paul Edward; PROCINSKY, Daryl Alex; PROCOPE, Cynthia Rosalie; PROCTOR, Trevor Bradley; PROCYSHYN, Dr. Alexander W.; PRODAN, Kathy; PRODANIUK, Connie Mary; PRODOR, Janice Marie; PROKOP, Christine Angella; PROKOPCHUK, Orest John W.; PROKOPUK, John George; PROKOS, Gus; PROSKOW, Raymond; PROSSER, Denis Kathleen; PROSTEBBY, Janice R.; PROTZ, Randy; PROTZ, Terry Roman Steve; PROULX, Carol; PROVEN, Maxine Marie; PROVENCAL, Caroline Joan; PROVOST, Lise Elizabeth; PROVOST, Roland; PROVOST, Valerie Anne; PROVOSTE, Victor Omar; PROWSE, Margaret Doris; PRUD'HOMME, David; PRYDE, Wendy Ann; PRYOR, Bonnie Joan; PRYSKO, Dennis PRYSTAWA, Barbara Marie; PRZBYISKI, Peter Stephen; PSHYK, Bernadette Marie; PSHYK, Judy; PSLANCE, Jean; PUA, Claudio; PUCCI, Elena; PUDAR, Iris Berna; PUDLOWSKI, Donna Miriam; PUDSEY, Gertrude Emma; PUECH, Bob Charles; PUECH, Daneka-Lee Marie; PUFFER, Kevin Gordon; PUGEDA, Dennis; PUGH, Bob; PUGH, Brenda Maxine; PUGH, Thora; PUIGNAU, Jorge; PUKANICH, Frank; PULKRABEK, John Theodore; PULLISHY, Peter Allen; PULLOCK, Richrd; PUNDIT, Manoi; PURCELL, Billie; PURCELL, Laurie Susznne; PURCELL, Mae Anna Geneva; PURCELL, Richard; PURCELL-LEWIS, Dr. John G.; PURDELL-LEWIS, Judith C.; PURDY, Elizabeth Rose; PURITCH, Rhonda-Lee; PURVE, Cecil J.; PURVES, Clare; PURVIS, Christine Susan; PURVIS, Gordon James; PUTTAGUNTA, Krishna Kumari; PUTTAGUNTA, Pardha Saradhi; PYLE, Danny Murray; PYLE, Elizabeth May; PYNE, Timothy Merrill; PYSYK, Rose Patricia;

Q

QIHELM, Kathleen; QUADRI, Wendy Jane; QUARTLY, Darrold Edwin; QUELCH, Charlotte; QUIGLEY, Therese Anne; QUILICHINI, Diane Rita; QUILLIAM, Harold; QUINLAN, Joan; QUINN, Betty Elynn; QUINN, Carolyn Mae; QUINN, Patrick Bruce; QUINN, Ron; QUINNEY, Norman Alfred Junior; QUIRING, Janet; QUIST, Sharon Ella; QUON, Angela; QUON, Donna; QUON, Monica Yat Hing; QURESHI, Irfan Haider;

R

RAAB, Gretel; RAAFLAUB, Arthur Ian; RABIK, Anne Victoria; RABIN, Chris; RABINOVICH, Emanuel; RABORN, Dr. George Wayne; RACE, Alban Thomas; RACE, Sylvia; RACHA, Nasser; RACKEL, Karen Margaret; RADASIC, Christine Susa; RADCLIFFE, Ted; RADDALGODA, Daya Asoka; RADEY, Valaree Elizabeth; RADKE, Cynthia; RADOMSKY, June Elisa; RADOSTITS, Karen A.; RADOSTITS, Lynne Teresa; RADVONY, Murv Allan; RAE, Allan Gordon; RAE, Barbara Elinor; RAE, James Duncan; RAFTER, Jennifer Elizabeth; RAFTIS, Roy; RAHMAN, John Blackwell; RAI, Gurmit; RAI, Harbax; RAI, Sukhvinder Singh; RAICHE, Jacques; RAINS, Paul Robert; RAITERI, Anita; RAI, Louie; RAI, Rajendra; RAJANI, Dr. Hasmukhial R.; RAJOTTE, Elaine A.; RAJOTTE, Ron; RAJU, Resham Singh; RAKOCHEY, Deborah Marie; RAKOCHEY, Patricia Ann; RAKOZ, Raymond Leo; RALEIGH, Suzanne Elaine; RALL, Randolph William; RALSTIN, Margaret Ann; RALSTON, Lynne F.; RAMAN-MAIR, Stephen; RAMDHANIE, Edward; RAMDHANIE Neera; RAMIREZ, Camilo Francisco; RAMIREZ, Lucia Patricia; RAMKISHUN, Dyual; RAMIAL, Annie; RAMOUTAR, Leah Marietta; RAMSANKAR, Monica Diane; RAMSAROOP, Phillip; RAMSAY, Janice; RAMSAY, Thomas Wilson; RAMSDELL, Lee George; RAMSEY, Bonnie; RAMSEY, Carol Ann; RAMSEY, Dr. Colin George; RAMSEY, Dr. Ronald Keith; RAMSEY, John Charles; RAMSEY, Marion Constance; RAMSEY, Marlene; RAMSLEY, Alison; RAMSLEY, Sandra; RANDOLPH, Gordon Hugh; RANDOLPH, John Robert; RANGER, Gary Ernest; RANIERI, Sandi; RANKEL, Carol Lee; RANKIN, Brian; RANKIN, John Howard; RANKINE, Douglas H.G.; RAPOSO, Claudia Tavares; RAPP, Christine G.; RASHBROOK, Angelina Andree; RASHBROOK, Sid Arthur; RASMUSSEN, Howard Glenn; RASMUSSEN, Lois Marie; RATCLIFFE, Antony Ewart; RATCLIFFE, Tana Margaret; RATERSON, Edna; RATH, G. Gilda; RATH, Roslyn; RATNASINGHAM, Girl S.; RATTAN, R. Nav P.S.; RATTIE, Edgar-Andre; RATTLESNAKE, Jerry Roger; RATTRAY, Mary-Ann Margaret; RATTRAY, William Davis; RATUSZ, Jan;

RATZ, Darren Edward; RATZ, Elizabeth; RATZLAFF, Leonard Peter; RATZLAFF, Paula Loraine; RAUGUST, Shelly E.; RAUSCH, Ursula; RAVEN, Heather; RAWDING, Elizabeth; RAWSON, Krista Denise; RAYMENT, Thomas A.; RAYMOND, Kendra Elaine; RAYNARD, G. Lloyd; REA, James Michael: READ, Jane Elizabeth; READ, Suzanna Helena; READE, Maurianne; REBALKIN, Denis Samuel; REBARGE, Joe James; REBNORD, Fraser B.; REBNORD, Joan Louise; REBONNE, Luis Leopold; RECHSTEINER, Yvonne; REDDINGTON, Bob; REDDINGTON, Wendy; REDEKOP, Jack L. REDEKOP, Sharon H. REDEKOP, Tannis Pearl REDMOND, Gerald; REDMOND, Margaret Eileen; REDMOND, Vivian Lilian; REDOCKA, David Casey; REDUCKA, Florence; REED, James Ross; REED, Melanie Lynn; REED, Robert Henry; REED, Shirley; REEKI, James Ross; REEMS, Dr. Hank; REES, David Albert; REES, Margaret Anne; REES, William John Edward; REEVE, Charlene; REEVE, Charelen Judith; REEVE, Corey Edward; REEVE, Gordon E.; REEVES, John; REGAMEY, Jean Alice; REGHELINI, Zarelda; REHLAU, Martin; REHMAN, James Dougal; REIB, Bonnie; REIB, Brett Cameron; REIB, Elisabeth; REICHE, Deborah June; REICHELT, David Harry; REICHELT, Jean Edith; REICHWEIN, Pearl Ann; REID, B. Shirley; REID, Catherine; REID, David William James; REID, Douglas Andrew; REID, Dr. David Albert; REID, Dr. David Collison; REID, Dwayne Alan; REID, Kathleen Virginia; REID, Linda; REID, William Morrison; REIDIE, David Michael; REIMER, Tina; REIMER, Werner David; REINART, Carson I.; REINBERG, Michael; REINELT, Barbara; REINHOLD, Timothy Shawn; REITNE, Marolyn A.; REITH, Karen Jean; REITH, Kathie Ann; REITMEYER, Hilda; REITMEYER, Patricia; RELF, Kimberly; REMBOWSKI, Mitchell John; REMEIKA, Linda Eleanor; REMPEL, Dr. Donald John; RENAUD-GAGNIER, Corinne; RENFORTH, J. Elaine; RENNEBOHM, Robert Eugene; RENNER, Annamary; RENNIE, Brenda; RENNIE, Gordon H.; RENNIE, Janice Gaye; RENNIE, John Hamilton; RENNIE, Karen; RENNIE, Margaret Marie; RENNIE, Sandy; RENOUF, Lori Joan; RENOUF, Stacy Lynn; RENTZ, Garry Douglas; REPCHUK Debbie Karen; REPCHUK, James Allan; RESAUL, Katheryn Denise; RESHEF, Elazar, RESTA, Janet Elaine; RETALLACK, Yvonne; RETZLAFF, Liana Lesley; RETZLAFF, Norm George; REUKEMA, Peter Bernardus; REVILLA, Luisa Rowena; REYE, Enrique R.; REYES, Enrique; REYNOLDS, D. Vincent; REYNOLDS, Krista Michele; REYNOLDS, William Thomas; RHEMTULLA, Toine; RHODES, Helen Muriel; RHODES, Jacalyn May; RHODES, Marilyn Louise; RIAR, Kulwant Singh; RIAR, Narindar Singh; RIAR, Ranjit Singh; RICARDO, Manuel; RICCA, Connie; RICCA, Tana; RICCI, Lucy C.; RICE, Daniel Cameron; RICE, Harry Peter; RICE, Shirley Ann; RICH, D. Merle; RICH, J. R. Kelly; RICH, Kimberlee Ann; RICH, Teresa Lynn; RICHARD, Beverley jEllalane; RICHARD, Dr. Harold; RICHARD, Dr. Lance Burnard; RICHARD, Ron; RICHARDS, E. Louise; RICHARDS, Elizabeth Margaret; RICHARDS, Hellen Voley; RICHARDS, James Alexis; RICHARDS, Jim Edward; RICHARDSON, Dr. Alan John; RICHARDSON, Katherine Ann; RICHARDSON, Scott; RICHMOND, Bob G.; RICHMOND, Christine Avalon; RICHMOND, Valerie Ann; RICHTER, Sherrylyn Bertha; RICKETT, Marion Martha; RICOT, Ryo A.; RIDDELL, Heather; RIDDELL, Michelle Lee; RIDDLE, Betty Irene; RIDDLE, Robert Dennis; RIDER, Marjorie Murry; RIDGWAY, Dianne R.; RIDGWAY, Wendy E.; RIDLEY, Kenneth G.; RIEDER, Diane Marie; RIEDER, Dianne Marie; RIEDIGER-DUEBEL, Joanne E.; RIEDMUELLER, Manfred W.; RIEMER, Dr. Lowell Brendon; RIES, Brenda Louise; RIESEL, Gabriela; RIESEL, Pauline Jane; RIEWE, Marlene Alice; RIGAL, Dr. Wynne M.; RIGGS, Stephen I.W.; RIJAVEC, Sharon Helena; RILEY, Annette Valerie; RILEY, John Ken; RILEY, Kimberly; RING, James Lewis; RING, Leslie Karen; RINGROSE, C.A. Douglas; RINTOUL, Beverly Joan; RIPKA, Leslie Michael; RIPLEY, Pamela Jean; RIPPON, Ann; RISPLER, Kenneth Charles; RITCHIE, A. Christine; RITCHIE, Beverley Anne; RITCHIE, David; RITCHIE, Donna Catherine; RITCHIE, Dr. Brian Douglas; RITCHIE, Dr. William L.; RITCHIE, Dr. William Legget; RITCHIE, June Virginia; RITCHIE, Marguerite Ann; RITCHIE, William; RITTER, Elizabeth Catherine; RITTER, Linda Darlene; RIVERS, Caroll Dianne; RIVEST, Michelle; RIVEST, R. John; ROACH, Elaine Beverley; ROACH, Elaine Beverly; ROAKE, Jeffery Scott; ROBB, Patricia; ROBBINS, Carol Lynne; ROBBINS, Karen Gertrude; ROBBINS, Sheila Kimberly; ROBERGE, Gerald; ROBERT-PEILLARD, Nathalie Anne; ROBERT, Michel; ROBERT, Nicole; ROBERTS, Bill Ken; ROBERTS, Bruce Edwards; ROBERTS, Curtis Munson; ROBERTS, Daryle James; ROBERTS, Donald Victor; ROBERTS, Karen Marina; ROBERTS, Nancy Jane; ROBERTS, Peter William; ROBERTS, Reg; ROBERTS, Susan Blair; ROBERTSON, Alan; ROBERTSON, Alan James; ROBERTSON, C. Richard; ROBERTSON, Caroline; ROBERTSON, Coleen; ROBERTSON, Dave K.; ROBERTSON, Elise; ROBERTSON, Grant; ROBERTSON, Gwendolyn C.S.; ROBERTSON, James Marvin; ROBERTSON, John Grant; ROBERTSON, Karen; ROBERTSON, Karen Elizabeth; ROBERTSON, Leane Michelle; ROBERTSON, Margaret Anne; ROBERTSON, Mary F.; ROBERTSON, Mary Fingland; ROBERTSON, Michael David; ROBERTSON, P. Beth; ROBERTSON, Sharon; ROBERTSON, Stewart G.; ROBERTSON, Susan Dawn; ROBICHAUD, David Nobert; ROBINE-DUE, Sherry; ROBINS, Larry Norman; ROBINSON-SMITH, Margo F.; ROBINSON, Beverley Ann; ROBINSON, Cathlyn Elizabeth; ROBINSON, Christopher; ROBINSON, David Alexander; ROBINSON, Denise Rosemary; ROBINSON, Daine; ROBINSON, Dr. Jeffery Mark; ROBINSON, Ellen C.; ROBINSON, Hazel Margaret; ROBINSON, Jeff; ROBINSON, Jon Clare; ROBINSON, Kathy Mary; ROBINSON, Kelly Ann; ROBINSON, Kenneth; ROBINSON, Lisa Joy; ROBINSON, Maureen Delanie; ROBINSON, Michael John; ROBINSON, Ronald Grant; ROBINSON, Ronalee; ROBINSON, Samantha Lynn; ROBINSON, Shelley Anne; ROBINSON, Barry A.; ROBITAILLE, Janet Karen; ROBSON, Dr. Alex; ROBSON, Jean R.; ROBSON, Jeanette Ann; ROBSON, Wes Norval; ROCCHIO, Pasquale James; ROCH, Connie Katherine; ROCHE, Dwayne James; ROCHE, Mary Anne Monica; ROCKETT, Melanie; ROCKLIFF, Jonathan; RODDELT, Wendy Dawn; RODEN, Shannon Marie; RODGERS, Kevin L. RODGERS, Wendy Elizabeth; RODRIGUE, Michelle Susan; RODRIGUES, Leonard Oliver; RODRIGUEZ, Juan David; RODYNIUK, Andriy Varema; ROED, Diane Lousie; ROED, Shannon Lauren; ROED, Tracy Lyn; ROELOFS, Joyce Diana; ROESTI, Karen pearl; ROETMAN, Albertus; ROGERS, James Douglas; ROGERS, Kathleen June; ROGERS, Kim; ROGERS, Kimberley Ann; ROGERS, Tim; ROGNVALDSON, Douglas James; ROJAS, Benjamin Humberto; ROLAND, Olga; ROLES, Carol Lynn; ROLFE, Kevin Duane; ROLHEISER, George; ROLHEISER, Jeffrey Gerald; ROLINGHER, Shawn; ROLLANS, Richard Shane; ROLLINGHER, Larry; ROLLINGHER, Tulane; ROMAIN, Brian David; ROMANCHUK, Florence; ROMANCHUK, Katherine; ROMANIUK, Douglas Anthony; ROMANIUK, Elaine Doreen; ROMANIUK, Karen Marie; ROMANIUK, Lillian Marie; ROMANKO, Mary; ROMANOWSKI, Barbara; ROMANOWSKI, Edward Thomas; ROMANOWSKI, Francis Jadwiga; ROMANYSHYN, Penny; ROMANYSHYN, Peter; ROMBOUGH, Colin Robert; ROMOREN, Lillian; RONAN, Cheryl; RONAN, Peggy M.; RONAN, Roxanne; RONNIE, Daryl Lynn; ROONEY, Douglas Charles; ROOPNARINE, Indira; ROOTSAERT, Christine Theresa; ROOTSAERT, Corinne Mary-Anne; ROPCHAN, Don; ROPER, Alyson; ROPER, Anne Marie; ROPER, Daniel A.; ROPER, Margaret Louise; ROPER, Sherry Anne; ROPPO, Luisa; RORKE, Libby; ROSALES, Sarella Zorka; ROSARIO, Carla Soriano; ROSBOROUGH, Richard Glen; ROSE, Garry; ROSE, Gary; ROSE, Lincoln Garrick; ROSE, Liz; ROSEN, Anne Louise; ROSEN, Robert Waine; ROSENAU, Terri Lynn; ROSENBERGER, Lucy; ROSENTHAL, Terri Lynne Marie; ROSICH, Geroge; ROSKEY, Adeline; ROSS, Alenander David; ROSS, Betty Grace; ROSS, Carl; ROSS, Carolynne Elizabeth; ROSS, Conny Ann; ROSS, David; ROSS, Donna Louise; ROSS, Doreen Marie; ROSS, Evlynn; ROSS, Forence Kaila; ROSS, Heidi; ROSS, Hugo Alan; ROSS, Jackie; ROSS, Joanna; ROSS, Karen; ROSS, Kate Una; ROSS, Patrick Felix; ROSS, Philip Villiam; ROSS, Sara C.; ROSS, Sarah Joan; ROSS, Shannon Mary; ROSS, William John; ROSSALL, Joan Josephine; ROSSALL, JONATHAN; ROSSER, Blair; ROSSER, Grace Lucille; ROSSER, Ian M.; ROSSI, Severina; ROSSITER, Deborah Anne; ROSSMENN, James G.; ROSTAD, Faith; ROSTAD, Terryl; ROSYCHUK, Shirlee Anne;

ROTH, Elizabeth Helen; ROTHSCHILD, Alexis Joan; ROULSON, Dorothy Louise;
ROUSELL, Laura Margaret; ROUSELL, Michael Andrew; ROUSSEAU, Alain Normand;
ROUSSEAU, Carolin L.; ROUSSIN, Pamela Joanne; ROUTLEDGE, Carolyn Doreen;
ROUTLEDGE, Gladys Irene; ROUTLEDGE, James Edward; ROWAN, Emily Philomena;
ROWAN, Margery; ROWAN, Olive Joan; ROWE, Helen Doreen; ROWE, Margaret Lucy;
ROWLAND, Corinne Lee; ROWLAND, Heather Ann; ROWLAND, Penny; ROWSE, Gordon H.; ROY-OBRIEN, Megan G.; ROY, Carole Noella; ROY, Diane Christine; ROY, Jennifer Ann;
ROY, Lawrence Keith; ROY, Linda Jayne; ROYAL, Cory; ROYCE, Bonny; ROYLE, Arthur Joseph;
ROZAK, Katherine; ROZENHART, Leslie Anne; ROZENHART, Robert Nicholas: ROZYCKI, Bogdan;
RUBAN, Francoise T.; RUDDICK, Martha J.; RUDDICK, Martha Janet; RUDE, Karen Dale;
RUDKOWSKI, D. Victor; RUDOIFSEN, Beverly Lynn; RUDOLF, Gregory; RUDOLPH, Gwen Eunice;
RUDOVICS, Ena; RUDY, Donna Jean; RUDY, Greg Allan; RUDY, Kenneth Wayne;
RUDZCKI, Deana Grace; RUECK, Gilbert; RUECK, Heinz; RUECK, Helga; RUECK, Sandra;
RUFF, Audrey A.; RUI, Liao; RUMBOLD, Kathryn Joy; RUMLEY, Jack; RUMOHR, Kenneth J.;
RUMOHR, Richard Kenneth; RUMSEY, Francis Eugene; RUNCK, Gloria J.; RUNCO, Angela;
RUNDLE, Patricia Jean; RUNISH, Varma; RUNYON, Jean M.; RUPERT, Michele Dawn;
RUPTASH, Deserrie; RUPTASH, Susan Marie; RURKA, Sheila M.; RUSHDY, Amgad W.;
RUSICH, John; RUSINKO, Carole Penny; RUSINKO, Jill Marie; RUSSELL, Ann Cecilia;
RUSSELL, Anne; RUSSELL, Barbara Lynn; RUSSELL, Bob A. RUSSELL, Dorene Gloria;
RUSSELL, Dr. Donald B.; RUSSELL, Fern Joanne; RUSSELL, Judith Marie; RUSSELL, Kevin John;
RUSSELL, Lisa Jane; RUSSELL, Lois Darlene; RUSSELL, Paul; RUSSELL, Richard David;
RUSSELL, Sally; RUSSELL, Stacey Leigh; RUSSELL, Thompson Harvey;
RUSTEMEIER, Catherine Claudia; RUTHERFORD, Russell Alexander; RUTSCH, Edmund;
RUTTAN, Julia Ann; RUTTAN, Karen Miriam; RUTTER, Jacquelyn; RUZICKA, Lorne Joseph;
RUZYCKI, Brian Ronald; RYAN, David; RYAN, Denise Mary; RYAN, Doreen Delores; RYAN, Gregory F.;
RYKS, Marian; RYL, Rosie; RYLAND, Carol A.; RYLAND, Mark James; RYLAND, Ralph Edgar;
RYMER, John Ewan; RYTON, Eileen; RYZIUK, Donald Ray; RYZUK, Marguerite Elizabeth;

S

SABOURIN, Dennis Brian; SABOURIN, Jacqueline Marie; SABOV, David; SABULA, Mabula Maseni;
SACCO, Tom; SACCOMANI, Angela; SACCOMANI, Silvana; SACH, Irma; SACHER, Angela;
SACKMAN, Paul; SACUTA, Janet Marie; SADEE, Eric Leonard; SADESKY, Natalie; SADGROVE, Roy;
SADOWNIK, Leslie Ann; SAFFRAN, Denis Alvin; SAGANSKY, Andrea M.; SAGE, Cynthia;
SAGE, Kevin Mason; SAGRIFF, Don; SAIK, Jackie; SAIK, Jean; SAIK, Jean Mary; SAIK, Walter John;
SAIKO, Shari Lee; SAITO, Eleanor C.; SAITO, James Christopher; SAKOUSKY, Joanne Marie;
SALAMANDICK, June; SALDANHA, Eugene; SALDANHA, Louise Theresa; SALE, Lorraine Anne;
SALEEM, Mohammed; SALEM, Rodney Joseph; SALEY, Olga R.: SALFI, Peter;
SALIBA, Cathy Madeline; SALKIE, Dr. Mark Louis; SALKIE, Fiona Jane; SALKIE, Mark Louis;
SALLOUM, Joseph Georges; SALLS, Delmar Arthur; SALLS, Melba Frances; SALM, Mary Jane;
SALO, Leona M.; SALOPEK, Marijan; SALTER, Cheryl-Lynn; SALTER, Julie; SALTER, Olive A.;
SALVADOR, Christopher; SALVALAGGIA, George Martin; SALVALAGGIO, Jo Kay;
SALVALAGGIO, S. E. Germaine; SAM, Cathie Leslie; SAMAHA, Nicholas Joseph;
SAMALACK, Steven C.; SAMBOR, Carla Collette; SAMBOR, Corine Marie; SAMBOR, Sharon Patricia;
SAMMONS, Jody Melissa; SAMMONS, Margot; SAMOIL, Carrie Anne; SAMOIL, George Eugene;
SAMORDIN, Fredric, Timothy; SAMPLE, Edward Burton; SAMPLE, Jeanetta Mae;
SAMPLE, Robert Edwin; SAMS, Irene Patricia; SAMUEL, Al; SAMUEL, Gerald B.;
SAMUEL, Therese Marie; SAMYCIA, Caroline; SAMYCIA, Daryl Nestor; SANCHE, Simone Lilvee;
SANCHEZ, Jose Miguel; SANDAHL, Norman John Lars; SANDE, Barbara Jean; SANDE, Karen;
SANDE, Nell David; SANDEN, Susan Jeannette; SANDER, Adrienne Marie; SANDERS, Carolee Ann;
SANDERS, Douglas Norman; SANDERS, Murray W.; SANDERS Norm, Ray; SANDERS, Shelley Lynn;
SANDERSON, Kenneth James; SANDERSON, Myron Noel; SANDERSON, Penny Eleanor;
SANDERSON, Tammy Jeanne; SANDERSON, Todd James; SANDHAM, Kenneth Albert;
SANDHAM, Robert Ian; SANDHU, Harpreet Kaur; SANDOUKA, Hani M.; SANDS, Cynthia Blanche;
SANDS Keziah Mary; SANDS, Sandra Audrie; SANDS, Sandra Dee; SANDS Sandra Sharon;
SANDUGA, Ized-Din; SANDULESCU, Mihai Otto; SANDY, Louise; SANDY, Louise H.; SANELLI, Bruno;
SANFORD, Lincoln John; SANFORD, Wilma Anne; SANGSTER, Judith Lynn;
SANHUEZA, Maria Mercedes; SANKO, Barbara Jane; SANREGRET, Michelle Terese;
SAPIC, Michael; SARA, Ted Mike; SARACH, Marian; SARATH, Ou; SARETSKY, Patricia Anne;
SARGENT, John Ernest; SARGENT, Lillian mary; SARIC, Katica; SARIC, Valerie; SARNECKI, Theresa;
SARSFIELD, Kim; SARTOR, Debbie Ann; SARUK, Shirley Marie; SASADA, Hanako;
SASAKI, Gregory Lyle; SASHUK, Kelly Joan; SASS, June Anne; SASYN, Helen Elizabeth;
SATHER, Marin; SATHER, Sandra Ruth; SATURLEY, Edward Paul; SAUNDERS, Darlene;
SAUNDERS, Krista Gale; SAUNDERS: Susan Kathryn; SAVAGE, Fiona Mary; SAVAGE, Jack;
SAVAGE, Susan Jennifer; SAVOS, Catherine H.; SAVERAUX, Robert Henry; SAVOIE, Aline M. E.;
SAVOIE, Denis F.; SAWATZKY, Bernard; SAWATSKY, David Allan; SAWATZKY, Donald Kenneth;
SAWATZKY, Dwayne Alan; SAWATZKY, Greg Jay; SAWATZKY, June Elaine; SAWATZKY, Susan Gail;
SAWCHENKO, Ludwig Paul; SAWCHUK, Ann; SAWCHUK, Ariette Katherine;
SAWCHUK, Brenda Karen; SAWCHUK, Debra; SAWCHUK, Elizabeth Eva; SAWCHUK, Irene Catherine;
SAWCHUK, Judy-Lynn Marie; SAWACHUK, Ken J.; SAWCHUK, Teresa Stephanie; SAWCHYN, Mark;
SAWCHYN, Monica; SAWICKA, Greta Teresa; SAWKA, Michael; SAWYER, William Gerald;
SAYERS, Reanna; SAYLE, Shirley Ann; SCACCIA, Antonella; SCAFE, Velma Georgine;
SCAMBLER, Murray W.; SCAPETORACHIS, Angelo; SCARPELLI, Rosie; SCHADE, Crystal Denise;
SCAEBIE, Michael Peter; SCAEFER, Susanne Eva; SCHALLIG, Leslie Ronald; SCHALM, Alfred;
SCHALM, Andrew; SCHALM, Colleen Ruth; SCHAMBER, Blaine; SCHAMUHN, Bonnie Gail;
SCHAPPERT, Chess; SCHAPPY, Camille Jeannette; SCHARABUN, Elizabeth;
SCHARABUN, Roman Victor; SCHARFENBERGER, Angela V.; SCHEFFER, Lisa; SCHEFER, Paul;
SCHEIE, Mildred; SCHELL, Janet Mary; SCHEPENS, Janice; SCHERER, Lorrie Jeanne;
SCHERGER, Coreen F.; SCHERGER, Eileen; SCHERMANN, Brenda Ann; SCHERMANN, Elizabeth A.;
SCHEUNERT, Sherry Pearl; SCHEWCIK-GREEN, Ingrid B.; SCHIENBEIN, Allan John; SCHIEWE, Gwen;
SCHILER, Ginny Colleen; SCHILLER, Kevin James; SCHILL, Margaret Ann; SCHILLER, Laverne;
SCHIMPF, Heather Lynne; SCHLADER, Roy Andrew; SCHLAG, Paul Norman;
SCHLAMP, Emilie Patricia; SCHLAMP, Holly Ann; SCHLECKER, Michele Anne;
SCHLIECHER, Bruce Theodore; SCHLEINDL, Val; SCHLEINOL, David Richard; SCHLENDER, Duana Lee;
SCHLERETH, Dave Patrick; SDCHLOSS, Dr. Eric; SCHLOSSER, John L.; SCHLOSSER, Kathleen;
SCHMALZ, Arlene Anita; SCHMEELKE, Laura Ula; SCHMIDKE, Elizabeth Lavina; SCHMIDT-IHMS, Maria; SCHMIDT, Camela V.; SCHMIDT, Cheryl D.; SCHMIDT, Doreen Elaine;
SCHMIDT, E. Lucille; SCHMIDT, Frieda; SCHMIDT, Jackie; SCHMIDT, John Kenneth;
SCHMIDT, Karen Elizabeth; SCHMIDT, Ken; SCHMIDT, Lawrence Oscar; SCHMIDT, Lucille;
SCHMIDT, Melinda; SCHMIDT, Norman Kenneth; SCHMIDT, Patricia Veronica;
SCHMIDT, Robert Glen; SCHMIDT, Rudi; SCHMIDT, Sherri; SCHMIDT, Sylvia Karin;
SCHMIDT, Sylvia Rosemarie; SCHMIDT, Tim; SCHMIDT, Tracy Elizabeth; SCHMIDT, Ursula Kathleen;
SCHMIDTKE, Dieter; SCHMITKE, Calvin D.; SCHMITKE, Glen Murray; SCHMITKE, Sheila Marie;
SCHMITT, Margo Ann; SCHMITZ, John J; SCHMITZ, Peter Raymond; SCHNAUTZ, Antonio F.;
SCHNEIDER, Craig Vincent; SCHNEIDER, David M.; SCHNEIDER, Janice Christine; SCHNEIDER, Karl;
SCHNEIDER, Patti Jean; SCHNELLBACK, Janet Marie; SCHOENEMANN, Patricia G.;
SCHOENING, Juanita Doreen; SCHOENING, William Richard; SCHOENROTH, Jeff;
SCHOFIELD, Gerald W.; SCHOLTEN, Anselmo Antonius; SCHORATH, Nelita Marie; SCHRA, Eric;
SCHRADER, Jacqueline Anne; SCHRAM, Tracy Lynne; SCHRAM, Valeria; SCHREIBER, Allen Joe;
SCHREINER:, Pearl G.; SCHRETTLINGER, Anita Christine; SCHRODER, D. Joy;
SCHROEDER, Eric Mitchell; SCHROEN, Maxine Wilhelmina; SCHROTEN, Susan; SCHROTER, Carol;
SCHRYVERS, James; SCHRYVERS, Robert; SCHUBERT, Barbara Claire; SCHUBERT, Gwendolyn Ruth;
SCHUBERT, Heidi F.; SCHUBERT, Jim Wayne; SCHUBERT, Kevin Gordon; SCHUH, David Bert;
SCHULDES, Beverley; SCHULDES, Nancy Dawn; SCHULDHAUS, Perry F.; SCHULER, Ken James;
SCHULLER, Michael Guy; SCHULTA, Wendy Joan; SCHULTZ, Cheryl Lynn; SCHULTZ, Dean James;
SCHULTZ, Gordon Harold; SCHULTZ, Jackie Denise; SCHULTZ, Keith Robert; SCHULTZ, Leanne;
SCHULTZ, Lynda Margaret; SCHULTZ, Ray Harvey; SCHULTZ, Sharon Elaine; SCHULZ, Garth Irwin;
SCHULZ, Lorry Donna Dee; SCHULZ, Thomas; SCHUR, Robert; SCHUR: Sylvia;
SCHURMAN, Kenneth Duane; SCHURMAN, Marjorie Ann; SCHUSTER, Andy;
SCHWABE, Marcus Christopher; SCHWAIGER, Dorothy J.; SCHWALFENBERG, Dr. Gerry Kurt;
SCHWARZ, Harald Alfred Johann; SCHWARZKOPF, Jane; SCHWARZKOPF, Thomas Edward;
SCHWINDT, Dr., George; SCINTA, Ruth Caroline; SCOBIE, Dianne Marie; SCORGIE, David;
SCOTT, Caroll J oan; SCOTT, Cathy Lynn; SCOTT, Don L.; SCOTT, Donald David; SCOTT, Harvey A.;
SCOTT, Joan Ann; SCOTT, Joanne Ruth; SCOTT, Kevin Garnet; SCOTT,Peggy Ann;
SCOTT, Robert Alan; SCOTT, Robert Gray; SCOTT, Rodney robert; SCOTT, Sandra L.; SCOTT, Thomas;
SCOTT, Thomas Wayne; SCOTTER, Troy George; SCREEN, David Gordon; SCUDDER, Brian Leslie;
SCULLY, Lowell; SDAO, Teresa Guiseppina; SEABROOK, David John; SEALE, Paula Jane;
SEALE, Robert Jason; SEARS, Bertha Allison; SEARS, Susan J.; SEBZDA, Andrea Laurel;
SEBZDA, Dan; SEEBER, Maria Luz; SEED, Mariette Denise; SEEHAGEN, Audrey;
SEEMANN, Jennifer A.; SEEPISH, Robin Christine; SEGAL, Lawrence Murray;
SEIBOLD, Myron Ladell Li; SEIFELDIN, Ali Assaad; SEIFERT, Alice; SEIFRIED, Neil R.; SEIGEL, Sharon;
SEIKER, Paul Edward; SELL, Jennifer Yvonne; SELLECK, Alison Jane; SELLES, Rein;
SELVARATNAM, Mary Jecintha; SEIZLER, A. Meigel; SELZLER, Teresa; SEMBALIUK, Andrea;
SEMBALIUK, PATRICIA: SEMBALIUK, Paul M.; SEMCHUK, Peter; SEMENIUK, Betty A.;
SEMENIUK, Greg; SEMENIUK, Iris Esther; SEMENIUK, Jon R.; SEMENIUK, Rommen Michaelo;
SEMENUIK, Orest; SEMENYNA, William James; SEMKOWICH, Sherri Lee E.;
SEMONICK, Jean Shirley; SEMONICK, Judi; SEMONICK, Peter; SEMPOVICH, Barbara Lee;
SEMWAL, Sudhanshu Kumar; SENDA, Ronald Eichi; SENGER, Carol Jean; SENGER, Cheryl Anne;
SENGER Shauna Marie; SENGER, Verna G.; SENKO, Virginia Mae; SENUIK, Douglas James;
SENYK, Cheryl Lynne; SEPT, Gerry James; SEPT, Janet Teresa; SEPULVEDA, Pat Enriquez;
SEQUEIRA, Aroon; SERBANESCU, Alina Michele; SERBANESCU, Maria-Doina;
SERBANESCU, Nicolae; SERBU, Jackie; SERBU, Samson Metro; SEREDA, Colleen Gail;
SEREDA, Glenn Peter; SEREDA, Terry Herta; SERINK, Debbie; SERNA, Carol Andrea;
SERREDA, Karen; SERVICE, Dan Bond; SERVICE, Jamie Allan; SERVOLD, Niel Kristen;
SETILOAN, Busang Peter; SETO, Gary Allan; SETO, Hing Kwak; SETTER, Michelle Ann;
SEUTTER Joseph; SEVERIN, David; SEVERIN, Gordon; SEVIGNY, Loyed Jimmy;
SEVIGNY, Steeve Geatan; SEWARD, Donna; SEXSMITH, James Richard; SEYLER, Valerie Ann;
SEYMOUR, Louisa Mabel; SEYMOUR, Ricki Patrick Steven; SEYMOUR, Wanda G.;
SHABELSKI, Debbie Anne; SHAHEDI, Esmail; SHAHNAWAZ, Ahmad; SHALAPAY, Carol;
SHALAPAY, Kenneth Patrick; SHALLWANI, Mehdi Azizali; SHALONIK, Lynda Joan;
SHAMESS, Jane Mary; SHANAHAN, Ernie Jerry; SHANDRO, Barry William; SHANDRO, Beverly D.;
SHANDRO, Elsie; SHANDRO, Lorne Dale; SHANDRO, Nicholas H.; SHANDRO, William Thomas;
SHANK, Elise Jeanne; SHANKS, Niall; SHAPIRO, Jacob; SHAPIRO, Lyucov;
SHAPKA, Brian Alexander; SHAPKA, David; SHAPKA, David Alexander SHAPKA, Elizabeth;
SHAPKA, Joy Lynne; SHAPKA, Kathreen Ann; SHARAM, Earle Scott; SHARIFF, Amin Pyarali;
SHARMA, Naresh Chander; SHARMAN, Paul Savid; SHARP, Michele Kim;
SHARP, Natalie Marguerite; SHARP, Penny Suzanne; SHARPE, Erica Joanne; SHARPE, Karen;
SHARPE, Maureen; SHARPE, Natalie Paula Anne; SHARPE, Niall Kd; SHARPLES, Frederick Glenn;
SHARPLIN, Bonnie Lynn; SHARRATT, Lisa Jayne; SHARRUN, Donna Lynn; SHARUGA, Ann;
SHARUN, Angela; SHARUN, Loria Ruth; SHAVE, Linda Mary; SHAVER, J. Myles; SHAVER, Jane Ann;
SHAVER, Jodi Anne; SHAW, Albert S.C.; SHAW, Bill John; SHAW, Brian G.; SHAW, Charles;
SHAW, Deborah Lynn; SHAW, Denise; SHAW, Geraldene; SHAW, Joanne; SHAW, Joyce Marie;
SHAW, Lawrence Ernest; SHAW Quentin Harold; SHAW, Renee; SHAW, Roger L.;
SHAW, Sandra June; SHAW, Walter R.; SHAW, Warren Robert; SHAW, William John;
SHEA, Anne Marie; SHEA, Dorothy; SHEA, Linda M.; SHEA, Michael William;
SHEDDEN, Jeannette Morton; SHEEHAN, Jeffrey T.; SHEEHAN, Todd J.; SHEEN, Brenda Delores;
SHEETS, Lynn; SHEIL, Hilary; SHEKHTER, Eugeny; SHELEFONTIUK, Paul; SHELTON, Allan B.;
SHELTON, Alleyne Margaret; SHELTON, Marnie Rose; SHELTON, Maureen Elizabeth;
SHELTON, Susan Lee; SHEPARD, Andrea Lynne; SHEPARD, Janet Gay; SHEPARD, Karen Elizabeth;
SHEPARD, Sheila; SHEPHERD, Dr. John Thomas; SHEPHERD, Jeremy Michael; SHEPHERD, Scott;
SHEPP, Dennis Douglas; SHEPP, Rae Elizabeth; SHEPPARD, Debbie Ann; SHEPPARD, Jim;
SHEPPARD, Pauline Sharron; SHEPPARD, Rainy; THEPPY, Alan Gerald; SHERBACK, Karin Louise;
SHERIDAN, Janette Veronica; SHERMAN, Inger; SHERMAN, Philip vincent; SHERMAN, Rose-Marie J.; SHEROO, Elavia; SHERRET, John Andrew; SHERRIN, Jo; SHERRINGTON, Pamela Lorraine;
SHERRIS, Keith Edwrd; SHERSTIANKO, Alison M.; SHERWIN, Doris; SHESTERNIK, Joseph Gordon;
SHEVLOUP, Larry D.; SHEVLOUP, Morris A.; SHEWCHUK, Debbie I.; SHEWCHUK, Gail Catherine;
SHEWCHUK, Laura; SHEWCHUK, Lisa; SHEWCHUK, Mary; SHEWCHUK, Michelle;
SHEWCHUK, Robyn Rae; SHEWCHUK, Sharon Lynn; SHEWCHUK, Stella Sylvia; SHEWCHUK, Victoria;
SHEWFELT, Leslie Ann; SHICKLUNA, Paul M.; SHIELDS, Bryan Thomas; SHIELDS, Derek Robert;
SHIELDS, George Edward; SHIELDS, Michael L.; SHIELDS, Terri-Lynn; SHIER, Anne Linda;
SHIFFLETT, David H.; SHIGEHIRO, Edie; SHILLABEER, John Ernest; SHILLINGTON, John M.;
SHIM, Carey; SHIMIZU, Joan; SHINDELKA, Irene S.; SHIPKA, Bernie Alexander;
SHIPKA, Judith Lorraine; SHIPKA, Karen Irene; SHPKA, Lorraine; SHIPLEY, George Richards;
SHIPLEY, Marion Agnes; SHIVAK, Marianne; SHOGAN, Roger K.; SHORE, Gregory Bruce;
SHORE, Kimberly Anne; SHORE, Stewart Graham; SHORT, Kathleen Rae; SHORT, Kenneth Gordon;
SHORT, Lorna Marie; SHORT, Rigmor; SHOSTAK, Nick; SHRAGGE, Dr. David; SHRAGGE, Mia;
SHUKALEK, Lori Maureen; SHUKALIAK, Charline Barbara; SHULER, Anne; SHULKO, Louise;
SHULTIS, Bonita Louise; SHUM, Nancy Lai Kwan, SHUMAKER, R. Matthew; SHUMLICH, Laurie Ann;
SHUPE, Mark E.; SHUPENIA, Stella; SHUR, Elena; SHUYA, Dale; SHUYA, John;
SHYMKO, Monica Fay; SIDLICK, Patricia Anne; SIDOR, Tommy Lynn; SEIG, Sandra Christina;
SIEGEL, Cheryl Gayle; SIEMENS, Richard Haven; SIEMENS, Valerie L.; SIEVE, Lois Ann;
SIGFSTEAD, Bryun; SIGFSTEAD, Dianne; SIGURDSON, Lana; SIGURDSON, Terence Gil;
SIGURDSON, Wendy; SIHVO, Tim Topani; SIKORA, Frank; SIKORSKI, Zanette Marie;
SIKSTROM, Sari; SILK, Evelyn Frances; SILLIPHANT, Stephen Barrie; SILLS, Barbara Dorise;
SILVER, Susan Diane; SILZER, Brian; SILZER, Cecile; SILZER, Michael James; SIM, Leona Ann;
SIMANOVSKIS, Janis; SIMAO, Humberto P. Guimaraes; SIMARD, Jocelyn Leda; SIMARD, Marc;
SIMARD, Sandra; SIME, Thomas James; SIMISON, M. Magdalen;
SIMMONDS, David Robert, SIMMONDS, Ellen Mae; SIMMONDS, Jacqueline; SIMMONDS, Lee-Ann Helen; SIMMNDS, Wendy; SIMMONS, Harold James; SIMMONS, Malcolm Warner;
SIMMONS, Nancy Irene; SIMON, Valerie Jill; SIMONOT, Adrien Gilbert; SIMONSON, Marilyn Jean;
SIMONYI, Gabar; SIMPKIN, Frederic Benjamin; SIMPKIN, Jane; SIMPSON, Angus Walker;
SIMPSON, Brian Ross; SIMPSON, David; SIMPSON, Daine Elizabeth; SIMPSON, Gayle Ann;

SIMPSON, Iain; SIMPSON, James Ernest; SIMPSON, John; SIMPSON, Lynda Dianne;
SIMPSON, Marilyn Irene; SIMPSON, Robert Wayne; SIMPSON, Sandra Gay;
SIMPSON, Thomas Edgar; SIMS, Barb Corinne; SIMS, Leland Glen; SIMUNKOVIC, Gary John;
SIMUNKOVIC, Paul, David; SINAL, Perri Martine; SINCLAIR, Catherine; SINCLAIR, Edward;
SINCLAIR, Grant; SINCLAIR, Jack Lenwood; SINCLAIR, Leila M.; SINCLAIR, Lori Ann;
SINCLAIR, Myrna Lee; SINGER-JORDAN, Dr. Jonathan; SINGER, Kenneth Gordon; SINGER, Millie H.;
SINGER, Paul Arthur; SINGH, Jitemdra; SINGH, Mohan; SINGH, Nikhilegh; SINGH, Solinder;
SINGH, Sulinder; SINGH, Teja; SINGLETON, Margaret C.; SINKWICH, Don Alexander W.;
SINNOTT, Judy; SIRDAR, Sheila Maureen; SIROIS, Audrey Mae; SIROIS, Ghislaine Aline;
SIROIS, Helen Dolores; SIROIS, Lina; SISKA, Valerie Dawn; SISSON, Gordon Paul;
SISSON, Larry Gordon; SISSON, Lindy R.; SISSONS, Tracie Lynn; SITTLER, Arlene Glenda;
SITTLER, Thelma Mary Theresa; SIVAK, Kay; SJULSTAD, Heather Jane; SKAGOS, Jimmy;
SKAKEN, Luci; SKARECKY, Simona Jirina; SKEELS, Lenard; SKERRA, Susanne Barbara;
SKETT, Margaret Peggy; SKILLEN, Lynn; SKILLINGS, James; SKINBERG, Pamela Ann;
SKINBERG, Patricia May; SKINBERG, Terry; SKINNER, Barbara Gail; SKITSKO, Ann Janet;
SKOG, Corry Dawn; SKOGG, Patricia Evelyn; SKOLSKI, Patrick Allan; SKONE, Susan Helen;
SKREPNEK, Peggy; SKROBOT, Denise; SKULMOSKI, Sharon; SKWAREK, Reg John;
RLABYSZ, Richard; SLACK, Trevor; SLAGHT, Linda Ann; SLATER, Vikki Joan; SLATOR, Cheryl;
SLATOR, Karen Ann; SLATTER, Elizabeth Anne; SLAVEN, Maureen Rose; SLAVIK, Guy Louis;
SLAVIK, Veronica Marian; SLECZKA, Patricia Lynn; SLECZKO, Sandra Joan; SLEIGHT, Terri;
SLELLEN, Pronyk; SLEMKO, Debra; SLEMKO, Derrick Wayne; SLEMKO, Russ; SLEMKO, Terry;
SLEMKO, Yvonne; SLINN, Patrick Alexander; SLIPEC, Cathy; SLIPP, Marke L.; SLOAN, Robert;
SLOBODAN, Michael Russell: SLOBODAN, Myrna Dianne; SLOMP, Florence; SLUPEK, John W.;
SLUPEK, John W.; SLYWKA, Larry Nestor; SMALIAN, Ernest; SMALL, Brenda Lynn; SMALL, Brian;
SMALL, Cecile S.; SMALL, Darlene Reda Mae; SMALL, Dave; SMALL, David Bruce;
SMALL, Evelyn Elsie; SMALL, Fred; SMALL, Geo Roger; SMALL, Marilyn; SMALLWOOD, Cheryl;
SMARSH, Robert Gordon; SMART, Susan Maria; SMATHERS, Tonya; SMECKO, Joe; SMEDSTAD, Oli;
SMEREK, Irene A.; SMEREKA, Wendy Candace; SMIRNOV, Polina; SMIT, Nick Hubert;
SMITH, Allen Gordon; SMITH, Allison; SMITH, Anita Lana; SMITH, Ann; SMITH, Annette;
SMITH, Anthony Marvin; SMITH, Arthur Raymond; SMITH, Beverly; SMITH, Beverly Lynn;
SMITH, Brenda; SMITH, Bruce David N.; SMITH, Bruce T.; SMITH, C.R. Randy; SMITH, Car La Maria;
SMITH, Carmen Loretta; SMITH, Catherine Ann; SMITH, Cecil; SMITH, Christopher Stanley;
SMITH, Cindy Joyce; SMITH, Colin James; SMITH, Daryl; SMITH, Denise Gale;
SMITH, Donald James; SMITH Donald L.; SMITH, Donna Helen; SMITH, Donna Lynn;
SMITH, Dorothy; SMITH, Douglas Allan; SMITH, Douglas Brian; SMITH, Dr. Bruce Douglas;
SMITH, Dr. Margaret Grace; SMITH Dwayne Robert; SMITH, Eileen Ruth Emma; SMITH, Ellen Vivian;
SMITH, Florence Ruth; SMITH, Garry John; SMITH, Gary Clifford; SMITH, Graham;
SMITH, Grant Herbert; SMITH, Guy Anthony; SMITH, Guy Leonard; SMITH, Heather;
SMITH, Isabel Alexandra; SMITH, Jacqueline Alethea; SMITH, Jacqueline Patricia;
SMITH, Jacqueline Susan; SMITH, James Deean; SMITH, Janet; SMITH, Janet Christine;
SMITH, Janet Rae; SMITH, Jason Lindsay; SMITH, Jay David; SMITH, Jean M.; SMITH, Jeffrey Neil;
SMITH, Jeffrey William; SMITH, Jennifer; SMITH, John Mcaree; SMITH, Juanita Gladys;
SMITH, Judy; SMITH, Judy Patricha Anne; SMITH, Karen Jean; SMITH, Katherine Jane;
SMITH, Kathy; SMITH, Kathy Diann; SMITH, Katrina; SMITH, Keith; SMITH, Lawrence L.;
SMITH, Leoda; SMITH, Linda Darlene; SMITH, Lorna Ann; SMITH, Margaret; SMITH, Margaret Ann;
SMITH, Margaret Elizabeth; SMITH, Margaret Karen; SMITH, Marlene Alice; SMITH, Mary Frances;
SMITH, Maureen Patricia; SMITH, Mel Gordon; SMITH, Melanie; SMITH, Michael R.;
SMITH, Monica Jean; SMITH, Murray; SMITH, Niall Charles; SMITH, Nicolle Dorothy;
SMITH, Norma Jean; SMITH, Norman; SMITH, Norman Bailey; SMITH, Pamela Muriel Rebecca;
SMITH, Patricia Ann; SMITH, Phyllis A.; SMITH, Raymond S.; SMITH, Renee Carmina;
SMITH, Ricks Sloan; SMITH, Robert Alexander; SMITH, Robert Donald; SMITH, Roxanne Kismean;
SMITH, Roy; SMITH, Ruby Alethea; SMITH, Ryan Kenneth; SMITH, Sharon D. SMITH, Siobhan;
SMITH, Stacey C.; SMITH, Sylvia; SMITH, Tracey Jo; SMITH, Wayne Curtis;
SMITH, Wesley Gwynne; SMITH, William Allen; SMITH, Wilma A.; SMITH, Yvonne Jeanne;
SMITS, Hans; SMITTEN, Lesley; SMOK, Cindy; SMOLAK, Edward James;
SMOICIC, Margaret Caroline; SMORDIN, Shelby; SMRECIU, Nicholas Germain;
SMYTH, James William; SMYTH, Lorraine Ruth; SMYTH, Robert H.; SNART, Myrna Louise;
SNAYCHUYK, Darryl Orest; SNELL, Edna; SNELL, Laurie Rose; SNIDER, Donald Philip;
SNOW, Debra Anne; SNOW, Donald; SNOW, Gary Howard; SNOW, Roxanna;
SNOWADZKI, Jeff Walter; SMNYDER, Amy Beth; SNYDER, Audrey Angela; SNYDER, Delores;
SNYDER, Marlene Dianne; SNYDER, Nancy Jeanne; SNYDER, Robert Allen; SOARS, John Berry;
SOBON, Sophie C.; SOBON, Sophie Christine; SOBATTKA, Kurt Jurgen; SODKE, Karen Holly;
SOETAERT, Joanne Phillis; SOFONOFF, Joan M.; SOKOL, Alexis Mary; SOKOLOSKI, Audrey May;
SOKOLUK, Kimberly Novice; SOKOLUK, Lisa Jane; SOKOLUK, Lori; SOKOLUK, Lori Roxanne;
SOLBERG, Wayne H.; SOLDAN, Anita Jean; SOLEM, Roberta B.A.; SOLI, Sharen Ann; SOLISKI, Gail;
SOLISKI, Ronald Wayne; SOLLEREDER, Karen Phyllis; SOLLOSY, Russell W.; SOLLWAY, Perry Gale;
SOLOJUK, Leslie Rae; SOLOMON, Dan; SOLONYNKO, Garry Heath; SOLONYNKO, Michael Keith;
SOLOWAN, Mabel; SOLOWAN, Ron Nick; SOLTESZ, Cindy Marie; SOLTICE, Susan;
SOLTYKEWYCH, Orest Constant; SOLTYS, Elizabeth; SOLYLO, Fred M.; SOMERSET, Jane Elizabeth;
SOMERVILLE, Kathy Ann: SOMLAI, Ivan D.; SOMMER, Michelle Dawn; SOMMER, Shelly Marie;
SOMMERFELDT, Susan Champion; SOMOGYVARI, Bill V.; SONEFF, Linda Olivia; SONG, Cook;
SONG, Hiju; SONNEN, Lesley Ann: SOO, Siew Christine Thau; SOOD, Prem Sagar;
SOPCHYSHYN, Olga Helen; SOPCZAK, Peter; SORENSEN, Birte; SORENSEN, Chet Clayton;
SORENSEN, John; SORENSON, Karen; SORENSEN, M. Janette; SORENSON, Brian Richard;
SOROBEY, William; SOROCHAN, Patricia Joan; SOROKA, Shaun; SOROKIN, Hershel;
SOSNIUK, Elaine Marian; SOSNOWSKI, Dr. Terry David; SOTO-ADOLFO, Fernando; SOTO, Ivan;
SOTO, Victor Alexander; SOUCY, Jean-Luc; SOUCY, Roland; SOUKUP, Hana;
SOULEIRE, Delie Dawn: SOULIERE, Maurice Patrick; SOUSTER, Joan Leslie; SOUTH, Karen;
SOUTHAM, Lyle; SOUTHWORTH, Christine Carol; SPADAUECCHIA, Rosanna; SPAK, Bernie William;
SPAK, Harvey Leonard; SPAK, Vivian; SPALDING, James Charles; SPANER, Donna Ann;
SPANER, Shelley Jane; SPANGGAARD, Finn Bjorn; SPANOPULOS, Gabriele;
SPARROW, Bonnie Lynn: SPECHT, Hans-Jurgen; SPEELMAN, Leah L.; SPENCE, Susan May;
SPENCER, Joseph Henry Prince; SPENCER, Kathryn Ann; SPENCER, Marion;
SPENCER, Mary Gervaise E.; SPENCER, Michelle Julia; SPENCER, Nicola Jane;
SPENDELOW, Brian Dennis; SPENRATH, Henry, E.; SPENRATH, Kathy Ann;
SPENRATH, Lorraine Marie; SPENRATH, Louise Genevieve; SPERLING, Les Michael;
SPERLING, Ronald Alexander; SPERRY, Wayne Howard; SPIEGELHANN, Steve Michael;
SPILLER, Paul Joseph; SPILSTED, Karla; SPINK, David; SPINK, Valerie Jacinte; SPITZ, Nancy Ann;
SPLAWSKY, William B.; SPONAGLE, Rand John; SPOONER, Ruth Davies; SPORCIC, Mary C.;
SPOT, Virginia; SPOTOWSKI, Andrea; SPRACKLIN, Kevin William; SPRAGUE, Donald Howard;
SPRAGUE, Grant; SPRAGUE, Kenneth Howard; SPRAGUE, Sandra Alverne; SPRAGUE, Sherrill Ann;
SPREAD, Carolyn Yvonne; SPREAD, Yvonne-Marie; SPRING, Sharon Lee; SPRINGER, Brenda Susan;
SPRINGER, Kristine Lee; SPRINKLING, Tracy E.; SPROAT, Lyle Emerson; SPROULE, Barbara Lillian;
SPROULE, Marnie; SPROULE, Shannon D.; SPROULE, Valerie Hilda; SPROULL, Iain M.;
SPYSZNYK, Carlos Eduardo; SPYSZNYK, Pedra; SQUAROK, Andy; SQUAROK, Mary Jacqueline;
SRIRANGAPATNA, Narayana; ST. AMAND, Serge Albert; ST. AMANT, Helen Marie Therese;
ST. ANDRE, Jacqueline Marie; ST. ARNAUD, Germaine; ST. GEORGE-RENNIE, Jacqueline;
ST. PIERRE, Kathy Evelyn; STACHNIAK, Cindy; STACK, G. Ronnie; STACK, Margaret-Anne Winifred;
STACK, Philip Gerard; STACK, Walter William; STADNYK, John; STADNYK, Maria Irena;
STAHL, Dawn; STAHLER, Barbara; STAINES, Lara Jean; STALKER, Rhona; STAMMER, Ingrid;
STAMP, Holly Jean; STAMP, Kenneth Jack; STAN, Betty Jean;
STANDISH, Arthur Stanley: STANDISH, Laurie Jayne; STANECKI, Joanne Elaine;
STANFORD, Linda Kay; STANG, Christina Marie; STANG, Joyce B.; STANGROOM, Randi;
STANHOPE, Joan Margaret; STANHOPE, Wendy B.; STANLEY, Ann; STANLEY, Brenda Louise;
STANLEY, Donald Wesguarth; STANLEY, Doris Evelyn; STANLEY, Gordon Richard M.;
STANLEY, Kimberly A.; STANLEY, Maryalice Catherine; STANLEY, Michael Andrew;
STANNERS, Donald A. STANNERS, Donald Alexander; STANNERS, Karales Lloy; STANNERS, Michele;
STANNERS, Roxane Jacqueline; STANNERS, Tamara Joy; STANTON, Ann;
STANTON, Charles Austin; STANTON, Dawn Carolyne; STANTON, Kenneth James;
STANTON, Lou Claire; STANTON, Margaret; STAPLES, Jeanette Nora; STAPLES, Richard Lee;
STAPLETON, Jeanette; STAPLETON, Kevin Walter; STAPLETON, Lisa; STARING, Cathryn Elizabeth;
STARING, Gerald Craig; STARING, M. Jean; STARK, Eduard; STARK, Hebert; STARK, Laura Lee;
STARK, Patricia Evelyn; STARK, Shelly Theresa; STARK, Tom; STARKE, Regina Margarete;
STARKMAN, Daniel Charles; STARKMAN, Sophie; STAROSELSKY, Regina; STARR, Audrey L.;
STARR, Jane Ellen; STARR, Lea Katharine; STARR, Mary Frances; STARRATT, Rene Colette;
STASESON, Janice Margaret; STATHIS, Gus; STAUDT, Hilde; STAWNYCHKA, Paulette Ann;
STEAD, Albert Edward; STEAD, Ivy M.; STEAD, M. Elaine; STEADWARD, Deborah; STEARNS, Joan;
STEARNS, John Roy; STEBELSKY, Luba Kristine; STEBLYK, Anne Laureen;
STEBLYK, Carolyn Mary Ann; STEBLYK, Cathy P. STEBLYK, Joann Margaret; STEBLYK, Patricia;
STECYK, Alice Mary; STEEDMAN, Shelley Anne; STEEDSMAN, Hannah Beatrice; STEELE, Dianna L.;
STEELE, Erin Hugh; STEELE, Gail Elaine; STEELE, Hugh; STEELE, Raeanne Lynn;
STEELE, William Scott; STEENVELD, Cameron Ivan; STEENVELD, Wendy Lee; STEER, Rena Kathleen;
STEEVES, Dale; STEEVES, Debby; STEEVES, Jody Lee; STEEVES, Marlene P.;
STEFANCICK, Mark Andrew; STEFANICK, George; STEFANICK, Millie R.; STEFANICZAN, Debra;
STEFANYK, Lucille Claire; STEFURA, Ann; STEFURA, Donna; STEIL, Lavonna June; STEIN, Edith C.;
STEIN, Janet Lee; STEINBERGER, Tibor; STEINBRING, Edwin Gary; STEINBRING, Karen Marie;
STEINKE, Cheryl Lynn; STEISKAL, Maryann Rose; STELFOX, Harry Anderson; STELMACH, Angeline;
STELMACH, Lew B.; STELTER, Marion Myrtle; STEMP, Robert Charles; STENGEL, Ingrid;
STENSON, Yvonne Charlene; STENSRUD, Kenneth Lyman; STENSRUD, Shirley Joyce;
STEPHEN, Deborah L.; STEPHEN, Frank; STEPHEN, Robert Mark; STEPHENS, Alexander;
STEPHENS, Cher A. STEPHENS, Derek Thomas; STEPHENSON, Ann; STEPHENSON, Larry Paul;
STEPHENSON, Lynne; STEPHENSON, Tina; STERK, John; STERLING, Glenn Michael; STERLING, Ian;
STERLING, Janet; STERNBERG, Dr. Harvey Hayes; STERNBERG, Ester Macca;
STERNS, Dr. Lawrence Perrin; STETSON, Marlene Louise; STEUDEL, Cecile Lydia; STEUDEL, Jeffrey;
STEVENS-GUILLE, C.R. Marcella; STEVENS-GUILLE, Desmond Philip; STEVENS, Edith;
STEVENS, Ernie; STEVENS, Joyce Annette; STEVENS, Linda; STEVENS, Paul A.;
STEVENS, Peggie Jean; STEVENS, Sandi; STEVENSON, Carole; STEVENSON, Debbie;
STEVENSEN, John; STEVENSON, John Hollett; STEVENSON, Kevin Russell;
STEVENSON, Merilyn Gail; STEVENSON, Sarah Anne; STEVENSON, Sherry Lynn;
STEVENSON, Vivian Ruth; STEVENSON, Wilma; STEWART, Beth M.; STEWART, Brenda Joyce;
STEWART, David R.; STEWART, Donna; STEWART, Doris Irene; STEWART, Douglas Stanley;
STEWART, R. Darrel; STEWART, Duane David; STEWART, Gail Susan; STEWART, Gerald David;
STEWART, Irene W.; STEWART, James H.; STEWART, Jay; STEWART, Jan Malcolm Bryan;
STEWART, Joycelyn Christine; STEWART, Leslie Catherine; STEWART, Linda Ann; STEWART, Loral;
STEWART, Lynda Layne; STEWART, Michael; STEWART, Pearl; STEWART, Rob David;
STEWART, William Kenneth; STIFT, Sandra Barbara; STILES, Dean James; STILES, Max William;
STILES, Peggy Edith; STILLWELL, Alan; STILLWELL, Alan Lloyd; STILWELL, Reginald;
STINSON, Robert Anthony; STIRJA, Nora; STIRLING, Glen; STIRLING, Joan Florence;
STIRLING, Linda; STIRRUP, Mike David; STITT, Terrence Deimer; STOBBE, Corinne Cheryl;
STOBY, Janet Christine; STOCHINSKY, Ava Marion; STOCHINSKY, Erin; STOCHINSKY, Lara Maureen;
STOCKDALE, D. Roxanne; STOCKDALE, Grace H.; STOCKWELL, Diane Lee; STOCKWELL, Lola Joy;
STODDARD, Ronald Lawrence; STODDART, Andrew William; STODDART, Carol Christina;
STODDART, Cindy Christina; STODDART, Ian G.; STOETZEL, Leonard J.; STOKES, Shelley Marie;
STOLL, Audrey J.; STOLLERY, Richard Andrew; STOLLINGS, Darren; STONE, Elena Gale;
STONE, Shaunnah; STONE, Susan Mary; STONEHOUSE, George Lewis;
STONELAKE, David Alexander; STORESHAW, Barry James; STORESHAW, Janice Elaine;
STOREY, Cathy; STORIE, Dwight C.; STOROSCHUK, Joanne Marie; STOROSCHUK, Susan Margaret;
SORRIER, Betty Margaret; STORRIER, Bob; STORRIER, Colleen Michelle; STORRIER, Linda Jo;
STOTHART, George Gilmour; STOTHART, Margaret; STOTT, Andrew; STOTT, Andrew Thomas;
STOTT, Clare; STOTT, Clare Katharine; STOTT, Jon Copeland; STOUT, Carolyn; STOUT, Monte H.;
STOUT, Monte Harold; STOWE, Mark Thomas; STOWE, Sandra Lee; STOWKOWY, Allen William;
STOWKOWY, Bonnie; STOWKOWY, Keitie Maureen; STOWKOWY, Stephen; STRAIN, Hart Robert;
STRAIN, Laura; STRAKA, Alena V.; STRAND, Greg John; STRAND, Sheila; STRAND, Sheila K.;
STRANG, Lisa Marie; STRANG, Marie Jane; STRANGMAN, Sandra Gwennen;
STRASHOK, Taras John; STRASS, Peggy L.; STRASS, Rae A.; STRATTON, Nancy Beith;
STRAUSS, Lori; STRAUSS, Ron William; STRAUTMAN, Julia Lynn; STREADWICK, John Paul;
STRELKOV, Alicia Beatriz; STRETCH, Herbert Charles; STRIBRNY, Jaromir K.; STRICKLER, Karl;
STRIEGLER, Susanne P.; STRIFLER, Jay-Jon Irwin; STRIFLER, Joyce Marie; STRIFLER, Kym-Shae Joyce; STRIFLER, LeeJay Irwin; STIFLER, Shae-Lee Joyce; STRINGAM, Esther A.;
STROICH, Terrance Stephen: STROJEK,Sylvia; STROME, Marvey Lavern; STROMSMOE, Marcia;
STRONACH, Donna; STRONG, James P.; STRONG, Joyce M.; STRONG, Lawrence;
STRONG, Marcy Dawn; STRONG, Marlene Patricia; STROUD, Lynda Joyce; STRUCK, Irene;
STRUDWICK, Doris; STRUGER, John M.; STRUK, Linda Ann; STRYNADKA, Hazel Ann;
STRYNADKA, Ken Dave; STUART, Agnes W.; STUART, Aileen; STUART Alan Grant;
STUART, Dave Charles; STUART, James Stephen; STUAR, Patricia Joan;
STUBBINGTON, June Joanne; STUBBS, Dr. Robert Lloyd; STUDER, Doris; stuhl, Barbara Anne;
STUMP, Lorna Rose; STUMPH, Brent; STUNDEN, Cathy S.; STURGEON, E. Jane;
STURGEON, William L.C.; STURGES, Patricia Margaret; STURGES, Philip Terence;
STURGESS, Nancy Jane; STURKO, Danni; STURKO, Micheal; SURMAY, Ross Michael;
SUBBARAO, Suseela; SUCH, Elsie G.; SUCHODOLSKI, Fred; SUDDARDS, Brian Robert;
SUDYK, Walter; SUECROFT, Audrey Eileen; SUGDEN, Carolyn; SUGDEN, Lynn Kenneth;
SUKALSKY, Boris; SUKONNIK, Peter; SULAK, George; SULAK, Shirley Tina; SULLIVAN, Carol Anne;
SULLIVAN, Juhn Patrick; SULLIVAN maurine; SULLIVAN, Paul Frederich; SULLIVAN, Robert John;
SULLIVAN, Susan Jean; SULYMA, Joseph Danial SULYMA, Wayne; SUMBAR, Edmund;
SUMMERS, Douglas Beryl; SUMMERS, Jerry; SUMMERS, Mary; SUMNER, Topdd Michael;
SUN, Zheng Ping; SUNDBY, Roy; SUNDMARK, Dana Luther; SURGENOR, Susan Marjorie;
SURGIN, Alan Kerr; SUROWIAK, Janet; SUSHYNSKI, Cheryl Lynn; SUSHNSKI, W. Allan;
SUSINSKI, Ann; SUTER, Elsie Edith; SUTHERLAND, Jack Alexander; SUTHERLAND, Judy;
SUTHERLAND, Lisa Dawn; SUTHERLAND, Lynn Ann; SUTTON, Ann; SITTON, Iris;
SUVA, Cesar Antonio Guzman; SUWALA, Jerome; SVARICH, Susan; SVEN, Wai Yeung;
SVENDGAARD, Marianne B.; SVENDSEN, Richard Alan; Svengaard, Esther Marie;
SVERDAHL, Daine Lynn; SWADRON, Mary; SWAIN, Duncan James; SWAN, Roseanne;
SWANN, Joan; SWANN, Susan; SWANSON, Leonard; SWANSON, Lorne; SWANSON, Ruby;
SWARBRICK, Brian; SWARE, Judith Dianne; SWAREN, Lisa; SWAREN, Tanya Simone;

SWART, Kelly Lynn; SWARTZ, Ray Kenneth; SWEETNAM, Maureen; SWEETNAM, Maureen Grace; SWENARCHUK, Walter A.; SWENSON, Barbara Anne; SWENSON, Steven Brent; SWIFT, Hilton Roy; SWINAMER, Gary Andrew; SWINAMER, Marlene M.; SWINIARSKI, Stacey; SWINSTEINICKI, Karen L.; SWITZER, Gary Peter; SWITZER, Jean; SWITZER, Keith; SWITZER, Leonard G.; SWORD, Karin Joyce; SWORD, L. Deborah; SWORD, Michael; SWORD, William Ralph; SY, T.W. Barre; SYCH, Brenda Lynn; SYCH Diane; SYDOR, Carol Joan; SYDOR, Caroline Joan; SYKES, Barbara; SYKES, Celeste M.C.; SYKES, Lorraine Gail; SYKES, Thomasl; SYLVESTER, Robert Neil; SYME, Marcie Lynn; SYMON, Lawrence; SYMONS, Julia Anne; SYMONS, Peter; SYSAK, Kelly Ann; SYSAK, Terry S.; SZALAY, Peter Alexander; SZASZKIEWICZ, marie Elizabeth; SZASZKIEWICZ, Paul Joseph; SZENTHE, Anna; SZEPESI, Susan; SZEPESI, William Andrew; SZIABEY, Dianne; SZOJKA, Michael Glenn; SZPYTMA, Mark; SZRAM Pauline; SZUCS, Joseph Leonard; SZUCS, Leslie Lynn; SZULC, Bogumila; SZUMIK, Peter; SZWENDER, Alice Sophia; SZWPONSKI, Jim Alfred; SZYBUNIA, Christianna;

T

TABASHNIUK, Conrad Daniel; TABIN, Arnie; TABOR, Lemont John; TABOR, Michele Renee; TADVALKAR, Prakash; TAETS-VAN AMERONGEN, John; TAETS-VAN AMERONGEN, Mary-Lou; TAILLEUR, Leo Joseph; TAILLEUR, Robert Henry; TAIT, Clifton William; TAIT, Karen Elaine; TAIT, Murray F.; TAKAHASHI, Ingrid Marie; TAKAHASHI, John; TAKAHASKI, Hank; TAKAPACKI, Joe-Marie; TALALA, Tareef Ata; TALARICO, Anthony John; TALARICO, Sandy; TALBOT, Jocelyne; TALBOT, Randall; TALBOT, Richard Robert; TALLMAN, Allan E.; TALLON, Frances Irene; TALLY, Karen Jo-Ann; TALLY, Pamela M.; TAM, David; TAMER-SALLOUM, Odette; TAN, Buan Chuan; TAN, Chor Boon; TAN, Cisilia Rahmawati; TANASICHUK, Adrian Keith; TANASICHUK, Hilary Ann; TANASIUK, Mike; TANCHUK, Donald Michael; TANG, Alice Po-Lin; TANG, Charles Ngi Wah; TANG, Deborah; TANG, Qian; TANGEN, Agnes; TANNER, Helen Adele; TANNER, Kathryn; TANSEY, Maureen Joan; TANTI, Victor; TAPLIN, Janice Anne; TAPPAUF, Elsie Anne; TAPPAUF, Emma; TARASOFF, Shelley Doris; TARNAWSKI, Amanda; TARNAWSKI, Vlodek; TARNOW, Shannon Holly-Kay; TARON, Dianne; TARRABAIN, Mike; TASCHUK, Diana Lee; TASCHUK, Sharon Ann; TASKEY, Esther Ann; TASKINEN, Sonja; TATARCHUK, Erik; TATARYN, Ivanna Viola; TATARYN, Larry; TATARYN, Linda Diane; TATE, Judy; TATE, Noreen Louise; TAUSCHER, Ursula; TAUSCHER, Ursula Marie; TAVANO, Ninetta; TAVERNER, Marina; TAYLOR, Alison J. Elizabeth; TAYLOR, Brian James; TAYLOR, Carolyn Jaye; TAYLOR, Christine Arlene; TAYLOR, Christy; TAYLOR, David K.; TAYLOR, Donald Milton; TAYLOR, Doris Jean; TAYLOR, Dr. Michael Herbert; TAYLOR, Dr. William J.B.; TAYLOR, Dr. William P.; TAYLOR, Elva; TAYLOR, Ian James; TAYLOR, Jenny; TAYLOR, Julie; TAYLOR, Mario V.; TAYLOR, Nancy; TAYLOR, Pamela; TAYLOR, Penelope L.; TAYLOR, Robert C.; TAYLOR, Rodney Sherwood; TAYLOR, Russell Frederick; TAYLOR, Sandra Diane; TAYLOR, Sandy; TAYLOR, Shem Guiou; TAYLOR, Wayne E.; TAYLOR, William Henry; TAYLOR, William Joseph; TE, Dr. Luis; TEAGLE, Roy; TEAGUE, Margaret Joan; TEASDALE, Lennie; TEASDALE, Peter; TEASE, Barbara Myrl; TEEUWSEN-HARTFORD, Glenn; TEICHGRABER, Anne; TEICHGRABER, Reinholt; TELFORD, Lorraine A.; TELFORD, Patricia Ann; TELIDETZKI, Rita Doris; TEMPLE, Becky; TEMPLE, Evelyn; TEMPLE, Janice Anita; TEMPLEMAN, Marleen Joan; TEMPLEMAN, Thomas Neil; TEMPLETON, Carolle Edna; TEMPLETON, Robin Bennett; TENETULK, Todd; TENG, Li-Ping Tracy; TENNANT, Adrienne Rae; TENNANT, Kathleen June; TEO, Koon-Hoo; TERCIER, Shirley Anne; TERNER, Kurt F.G.; TERRILL, Charles Jay; TERSMETTE, Gerard A.; TERSMETTE, Joan; TERZIANA, Catherine; TESSMER, Mavis Ardelle; TETU, Louis; TETZLAFF, Corrine Catherine; TEWS, Tami Lynn; THAO, Pham Van; THATCHER, Jonathan James; THEOPHILUS, Shirley Marie; THEORET, Chantelle Monique; THEORET, Richard Leon; THERIAULT, Allan James; THERIAULT, John Paul; THERIAULT, Patricia Anne; THERIAULT, Susan Marie; THEUSS, Norman W.; THIBAUDEAU, Anthony V.; THIBAULT, Barbara; THIBAULT, Sally M.; THIBAULT, Serge; THIBERT, Robert Allen; THIBODEAU, Peter Charles; THIEM, James; THIEVEN, Yvette Paula; THIRKILL-HOBSON, Charles; THIVERGE, Ann-Marie A.; THOEN, Joanne Veneda; THOM, Donald; THOMAN, Louise Anne; THOMAS, Dave; THOMAS, Deborah Diane; THOMAS, Derri; THOMAS, Elizabeth Ann; THOMAS, Geoff; THOMAS, Myrna R.J.; THOMAS, Nancy; THOMAS, Neil G.; THOMAS, Petra Anna; THOMAS, Terry J.A.; THOMASON, Kari Lee; THOMLINSON, Kristine Bevery; THOMPSON, Cindie J.; THOMPSON, David Gordon; THOMPSON, Deryl E.F.; THOMPSON, Doris Elizabeth; THOMPSON, Frances; THOMPSON, Gary Wayne; THOMPSON, Gordon William; THOMPSON, James Wilke; THOMPSON, Judith Ann; THOMPSON, Judith Rae; THOMPSON, Kathy; THOMPSON, Laura B.; THOMPSON, Lee; THOMPSON, Leonard Andrew; THOMPSON, Lorne N.; THOMPSON, Margare Teresa; THOMPSON, Margaret Elaine; THOMPSON, Maureen Joselyn; THOMPSON, Patricia Louise; THOMPSON, Patty Gail; THOMPSON, Robert John; THOMPSON, Shailene Elizabeth; THOMPSON, Shannon Judith; THOMPSON, Shirley Ellen; THOMPSON, Suzanne Adele; THOMSON, Charles; THOMSON, Colleen; THOMSON, Doreen Norma; THOMSON, Duncan John; THOMSON, Ian Miller; THOMSON, Janis Dawn; THOMSON, Jennifer Grace; THOMSON, Joanna Louise; THOMSON, Joanne L.; THOMSON, Mary Lou; THOMSON, Sharon Ann; THOMSON, Shauna Gaylene; THOMSON, Thomas Richard; THORARINSON, Gene; THORARINSON, Sylvia J.S.: THORKELSSON, Paul; THORIAKSON, Barney A.; THORIAKSON, Doug Michael; THORIAKSON, Jean Barbara; THORIAKSON, Marlene S.; THORNBOROUGH, M. Brenda; THORNBOROUGH, Ronald William; THORNE, Linda M.; THORNEWELL, Donna Jean; THORNTON, Candy Eva; THORNTON, Lorna May; THORNTON, Paula Mary; THORPE, Shirley Isabell; THORSELL, Steve; THORSON, Darrell Wayne; THORSON, Karin; THOW, Kelli Lee Ann; THOW, Sherry Dawn Marie; THRALL, Richard Henry; THRESHER, Ted Edward; THRIFT, Julie Lucille; THRONDSON, Cathy Lynne; THURSTON, Ted; TIENKAMP, Trudy; TIEULIE, Darcy Real; TIEULIE, Gerard Gabriel; TIEULIE, Lynn Fern; TIEULIE, Paulette Vivian; TIGHE, Shannon Maureen; TILBURY, Trudy Ann; TILLAPAUGH, Sheila Mae; TILLNER, Katherine Susan; TIMANSON, Kent Alan; TIMLECK, Cindy Anne; TIMLECK, David Doran; TIMMER, John; TIMMER, Patricia Anne Marie; TIMMERMAN, Bobbi Wynne; TIMMONS, Karen Dawn; TIMMONS, Kristen Suzanne; TIMMONS, Patricia Lynn; TIMMS, Fae-Lynn; TIMOTEO, Enzo; TINKLER, Thomas Maurice; TITHECOTT, Ronald Gordon; TJOSVOLD, Ken E.; TKACHENKO, Helen; TKACHUK, Dolores Eleanor; TKACHUK, Donald Gordon; TKACHUK, Marilyn Beryl; TKACHUK, Ronald David; TKACHUK, Ronald E.; TKACHUK, Shawn; TKACHUK, Ted J.; TKACHUK, William; TO, Dominic; TO, Huan Thanh; TOAL, Dr. Kevin; TOBAR, Anna Marina; TOBEY, Irene Marjory; TOBEY, William Alfred; TOCHENIUK, Laureen; TOCHENIUK, Steven; TOCHENIUK, Valerie; TOCHENUIK, Iona; TOD, Brian; TOD, Brian William Leslie; TOES, Kristiana Monique; TOFIN, Elinor Anne Frances; TOKARYK, Lily; TOKER, Shirley; TOLBOOM, Cornelius; TOLLER, Rob Campbell; TOLLEY, Deborah Tui; TOLMIE-THOMPSON, Jana Lee; TOM, Mei; TOME, Kesi; TOMKINS, Tanya; TOMKO, Dianne Cheryl; TOMLINSON, David Brian; TOMLINSON, George Henry; TOMLINSON, Jill Karen; TOMLJANOVIC, Goran; TOMM, Alma Alice; TOMNEY, Marilyn Iris; TOMNIUK, Bob; TONAI, Tammy; TONG, Sam S.Y.; TOOGOOD, John Alfred; TOOKEY, Ronald Alvin; TOOLE, Susan Mary; TOOTH, Jean Ellen; TOPOLNISKY, Metro; TOPOLNISKY, Teresa May; TOPP, Eileen; TOPPING, Anne Bernadette; TOPPING, John Arthur; TOPPING, Maureen Edith Elaine; TORGERSON, Vigi; TOROK-BATH, George A.; TORONCHUK, Allison W.; TOSHIAKI, Oda; TOTH, Cecilia; TOTH, Ferenc; TOTH, Peter Richard; TOTINO, Aileen Wilhelmina; TOTINO, Frank Carmen; TOTTRUP, Lois Evelyn; TOUCHETTE, Jeann; TOUGAS, Diane Michelle; TOUPIN, Gloria Marguerite; TOURANGEAU, Patricia Anne; TOWELL, Ronald John; TOWERS, Kristine Louise; TOWLE, Jerry Anthony; TOWLE, Roberta Erin; TOWNS, Maureen L.; TOWNSEND, Joyce; TOWNSEND, Joyce Ann; TOWNSEND, Lisa Michelle; TOWNSEND, Robert Kingsley; TOWSIGNANT, Judy Anne; TOY, Debbie; TOY, Patty; TOY, Pearl; TRAC, Hue Bach; TRACE, John A.; TRACEY, Kim; TRACH, Jacob; TRACHUK, Leslie Harry; TRAISH, John L.; TRAISH, Patricia Ann; TRAN, Jane; TRAQUAIR, Barry; TRAQUAIR, Janet; TRAQUAIR, Robert; TRASK, Jeffrey Kym; TRAUB, David Emerson; TRAVES, Edna Louise; TREACY, Patricia; TREEN, Bryan; TREFANENKO, Stephen; TREFANENKO, William; TREFFRY, Arthur Murray; TREFFRY, Diane Margaret; TREIJS, Deborah Anne; TREMAIN, Loretta Fayre; TREMBATH, Gord; TREMBLAY, Carole; TREMBLAY, Christian Arthur; TREMBLAY, Jacquie Lucille; TREMBLAY, Louise C.; TREMBLAY, Margaret M.; TREMBLEY, Sophie; TRENDEL, Brenda May; TRENT, Michael Charles; TREPANIER, Cheryl A.; TREPANIER, Cheryl Anne; TREMPANIER, Elaine Marie; TREPANIER, Troy Christian; TREVOR, Bernard; TREVOR, Tiffany; TRIBBLE, Arlene; TRIBBLE, Bruce; TRIBBLE, Donna Lynne; TRIBBLE, Gary A.; TRIFFO, Dorothy; TRIGG, Heather Lee; TRIGG, Nancy Elizabeth; TRIMBLE, Martin Alan; TRIMBLE, Wendy; TRIMMER, Delphi Suzanne; TRIP-DE-ROCHE, Anne Marie; TRIPP, Darlene Blanche; TRIPP, David Wayne; TRIPP, Kevin Stuart; TROCENKO, Walter William; TROFIMUCK, Tom; TROFIMUK, Maryanne; TRONT, Darryl W.; TROONCK, Barbara Nicolette; TROOCK, Marilyne; TROTT, Eve; TROTT, George Edward; TROTTER, Richard Ward; TROUGHTON, Dennis John; TROUGHTON, Patricia M.; TROUT, Brenda Jean; TROUT, Terri Lynn; TRUDEAU, Jose Renee; TRUDEL, Mike; TRUDGEON, Kenneth Barry; TRUDGEON, Marilyn; TRUEMAN, Andrea Lynne; TRUEMAN, Scott Cline; TRUPP, Sandra Mary-Ellen; TRUSSART, Francyne Danielle; TRY, Alan; TRYAN, Michael Keith; TRYON, Michelle Kathleen; TRYON, Shirley Irene; TSANG, Lawrence; TSANG, Shirley Hing-Ping; TSANG, Steven Chun-Ho; TSANG, Tiffany Pui-Kee; TSIANDOS, Jenny; TSIVUNIN, Sergei Nikolaievich; TSOUKALAS, Melanie Beatrice; TUBINSHIAK, Emil; TUBINSLAK, Abrarn; TUCCI, Marilena; TUCHSEN, Edward Hans; TUCHSEN, Luanne; TUCK, Marjorie Rose; TUCKER, Allison; TUCKER, Audrey; TUCKER, Debbie; TUCKER, Patrick; TUFF, Joy; TULLY, Glen; TULODZIECKI, Frank Jeseph; JULOKAS, Sylvia Esther; TUNG, Parrish Chi-Kin; TUNNICLIFFE, Gale Ardele; TUPPER, Shelley Carmen; TURCOTTE, Leonard Emile; TURKO, Susan Carol; TURLEY, Donna; TURNBULL, Cathy; TURNBULL, Sandra Jane; TURNER, Anthony Raymond; TURNER, Connie Jane; TURNER, Anthony Raymond; TURNER, Connie Jane; TURNER, Dr. Andrew Robert; TURNER, Eve Jeanette; TURNER, Gilbert Alexander; TURNER, John Arthur G.; TURNER, Kimberley Ann; TURNER, Lance A.; TURNER, Leo Robert; TURNER, Lucy; TURNER, Mary S.; TURNER, Scott Bradley; TURNINGA, C. Leon; TURNOCK, Brian Kenneth; TURTA, Michael William; TURZANSKY, Andrew; TUSTIAN, Joyce Eleanor; TUSTIN, Sheila Elizabeth; TUTT, George F.; TUTTLE, Darlene Marie; TUTTLE, Jean Margaret, TWEDDLE, Ann L.; TWEDDLE, Elizabeth C.; TWERDIN, Shirley; TWERDOFF, Patricia Anne; TWOLAN-BROWN, Connie Ann; TWOMBLY, Michael Albert; TYCHY, Darryl Robert; TYL, Ivona; TYLER, John Richard; TYLER, Stephen Roger; TYLER, Tuppy; TYLOR, Moneca; TYLOR, Robbin; TYLOR, Toby; TYLOR, Woneta; TYMKO, Lesa Mary; TYMO, Sharon Ann; TYMOCZKO, Helen Sophie; TYMOFICHUK, Janis; TYRKALO, Bessie; TYRKALO, Marion Joseph; TYRRELL, David L.J.; TYRRELL, Janice; TYRRELL, Lee Ann;

U

UBBING, Ben; UDVARDY, Louis Charles; UGOII, Claudette; UGOII, Karen Chinyere; ULAN, Stephanie Jane; ULLAH, Raza; ULLIAC, Anita Denise; UMRYSH, Leanne Maria; UNDERHILL, Jackie Mae; UNDERHILL, John B.; UNDERSCHULTZ, John P.; UNDERWOOD, Arthur Howard; UNDERWOOD Diane Ruth; UNDERWOOD, Muriel May; UNGER, Dianne Vera; UNGER, Linda Louise; UNGERAN, Lloyd Crayford; UNRAU, Audrey Helen; UNSWORTH, Maria; UNWIN, Pam; UNWIN, Patricia Jean; UPRIGHT, Dennis B.; URBAN, Monica Eleanora; URBANOSKI James Joseph; URBINA, Eileen Elizebeth; URBINO, Mario; URCH, Corinne Marie; URE, Daniel James; URSCHEL, Dr. John Wilfred; URSCHEL, Sandi Jane; URSU, Judith Fay; URSULAK, Karen; URTASUN, Dr. Raul; USENIK, Blaine; USISKIN, Sidney R.; USTENOV, James William; UZWYSHYN, Constance Helen; UZWYSHYN, Tanis Audra;

V

VAAGE, Lois Jean; VAAGE, Sarah; VAASIO, Wayne Albert; VAGUE, Claudette Anne; VAITKUNAS, Joseph Raymond; VAITKUNAS, Vanessa; VAITKUNAS, Victoria; VALDEZ, Gonzalez Gerardo; VALENTIJN, Gerry Napoleon; VALLI, Gilda Lois; VAN AMSTERDAM, Ronald P.; VAN ARMAN, George R.; VAN BRABANT, Adeline Marie; VAN BRUNSCHOT, Paul; VAN DE LIGT, Bill; VAN DE VLIERT, Garry; VAN DEN BOOGAARD, Berthold; VAN DEN HEUVEL, Ronald; VAN DER WEIDE, Thomas; VAN DUSEN, Florrie; VAN DYKE, Deborah Ruth; VAN EEKEN, Jenny; VAN EEKEN, M. Ted; VAN ESSEN, Isabel; VAN HEMERT, Aldagonda B.; VAN HEMERT, Jack; VAN HEMERT, Pauline; VAN LUVEN, Lynne; VAN MEURS, Helga; VAN MEURS, John A.; VAN MUYDEN, Jordyce Carol; VAN PRAET, Danielle; VAN SCHOOR, Holly Elizabeth; VAN SICKLE, Nola Elsie; VAN SOEST, Theresa Maria; VAN STAVEREN, Harriet; VAN STIPHOUT, Karen; VAN TIENEN, Lenette; VAN VEEN, Vera; VAN VLIET, Virginia; VAN WEELDEN, Geraldine; VAN WEELDEN, Henry; VAN WOUDEMBERG, Tina; VAN-STRAATEN, Christine; VAN, Den Brakel Everhard; VAN, Niekert Hubert John; VANALSTYNE, Merle Agnes; VANBAKEL, Margaret Kathleen; VANBAKEL, Paul Robert; VANBAKEL, Robert William; VANCE, Karen Janette; VANDAMENT, Jack Boyd; VANDAMENT, Marcy Lynn; VANDE KLEUT, John; VANDENBROEK, Barend; VANDEPOLDER, Maria; VANDERGOUWE, Miriam; VANDERKRUK, Gary John; VANDERKRUK, Julie Rose Marie; VANDERLEELIE, Jennifer Jill; VANDERMEER, Bill; VANDERZYL, Margaret Diana; VANDRUNEN, Shirley Ann; VANHEUKELOM, Janleen Karoline; VANHOGEZAND, Jan Peter; VANHUUKSLOOT, Teuntie; VANKATRAMAN, Malanie; VANT KLAPHEK, Gerty Colinde; VARMA, Meena; VARMA, Neerai; VASKO, Kathy; VASS, Sherril May; VASSILIOU, Jason Paul; VAUGHAN, Tracy Maureen; VAWTER, Dianne Gail; VEALE, Christopher; VEALE, Glenn Howard; VEALE, Sandra; VEEKEN, Priscilla Maria; VEENEMAN, Gary Edward; VEENSTRA, Debra Janet; VEENSTRA, Marianne; VEER, Nicloe; VEILLETTE, Marc Joseph; VEINOT, Vernon Alvin; VEITCH, Colin; VEITCH, Linda Grace; VELII, Karim Sadrudin; VELT, Charles; VELTHOEN, Christiaan A.; VELTHOEN, Christiaan Alexander; VENDITTELLI, Battista; VENDITTELLI, Luanne Joy; VENKATARAM, Suresh; VENNE, Rachelle; VENNER, Ellen Elizabeth; VENTIMILLA, Alberto; VERBITSKY, Marilyn Donna; VERCHOMIN, Lois Patricia; VERCHOMIN, Michael Stephen; VERCHOMIN, Orest John; VERDON, Stephen Herbert C.; VERESCHAGIN, Walt John; VERGARA, Raul Jose; VERHULST, Susan J.; VERMEE, Terry Louise; VERMEGEN, Zwanette Hendrike; VERMEULEN, Lorraine Christine; VERNON, Casey; VERRIER, Ed; VERRIER, Marion Jean; VERSCHUREN, Joanne Helen; VERSLUYS, Helen; VESPRINI, Alan Carlo; VESPRINI, Patti L.; VETHA, Charles Marcellus; VETTESE, Amanda Leigh; VETTESE, Shelley Barbara; VIANA, Andres; VICKERS, Katharine Alice; VICKERSON, Donald S.; VICKERSON, Laura; VICKOVIC, Micheal;

VICTOOR, Dolores Margaret; VICTOOR, Elsie Mary; VICTOOR, Sherri-Lynn Anne; VIEN, Helene;
VIK, Janice Helen; VIKSE, Gordon Milton; VIKSE, Rodney Kenneth; VINAYAK, Ravi Shankar;
VINCE, Cindy Diane; VINCENT, Anne; VINCENT, Bruce R.; VINET, Stan; VINK, Harry M.A.;
VIS, Shirley Patricia; VISSER, Audrey G.; VISSERS, Randall Lor; VISWANATHAN, Padma;
VITEYCHUK, Trudy; VICHEK, Violet; VLIEG, Gordon Edward; VOAKLANDER, Vanore; VOELKER, Bruce;
VOGELESANG, Tannis May; VOGL, Keith Gordon; VOGT, Kathy; VOIVODICH, Sandy;
VOL HOLLEN, Shelda Marlaine; VOLLRATH, Carl Christiaan; VOLLRATH, Karin;
VON EICKEN, Herbert Stanley; VON INNEREBNER, Renata; VON ODER, Gail Vivian;
VON WESTARP, Monique Elise; VAN ZUR GATHEN, Teresita; VONA Margaret; VOSS, Jerry R.;
VOTH, Pamela Elaine; VOUSDEN, Colin Charles; VOUSDEN, Sandra; VOUVE, Isabelle Francoise;
VOYCE, Dr. Clyde D.; VRABEL, Sharon Marie; VRETENAR, Doris Franka; VUKELIC, Kresimir;
VUKOVIC, Mary Anne;

W

WABASCA, Sheila Sandra; WACH, Grant Douglas; WACOWICH, David Joseph;
WACOWICH, Edward R.; WACOWICH, Nancy; WACOWICZ, Teresa Lynn V.; WADDELL, Cherryle Mae;
WADDELL, Lillian; WADDEN, Olive; WADE, Donald W.; WADE, Sandra Lynn; WADE, Sherri Dawne;
WADSWORTH, Larry Richard; WAGNER, Janene Vanessa; WAGNER, Leanne Rose;
WAGSTAFF, Jacqueline Jackie; WAHL, Debra Lynne; WAIDA, Eiko; WAIDMAN, Al George;
WAIDMAN, Linda Marie; WAILOO, Zephine Marion; WAINAINA, Paul Kuria; WAKAL, James William;
WAKARUK, Rudy; WAKE, Joyce L; WAKEFIELD, Martha Jean; WAKEHAM, R. Hugh; WALDEC, Steve;
WALDIE, M. Patricia; WALDON, Lance Eric Y.; WALDRON, Ross Murdoch;
WALEWSKI, Joanna Magdelena; WALKEDEN, Nona; WALKER, Barbara; WALKER, Barbara Ann,
WALKER Beatrice Veraline; WALKER, Bob; WALKER, Debby Leigh; WALKER, Debra Lee;
WALKER, Diane Laurie; WALKER, Donald Stephen; WALKER, Douglas George; WALKER, Dr. Allan F.;
WALKER, Dr. Jeanne M.; WALKER, Dr. Keith; WALKER, Gregory Alexander;
WALKER, Gregory Andrew; WALKER, Helen Louise; WALKER, Iris Marie; WALKER, Janet;
WALKER, John Anthony; WALKER, John Hilary; WALKER Kendall Anthony;
WALKER, Leonard Anthony; WALKER, Lloanne Gayle; WALKER, Lynn; WALKER, Lynn Irene;
WALKER, Nancy; WALKER, Patricia Catherine; WALKER, Patricia Mary; WALKER, Robert Christopher;
WALKER, Robert Donald; WALKER, Ronald K.; WALKER, Suzanne; WALKEY, Christopher John;
WALKEY, Judith Bel; WALKEY, Michael; WALL, Anne Margaret; WALL, Calvin Lee Michael;
WALL, Mark Anthony Woodrow; WALL, Robert Baden; WALL, Stephen; WALLACE, Barbara;
WALLACE, Brian Douglas; WALLACE, Dick; WALLACE, Florence; WALLACE, Heather;
WALLACE, Jack; WALLACE, Lorne Alexander; WALLACE, Lynda May; WALLACE, Tammy Margaret;
WALLIS, William John; WALLS, Clayton Albert; WALLS, Janice; WALMSLEY, Gail Patricia;
WALPER, Wynne June; WALSH, Brenda; WALSH, Cathy; WALSH, Harold James; WALSH, Ken;
WALSH, Valerie Louise; WALTER, Janet M.E.; WALTER, Karen; WALTERS, John Paul Murray;
WALTERS, Keirra Noelle; WALTERS, Marylu; WALTERS, Renate; WALTON, Charles;
WALTON, Diane Leslie; WALTON, Ivy Jane; WALTON, Joan; WAMSLEY, Gwen Elaine;
WAMSLEY, Kenneth L.; WAMSLEY, Kerry Ann; WANG, Angela En-Chi; WANG, Dr. Peter;
WANG, Jacqueline; WANG, Shujie; WANG, Xiaoning; WANGLER, Margaret Ann;
WARD, Allison Margaret; WARD, Bill; WARD, David Charles; WARD, Dixon Scott; WARD, Don Earl;
WARD, George Frederick; WARD, Janet Elizabeth; WARD, Laurene Margaret; WARD, Lynda;
WARD, Terry; WARDELL, Perry A.; WARDS, Shana Barbara; WARE, Barbara Jean;
WARE, Christopher Shaun; WARE, Jacqueline; WARE, Jacqueline Grace; WARE, Raymond F.;
WARHAFT, David Ashley; WARING, Hal Martin; WARING, Katherine; WARITSKY, Marie Martha;
WARITSKY, Michelle Anne; WARKE, J. Lewis; WARKE, Valerie E.; WARMAN, Margaret;
WARMAN, Margaret Rose; WARNER, Carol; WARNER, David William; WARNER, Heath Alan;
WARNER, Walter Roys; WARNING, Joan Margaret; WARNKE, Sandra Ann; WARREN, Donald R.;
WARREN, Jori Lynn; WARREN, Margaret Louise; WARREN, Marjorie; WARREN, Mary Ann;
WARREN, Monica Francine; WARREN, Richard; WARRING, Jr. Richard; WARRING, Rod Gordon;
WARRIOR, Stuart; WARSHAWSKI, Carol; WARSHAWSKI, Lisa; WARUNKY, Debbie Lynn;
WARUNKY, Katherine; WARWICH, Richard Rudolph; WARZIN, Elaine K.; WASALA, Ann Mary;
WASALA, Joe M.; WASHYIK, Irene Sonja; WASIK, Cheryl Ann; WASNEA, Allen Douglas;
WASSON, Julie Anne; WASYLASKO, Emily Eugenia; WASYLYNCHUK, Mary Ann;
WASYLYSHYN, Katherine Marie; WATAMANIUK, Carol Ann; WATCH, Carol Roxanne;
WATERHOUSE, Scott Jason; WATERS, Adrienne Shelley; WATERS, John R.; WATERS, Keryl;
WATERS, Tex; WATERSON, Cindy Colette; WATERSON, Richard Allan; WATSON, Annette Julia;
WATSON, Brian Mitchell; WATSON, Christie Mitchell; WATSON, D. Tiffany; WATSON, D. Tracey;
WATSON, Doug; WATSON, Elizabeth; WATSON, Jack John; WATSON, John Stannard;
WATSON, Jannette; WATSON, Marian Audrey; WATSON, Marjorie D.; WATSON, Ronald L.;
WATSON, Shelley; WATT, Anne; WATT, Cathy Anne; WATT, Florence Dorothy; WATT, Heather;
WATT, Keith; WATT, Viola Catherine; WATT, Wallace William; WATTERS, Jim Edwin;
WATTERWORTH, Jack Arthur; WATTERWORTH, Muriel; WATTERWORTH, Muriel Alexandria;
WATTON, Richard Wayne; WATTON, Robert Gordon; WATTS, Annike Elisabeth;
WATTS, Jessica Judith; WAUN, Evelyn Mary; WAUN, Lyle John; WAWRYKOW, Bonnie Marie;
WAY, Gerald J.; WAYE, Allan; WEATHERALL, Ann Elizabeth; WEATHERDON, Rosalind;
WEAVER, Lynne Marie; WEBB, Kenneth Clair; WEBB, Michael Bradley; WEBB, Patricia Gail;
WEBB, Robert G; WEBB, Robert Gordon; WEBBER, Diane Joan; WEBBER, John Robert;
WEBBER, Penny Joan; WEBER, Denise M.; WEBER, Irvin W.; WEBER, Monica Lyn;
WEBER, Philip Emberson; WEBSTER, Bill; WEBSTER, Brenda Alice; WEBSTER, Bruce William;
WEBSTER, Donna Leigh; WEBSTER, Douglas Scott; WEBSTER, Grace Jones; WEBSTER, Joanne Lee;
WEBSTER, John Thomas; WEBSTER, Mary Isabella; WEEKS, Chuck; WEENK, Judith Louise;
WEESE, Kevin Clinton; WEGERT, Wade; WEGNER, Charles Richard; WEGNER, Warren Charles;
WEICKER, Dianne Louise; WEIDEMAN, Donald James; WEIDMAN, Teresa Lynne;
WEIDNER, Hans Wolfgang; WEIDNER, Karin; WEINBERGER, Christine Carol;
WEINBERGER, Mary Ann; WEINZIERL, Deanne Shirley, WEINZIERL, Shirley Elaine; WEIR, Betty Lou;
WEIR, Colleen; WEIR, Dr. Bryce; WEIR, Judy Marie; WEIR, Sandra J.; WEIR, Sandra Joyce;
WEIR, William A.; WEISBERG, Deborah Joan; WEISE, Jim A.; WEISER, Thomas; WEISS, Judy;
WEISS, Julie; WEISS, Margie Dawn; WEITZEL, Sharon Diane; WELCH, Colin Robert; WELCH, Cy;
WELCH, Gordon John; WELCH, Lil; WELDON, Patricia Anne; WELGUZ, Dale; WELLER, Dean;
WELLMAN, Harriet Lillian; WELLS, Debra Anne; WELLS, Karen Anne; WELSH, Elizabeth;
WELSH, Kathleen Muriel; WELSH, Kelli Lynn; WELTON, Earl Hubert; WENDEL, Colleen A.;
WENGER, Christopher Scott; WENGER, Claude Randy; WENGRYN, Brad Harold; WENK, John Edward;
WENSCHLAG, Lesley; WENSCHLAG, Cameron Bruce; WENSTOB, Corrine Gay;
WENSTOB, Lisa Norinne; WENTAO, Xie; WENTWORTH, Mel E.; WENTWORTH, Neil G.;
WENTZEL, Hardy Herbert; WENZEL, Kevin Alfred; WEPPLER, Judith Kathryn;
WERBINSKY, Brian William; WERBISKI, Patricia; WERHUN, Jerry William; WERNER-
KING, Janeen Anne; WERNER, Brenda Lydia; WERNER, Erica; WERNER, Gladys Elizabeth;
WERNER, Renata; WERNICKE, Stephen Craig; WERRING, AnnaChristina; WERSHAF, Charlotte;
WERSTIUK, Kevin William; WERTH, Elin; WESELAK, Jackie V.; WEST, Geoff; WEST, Gigi Clotilde;
WEST, Lillian Dora; WEST, Timothy Wayne; WEST, Walter Ambrosie; WESTACOTT, David;
WESTBURY, Richard George; WESTERLUND, Charles K.; WESTGAARD, Lissi;
WESTLAKE, Donald W. S.; WETMORE, Shirley Ann; WETTERBERG, Donna;
WETTERBERG, Shelley Dawn; WETTLAUFER, Ron; WEYTS, Terrance Marcel;
WHARTON, Paul Geoffrey; WHARTON, Wynyard Oscar Leslie; WHATTAM, Tracey Ann;
WHEADON, Patricia J.; WHEATLEY, Darlene May; WHEELANS, Lyndsay Margaret;
WHEELANS, Ruth Enid; WHEELER, Dorothy Anne; WHELAN, Corinne; WHELAN, Stephen Douglas;
WHELAND, Terese Mary; WHILLIER, David; WHILLIER, Dexter; WHILLIER, Oda; WHILLIER, Randy;
WHISKIN, Jane Marie; WHITBOURNE, Sonja Kathryn; WHITBY, Ronald Franklin;
WHITBY, Shirley Patricia; WHITE, Anna A.E.; WHITE, Betty Jeanne; WHITE, Bonnie Heather;
WHITE, Bradley Steven; WHITE, Carleen; WHITE, Christy Lynne; WHITE, Don; WHITE, Dr. M. Lilliam;
WHITE, Edwin Jams; WHITE, Elsie Irene; WHITE, Frank; WHITE, Glenn; WHITE, Gordon;
WHITE, Gwendolynne Christine; WHITE, Helen Anne; WHITE, Jill; WHITE, Lawrence John;
WHITE, Linda Lorraine; WHITE, Linda Rae; WHITE, Lorianne Lisa; WHITE, Mark; WHITE, Maurice D;
WHITE, Naomi; WHITE, Peter; WHITE, Richard Murray; WHITE, Robert Dale;
WHITE, Ronald Matthew; WHITE, Shelley Melinda; WHITE, Walder G.W.; WHITE, William Stewart;
WHITEHORN, Karen; WHITELEY, Les Wynn; WHITEMAN, Mark William; WHITESIDE, B. Marie;
WHITFIELD, David Murdo; WHITFIELD, Erin Maria; WHITFIELD, George; WHITFIELD, Kendra Cammell;
WHITFORD, Blaine Rodney; WHITING, Kenneth Ross; WHITMAN, John Alton; WHITNEY, Susan;
WHITNEY, Terry; WHITTAKER, Joel Derrick; WHITTEN, Sheila Louise; WHITWORTH, Michael John;
WHITWORTH, Tracey; WIBER, Bruce Allen; WICENTOWICH, Cherise Leah;
WICKENCAMP, Esther Lucille; WICKERT, Casey; WICKETT, Susan Therese; WICKEY, Andy;
WIDAS, Diane; WIDGIZ, Sandra Louise; WIDYNOWSKI, Gary; WIEBE, Beverly Ann;
WIEBE, Cydney Maureen; WIEBE, Douglas James; WIEBE, Patricia Karen; WIENS, Hank;
WIENS, Patrick John; WIENS, Shirley M.; WIESENBERG, Faye; WIESNER, James E.;
WIGEMYR, Cheryl Anne; WIGGINS, Samuel Mark; WIGHT, Blaine Irvine; WIGHT, Lillian Beatrice;
WIGHT, Marilyn Louise; WIGHTMAN, Daryl M.; WIGLEY, Cindy Lea; WILBERG, Barbara Maud;
WILBERG, Chris Ross; WILBERG, Curtis James; WILBERG, Karl Robert; WILCER, Armin,;
WILCER, Sharon; WILDE, Susan Maureen; WILDENHOFF, Anne Kirstine; WILDGOOSE, G. Norman;
WILES, David William; WILFORD, Jeff N.P.; WILHELM, Barry Evan; WILHELM, Rita; WILINSKI, Helen;
WILKES, Gordon Henderson; WILKES, Peter Stewart; WILKINS, Carla; WILKINS, Frank Anthony;
WILKINS, James Douglas; WILKINS, Linda Gail; WILKINSON, C. James; WILKINSON, Diana Joan;
WILKINSON, Elizabeth Jean; WILKINSON, Marjorie Anne; WILKINSON, Neil Rudell;
WILKINSON, Ruby; WILKINSON, Sandy Lynn; WILKINSON, Shirley Ann; WILKINSON, Thomas Wayne;
WILKS, Cameron David; WILLARD, Linda Jean; WILLERT, Ivan C.; WILLEY, Christine Noel;
WILLIAM, John Smith; WILLIAMS, Allen Dale; WILLIAMS, Anthony John; WILLIAMS, Brent Douglas;
WILLIAMS, Charlene Marie; WILLIAMS, Charlene Michelle; WILLIAMS, Christopher James;
WILLIAMS, Dana Ray; WILLIAMS, Dawn; WILLIAMS, Della May; WILLIAMS, Dolores Kathleen;
WILLIAMS, Doris Margaret; WILLIAMS, Elva June; WILLIAMS, Ernest; WILLIAMS, Erskine;
WILLIAMS, Frances Helen; WILLIAMS, Geoffrey; WILLIAMS, George Stuart;
WILLIAMS, Gloria Louise; WILLIAMS, Gwen; WILLIAMS, Jim; WILLIAMS, Joan Marie;
WILLIAMS, Joanne Patricia; WILLIAMS, John David; WILLIAMS, June Marie;
WILLIAMS, Laurie Anne; WILLIAMS, Lori Anne; WILLIAMS, Lorraine; WILLIAMS, Lowell;
WILLIAMS, Mary Jo; WILLIAMS, Natasha; WILLIAMS, Pamela; WILLIAMS, Pamela Wendy;
WILLIAMS, Paul; WILLIAMS, Peter Charles; WILLIAMS, Preston Ivor; WILLIAMS, Ray;
WILLIAMS, Renate Soraya Yvette; WILLIAMS, Rose; WILLIAMS, Roy John David;
WILLIAMS, Sara Louise; WILLIAMS, Scott John; WILLIAMS, Thelma; WILLIAMS, Tom Arthur;
WILLIAMS, Trevor; WILLIAMS, Warren Wayne; WILLIAMSON, Carol Eleanor;
WILLIAMSON, Lorraine Doreen; WILLIAMSON, Owen David; WILLAMSON, Philip Charles;
WILLIAMSON, Rita; WILLAMSON, Robert Lee; WILLIAMSON, Sherri Ann; WILLIS, Allison;
WILLIS, Gordon K.; WILLIS, Linda; WILLIS, Lynn Alexandria Ann; WILLOUGHBY, Wanda;
WILLOWS, Donald Colin; WILLOX, Eva Louise; WILLS, Ken Joseph; WILLS, Lori-Ann;
WILMOT, Carrie; WILMOT, John Holt; WILMOT, M. Elizabeth; WILSON, Allen; WILSON, Andrew H.;
WILSON, Barbara Ann; WILSON, Barbara J.; WILSON, Brian R.; WILSON, Carolyn June;
WILSON, Christine; WILSON, David Michael; WILSON, Deborah; WILSON, Dennis Ralph;
WILSON, Donald Keith; WILSON, Donna Irene; WILSON, Doreen Mae; WILSON, Edith Diane;
WILSON, Emily; WILSON, Frank Davis; WILSON, Geoff; WILSON, Gregory Paul; WILSON, Hazel K.;
WILSON, Howard; WILSON, Jamie S.; WILSON, Joan Ellen; WILSON, Joan Montgomery;
WILSON, Karen E., WILSON, Kathleen Ann; WILSON, Ken Foster; WILSON, Leslie; WILSON, Leslie E.;
WILSON, Linda G.; WILSON, Lois; WILSON, Mark Vincent Hardman;
WILSON, Marlene, WILSON, Michael; WILSON, P. Daryl; WILSON: Pat Lorraine;
WILSON, Richard Roy; WILSON, Roxanne Lorraine; WILSON, Sarah Jane; WILSON, Stephanie;
WILSON, Stephanie Ruth; WILSON, Stephen Francis; WILSON, Suzanne Marie; WILSON Tracy Anne;
WILSON, William George; WILSON, William Richard; WILTSE, Wayne John;
WILTSHIRE, Harvie Ernest; WILTZEN, Hugh Oliver; WILTZEN, Janet Helen; WILTZEN, Robert C. A.;
WINCE, Pat; WINCENTOWICH, Joseph Edwin; WINCHESTER, Maureen Anne;
WINDEL, Carrie Kristine; WINDEL, Colleen; WINDJACK, Gail Margaret; WINDJACK, Orest;
WING, Jeanette; WINGER, Kim Jean; WINGET, Pam; WINGROVE, Darcy; WINGROVE, Darcy Louise;
WINKELAAR, Chris Sylvia; WINTER, Betty Ann; WINTER, Katie Bernadine; WINTER, Noel A.;
WINTER, Uwe; WISE, David Dale; WISHART, Patricia Joan; WISHART, Sandy Joan;
WISHEU, Simon Michael; WISNIEWSKI, Brenda Ann; WISPINSKI, Jo Anne Alice;
WITHROW, Debra Marie; WITTEL, Angie Lee; WITTEN, Mona Rose; WITTEN: Norman Lewis;
WITTEN, Randall Stewart; WITTENBERG, Joerg; WITTRUP, Gloria Xania; WLODYKA, Ronald Douglas;
WLODARKIEWICZ, Donna J.; WNAG, Coa An; WOELINGA, Gerald J.; Woeppel, Donald Gordon;
WOEPPEL, Jean; WAIMA, Laurie E.; WOITE, Elke Lucie; WOJOAK, Sonja Wanda;
WOITOWICZ, Dawn Michelle, WOLBERT, Friedrich Mathias; WOLD, Raymond Glen;
WOLF, Lorraine Marie; WOLFE, Brian Michael; WOLFE, Debbie Nadine; WOLFE, Donn Leanne;
WOLFE, Jeanne Wynn; WOLFE, Robert Franklin; WOLFMAN, Maxine Reva; WOLFMAN, Morley;
WOLFRAM, Joanne; WOLOSZYN, Betty Diane; WOLTER, Darryl; WOLTER, Lisa F.;
WOMACK, Katherine Diane; WOMACK, Larry Walter; WONG, Andrew O.; WONG, Anna;
WONG, Annie; WONG, Brian; WONG, Caroline Sue; WONG, Ching-Kwai; WONG, Claren Choy Ying;
WONG, Daisy LaiLing; WONG, Dennis Yinjit; WONG, Diane Chung Ki; WONG, Dick B.;
WONG, Dr. Paul Kinsang; WONG, James; WONG, Jenny; WONG, Juliana; WONG, June;
WONG, Kathleen; WONG, Kit Kennith; WONG, Margaret; WONG, Nyuk Ken; WONG, Perry;
WONG, Petty; WONG, Robert Chi; WONG Siu Lan; WONG, Stella; WONG, Susan;
WONG, Teck Cheong; WONG, Tony Fooknyad; WONG, Vanessa; WONG, Wendy Lai-Yee;
WONG, William George; WONG, Yoko Oike; WOO, Doris; WOOD, Marily; WOOD, Thompson Lee;
WOOD, Ven-Ding; WOOD, Alison Elizabeth; WOOD, Bette Jean; WOOD, Brenda Lee;
WOOD, Charlene Mary; WOOD, Colleen M.; WOOD, Diane Elizabeth; WOOD, Elizabeth Margaret;
WOOD H. Gary; WOOD, Helen E.; WOOD, Helen Elizabeth, WOOD, James Francis Evelyn;
WOOD, Janet Elizabeth; WOOD, Jayanne M.; WOOD, Kelly; WOOD, Lorne R.; WOOD, Melanie Ann;
WOOD, Robert Leonard; WOOD, Sarah Elizabeth; WOOD, Tracy Lynn; WOODCOCK, Dwayne Dale;
WOODCOCK, Sharon Alma; WOODFORD, Robert James; WOODGER, Jennifer;
WOODHEAD, Jason Weldon; WOODING, Colette Frances; WOODMAN, Herbert Men;
WOODMAN, Pamela Sue; WOODS, Catherine Isabel; WOODS, Colleen Mary; WOODS, Marcia Gaye;
WOODS, Willa Eva; WOODWARD, Blance Madeline; WOODRIDGE, Anthonie David;
WOOLHAM, Richard C.; WOOLARD, Laine Munroe; WOOLNOUGH, Gerald Edward;
WOOLSEY, Janice Lynn; WOOLSEY, John Thomas; WOOLSEY, Karen Marie, WOON, Leanne;
WOREN, Cathy May Rose; WOREN, Rodney Richard; WORKUN, Roman Bohdan;

WORONIUK, Christopher John; WOROSCHUK, Cynthia Marie Rose; WOROSCHUK, Lori Lynn;
WOROSCHUK, Sheri Ann; WORRALL, Les Houghton; WORTH, Debbie; WORTON, Tom;
WOTYPKA, Barbara; WOWK, Betty Mary; WOWK, Cheryl Marie; WOWK, Gerald Walter;
WOWK, Laverne Anne; WOWK, Todd Michael; WOYTENKO, Bill R.; WOYWITKA, Karen Lynn;
WOYWITKA, Sheenagh Lynn; WOZNIUK, Elizabeth; WOZNIUK, Kari-Lynne; WOZNIUK, Tara-Anne;
WOZNIUK, Valerie; WRAY, Donald George; WRIGHT, Anne Elizabeth; WRIGHT, Chris;
WRIGHT, Clara; WRIGHT, Darlene Ann; WRIGHT, Edith; WRIGHT, Glen Keith;
WRIGHT, Jane Catherine; WRIGHT, Joelle Ralene; WRIGHT, Joyce Virginia; WRIGHT, Kimberly Ann;
WRIGHT, Kristine Elizabeth; WRIGHT, Linda Marie; WRIGHT, Nancy Christine; WRIGHT, Nicole Marie;
WRIGHT, Sandra Lee; WRIGHT, Susan; WRIGHT, Susan Frances; WROBEL, Dean; WROTNIAK, Max;
WRUBLESKI, Jodi Diane; WRUBLESKI, Lyall; WU, Belinda; WU, Chaolun; WU, Lily; WUJCIK, Jean;
WUJCIK, Marie; WUJCIK, Mitchell; WUJCIK, Peter; WULF, Evelyn Joanne; WULFF, Clifford;
WULFF, Joan Sandra; WULFF, John F.; WUNDERLICH, Gerd; WUNSCH, Kirsten;
WURMANN, Hannelore Gail; WURMANN, Kirsten Anne; WUTZKE, Doris; WYATT, Barbara;
WYATT, Bob; WYATT, Karen; WYCOTT, Carolyn Leslie; WYGERA, Michele Grace;
WYLLIE, Marguerite Florence; WYLLIE, Robert; WYNN, Agnes Dickson; WYNNYK, Mike W.;
WYNYCHUK, Karin; WYSE, Glen Bryan; WYSOCKI, Linda;

Y

YACHNEY, Jeri-Lynn; YAGOS, Colleen Denise; YAKIMCHUK, Arlen; YAKIMETS, Katherine Anne;
YAKIMYSHYN, Patricia Marie; YAKISMISHYN, Maryanne; YAMAMOTO, Ann Marie;
YAMAMOTO, Isao; YAMAMOTO, Ken; YAMNIUK, John; YANCHAR, Natalie Lynn; YANDA, Marjorie;
YANDEAU, Lesley Joan; YANDRESKI, Laurie; YANO, May; YANO, May Mitsuko; YANOW, Steffie;
YAPP, Kimberly Kim-Liam; YAREMA, Maria Margaret; YAREMKEVICH, Annette Grace;
YAREMKO, Mark Alexander; YAREMKO, Patricia Anne; YARMAK, Grace Patsy; YARMOLUK, Ken L.;
YARMUCH, Sylvia; YASCHYSHYN, Rick Michael; YASINSKI, Claudette Marie; YASINSKI, Louis;
YASUHARA, Isao; YATES, Patricia Catherine; YATES, Stanley; YAU-YIN, Chow;
YAWORSKI, Cecilia J.; YAWORSKI, Jill Monica; YE, Shui-Ting; YEAMAN, George;
YEARWOOD, Wendy Lea; YEDLIN, Deborah Daphne; YEE, Carol Margaret; YEE, Karen Edna;
YEE, Linda; YEE, Lora; YEE, Lynn; YEE, Pauline; YEE, Pauline Man Han; YEE, Richard;
YEE, Sandra Marie; YEE, Tony Lipwing; YEGANI, Dilara; YEGANI, Nadir; YELLE, Margo Frances;
YENNEY, Richard Lim; YEO, Woon Boe; YEOMAN, Margaret; YEOMAN, Shaunda Lyn;
YEOMANS, Alice Maria; YEOMANS, Nancy; YEOMANS, William George; YEREMY, Maureen Louise;
YESKE, Nettie Anne Katherine; YEUNG, Jupiter; YEWCHUK, Gregory John; YIM, Patricia Catherine;
YIP, Koon-Kiu; YIP, Susan Tzeh-Ching; YIP, Wayne Dan; YJU, Hung Yee Margaret; YJU, Paul Pui-
Wan; YODA, Susumu; YONEDA, Dr. Janet Toyo; YOOS, Elke Dora; YOUNG, Alberta Grace;
YOUNG, Barbara Anne; YOUNG, Cameron Bruce; YOUNG, Cecile Paulina; YOUNG, Christine Mary;
YOUNG, Daniel James; YOUNG, David Bowman; YOUNG, Denise Marie; YOUNG, Douglas Montague;
YOUNG, Dr. Donald G.; YOUNG, Dr. Malcolm John; YOUNG, Heather Tracy Ann; YOUNG, Helen;
YOUNG, Isabel Margaret; YOUNG, Jennifer; YOUNG, Laurie; YOUNG, Maimie; YOUNG, Mary J.;
YOUNG, Molly Jardine; YOUNG, Patrick John; YOUNG, Ralph Gordon; YOUNG, Randy James;
YOUNG, Ruby; YOUNG, Shauna Anne; YOUNG, Susan Louise; YOUNG, Tim Wayne;
YOUNG, Victoria Lynn; YOUNG, Vincent Maclean; YOUNG, William Francis; YOUNG, Winifred Joan;
YOUNGER, Daisy Louise; YOUNGMAN, Christine E.; YOUNGS, Dave Jack; YOUNGS, Myron Anthony;
YOUNIE, Ruth Margaret; YOUNK, Karina; YOUNKER, Laurine; YOUSIF, Faiza; YOUSIF, Salwan Francis;
YU, Ling; YU, Polly Yuan Yuan; YU, Zavier Mingkang; YUCA, Romana Theresa; YUEN, Amy;
YUEN, Margaret; YUEN, Nancy; YUHASZ, Helen Marie; YUILL, Janet E.; YUILL, Wilda Elsie;
YUK, Dorothy; YUK, Janice; YUK, Raymond; YUN, Mina; YURKIW, Zane Laurence;
YUSHCHYSHYN, Cecile; YUSYPCHUK, Larysa Tamara; YUZWA, Gregory Michael;

Z

ZABLOSKI, Don; ZABORSKI, Andrew; ZACHARKO, David; ZACHARKO, Ronald William;
ZACHARUK, Gary; ZADECKI, Barbara Ann; ZAHARA, Amelia Dee; ZAHARIA, George Nick Steve;
ZAHARKO, Ian Adrian; ZAHARKO, Mike; ZAHARY, Suzanne; ZAHARY, William; ZAHN, Marg;
ZAHORODNY, Nancy; ZAHORULKO, Julia; ZAIDI, Asma; ZAINUL, Imtiaz; ZAITSOFF, Reva Louise;
ZAIWALLA, Sheroo; ZALAZAR, Rodolfo; ZALESKI, Paul John; ZALESKI, Susan Patricia;
ZALEWSKI, Barbara; ZALITACH, Leslie Ann; ZAN, Susan Ann; ZANELLO, Erika; ZANON, Tony;
ZAPF, Elli Freda; ZAPF, Eugene Ralph; ZAPF, Graham Noel; ZAPF, Margaret Louise;
ZAPH, Ruth Margurite; ZAPLACHINSKI, Warren Allen; ZAPS, Dolores A.; ZARAGOZA, Dean;
ZARAGOZA, Leticia; ZARSKY, Audrey May; ZATKO, June A.; ZAVISLAKE, Colleen Annette;
ZAWALAK, Terry Anne; ZAZULAK, Elson Paul; ZEBIC, Bob; ZEILINSKY, Gloria; ZEINER, Teresa Anne;
ZELANT, Allen Gordon; ZELENAK, Patrick John; ZELENY, Corinne Joann; ZELENY, Josie;
ZEMRAU, Jan Marie; ZELMAN, Robert; ZENARI, Elisabeth; ZENGO, Lydia; ZEPEDA, Carmen Elizabeth;
ZERR, Marion F.; ZETTER, Sheila Gayle; ZHAI, Hou Long; ZHANG, Qingnian; ZHONGSHAN, Wang;
ZHOU, Xianghe; ZIARKO, Nancy Caroline; ZICHY, Mike; ZIEBER, Rachelle Kathy;
ZIELINSKI, Andrea Marisa; ZIELINSKI, Tomasz Adam; ZIELSDORF, Margaret;
ZIERATH, Donna Kathleen; ZILINSKI, Judith; ZILM, Jennifer Ann; ZIMMEL, Vicki Lynn;
ZIMMER, Marjorie Isabelle; ZIMMERMAN, Bonnie Lynn; ZIMMERMAN, Linda Ruth;
ZIMMERMAN, Robert Wayne; ZINGLE, Darlene Anne; ZINGLE, Jeffrey Steven; ZINGLE, Randy Bert;
ZINIEWICZ, Alex; ZINIEWICZ, Alice; ZISMAN, Shmuel; ZITA, Ivana; ZIVKOVIC, Helen;
ZIVKOVIC, Helen Jelena; ZOHAIR, Maher Ammar; ZOHNER, Sandi Lee; ZOLNER, Mary;
ZOLTENKO, Charlene Debra; ZOMBOR, Joseph S.; ZOMBOR, Szilard; ZORZOS, Gerogia;
ZOTTENBERG, Dasha Godes; ZROBET, Caroline; ZROBOK, Dawn; ZUBYK, Peggy Rose;
ZUCHT, Walter; ZUHAIR, Ahmed; ZUKE, Daniel; ZUKE, Gene; ZUKIWSKI, Carol May;
ZUMBO, Adele Rose-Marie; ZUMBO, Vince; ZUPANCIC, Pamela Jane; ZURAWELL, Fern Thelma;
ZUTTER, Sabina; ZUTTER, Sabina Olive; ZUTTER, Susan Victoria; ZUTZ, Elaine; ZWICKER, Mary-Anne;
ZWICKER, Ron; ZWOZDESKY, Christine; ZYGUN, Alexander Andrew; ZYLENKO, Douglas Eugene;
ZYLSTRA, Ingrid Elaine; ZYP, Danielle Elizabeth; ZYP, John William

Flash Card Holders

A

AAB, Joanne; ABBOTT, Shawn; ABOUHASSAN, Hussein; ABOU-SHEHADEH, Houlio;
ABRAMYK, Patty; ACKERMAN, Kaye; ACKERMAN, Kit; ACTON, Cathy Lynn; ACTON, Donna;
ACTON, Jody James; ADAM, Linda; ADAMA, Wendy; ADAMKIEWICZ, Richard; ADAMS, Evelyn;
ADAMS, Judi; ADAMS, Mary; ADAMSON, Kelly; ADAMYK, Drusilla; ADILMAN, Audrey;
AFFELD, Marian; AGATE, Keitha; AGNEW, Edna; AGUILLON, Bernadette; AINSLIE, Kathy;
AITKIN, Judith; ALBARDA, Beatrix; ALBERTS, Pat; ALBURQUENUE, Carl; ALCOCK, Karen;
ALEXANDER, Colleen; ALFORD, Tamara; ALI, Renuma; ALI, Usman; ALLADIN, Aisha;
ALLADIN, Ibrahim; ALLEN, George; ALLEN, Kate; ALLEN, Keith; ALLEN, Rita; ALLER-STEAD, Gail;
ALLIN, Katherine; ALLORE, Sonia; AMENT, Molly; AMITA, Arora; ANCTIL, Carole;
ANDERSON, Anne; ANDERSON, Arlene; ANDERSON, Carolyn; ANDERSON, Cedric;
ANDERSON, Charlene; ANDERSON, Claire; ANDERSON, Dougie; ANDERSON, Douglas;
ANDERSON, Evelyn; ANDERSON, Jean; ANDERSON, Laura Lee; ANDERSON, Marion;
ANDERSON, Norm; ANDERSON, Sam; ANDO, Hikomatsu; ANDREAS, Albert; ANDREAS, Gladys;
ANDREAS, Holly; ANDRIETZ, Tracey; ANDRIUK, Fay; ANSU-KYEREMETH, Kwasi;
ANTONIO, Elizabeth; ANTONIO, Lori; ANTONIO, Marj; ANTONIUK, Andy; APEDAILE, Erik;
APEDAILE, Sarah; AQUAROK, Jacki; ARIAL, Richard; ARIAL, Ruth; ARMISTEAD, Norma;
ARMITAGE, Jill; ARMITAGE, Phyllis; ARMITAGE, Roy; ARMITSTEAD, Barb; ARMITSTEAD, Laurie;
ARMITSTEAD, Maureen; ARMITSTEAD, Mearl; ARMSTRONG, C.; ARMSTRONG, Dorothy;
ARMSTRONG, Kathy; ARMSTRONG, Kim; ARNOLD, David; ARNOLD, Wendy; ARONDA, Woodroffe;
ARPS, Esther; ARTHURS, Claudine; ASHTON, Dianne; ASHTON, Mane; ASSINEWE, Valerie;
ATKINSON, Cecile; ATKINSON, Cecile; ATKINSON, Helen; ATKINSON, Kerry; ATKINSON, Ralph;
ATKINSON, Terry; ATKIS, Margaret; ATKISON, Lindsay; AU, Joanne; AUBIN, Ron; AUER, Tom;
AUGUSTINE, Melissa; AUSTIN, Dave; AUSTIN, Leanne Susan; AXANI, Patricia; AYLIN, Elizabeth;
AYOUNG, Peter; AYOUNG, Wolston;

B

BABBIK, Rose; BABIUK, Jeanette; BABOWAL, Colleen;
BACCHUS, Rabena; BACH, Ryan; BADACH, Crystal; BADRY, Kathleen; BADRY, Sharlene;
BAECK, Marlynn; BAGGETT, Patricia; BAGSHAW, Karen; BAILES, Allison; BAILES, Bernadette;
BAILEY, Ester; BAILEY, Harold; BAILEY, Jennifer; BAKER, Gail; BAKER, Helen; BAKER, MaryAnne;
BAKER, Timothy; BAKER, Wendy; BAKKER, Stephen Wayne; BALAN, Deborah; BALL, Beatrice;
BALL, Eugene; BALL, Shirley; BALLANCE, Pamela; BANERJEE, Rajaree; BANH, Mai; BANKS, Anne;
BANKS, Kerri; BANNARD, Dawn; BARBARA, Bill; BARELAY, Mary; BARETT, Kelly; BARKER, Elsa;
BARKER, Marvin; BARLAGE, Gerald; BARNES, Judi; BARNES, Sally; BARNES, Susan;
BARON, Charlaine; BARRETT, Pat; BARRETTE, Arlette; BARRIGAN, Jill; BARRY, Eva;
BARRY, William; BARTCO, Mark; BARTCO, Mary; BARTCO, Walter; BARTEL, Linda;
BARTEL, William; BARTH, Leslie; BARTKO, June; BARTON, Michael; BAS, Josef;
BASARABA, Maria; BASARSKY, Karen; BASTIDAS, Milkka; BATEMAN, Diane; BATES, Anne P.;
BAUDER, Elaine; BAUDER, Morris; BAUDER, Stella; BAUEE, Darrell; BAUMGARTNER, Audra;
BAUTISTA, Heidi; BEACON, Bettina; BEAKHOUSE, Cathy; BEAMAN, Danny; BEATON, Heather;
BEAULNE, Suzanne, J.; BEAZLEY, Cali; BECKER, Susan; BECKETT, Shirley; BEGLEY, Theresa, Mary;
BEHIEL, Norman; BELAIR, Isabelle; BELANGER, Michael Paul; BELITSKY, Gwen; BELITSKY, Jeff;
BELITSKY, Kay; BELLAND, Laurelle; BELLOW, Jonathon; BENIUK, Andrew; BENNETT, Brooke;
BENNETT, Marion; BENOITON, Kene David; BENSON, Charles; BENTHAM, Anne; BENTT, Michelle;
BEREZAN, Orie; BEREZNICKI, Dr.; BERG, Darren Leif; BERG, June; BERG, Leif; BERG, Nolan Kendall;
BERG, Shane Lee; BERG, Sharon; BERNSTEIN, Ari; BERQUIST, Joyce; BERRETH, Sheryl;
BERRINGER, Jo-Ann; BERRY, Glenn; BERTOLIN, Diana; BERZINS, Lara; BETTEGER, Dharma;
BETTINO, Angela; BETTINO, Tony; BETTON, Carla; BEYER, Valerie; BHAIWALA, Nazeen;
BHAR, Amrita; BHAR, Joveena; BHATTA, Pradeep; BHATTA, Prakash; BHATTA, Preet;
BHATTA, Prem; BICKELL, Darren; BICKELL, Marion; BIELENY, Lorraine; BILESKI, Amy Marie;
BILLIG, Ed; BINCE, Gene; BINCE, Lori J.; BINDER, Heather; BING, Heddy; BINGLEY, Marilyn;
BINNIE, Pamela; BIRD, Sherry; BISCHELL, Nida; BISHOP, Larry; BISHOP, Lisa; BISHOP, M. Sharon;
BISHOP, Ron; BISHOP, Valerie; BISSONNET, Allison E.; BITAMBA, Goretti;
BLACHETTE, Bonnie Rose; BLACKNER, Leslie Anna; BLADON, Sheri A.; BLAIN, Nancy;
BLANCHARD, Susan; BLANCHETTE, Albert; BLEAKLEY, Betty Anne; BLEAKLEY, Corinne; BODIE, Jill;
BODNAR, Kathi Marie; BODOBOROZNY, Colleen; BOETCHER, Arnold; BOGWORTH, Lori;
BOISSONNAULT, Antoinette; BOKENFOHR, Kerry; BOLSTAD, Jane; BONEY, Rose; BONORA, Doris;
BONVALET, Yuain Marc; BOONAR, Eugene; BORCH, Florence; BORLE, Joyce; BORRELLI, Rudy;
BORRIS, Mary; BOSIAK, David; BOSS, Shelagh; BOSWORTH, Jean; BOSWORTH, Lori;
BOTCHETT, Enid; BOTCHETT, George; BOUCHER, Bonnie; BOUMAN, Maureen; BOURGEAULT, Dale;
BOURGEAULT, Guy; BOURKE, Maureen; BOWEN, Chris; BOWEN, Marg; BOWERS, Laurie;
BOWES, Deb; BOWLBY, Jeff; BOYACHUK, Edward; BOYD, Dan; BOYD, Deanne; BOYD, Denise;
BOYD, Eileen; BOYD, Laurie; BOYD, Sheila; BOYD, Stephen; BOYKO, Audrey; BOYKS, Natia;
BOYLE, Margaret; BOYLE, Ruth Ellen; BPROULE, Erin; BRADLEY, D. Ian; BRADLEY, Elizabeth;
BRADLEY, Emiline; BRADLEY, Noreen T.; BRADLEY, Walter; BRAMLEY, Lorna;
BRANDABURA, Deanne; BRANNEN, Rosemary Betty; BRASS, Donna; BRAUN, Doris;
BREITKVEIR, Jan; BRENNEIS, Crleen; BREWER, Michelle; BREZINSKI, Calvin; BREZINSKI, Isabelle;
BREZINSKI, Linda Elaine; BRIGIDGAR, Lorraine; BRILL, Margaret; BRIMACOMBE, Marg.;
BRIMER, Kathleen Ann; BRISEBOIS, Corrine; BRISPO, Philip; BRITTON, Lynda; BROERSEN, Ingrid;
BROMLEY, Charlene; BROMLEY, Graham; BROOKER, Delphine; BROOKES, Brenda Joyce;
BROOKES, Edward John; BROOKS, Eric Gerald; BROOKS, Kathryn Joanne; BROOKS, Laurie;
BROSSEAU, Lise; BROUWER, Linda; BROUWER, Rick; BROWN, Alice; BROWN, Ann;

BROWN, Caren; BROWN, Carleen; BROWN, Colette; BROWN, Corina; BROWN, Desiree; BROWN, Doreen; BROWN, Erin; BROWN, George A.; BROWN, Hugh; BROWN, Kerry; BROWN, Lorraine; BROWN, Martha; BROWN, Sheila; BROWN, Terry; BRUNEL, Patricia; BRYANT, Roni; BRYCE, George; BRYCE, Ta ee a; BRYDEN, Bernard; BRYDEN, Denise; BRYENTON, Bob; BRYENTON, Doug; BRYENTON, Evelyn; BRYER, Brigette; BRYGADYR, Maryanne; BUBA, Corina; BUCHANAN, Kathryn; BUCHANAN, Zelma; BUCHWALD, Herbert; BUCHWALD, Jason; BUCHWALD, Joyce; BUCK, Wendy Sue; BUCKWALD, Jonathon; BUCULAK, Bonita; BUECHNER, Michelle; BUECHNER, Monica; BUKOWSKI, Kim; BURBRIDGE, Korrie; BURGHARDT, Brenda; BURGHARDT, Marie; BURKE, Dave; BURNS, Anne; BURNS, David; BURNS, Margaret; BURNS, Peter; BURNS, Susan; BURT, Agnes J.; BURT, Bob; BURT, Karen; BURTON, Duane; BURYN, Peter; BUSE, Carmen F.; BUSSIERE, Lise; BUTT, Mary Lou; BUXTON, Laurie; BUXTON, Nona; BUZA, Hilda; BUZAK, Ernest; BUZAK, Lawrence; BUZAK, Vera; BYKOWSKI, Gail; BYRON, Jeanne;

C

CALLAGHAN, John; CALLAGHAN, Lesia; CALVERT, Charlene;
CAMENZIND, Donna; CAMENZIND, Marcelle; CAMPBELL, Anne; CAMPBELL, Beverly; CAMPBELL, Colin; CAMPBELL, Grace; CAMPBELL, Hester; CAMPBELL, Hester; CAMPBELL, James; CAMPBELL, Ken; CAMPBELL, Mary; CAMPBELL, Sylvia; CAMPBELL-FOWLER, Sheila; CANU, John; CAOUETTE, Doris; CAOUST, Diane; CARDINAL, Lewis; CAREY, Philip John; CARFANTAN, Diana; CARINELLI, Tiziana; CARLE, Karen; CARLESON, Grant; CARLETON, Tammy; CARLINE, John; CARLINE, Sally; CARLSON, Grant; CARMICHAEL, Susan; CARNAHAN, Ken W.; CARROZZA, Carmelina; CARTIER, Ritor; CARVER, Kelly; CATHCART, Cori-Lyn; CATIE, Allan; CENA, Preston; CENA, Preston; CENA, Stan; CHAN, Elenore; CHAN, Paul; CHAN, Pearlie; CHAN, Peter; CHANNON, Corinne; CHAPMAN, Bob; CHAPMAN, Colleen; CHAPMAN, Denise; CHAPMAN, Jack; CHARLESWORTH, Robin; CHARTRAND, Tracy; CHASE, Gord; CHAU, Fern; CHEZ, Irene; CHILDS, Bonny; CHILKOWICH, Andrew; CHILKOWICH, Carol Lynn; CHILKOWICH, Teresa; CHIMKO, Philomena; CHIN, Barry; CHIN, Suzanne; CHINN, Brenda; CHIODO, Frances; CHISWELL, Albert; CHISWELL, Geneva B.; CHIU, Cyril K.K.; CHMILAR, Catherine P.; CHOMA, Angela; CHOMA, Joe; CHOMA, Minnie; CHOMIAK, Larysa; CHOMIAK, Myroslava; CHONG, Penelope; CHORNEY, Olga; CHOW, Karen; CHOW, Yenny; CHRISTENSON, Keith; CHRISTIANSEN, Karen; CHRISTIE, Carolina; CHRISTIE, Paula; CHRISTOPHER, Joyce; CHUPA, Charlie; CHURCILL, Sandy; CIONA, Iris; CIONA, Steve; CIPIN, Jennifer; CIUZ, Arlene; CLANCY, Eva; CLAPP, Bradley; CLARE, L.; CLARE, M.; CLARK, Bernie; CLARK, Darlene; CLARK, Janet; CLARK, Margaret; CLARK, Stephen; CLARKE, Bev; CLEASBY, Lisa; CLEE, Barbera; CLEGG, Wendy; CLIFTON, Carrie; CLIFTON, Joan; CLOUTIER, Jean; CLOUTIER, Vivian; COCKRALL, Barbara Anne; COCKRALL, Frank; COCKRALL, Jennifer Anne; COCKRALL, Michael Anthony; COCKRALL, Terrence A.; CODNER, Michele; COFFIN, Tracy; COHEN, Hoda; COHEN, Mandy; COLE, Pat; COLEMAN, Deanna; COLLEGHAN, Linda; COLLINS, Alison; COLLINS, Allison; COLLINSON, Patrick; COLTMAN, Kim; COLUMBE, Monique; COLVILLE, Susan; COMBS, Bertina; COMPASSI, Paul; CONNERY, Connie; CONNIE, Donald; CONNIE, Ella; CONSTANTINESCU, Vasile; CONSTANTINESQUE, Elana; CONVERSE, Alberta; CONVEY-LYONS, Loretta; COOK, Dellis; COOK, Howard; COOK, Maria; COOKE, Ed; COOKE, John; COOKE, Julie; COOKE, Nine; COOMBES, Joan E.; COOPER, Charlotte; COOPER, Eileen; COOPER, Eileen; COOPER, Howard E.; COOPER, Rueben; COOR, Joan; CORBEIL, Sylvie; CORBETT, Sandra; CORBETT, Tracey; CORNESS, Donald; CORNFIELD, Debbie; CORRADO, Sylvia; CORRIEAN, Rob Michael; COTT, T.G.; COTTMAN, Kim; COULOMBE, Brenda; COULOMBE, Roland; COULOMBE, Ron; COURTNEY, Lisa; COUTE, Terry; COUTTS, Marion; COUTTS, Sheenah; COWAN, Barbara Jean; COWIE, Heather; COX, Suzanne; CRAIG, Caroline; CRAIG, Jane; CRAWFORD, Leona; CRAWFORD, Marilyn J.; CRAWLEY, Claudia; CRAWLEY, Jack; CROCKER, Sheila; CROCKETT, Don; CROCKETT, Jay; CROCKETT, Leigh; CROCKETT, Lynn; CROSBY, Lori; CROTEAU, Mark; CRYDERMAN, Stella; CSILICS, Mrs. Tony; CSILICS, Tony; CUGLIETTA, Anna; CUGLIETTA, Francesca; CULO, Drina; CULVER, Fram; CUMMING, Dwight; CUNNINGHAM, Lorna; CURREY, Brenda; CUSACK, Marie; CUSH, Carolyn; CUYLER, Barbara; CUYLER, Bruce; CYMBALUK, Miles; CYR, Kelli;

D

DABIE, Anne; DAHLQUIST, Carina; DAIBER, Carola;
DALLOW, Joanne Elaine; DAME, Joan; DAMMANN, John; DANBROOK, Carla; DANCHUK, Max; DANIELS, Carol; DANIELS, Diane; DANIELS, Marla; DARIUS, Rolanda; DAVIDSON, Dianne; DAVIDSON, Heather; DAVIDSON, Kerry; DAVIDSON, Nigel; DAVIE, Isabel; DAVIES, Caroline; DAVIS, Bonnie; DAVIS, Glen; DAVIS, Wendy; DAVISON, Linda; DAWSON, Linda; DAWSON, Michael Bruce; DAWSON, Stewart Leonard; DAY, Maureen; DAY, Shannon; DAYMAN, Marlee; DE BEURS, Della; DE HAAS, Pat; DE JONGH, Elly; DE LEON, Leticia Isabel; DEAN, Rita; DEANE, Robert; DEBEURS, Leona; DeBRINSKI, John; DECHAINE, Lise; DECOCQ, Gerald; DEE, Heather; DEEGAN, Gwen; DEGEER, Shelley; DELANEY, Vera; DELAROSBEL, Gloria; DeLEEUW, Jake; DeLEEUW, Maria; DeLEEUW, Mark; DeLEEUW, Michelle; DeLEEUW, Trix; DELEON, Arcelli; DELFOSSE, Arlene; DEMERS, Janet; DeMUNNIK, Betty; DENISON, Samme; DENT, Aileen R.; DEPNER, Aaron; DEREWONKO, Jerry; DERKATCH, Cecile M.; DERWOOD, Kim; DERY, Monique; DESFOSSES, Suzanne; DESHAYE, Audrey; DESJARDINES, Pam; DESJARDINES, Ronald; DEUTSCHER, Carol; DEVILLE, Mark; DEVLIN, Gail Theresa; DEVLIN, Randy; DEVRIES, Fran; DEVRIES, Peter; DEWAR, Marion; DICK, Margaret Dawn; DICK, Pat; DICKIE, Marg; DICKSON, Bill; DICKSON, Dick; DICKSON, Shane; DICKSON, Sybil; DIELMAN, Caroline; DIESING, Karen; DIETRE, Connie; DIMITROFF, Jane; DINER, Mark; DING, Julianna; DINWOODIE, Gen.; DITT, Michelle; DIVELL, Doug; DIWISCH, Carmen; DIXON, Deanna; DIXON, John; DIXON, Leanne Marie; DIXON, Michael; DMYTRUK, Leslie; DMYTRUK, Orysia; DOBKO, Eleanor; DOBKO, Kelly; DOBKO, Nester; DOBRESCU, Kendra; DOBSON, Carol; DOBSON, Glenn; DOCKERTY, Betty-Lou; DODDS, Elaine; DODDS, Nora; DoGROOT, Henny; DOHORAN, Michael; DOLYNCHUK, Shelley; DOMBOWSKY, Carrie; DOMBROSKI, Emil; DONADT, Anita; DONALD, Sharon; DONNELLY, Todd Douglas; DONOVAN, Allan; DONOVAN, Emma; DOROSH, Dale; DORTCH, Stephanie; DOSSER, Barb; DOTTER, Paula; DOUCET, Helene; DOURISH, Barbara; DOURISH, Colin; DOWKER, Karen; DRADER, Marilyn; DREFS, Stacey William; DREW, Kevin; DREW, Tanya; DREWS, Marily; DROBOT, Vera; DRUMMOND, Alison; DRUMMOND, R. Clare; DRUMMOND, William; DRYSDALE, Margie; DUCHARME, Pierre; DUE, Brendan; DUFRESNE, Beth; DUMA, Linda; DUMONT, Donna; DUMOUCHEL, Dailene Marie; DUNBAR, Kathleen; DUNBAR, Rosemary; DUNN, Pat; DUNN, William; DUONG, Hung; DUPUIS, Cheryl Fay; DYCK, Jill; DYCK, Verline; DYER, Sharon; DYJUR, Dave; DYJUR, Diane; DYKSTRA, Yvonne; DZENICK, Margaret F.; DZIWENKA, Lee Nicholas; D'AMUR, Patricia;

E

EASTMAN, Merv; EDGAR, Daryn; EDMONDS, Lara; EDRIDGE, Laura; EDWARDS, Mary Anne; EDWARDS, Sandra; EDWARDS, Susan; EDWARDS, Tammy; EGAN, Colleen; EGAN, Doug; EGGERTSON, Betty; EGGERTSON, Tom; EGGLESTONE, Augustina; EGGLESTONE, Donna; EISLER, Ann; EL ALAWA, Virginia; ELAVIA, Sheroo; ELGER, Bruce; ELGIE, Brian; ELING, Carice; ELKOW, Marie; ELKOW, Marilyn; ELL, Lorinda; ELLIOTT, Madeleine; ELLIS, Christopher; ELLIS, Joanne; ELLIS, Mary Lou; EMERSON, Eldon; EMERSON, Marlene Sharon; ENFIELD, Christine Leanne; ENGEN, Raylene; ENNIS, Carolyn; ERIKSON, Lloyd; ERNICK, Lena; ESSIEN, Elaine; ESTABROOKS, Patricia; ETHERINGTON, David; ETHINGTON, Heather; EVANS, Darrel Vern Jr.; EVANS, Darrel Vern; EVANS, Lisa Ann Marie; EVANS, Marilyn Norma Ann; EVANS, Shannon Elizabeth; EVENSON, Richell; EVERETT, Carol; EWASIUK, Dennis; EWASIW, Joe; EWENSON, Betty; EWENSON, Pat; EWENSON, Susan; EWONIAK, Nadien;

F

FABCO, Jerhert;
FADIN, Pierina; FAHLMAN, Lila; FAHMY, Sami; FAIRBAIRN, Gail; FAISY, Diane; FAISY, Renee; FALCONER, Isabelle; FALCONER, John; FALCONER, Lucy; FALCONER, Luie; FALCONER, Ron; FALCONER, Ron; FALLIS, Bruce; FALLIS, Corinne; FARBIRDGE, Florence; FARYON, Richard R.; FAULDER, Betty; FAZIO, Stephan Heidi; FEDECHKO, Douglas; FEDECHKO, Marienne; FEDORATION, Cindy; FEDORATION, jean; FEDORATION, Willy; FEHELEY, Carol J.; FENEAK, Louise; FENIAK, Louise; FERGUSON, Olga; FERGUSON, Stanley; FERGUSON, Stan; FERNANDES, Maurice FERNANDEZ, Elly; FERREIRA, Albano; FERRERO, Sally; FERRIER, Rebecca; FIELDING, Christine; FILER, Wendy; FILEWICH, Kathy; FILIPPELLI, Vicky; FILLION, Jume; FILMOUR, Jeannie; FINCH, Morag; FINCHAK, Darcy; FINDLATER, Barry; FINDLATER, Barry; FINDLATER, Donna; FINDLATER, Donna; FINSTAD, Jackie; FINSTAD, Leanne; FIORILLO, Adeline; FISCHER, Donna; FISCHER, Olga; FISHER, Darrin Kent; FISLASON, Corinne; FITL, Mary; FITZGERALD, Paul; FITZPATRICK, Bea; FITZPATRICK, James; FITZPATRICK, Maretta; FITZPATRICK, Sue; FITZPATRICK, Wilf; FLAMAN, Janelle; FLASHA, Michelle; FLATERUD, Gordon; FLEGER, Marilyn; FLEGER, Mrs. W.W.; FLEGER, Mr. W.W.; FLEMING, Brenda; FLEMING, Shirley FLEMING, Wayne; FLESHER, Jay; FLEUREN, Carmen; FLOYD, Jeff Norman; FODCHUK, Barbara; FOGH, Liana; FOLDES, Cynthia; FONTAINE, Lynn; FOO, Robert; FORD, Arlene; FORD, Elmer; FORD, Fred; FORD, Lydia; FOREMAN, Pat L.; FOREMAN, Todd; FOREST, Betty; FORRE, Cindy; FORSS, Bernice; FORSS, Terence; FORSTER, Sharon; FOSSEY, Brent; FOSTER, Evelyn Jean; FOSTER, Joseph; FOSTER, Karen; FOSTER, Liz; FOSTER, Pamela; FOULTEN, Kim; FOUTS, Kimberly; FOWLER, Brenda; FOX, Bonnie; FOX, Loree; FRANCIS, Brian; FRANCIS, Doris; FRANKUM, Louise T.; FRASER, Joan; FRASER, Linda; FRASER, Olga; FRAZER, Elsa-Marie; FREED, Irene Opal; FREEDMAN, Dena; FRENCH, Derek; FRENCH, Mrs. Lois; FRENKE, Bill; FRENKE, Leslie; FREY, David; FREY, Jane; FREY, Kathryn; FRICKER, Rebekah; FRIDEL, Stephina-Anne; FRIEDENSTAD, Birgit; FRIEDMAN, Jacki; FRIEND, Larissa Joyce; FRIESE, Nadeen; FRIESEN, Cheryl; FUCHS, Kay; FUHR, Allison; FUJII, Juanita; FULMORE, Shari; FUNDYTUS, Trish; FUNG, Larry; FUNG, Simon; FUNK, Joan; FUNK, Joan;

G

GAEIUK, Donna; GAGNE, Irene;
GAGNON, Shirley; GAINER, Flo; GAINER, Jerry; GAJDA, Shelley-Anne; GALANT, Lucille; GALDRAITH, Heather GALDRAITH, Sylvia; GALL, Dorothy Simpson; GALL, Mancy-Rae; GALL, Tom; GALLANT, Murray; GALLOWAY, M.; GAMACHE, Lise; GANTON, Jodi; GAORIAN, Mila GARIEFSY, Pat; GARNEAU, Janet; GARRAWAY, Naisan; GATES, Cara; GATES, Virginia; GATIEN, Angele; GAUNT, Jennifer; GAUTHIER, Marie; GAVINCHUK, A. Patricia; GAWRYJAL, Eva; GAYLERD, Cindy; GEE, Emily; GEE, Yankui; GENEST, Tony; GEORGE, Jacqueline; GERHART, William Fabro; GERLACH, James; GERLACH, Larvat; GERLACH, Lois; GERLACH, Nancy; GERLACH, Nancy; GERMAIN, Denise; GERMAIN, Ken; GERMAIN, Marc; GERMAIN, Sandy; GERMAN, Margaret; GERMANIUK, Connie; GERMANIUK, Debbie; GERMANIUK, Merrill; GERMANIUK, Walter; GERRITSEN, Shelley Rae; GERRITSEN, William; GIACOBBO, Marisa; GIBBON, Iniyaz; GIBSON, Cheryl; GIBSON, Dorothy J.; GIBSON, Frank; GIESBRECHT, Lorne; GIESBRECHT, Margaret; GIESE, Gail; GIESE, Vivian; GILES, Florence; GILLESPIE, Ann; GILLESPIE, Muriel GILLIES, Margaret Sr.; GILLIS, Bethany; GILLIS, Janet; GILLIS, Yvonne; GILLISON, Eileen; GIRARD, Cindy; GIROUD, Ellen; GIVENS, Christine; GLAZIER, Irene; GLENNY, David S.; GLENNY, Dawn; GLENNY, Nancy; GLOECKLER, Wally; GLOVER, Ron; GOBEIL, Brigitte Helene; GOBEIL, Juliet; GOBIEL, Michelle Renee; GOBIN, Irene; GODFREY, Allison; GOERTZ, Kay; GOETTLER, Sue Doreen; GOETZ, Mona; GOLAN, Doron; GOLDBECK, Rob; GOLDSTICK, Betsy; GOLEC, Karen; GOLEMBLASKI, Kelly; GOLEY, Henryk; GOMME, Graham; GOMME, Heather; GOMME, Robbie; GOOCH, Ed; GOOCH, Liz; GOOD, Ed; GOOD, Grace; GOOD, Judith; GOOSELIN, Renee; GORCHOLSKI, Michelle; GORDEY, Brandy; GORDHOLSKI,; GORDICHUK, Christie; GORDICHUK, Christie; GORDICHUK, Jude; GORDICHUK, Sue; GORDICHUK, Susan; GORDILUK, Doug; GORDILUK, Pam; GORDON, Colin; GORDON, Dick; GOSS, Stephen; GOULD, George; GOULD, Margaret; GOULET, Bonnie Lynn; GOURLAY, Blanche; GOURLAY, Charles; GOURLEY, Jeff; GRACE, Howie; GRAHAM, Charlene; GRAHAM, Christopher; GRAHAM, Corrie; GRAHAM, Karen; GRAHAM, Maryse; GRAHAM, Michelle; GRAHAM, Susan; GRAMLICH, Paulette; GRANDE, Lina; GRANDFIELD, Shirley; GRANT, Carol; GRASDAL, Rod; GRAY, Michele M.; GREEN, Amanda; GREEN, Caroline; GREEN, Gordon; GREEN, Leslie; GREEN, Ron; GREGOIRE, Marjolaine; GREGOIRE, Patricia; GREIDANUS, Nelson Victor; GREIDANUS, Robert Ian; GREIDANUS, Tom Gless; GREKUL, Helen; GRETHEN, Brigitte; GRIFFITHS, Sherry; GRIGAT, Margie; GROOT, Helen; GROOT, Marian; GROTSKI, Helen; GROTSKI, Maryanne; GROVES, Tracy; GRULL, Bertha; GRUSIE, Rose Marie; GUENETTE, Mark; GUIGNON, Diane; GUILD, Brenda; GUILFOYLE, Marian E.; GUINDON, Sue; GUKSHARK, Darwin; GULAYETS, Kevin; GULLICKSON, ARLENE; GULLY, Tina Violet; GUNN, Barb; GUNN, Patricia; GUNN, Robert Nicholl; GUNRAI, Joan; GURLEY, Debbie E.; GUSHATY, George; GUSHATY, June; GUSKE, Brian; GUST, Debra; GUST, Doreen; GUSTAFSON, Carina; GUSTAFSON, Corina; GUTERSON, Cathie; GUZZO, Silvano;

H

HABIB, Rozmina; HAGEDORN, Bruce; HAGEMAN, Thomas J.; HAGEN, Cheryl; HAGEN, Jacqueline; HAGERMAN, Laurie J.; HAGERTY, Jane; HAGERTY, Patricia; HAGIST, Edith Vivian; HAGSTROM, Joan; HAIGHT, Loria; HAJAR, Mona; HALABI, Kamal J.; HALKO, Pauline; HALKO, Sherry; HALKO, Trevor; HALL, Faye; HALL, John; HALL, Lynda; HALL, Manci; HALLIDAY, Jan; HAMBLIN, Vickie J.; HANCAR, Cheryl; HANCAR, Colleen; HANCAR, Mike; HANCAR, Tod; HANCOCK, Janet; HANELT, Gordon; HANELT, Kelly; HANELT, Marion; HANELT, Shannon; HANNA, Jessica; HANSEN, Caroline; HANSON, Loreen; HANSON, Martha; HANSON, Russell; HARBIN, Jennifer J.; HARDY, Alberta Mark; HARDY, Brenda D.; HARDY, Evelyn; HARDY, Janice; HARDY, John; HARDY, Richard; HARDY, Scott; HARGREAVES, Laura: HARIPERSAD, Ishana; HARPER, Bradley John; HARRIS, Irene; HARRIS, Minnie; HARRIS, Neil; HARRIS, Stephanie Shannon; HARRIS, Suzanne; HARRISON, Jeff; HARRY, Beth; HARTMANN, Christa; HARVEY, Doreen; HARVEY, Dorothy; HARWOOD-LYNN, Monique; HARYSH, John; HASHIMOTO, Kenji; HASSAN, Greg; HASSAN, Jack; HASSAN, Leslie; HASSAN, Nadine; HASSAN, Vivian; HATCH, Joseph; HATNER, Betty; HATTERSLY, Nancy; HAUSCH, Martin Alberta; HAUSE, Eileen; HAWK, Lise HAWKER, Dawn; HAWKER, Ena;

HAWKERS, Helen; HAWKSWELL, Philip; HAY, Glenn; HAY, Shelley; HAY, Susan; HAYASHI, Lynda;
HAYDEN, Alix; HAYES, Brian; HAYES, Brian; HAYES, Onnolee; HAYES, Onnolee;
HAYMAN, Laverne Lillian; HEADLEY, Randolph; HEADLY, Neville; HEAPS, Randy; HEATH, Gillian;
HEATHERINGTON, Gerry; HEATHERINGTON, Jared; HEATHERINGTON, Pat; HEATHFIELD, Ken N.;
HEDLUND, Jodi; HEEKS, Jim D.; HEGER, Helen; HEIR, Lillian; HEISLER, Cindy; HELM, David;
HENDERSON, Jill; HENDERSON, Joyce; HENDERSON, Rob; HENKLMAN, Maureen L.;
HENNIG, Brenda; HENNIG, Lois; HENNING, Mervin; HENNIS, Jean; HENRIQUEZ, Claudia;
HENRIQUEZ, Lorena; HENRIQUEZ, Sandra; HENRY, Doris; HERGBERT, Albert; HERGBERT, Daphne;
HERGOTT, Glenn; HERGOTT, Neil; HESP, Kevin; HESTON, Dee; HESTON, Maurice; HEWITT, Larry;
HEWLETT, Douglas; HIBBARD, Jeannette; HIBBARD, Jody; HIBBELN, David; HIBBERD, Mike;
HILL, Hazel; HILL, Patricia; HILTON, Anne; HILTON, W.J.; HIMSCHOOT, Shirley D.; HINDS, Kevin;
HIRUKI, Lisa; HISLOP, Edith; HISLOP, George; HISLOP, Jessie; HISLOP, Winn; HITE, Brent;
HJYNH, Duc-Nhi; HLUS, Joseph; HNYBIDA, Arianne; HO, Joan; HOBAL, Jacqueline;
HOCKSTRA, Jackie; HODGESON, Lisa; HODGINS, Allyson; HODGINS, Jim; HODGKINSON, Jean;
HODGSON, Glenna; HODGSON, Karen; HODGSON-WARD, Audrey; HOEBER, Lorraine;
HOFFMAN, Karen; HOFFMAN, Linda; HOFFMAN, Susan; HOGARTH, Teresa; HOGSON, Ken;
HOHNES, Sherron; HOHOL, Tina; HOLE, Harry; HOLLAND, Brenda Jean; HOLLAND, Shelley;
HOLM, Dorothy; HOLM, Sheila; HOLMES, Tracy; HOLT, Kate; HOLT, Phyllis; HOLZER, Michael;
HOMYNYK, Jill; HOMYNYK, Lily; HOOD, Kevin; HOOK, Wanda; HOOVER, Morris; HOOVER, Pearl;
HOPKINS, Linda; HOPKINSON, Shirley; HORE, Diane; HORE, Lewis; HORMADY, Myrtle;
HORNE, Vivienne; HORNER, Ann; HORRICKS, Wendy; HORUDKO, Terry John; HOSKINS, Todd;
HOTRA, Rose; HOTTE, Darrin; HOUG, Lorraine; HOULDEN, Evelyn; HOULE, Catherine;
HOULE, Doreen; HOULE, May; HOUSDORFF, Cathy; HOUSTON, Bill; HOUSTON, Chris;
HOUT, Suzanne; HOW, Wanda; HOWE, Art; HOWE, Luella; HOWE, Sharon; HOYLE, Heather;
HOYLE, Michelle; HRABI, David; HRABI, Jim; HRABI, Lyria; HRITZUK, Daisy; HRYCHUK, Carol;
HRYCHUK, Susan; HRYCYSCHYN, Sandy; HRYNCHUK, Laurie; HRYSTAK, Jamie; HSUNG, Yew-Har;
HUBER, Len; HUBER, Margaret; HUBER, Vera; HUCULAH, Liz; HUCULAH, Terry; HUE LYE, Koon;
HUMBLE, Betty; HUMBLE, David; HUMMEL, Gloria; HUMMEL, Keith;
HUNCHAK, Kelly HUNG, William; HUNKA, Leanne; HUNT, Bill; HUNT, Brian; HUNT, Jody;
HUNT, Laurie; HUNTER, George; HUNTER, Ian; HUNTER, Jim; HUNTER, Joe; HUNTER, Kate;
HUNTER, Michele; HURSHOY, MARY: HURST, Don; HUSER, Glen; HUSS, Dennis; HUSS, Elizabeth;
HUTCHINGS, Colleen; HUTCHINGS, Sharon; HUTCHINGS, Ted; HYRCHUK, Beth Irene;

I

IBRAHAM, Sadrych; ICULA, Dawn; IDICULA, Faith; IGGULDEN, Bruce; IGGULDEN, Kathy;
ILES, Catherine; INGIBERGSSON, Asgar; INGRAM, Paul; INGROSSO, Delores; INGROSSO, Maria;
INMAN, Ann; INMAN, Christine; INMAN, Dean; INMAN, Mark; INMAN, Ron; IRVINE, Tom;
IRVING, Hazel; IRVING, Reg; ISEKE, Caroline; ISWYSHYN, Audrey; ISWYSHYN, Janis;
ITO, Catherine; ITO, Daniel;

J

JACKNICKE, Cassie; JACKNISKY, Ann; JACKSON, Diane;
JACKSON, Dianne; JACKSON, Karen; JACKSON, Laurance; JACKSON, Renate Christine;
JACOBSON, Bob; JAGGARNAUT, Dianne; JAHANS, Bev; JAINARINE, Dee; JAJCZAY, Victoria;
JAMAL, Samina; JANI, Noreen; JANUEL, Len; JAQUES, Jo Ann Monica; JARBEAU, Greg;
JARDINE, Lynne; JAREMA, Joanne; JARMOLICZ, Linda; JARRETT, Doug; JARVIS, Joann;
JARVIS, Patricia; JASON, Edward; JAY, Wendy; JEAN-LUIS, Judy; JEDE, Lorrie; JEFFREY, Verona;
JELEN, Blanka; JELEN, Sarka; JENKINS, Betty; JENKINS, Bob; JENKINS, Joan; JENKINS, Sandi;
JENKINS, Susan; JENKINS, Ted; JENKINSON, Dr. Jarion; JENSEN, Chris; JENSEN, Susan;
JERIA, Manuael J.; JERKE, Keith; JEVNY, Connie; JEWELL, Joan; JEWETT, Ron; JEWETT, Sandy;
JIM, Carolyn G.; JIM, Cheryl L.; JIMENEZ, Ma; JIN, Pearl; JIRY, Marie-Louise; JIRY, Neidi-Lynne;
JIRY, Robin; JIRY, Ronald JODOIN, Paul; JOE, Betty; JOE, Greg; JOE, Hugh; JOE, Pearl;
JOFRE, Ingrid; JOHAL, Gurpreet; JOHN, Christina; JOHN, Christina; JOHN, Susan; JOHNSON, Cliff;
JOHNSON, JEFF: JOHNSON, Margo; JOHNSON, Randy; JOHNSON, Ron; JOHNSON, Sandra;
JOHNSON, Sandy; JOHNSTON, Brian; JOHNSTON, Jenny; JOHNSTONE, Beryl; JONES, Armande;
JONES, David Sharron; JONES, Renee Francis; JORDAN, Elsie; JORDAN, Kelly; JORDEN, Juliette;
JORDEN, Susan; JOSEY, Diane; JOSEY, Kenneth; JOSLIN, Gertie; JOURNAULT, Lucile;
JULLEN, Linda; JUNELL, Joan; JURRAY, Lynn;

K

KACHUR, Anne; KACUR, Gerrie; KADATE, Lyle;
KADERLE, Diana Lynn; KAGANOVSKAYA, Sophia; KAGANOVSKY, Boris; KALAMANOVITCH, Michael;
KALINOWSKI, Heidy S.; KALINOWSKI, Kathy; KALINOWSKI, Michael; KALINOWSKY, Avril;
KALINOWSKY, Laurissa; KAMININSKI, Karen; KAMLESH, Verna; KAPALANSKY, Anna;
KAPLANSKY, Anna; KAPLANSKY, Greg; KAPLER, Lloyd; KAPLER, Merna; KARBONIK, Colin;
KARBONIK, Kevin; KARL, Frances E.; KARPETZ, Heather; KASHUBA, Maryilyn; KASHUBA, Patricia;
KASOWSKI, Mike; KASSIAN, Darlene; KASSOWAN, Carmelle; KATSMAR, Dian; KAWALILAK, Kathy;
KAWASHIMA, Jun; KAWASHIMA, Ken; KAWULYCH, Elsie; KAWULYCH, Margaret L.; KAY, Bill;
KAY, Margaret; KAYE, Annette; KAYE, Roy; KEARNS, Carol; KEELEY, Elain; KEELEY, Wing;
KEEN, Sandra; KEHOE, Nancy; KEICHINGER, Charmaine; KEIL, Howard; KELL, Audrey; KELLER, Mae;
KELLY, Colin; KELLY, Corrine; KELLY, Craig; KELLY, Jean; KELLY, Mike; KELLY, Philip; KELLY, Sarah;
KELLY, Sharon; KELLY, Sheila; KENDALL, Hazel; KENDALL, Stanley; KENNEDY, Anne;
KENNEDY, Brenda; KENNEDY, Carol; KENNEDY, Carol; KENNEDY, Marjorie R.; KENNEDY, Mike;
KENNEDY, Rubina jane; KENNEDY, Shelagh; KENNIE, Margarot; KENT, John; KEOWN, Brendan;
KEOWN, Pat; KEROACK, Jacqueline; KERR, Astley G.; KERSLAKE, Mimi; KEYS, Judy; KEYS, Kerrie;
KEYS, Tracy; KHADIM, Shabnam; KHAN, Mona; KICHTON, Vera; KIERAN, Danny; KIHARA, Hilda;
KILPATRICK, Lynn; KILPATRICK, Shirley; KINMOND, Stuart; KINMOND, STuart; KIRIAKA, Lorna;
KIRILLO, Elizabeth; KIRK, Sheila; KISH, Doug; KISH, Gail; KISILEVICH, Dave; KISILEVICH, Karen;
KISILEVICH, Veronica; KITTLE, Grace; KITTLE, Grace; KLAPSTEIN, Carol; KLAPSTEIN, Elmar;
KLAPSTEIN, Elmar; KLAPSTEIN, Fred; KLAPSTEIN, Keith; KLAPSTEIN, Kent; KLAPSTEIN, Kim;
KLAPSTEIN, Kristi; KLATSTEIN, Elmer; KLAUS, Norma; KLAVER, W.H.; KLEIN, Arlene; KLEIN, Arlene;
KLEIN, A.L.; KLEIN, G.J.; KLINE, Gloria; KLINE, Gloria; KLINE, Loren; KLINE, Lorne;
KLINGBEIL, Doris; KLOOS, Norma; KLUCK, Andrea Lynn; KLUCK, Andrea; KLUCK, Cheryl Lee;
KLUCK, Cheryl; KLUCK, Pearl; KLUCK, Pearl; KLUTHE, Carol; KLUTHE, Norman; KNAPIK, Lisa;
KNEBAL, John; KNEBAL, Valerie; KNEIL, John; KNIEL, John; KNIGHT, Harry; KNIGHT, Irene;
KNIGHT, Wendy; KNOX, Sherri; KOBYLANSKI, Debbie; KOBYLKA, Deborah; KOCHAN, Corinna;
KOCHAN, Louise; KOEHLI, Allen; KOENIG, Shirley; KOHUT, Phyllis; KOKOTILO, Joanne;
KOLBA, Cathy; KOLTHAMMER, Helen-Rae; KONRAD, Wendy; KORBUT, Colleen; KORBUT, Michelle;
KORBYL, Edward; KORBYL, Richard; KORBYL, Robert; KORBYL, Vicki; KORDY, Sandi;
KORENIC, Ann KORETSCH, Veronica Caroline; KOROLUK, Debbie; KOROLUK, Janet; KORTES, Marien;
KOSCINK, George; KOSKA, Sandy; KOSSMAN, Katherine; KOSTENUK, Marrion Lynn;
KOWALCHUK, Barry; KOWALCHUK, Marjorie; KOZIAK, Anna; KOZIAK, Basil; KOZIAK, Don;
KOZIAL, Albert; KOZIAL, Stella; KRAEMER, Cheryl; KRAM, Tillie; KRAMER, Carol;
KRAUSHAR, Cheryl; KRAUSKOPF, Judi; KRAUSKOPF, Judi; KRAWCHUK, Janet; KRAWCHUK, Janet;
KREBS, Lorri; KREBS, Patti; KRELL, Kari; KROETCH, Rebecca; KROL, Margaret; KROOK, Gwen;
KRPAN, Maggie; KRSTIC, Lil; KRUKEWICH, Pat; KRUPP, Judy: KRYZANOWSKI, Karen;
KRYZANOWSKI, Lil; KUBRAK, Shirley; KUCHERAWAY, Charlene; KULY, Chris; KUMAR, Anil;
KUMPF, L. Bella; KUNIK, Bal; KUNY, Michael KUNY, Penny; KURARNA, Marian;
KUSHNERYK, Wayne; KUSICH, Rita M.; KUTARNA, Liz; KUYT, Pamela; KUZYK, Rick; KWAN, Marvin;
KWONG, Jackson; KWONG, Regina; KYEREMANTENG, Ave.; KYLE, Blaine; KYLE, Edgar;
KYLE, Myrna; KYLYMOKOWICH, Lydia;

L

LABBY, Bryan David; LABBY, Diana-Irene;
LABOUCHAN, Darlene; LABRIE, Doris; LACKTON, Barry; LACKTON, Rosalie;
LaCOURSIERE, Terrance; LAFLECHE, Audra; LAFRANCE, Albert; LAFRANCE, Rene; LAIN, Cindy;
LAIN, Jack; LAING, Darryl; LAING, Dave; LALIBERTE, Dianna; LALONDE, Susan; LAM, Gilbert;
LAMB, Gerard; LAMBLE, Emily; LAMBLE, Wayne; LAMERS, Jackie; LAMONT, Rose;
LAMOUREUX, Stephen; LAMPARD, Dr. Dorothy; LAMPARD, Joyce; LANE, Rhoda; LANES, Alice E.;
LANGE, S. Florence; LANGLOIS, Claudia; LANGLOIS, Helen; LAO, Meiyann; LAPIERRE, Donna;
LAPLANTE, Daniel; LAPOINT, Kim; LARIO, Ann Margaret; LAROCQUE, Stephan; LaROQUE, Bonnie;
LARSON, Barb; LARSON, Ilene LARSON, Laurelle; LARSON, Lyn; LARSON, Richard; LARSON-
Ashworth, Sherril May; LASIC, Zora; LATHAM, Winifred; LATOSKI, Betty; LAVALLE, Susan;
LAVERGNE, Sharon; LAWRENCE, Ge-trude; LAWRENCE, Janis; LAYCOCK, Tena; LAYETZKE, Brent;
LAYETZKE, Maureen; LAYLOCK, Kerrie; LAZAR, Alexandra; LEARMONTH, Karen Anne;
LEBRAY, Colin; LEBUKE, James; LEBUKE, Marilyn; LECKY, Kathleen; LEDDY, Helen; LEDE, Jennifer;
LEDEY, Brice; LEDGER, Betty; LEE, Calvin; LEE, Dennis; LEE, Jaye; LEE, Katherin Chui Kiu;
LEE, MARILYN: LEE, Marlene; LEE, Regine; LEE YUEN, Margaret A.; LEECK, Irene; LEFEBURE, Helene;
LEFEVBRE, Rollande; LEGAULT, Frances; LEGROS, Angela; LEHMAN, John E.; LEMAN, Charles;
LENEY, Beverly; LENNOX, Bob; LENNOX, Pat; LENT, Frank; LENTZ, Kathleen; LEONG, Jimmy Wong;
LEPARD, Ross; LEPINE, Janice; LEROHL, Karen; LESTER, Maggie; LESTER, Mary; LETENDRE, Cindy;
LETENDRE, Jason; LETOURNEAU, Lisa-Marie; LEUNG, Esther; LEUNT, Andy; LEVANG, Christine;
LEVANG, Donna; LEVANG, Gordon; LEVESQUE, Adele; LEWICKI, Rose; LEWIS, Sharna Rae;
LIEW, James; LIGHTBODY, Margo Ellen; LILGE, Charlene; LILGE, Chris; LINCHET, Claudette;
LINCHET, Tony; LINDBERG, Wally; LINDBERT, Glenna; LINDSAY, Melody; LINDSAY-STEWART, Pege;
LINEKER, Robert; LINEKER, Ruth E.; LINES, Dan; LISTER, Betty; LISTER, Ron; LITKE, Dee;
LITTLE, Annie; LITVINCHUK, Michelle; LIZOTTE, Brenda; LIZOTTE, Joey; LIZOTTE, Melanie;
LOESCH, Diane; LOFQUIST, Don; LOGA, Julie; LOGSETTY, Sarvesh; LOMAS, Joyce;
LOMAX, Denis William; LONELY, Peter LOOSEMORE, Shawn; LOOV, Valerie; LOPUSHUNSKI, Heather;
LORD, Dorothy; LORINCZ, Denise; LOUIE, Bessie; LOUIE, Bill; LOUIE, Dorothy;
LOUIE, Jacquiline: LOUIE, Mark; LOUIE, Siri; LOVE, Kay; LOVERIDGE, Edna; LOWTHER, John;
LOWTHER, Pat; LOWTHER, Red; LOYER, Angela; LOYER, Ken; LOZON, Donna; LUBERT, Renie;
LUCHKA, Darlene; LUCIW, Jerry; LUDESCHIER, Hanna; LUIS, Delia; LUKA, Arno; LUMME, Bernie;
LUMME, Karen; LUNDMARK, Leslie Ellen; LUNQUIST, Terri; LUNSE, Charlotte; LUPASCHUK, Karen;
LUPUL, Cheryl L.; LUQUE, Lila; LURYE, Alina; LUSCOMBE, Karen; LUSCOMBE, Pamela;
LUSCOMBE, Patty; LYDERIK, Carrie; LYKE, Janet H.; LYKEN, Janet; LYNCH, Leslie LYNCH, Sharon;
LYOLL, Brenneis;

M

MA, Daniel; MA, Steven; MACCOSHAM, Corinne; MACCOSHAM, Greg;
MACCOSHAM, Spencer; MACCOSHAM, Terrie; MACCOSHAM, Tracy; MACDONALD, Anne-Marie;
MACDONALD, Bill; MACDONALD, Marilyn; MacEACHERN, Heather; MacEACHERN, Marilyn;
MacEACHERN, Robert; MACEACHERN, Roger; MACEACHERN, Tara; MacGREGOR, Heather;
MacGREGOR, Janet; MacGREGOR, Jim; MACIEYOWSKI, Marg; MACINNIS, Linda;
MACKELLAR, Mildred; MACKENZIE, Kathleen; MACKINNON, Kevin; MACKORUK, Larry;
MACKORUK, Larry; MACKOWETSZKY, Loran; MACLACHLAN, Howard; MACLACHLAN, Mary;
MACLEAN, Colin; MACLEAN, Helene; MACLEAN, Judy; MACLEAN, Roxanne; MacLEOD, Cliff;
MACLEOD, Sharon Anne; MacLEOD, Win; MACMILLAN, Laurie Anne; MACMILLAN, Lesley;
MACOLOR, Jose; MacPHERSON, Brian; MACPHERSON, Melody; MACPHERSON, Sharon;
MACRAE, Wendy MACRAY, Ken; MADAY, Charlcia; MADUK, Phyllis; MAGILL, Joyce;
MAGNAN, Huguette; MAGNAN, Martin; MAH, Cedar; MAH, Lily; MAH, Sandra; MAH, Sharon;
MAH, Suzannah; MAHE, Jocelyne; MAHON, Terry; MAIDEN, Heather; MAIDEN, Lionel;
MAJESKI, Debbie; MAJESKI, Kevin; MAKSIM, Don; MAKSIM, Liz; MAKSIM, Stella;
MALACHOWSKI, Dawn; MALHOTRA, C and 4 kids MALICK, Mary; MALKINSON, Elaine;
MALONE, Maureen; MALYSH, Marie; MANCHAK, Leonard; MANGINNE, Bob; MANGINNE, Edie;
MANKOW, David; MANKOW, Lisa; MANKOW, Rose; MANKOW, Serg; MANN, Greg D.J.;
MANN, Meera; MANNING, Ann; MANNING, Sarah; MANSFIELD, Mary; MANUEL, Angela;
MANUEL, Shirley; MANWARING, Anne; MAPPLEBECK, Elizabeth; MARBORD, Erna;
MARCHAND, Sharon; MARIAN, Dan; MARIER, jacqueline; MARION, Cheryl; MARION, Jeannine;
MARK, Dorothy; MARK, Hazel; MARK, Nancy Faye; MARKEVICH, Daria; MARKEVICH, Lubko;
MARKOWICH, Doreen Barbara; MARKOWICH, Kenny; MARKOWICH, Marsh; MARKOWICH, Mike;
MARKOWICH, Peggy; MARKOWSKI, John; MAROCCO, Linda; MARR, David; MARR, Vincent;
MARRAZO, Mario; MARSH, Glen; MARSH, Ruth; MARSHALL, Bev; MARSHALL, Dorothy;
MARSHALL, Kristin; MARSHALL, Robert; MARTEL, Carol-Ann; MARTEL, Jessie; MARTEL, Lisa;
MARTEL, Pat; MARTELL, Ed; MARTIN, Chris; MARTIN, Cindy Lee; MARTIN, Denise; MARTIN, Fran;
MARTIN, Irene; MARTIN, Jane; MARTIN, Jayne; MARTIN, Jeanette; MARTIN, John;
MARTIN, Susan; MARTIN, Trudy Lynn; MARTIN, Wendy; MARTZ, Irene;
MARVIN, Bill MARVIN, Donna; MARVIN, Tara; MARYN, John; MASH, Pat; MASKELL, Frances;
MASKEWICH, Joe MASKEWICH, Shirley; MASLYK, Barry; MASON, Sandra; MASSEY, Don;
MASSEY, Karen; MASTERVICK, Lorraine; MASTRONARDI, Silvana; MATANOVICK, Anna;
MATBICHUK, Olga; MATEJICEK, Leona; MATHEW, Jolly; MATHEWSON, Bruce;
MATHEWSON, Michele; MATHIEU, Tina; MATISHAK, Mark; MATLOCK, Ken John; MATSUBA, Eiko;
MATSUBUCHI, Akem; MAY, Laura; MAYALL, Arleen; MAYALL, Denise; MAYALL, Don;
MAYALL, Jeffrey; MAYER, Ethel; MAYES, Brenda; MAYFIELD, MArian; MAYKO, John;
MCAFEE, Anne; MCAFEE, Don; MCALEAR, Cathy; MCANDREW, Iris; MCARDLE, Lena;
MCATEER, David; MCBAIN, Elizabeth; MCCAGHERTY, Judy; MCCANN, Michael; MCCAULEY, Patti;
MCCAY, Isobel; MCCLEARY, Christine; MCCLEARY, John; MCCLEARY, Katherine; MCCLEARY, Philip;
MCCLELLAN, Sandra; MCCLURE, Rae; MCCOLL, Dawn; MCCOMAGHEY, Murray;
MCCORMACK, Jean; McCRORY, Wendy; McCUMBER, Suellen; MCCUTCHEON, Nancy A.;
McDERMOTT, Doreen; McDERMOTT, Gordy; MCDONALD, Eileen Margaret; MCDONALD, Ellen;
McDONALD, George; MCDONALD, Joan; MCDONALD, Kathy; McDONALD, Mary;
MCDOWELL, Vickie; MCEWEN, Bonnie; MCEWEN, Nelly; McFADDEN, Deanna; McFADDEN, Lorne;
MCFADDEN, Pamela; MCFALL, Patricia; MCFARLANE, Bruce; MCFARLANE, Gordon;
MCFARLANE, Mary; MCGALE, Debbie; McGHEE, Alison; McGILVERY, Denise; McGILVERY, Sally;
MCGINNIS, Jackie; MCGOVERN, Michele Marie; McGREGOR, Fiona; MCGREGOR, Peter;
MCINALL, Margaret; MCINTOSH, Ann; MCINTOSH, Diane Paula; MCINTOSH, George;
MCINTOSH, Laurie; MCINTOSH, Maureen; MCISAAC, Colin; McISAAC, Eleanor; MCISAAC, Karen;
McISAAC, Lilian; MCKAGUE, Ruby Kathleen; MCKEEN, Roberta; MCKENDRY, Kevin;

MCKENDRY, Tom; MCKENNA, Paul; MCKERNAN, Maureen; MCKINLEY, Al; MCKINLEY, Marlene; McKINNEY, Connie; McKINNEY, Kelly; McKINNEY, Lisa; McKINNEY, Sid; MCKINNON, Cameron; MCKINNON, Graham; MCKINNON, Patricia; McLAUGHLIN, Mary; McLAUGHLIN, Ronald; MCLEAN, Lavanda; McLEAN, Marilyn; McLENNAN, Donald; MCLENNAN, Donald; McLENNAN, John MCLEOD, Dorothy L.; MCLEOD, Gordon; MCLEOD, Graham; MCLEOD, Kristin; MCLEOD, Liz; MCLEOD, Patricia; McMAHON, Janelle; MCMANN, Neil; MCMILLAN, Adelaide; MCMULLIN, Tamaris Marilynne; MCMURRAY, DONNE: McNAB, Elizabeth; McNEIL, Vicki; MCNISH, Brian; MCNISH, Val; MCNULTY, Patricia; MCPHEE, Edward (Ted); MCQUARRIE, Steve; MCRAE, Ken; McSHANE, Donna Joan; McSHANE, Tracy; MCTAVISH, Karen; MEDINA, Susanne; MEEHAN, Bonnie Mary Anne; MEGINNIS, Jacqueline; MEGINNIS, Michelle; MEHCLE, Alison; MEHTA, Mona; MEIDINGER, Cathy; MEIKLEJOHN, Andrea; MEIKO, Alison; MELAMED, Assir; MELENTIA, Mrs. E.; MELHAM, Kathie; MELMOCK, Peggy; MELNYCHUK, Linda; MELNYCHUK, Sonia; MELNYK, Brenda; MELNYK, Dorothy; MELNYK, Marie; MENI, Monique; MENSINK, Naomi; MERKOSKY, Roger; MESSIAK, Elizabeth; MESSIAK, Sandy; MESSIER, Jennifer; MESSIER, Marry; MESTON, Jan; METERS, Leanne; METHVEN, Flora; METZ, Diane; MEYER, Ann; MEYER, Brigitta; MEYER, Debbie; MEYER, Jean; MICHAELS, Diana; MICHAUD, Agnes; MICHAUD, John; MICHELIN, Lyn; MICKELSON, Angie; MICKO, Margaret; MICKO, Michael; MICKO, Michelle; MICZYNSKI, Isabelle; MIETZNER, Claudia; MILANOVICH, Steven; MILL, Tracy Louise; MILLARD, Beth; MILLARD, Doris; MILLARD, Jim; MILLER, Barb; MILLER, Cathy; MILLER, Darlene; MILLER, David; MILLER, Edith; MILLER, Frances; MILLER, Holly; MILLER, Janet; MILLER, Jenny; MILLER, kelly; MILLER, Teresa Elaine; MILLS, Audrey; MILLS, E.; MINAILO, Chris; MINCHIN, Margaret; MINSOS, Jennifer; MIREAULT, Joseph; MISKEW, Debbie; MISTAL, Clarence; MISZTAL, Zygmunt; MITCHELL, David; MITCHELL, Douglas; MITCHELL, Evelyn; MITCHELL, Jill; MITCHELL, John; MITCHELL, Kristie; MITCHELL, Lill; MITCHELL, Maggie; MITCHELL, Mary Ann; MITCHELL, Patricia; MITCHELL, Robin; MITCHELL, Russell; MITCHELL, Tammy; MITCHELL, Warren; MITTELSTADT, Angela; MIZERA, Dorina; MLCUCH, Bronislava; MOAN, Karen; MOEN, Judy; MOERTH, Karin Helen; MOHAN, Romesh; MOHAN, Skrishna; MOLLOY, Carmen; MOLLOY, Ken; MOMR, Eldeen Gail; MONCK, Barbara; MONCK, Jesse; MONCK, Vincent; MONTGOMERY, Donna; MONTGOMERY, Leanne; MOOLK, Cynthia; MOON, Donna Mah; MOORS, janet; MOORS, Josephine; MORAKAMI, Vincent; MORAN, Elsie; MORGULIS, Anton; MORIN, Debbie; MORIN, Guy Robert; MORIN, Holly; MORIN, Louis; MORIN, Mark; MORIN, Rhonda; MORIN, Susan; MORISSETTE, Rosanne Lynne; MOROKOVICH, Mike; MORRILL, Judy; MORRIS, Christine; MORRIS, Christine; MORRISON, Elissa; MORRISON, Joyce; MORRISON, Wally; MOSKALYK, Donna; MOULLEN, Bob; MUELLER, Janet; MUELLER, Randy; MUHLBIER, Cindy; MUHLBIER, Perry; MULAK, Maureen; MULLEN, Dan; MULLEN, Darrell; MULLEN, Don; MULLEN, Mrs.; MULLEN, Mr.; MULLEN, Susan; MULLIGAN, David; MULWANI, Deepak, Mike; MULWANI, Rajeev; MUNCHA, Kim; MUNCRO, Debbie; MURAKAMI, May; MURAKAMI, Sash; MURCH, Marijo; MURDOCK, Joanne; MURPHY, Janet; MURPHY, Kevin; MURPHY, Shawna; MURRAY, Doreen; MURRAY, Pearl; MURRAY, Stacey; MUSIC, Glen; MYCHOLAT, Doug; MYKITIUK, Roxanne; MYSHCHYSHYN, Irena;

N

NADON, Phylis; NAGY, Heather; NAGY, Lawrence; NAKONECZNY, Kathy; NARINSINGH, Peter; NATSUYAMA, Kasako; NAVAZ, Fazal; NEELANDS, Jill NEIL, Daniel; NEILSON, Lynn; NEILSON, Michelle; NELSON, Brent; NELSON, Bruce; NELSON, Jeff; NELSON, Ken; NELSON, Sandra; NELSON, Suzanne; NESS, Arnie; NETT, Arnold; NEUFELD, Bernice; NEUFELD, Blair; NEUFELD, Dorothy; NEUFELD, Gayle; NEUFELD, Peggy; NEUFELD, Rhonda; NEWEL, Douglas; NEWMAN, Betty; NGAT, Albert; NGUYEN-DINH, Phoung; NGVYER, Tvyet; NIBLET, Jessie; NICHOLS, Cheri; NICHOLS, Dayna; NICKEL, Violet; NICKEY, Andy; NIEHAVS, Daniel; NIELSON, Maggie; NIELSON, Wendy; NIKOLAYCHUK, Marion; NILSON, Louise; NIMMO, Lynda; NIXON, Greg; NIXON, Sarah; NOGA, Delores; NONAY, Laural; NORD, Fay; NORRIS, Garth; NORRIS, Liz; NOSEK, George; NOTDORFT, Erwin; NOTDORFT, Ingrid; NOTT, Kathy; NUTHACK, Francine; NYBERG, Janet; NYCHOLAT, Douglas; NYCOLYK, Alex; NYCOLYK, Nadia; NYHOLAT, Dang; NYHUS, Bernice;

O

OBERFELD, Alex; OBERFELD, Arkady; OBERFELD, Svetlana; OBREGON, Madeleine; ODYNSKI, Pat; OGRODNICK, Chantal; OGRODNICK, Sherry; OGSTON, Leslie; OHASHI, Bonnie; OHRN, Jocelyn; OHRN, Mary; OKEMAW, Laura; OLESEK, Jody-Anne; OLIJNYK, Bohdan; OLIVER, Kathy; OLNEY, Karen; OLNEY, Loreen; OLNEY, Walter; OLNEY, Walter; OLSON, Brian; OLSON, Corrie; OLSON, David; OLSON, Helen; OLSON, Jean; OLSON, Jennifer; OLSON, Judy; OLSON, Marla; OLSON, May; OLSON, Mildred; OLSON, Pauline; OLSON, Phyllis; OLSON, Randy; OLSON, Roger; ONESS, Edith; ONESS, Randy; ONUSKO, Linda; OPAZO, Jaime; OPAZO, Marcello; ORCHARD, Debra; ORCHESKI, Charlene; ORKUSZ, Darlene; ORLESKI, Georgia; OSAKA, Joann; OSBOURNE, Karen; OSIETKA, Lasha; OSTER, Roy; OSWALD, Caren; OTKINSON, Cecile; OTTO, Joanne; OUKYK, Myra; OVELLET, Marie; OWEN, Peter; OZORIO, Bill; OZORIO, Michael; OZORIO, Rene; O'BRIAN, Gilvert; O'BRIAN, Karen; O'BRIEN, Caroline; O'BRIEN, Karen; O'BRIEN, Paul; O'BYRNE, Dawn; O'BYRNE, Dean; O'BYRNE, Jeanne; O'BYRNE, Roy; O'CALLAGLAAN, Pat; O'CONNELL, Mary; O'CONNOR, Brian; O'HARA, Francis; O'HARA, Ron; O'LOUGHLAN, Julianne; O'SHEA, Darleen; O'SULLIVAN, Dan; O'SULLIVAN, Peg;

P

PACKER, Art; PACKER, Mary; PACKOLYK, Paulette; PADGET, Elizabeth; PAGE, Elaine; PAGE, James; PAGE, Roberta; PAGEE, David; PAGEE, Lorna; PAGLIAROLI, Palmira; PAGOLA, Delia; PALAHNIUK, Marian; PALEY, Mona Leonora; PALMER, Queenie; PALMER, Steven; PANCHISHIN, Janice; PANCYIA, Bonnie; PANESAR, Daljit; PANYCH, Merelee; PAPPAS, MARY: PAQUETTE, jenny; PARADIS, Diane; PARADIS, Lucien; PARAN, Helen; PARDEE, Mary; PARE, Elsie; PARE, Michael; PARE, Yvonne; PARFETT, B.; PARFETT, J.G.; PARITI, Annapurna; PARK, Betty; PARK, Darwin; PARK, Roxi; PARK, Ryan; PARK, Susan; PARKER, Bonnie; PARKER, Bonny; PARKER, Joan; PARKER, Ron; PARKS, Grant; PARKS, Sandra; PARRAGUEZ, Benjamin; PARRAGUEZ, Louise; PARROTTA, Linda; PARROTTA, Nicholas; PARSK, Heather; PARSLOW, Robert; PASEMKO, Peter; PASIN, Lisa; PASTUSZENKO, Christine; PASTUSZENKO, George; PASTUSZENKO, Vera; PASTUZYK, Carol; PASULA, Linda Anne; PATEL, Arun; PATRICK, Lisa; PATSULA, Anna; PATTERSON, Gary; PATTERSON, Leonora; PATTON, Anne; PATTON, Carol; PATTON, Cliff; PATTON, Tracey; PAWLICK, Anne; PAWLICK, John; PAWLIUK, Robert; PAWLYK, Vera; PEARSON, Dave; PEARSONS, Lea; PECHTOL, George; PEDERSON, George; PEDERSON, Karen; PEDERSON, Rob; PEDROLA, C.; PEERS, M.; PELECH, Fiona; PENNINGTON, Dex; PENNINGTON, Francis; PENONZEK, Debbie; PENSALOR, Edgar; PERERA, G.A.; PERERA, L.; PERKINS, Martha; PERL, John; PERMELIA, Parham; PERRY, Beth; PETER, Mark; PETERSON, Barbi; PETERSON, Beverly; PETERSON, Hazel; PETERSON, Jan; PETERSON, Margo; PETERSON, Vicki; PETRIW, Nester; PETRIW, Roman; PHAM, Trang; PHAMBHANI, Jyoti; PHILIPS, Greg; PHILIPS, Sylvia; PHILLIPS, Enid; PHILP, Dianne; PIDNER, Anne; PIERCY, Belva; PIERCY, Brian; PIKE, Shelagh; PIKE, Wendy; PIKE, Wendy; PINTO, Rosseti; PINTON, Cathy; PIPER, Barbara; PIPER, Douglas; PIPER, Suzanne; PIRZAK, Sandi; PISESKY, Irene; PISESKY, Laureen; PISKA, Norma; PLATO, Nancy; PLATZER, Bob; PLATZER, Krista; PLOSKINA, Yelena; PLUMB, Carole; POINS-LYBBE, Kathy; POINTE, Joanne; POINTE, Reg;

POIRIER, Marion; POIRIER, Sandy; POIVCHUK, Cynthia; POLOWY, Ardele; POLOWY, Edward; PON, Daisie; PON, Hester; PONCE, Waldo; PONICH, Dian; PONICH, Matthew; PONIEWOZIK, Adolph; PONIEWOZIK, James; PONIEWOZIK, Marilyn; POOHKAY, Mary; POOHKAY, Wm.; POOLER, Susan; POON, Cecilia; POON, Patti; POON, Pearl; POON, Rick; POON, Sally; POON, Susie; POONIA, Gurtek; POPAL, Marguerite; POPE, Larry; POPE, Nancy; POPOWICH, Janet; POPOWICH, Sandra; POPP, Carol; PORTER, Linda; PORTER, Tanya; PORTERFIELD, Kay; POSTON, Gail; POTTER, Ben (could be Ken); POTTS, Linda; POULIN, Cindy; POULIN, Ron; POULSEN, Mathild; POWELL, Elizabeth; POWER, Sandry; POWLESLAND, Larry; PRATLEY, Mary-Jean; PRATTER, Karl; PRENDERGAST, Angela; PREVOST, Thena; PREZOST, Maria; PRICE, Leslie; PRIDHAM, Barry; PRIDHAM, Lola; PRIDMORE, Barbara; PRIESTLY, Chris; PRIESTLY, Linda; PRIESTLY, Tom; PRIMA, Ray; PRIMEAU, Agnes; PRIMEAU, MARIE Louise; PRIMOSCH, Joan; PRIMOSCH, Richard; PRITCHARD, Dawn; PRITCHARD, Shawn; PROCHNAN, Byron; PRODAN, Gina; PRODEN, Anne; PRODEN, Janet; PRODEN, Mel; PRODMORE, Cedric; PRODMORE, Helen; PRODMORE, Tracy; PROKOP, John; PROKOPCHUK, Harry; PROKOPIW, Jacki; PROSKIW, G.; PROULX, Carol; PROVENCAL, Caroline; PROVOST, Shawn; PROVOST, Valerie; PRUDEN, Holly; PRUD'HOMME, David; PRUD'HOMME, Linda; PSALZ, Veronica; PULLISHY, Grant; PULLISHY, Jihn; PURCELL, Billie; PURCELL, Richard; PURDELL-LEWIS, Judith; PURDELL-LEWIS, Sandi; PURDELL-LEWIS, Sandi; PYLE, Esther;

Q

QUEVILLON, Lynn; QUILLIAM, Janet; QUILLIAM, Kelly; QUINONES, Patricia; QUON, May;

R

RABIN, Deanna; RACE, Alban; RACE, Sylvia; RADCLIFF, Charlotte; RADULESCU, Dora; RAMASHOYE, Max; RAMBARAN, Charlene Roselle; RAMCHANDANI, Aortie; RAMLAL, Annie; RAMOUTAR, Leah; RAMSEY, Bonnie; RAMSEY, Glenna; RAMSEY, Marlene; RAMSEY, Ronald; RANDLES, Darcy; RANKIN, Bill; RANKIN, Florie; RAUCH, Susan Leeann; REAUME, Joe; REDDINGTON, Wendy; REDMOND, Margaret; REED, Gord; REED, Jan; REGHELINI, Zarelda; REIB, Elisabeth; REICHE, Deborah; REID, Barb; REID, Cass; REID, Donna; REID, Jim; REID, Mike; REID, Paul; REIDIGER-DUEBAL, Joann; REIMER, Lowell; REIMER, Tina; REINBERG, Michel Enrique; REMBISH, Judy; REMEIKO, Linda; RENDELL, Valeri; RENFORTH, Elaine; RENNIE, Brenda; RENNIE, John; RICHARDS, Peter; RENOUF, Lori; RESHEF, Elazar; RETTIE, Susan; RETZLAFF, Llana; REYES, Danilo; REYNOLDS, Karen; RICCI, Tana; RICE, Shirley; RICH, Anthony; RICH, Katy; RICH, Mary; RICH, Meagn; RICH, Sheila; RICH, Susan; RICHARDS, Barbara; RICHARDS, Caroline; RICHARDS, Christie; RICHARDS, David; RICHARDS, Dawn; RICHARDS, Denny; RICHARDS, Sally; RICHARDSON, Katherine; RICHMAN, Janet; RICHMOND, Donna; RICHMOND, Murray; RICHTER, Ursula; RIDDELL, Michelle; RIES, Brenda; RIIVES, Roland; RIIVES, Sarah; RIJAVEC, Sharon; RILEV, Laura; RILEY, Annette; RILEY, John; RILEY, Loreen; RISSELADA, Dick; RIVERS, Dianne; ROBBINS-DUE, Sherry; ROBERTS, Bill; ROBERTSON, Bernice; ROBERTSON, Beryl; ROBERTSON, Catherine; ROBERTSON, Elise; ROBERTSON, Heather (Nychka); ROBERTSON, Hugh; ROBERTSON, John (Nychka); ROBERTSON, Ieane; ROBERTSON, Leslie (Nychka); ROBERTSON, Lynda; ROBERTSON, Norma; ROBINS, Tammy ROBINS, Todd; ROBINSON, Bill; ROBINSON, Connie; ROBINSON, Diane; ROBINSON, Jim; ROBINSON, Rob; ROBINSON, Vivien; ROBLIN, Grace; ROBSON, Jean; ROBSON, Shelly; ROCHE, Maryanne; ROCHELEAU, Ginette; RODEN, Athaide; RODEN, Shannon; RODEN, Tina; ROEHL, Dean; ROEHL, Lynne; ROELOFS, Susan Margaret; ROESTI, Karen; ROFFETTI, Pinto; ROGERS, Kate; ROJOWSKI, Alice; ROLSTON, Dia; ROMANCHUK, Kathy; ROMANO, Dawna Gail; ROSAK, Glenda; ROSALES, Sara Elaina; ROSATI, Barb; ROSI, Bossio; ROSS, Cynthia; ROSS, David; ROSS, Heather; ROSSI, Severina; ROSYCHUCK, Jarrett; ROSYCHUCK, Nadine; ROSYCHUCK, Pamela; ROULEAU, Dennis; ROULSON, Dorothy; ROULSTON, Rudy; ROUSE, Susan; ROUSSEAU, Leanord Paul; ROUT, Denise; ROVINSON, Cathlyn; ROWAN, Margery; ROWE, Elaine, Valerie; ROWE, Helen; ROWE, Margaret; ROWLAND, Debra Pauline; ROWLAND, Heather; ROWLEY, Debbie; ROY, Bobbi; ROYCE, Bonny; RUBERTS, Karen; RUBULIAK, Linda; RUBULIAK, Sharon; RUDOLPH, Karen; RUDOLPH, Linda; RUDOLPH, Lorraine; RUFFELL, Christine Anne; RUMOHR, Rich; RUMSEY, Frank; RUNDLE, Patty; RUSK, Evelyn; RUSK, Gail; RUSK, Michael; RYCKMAN, Joanne; RYMAK, David; RYSINKO, Carole; RYSINKO, Jill;

S

SABOURIN, Jacqueline; SACCOMANI, Angela; SAGE, Ashley; SAGE, Cynthia; SAGE, Robert; SAGRIFF, Don; SAIK, Gary; SAINCHUK, Barry; SAINCHUK, Carolyn; SAINCHUK, Lisa Marie; SAINCHUK, Marilyn; SALAHUB, Joan; SALAMANDICK, Jo; SALAMANDICK, Walter; SALFI, Peter; SALLOUM, Joseph; SALOPEK, Donna Mary; SALTER, Barry; SALVALAGGIO, Jo; SALZANO, Maria; SAMIS, Dawn; SAMKO, Barb; SAMYCIA, Mickey; SAMYCIA, Orest; SAMYCIA, Paul; SAMYCIA, Russell; SANDERSON, Janie; SANDHU, Sanjeevan; SANGSTER, Judith; SARANCHUK, Darlene; SARGENT, Ann; SARNER, Linda; SAUNDERS, Darlene; SAUNDERS, Doug; SAUNDERS, Karolee; SAUNDERS, Norman; SAUNDERS, Shelley; SAUNDERS, Sonya; SAUVE, Monique; SAVAGE, Fiona; SAVARD, Kim; SAVOIE, Monique; SAWARD, Kim; SAWATZKY, June; SAWCHUK, Barbara Ann; SAWCHUK, Elizabeth; SAWCHUK, Judy-Lynn; SAWCHUK, Teresa; SAWCHUK, William; SAWICKA, Greta; SAYER, Don; SAYER, Shirley; SCHAAF, Kara Ann; SCHAEFER, Susan; SCHAEFER, Suzanne; SCHALM, Colleen; SCHAVERTE, Gwen; SCHELL, Janet; SCHERMANN, Elizabeth; SCHIEWE, Gwen; SCHIMPF, Heather; SCHLACHT, Bill; Schlam, Alfred; SCHLAMP, E. Pat; SCHLENDER, Duana; SCHLENDER, Elizabeth; SCHLENDER, Ron; SCHMIDT, Anita; SCHMIDT, Christina; SCHMIDT, Karen; SCHMIDT, Sheldon; SCHMIDT, Sylvia R.; SCHMIDTKE, Ingrid; SCHNEIDER, PATTI: SCHNEIDER, Patti; SCHOELER, Andreas; SCHOENROTH, Jeff; SCHOOLEY, Dawn; SCHOOLEY, Jennifer; SCHOOLEY, Sherrie; SCHORATH, Velita; SCHOTTEN, Anselmo; SCHRA, Eric; SCHRETTLINGER, Anita; SCHRODER, Joy; SCHULDES, Beverly; SCHULTZ, Dawn; SCHULTZ, Jane; SCHULTZ, Lynda; SCHULTZ, Mrs.; SCHULTZ, Wilma; SCHUMACHER, Anthony; SCHWARTZ, David; SCMONICK, Judi; SCOTT, Aurilee; SCOTT, Joan; SCOTT, Joan; SCOTT, Kevin; SCOTT, Mac; SCOTT, Mitch; SCOTT, Nadia; SCOTT, Peggy; SCOTT, Terri; SCOTT, Thelma; SCUDDER, Brian; SCUDDER, Diane; SEARS, Bertha; SEATON, Jean; SEDDON, Laura; SEELER, Maria; SELL, Frances; SELL, Francis; SELZLER, Teresa; SEMBALIUK, Andrea; SEMBALIUK, George; SEMBALIUK, Patricia; SEMBALIUK, Paul; SEMBALIVK, Andrea; SEMBALUK, John; SEMBALUK, Mrs. John; SEMENIUK, Con; SEMENIUK, Dan; SEMENIUK, Diana; SEMENIUK, Vera; SEMWAL, Sudhanshu Kumar; SERGHE, John; SEYMOUR, Louisa; SFECLA, Mr. & Mrs.; SHAHNAWAZ, Ahmad; SHALAPAY, Carol; SHALAPAY, Ken; SHALLWANI, Medhi; SHANDRO, Bev; SHANDRO, Elsie; SHANDRO, Joanne; SHANK, Stan; SHANK, Yvonne; SHANTZ, Anne J.; SHAPKA, David; SHAPKA, Wlizabeth; SHARP, Kim; SHARP, Michelle; SHARP, Penny; SHARPE, Anne; SHARPE, Glenda; SHARPE, Tom; SHAW, Deborah; SHAW, Denise; SHAW, Geraldine; SHEEHAM,; SHELTON, Susan; SHENKAREK, Ernie; SHENKAREK, Maureen; SHERMAN, Greg; SHERMAN, Philip; SHERMANN, Paula; SHERRIN, Jo; SHEVCHUK, Stella; SHEWCHUK, Dawn; SHEWCHUK, Elaine; SHEWCHUK, Laura; SHEWCHUK, Stella; SHIPKA, Jude; SHORT, Irene; SHUKALIAK, Charlene; SHULAKEWYCH, Bohdan; SHUPENIA, Stella; SHYMKO, Monica; SIGURDSON, Terry; SIKORA, Frank;

SIKSTROM, Sari; SILTALA, Andrew; SIMAO, Humberto; SIMARD, Lon; SIMARD, Sandra; SIME, Tom; SIMMONS, Gina; SIMMONS, Harold; SIMMONS, Nancy; SIMON, Laura; SIMONSON, Marilyn; SIMPSON, Gayle; SIMPSON, Ian; SIMPSON, Lynda; SIMPSON, Wayne; SINCLAIR, Bernice; SINCLAIR, Jack; SINCLAIR, Leila; SINCLAIR, Myrna Lee; SINGH, Birbel; SINGH, Jitendra; SINGH, Sulinder; SITTLER, Thelma; SKELLY, Lorraine; SKELLY, Valerie; SKITSKO, Ann; SKREPNEK, Peggy; SKRIBIS, Liana; SLABYSZ, Richard; SLATER, Irene Mary; SLATTER, Beth; SLAVIK, Veronica; SLAVUTA, Sonia; SMANDYCH, Randy; SMEDSTAD, Oli; SMEREKA, Shelley; SMILKIE, Alison; SMITH, Allison; SMITH, Ann; SMITH, Arlene; SMITH, Arlene; SMITH, Beverly; SMITH, Brenda; SMITH, Catherine; SMITH, Cathy; SMITH, Eileen R.E.; SMITH, Juanita; SMITH, Karen; SMITH, Kay; SMITH, Kim; SMITH, Kristina; SMITH, Leverna; SMITH, Melani; SMITH, Norma; SMITH, Roxanne; SMITH, Sandra; SMITH, Sara; SMITH, Shirley; SMITH, Stacey; SMITH, Susan; SMITH, Susan; SMOK, Cindy; SMYTH, Lorraine; SNOW, Tracy; SNYDER, Audrey; SOBLEWICKI, Jay; SOBON, Sophie; SODKE, Karen; SOKIL, Kim; SOKOLOSKI, Elaine; SOKOLOSKI, Joanne; SOKOLUK, Kimberly; SOKOLUK, Lori; SOLISKI, Gail; SOLLERDER, Gertrude; SOLLEREDER, Karen; SOLTYKEWYCH, Orest; SOLYS, Elizabeth; SOMERSET, jane; SOMERVILLE, kathy; SONEFF, Linda; SOPCHYSHYN, Helen; SOPCHYSHYN, Wils; SORENSON, janette; SOROBEY, William; SOROCHAN, Joan; SOROCHUK, Marilyn; SOROCHUK, Peter; SOUCY, Roland; SOUKUP, Hana; SPEE, Ann; SPEE, Michael; SPEE, Rim; SPENCER, Kathryn; SPEROWKA, Colleen; SPILLER, Paul; SPILLETT, Ken; SPINK, David; SPINK, Valerie; SPINNER, Angel; SPIRANGAPATNA, Narayana Prasad; SPISAK, Robin; SPRAAKMAN, Candace; SPRATT, Doug; SPRATT, Flo; SPRING, Sharon Lee; SPRINGER, Brenda; STACHNIAK, Cathy; STACK, Marg; STACK, Philip; STAFF, Fran; STAHL, Dawn; STAINES, Iara; STAINTON, Yvette; STANG, Loretta; STANTAKE, Loreen; STANTON, Claire; STANTON, Dawn; STANTON, Kay; STAPLETON, Kevin; STARCHUK, John; STARING, Cathryn; STARING, Gerald; STARING, Jean; STARK, Eduard; STASCO, Mary; STASZENSKI, Donna; STAWNYCHKA, Paulette; STEARNS, John; STEELE, Raeanne; STEEVES, Dale; STEEVES, Debby; STEFAN, Krista; STEFANYK, Jennifer; STEIN, Edith; STEIN, Janet; STEINBRING, Karen; STEINKE, August; STEINTE, Lily; STELFOX, Elaine; STELFOX, Joyce; STENGEL, Dawn; STENGEL, Pat; STENGEL, Pat; STENSON, Yvonne; STEPHANSON, Leslie; STEPHANSON-QUONA, Larry; STEPHANYSAHYN, Betty; STEPHEN, Frank; STEPHENS, Cher; STEPHENSON, Alice; STEPHENSON-QUONG, Darlene; STETSON, Sandra; STEUBER, Holly; STEVENS, Barb; STEVENS, Cathy; STEVENS, David; STEVENS, Kathy; STEVENS, Kristie; STEVENS, Len; STEVENS, Roberta; STEWART, Duane; STEWART, Jill; STEWART, Jocelyn; STEWART, Leslie; STEWART, Linda; STEWART, Loral; STEWART, Wendy; STIEBRITZ, Brigette; STILWELL, Reg; STINSON, Alice; STIRLING, Joan; STOBBE, Corinne; STOBY, Janet; STOCHINSKY, Eric; STOCKDALE, Roxanne; STOEHR, Eric; STOEHR, Hilda; STONEHOUSE, Dorinda; STONEHOUSE, George Sr.; STONHOUSE, Corinne; STOTT, Agnes; STRAKA, Alena; STRAMBERG, Grant; STRAND, Angela; STRANDLIE, Linda; STRASS, Peggy; STRASS, Rae; STRAYER, Sharon; STRIBRNY, Jaromir; STRIFLER, Irwin; Strifler, Jay-Jon; STRIFLER, Joyce; STRIFLER, Kym-Shae; STRIFLER, Lee-Jay; STRUK, Borysia; STRUK, Ostap; ST. AMANT, Helen; ST. ANDRE, Jacqueline; SUAREZ, Elena; SUCHOCKI, Maria; SUKALSKY, Boris; SUNKU, Badri; SURBECK, Doris; SURGIN, Alan; SUROWIAK, Janet; SUSHYNSKI, Cheryl; SUTHERLAND, Tamara; SUVANTO, Scott; SVERDAHL, Diane; SWANN, Joan; SWANSON, Lori; SWARE, Judey; SWENARCHUK, Walter; SWICKAS, Toni; SWICKIS, Jim; SWIFT, Roy; SWINAMER, Deanna; SWINAMER, Gary; SWINAMER, Marlene; SWINAMER, Stuart; SWINIARSKI, Stacey; SWINTON, Ruth; SWIREDOWSKY, Len; SWIREDOWSKY, Lilian; SWONEK, Deborah; SYDEL, Eva; SYEDA, Hameed; SYRO, Jo Ann; SZABO, Kim; SZUCS, Joe; SZUCS, Leslie;

T

TABASHNIUK, William; TAIRNEY, Shannon; TAKHAR, Kiran; TAMER-SALLOUM, Odette; TANG, Deborah; TAPPAUF, Elsie; TARNOWSKI, Angelique; TASKINEN, Sonja; TASSONE, Iolanda; TATARIN, Gloria; TATARIN, Janice; TATARIN, Wendy; TAYLOR, Audrey; TAYLOR, Bryanne; TAYLOR, Christy; TAYLOR, David; TAYLOR, Deborah; TAYLOR, Debra; TAYLOR, Dr. Bill; TAYLOR, Fern; TAYLOR, John E.k.; TAYLOR, Robert C.; TAYLOR, Sandy; TAYLOR, Suzanne; TAYLOR, Tara; TAYLOR, Tina; TAYLOR, Tracy; TCHIR, Shelly; TEASE, Barb; TENNEY, Tina; TESSMER, Mavis; THELISS, Norman; THERIAULT, Allan; THERIAULT, Patricia; THERIAULT, Susan; THIERMAN, Debbie; THOM, Marina; THOMAS, Elizabeth; THOMAS, Myrna; THOMASSON, Brenda; THOMLINSON, Kristine; THOMPSON, Ann; THOMPSON, Cindie; THOMPSON, David G.; THOMPSON, David; THOMPSON, Deryl; THOMPSON, Gary; THOMPSON, Gay; THOMPSON, Gordon; THOMPSON, Heather; THOMPSON, Janet; THOMPSON, Jay; THOMPSON, Jim; THOMPSON, Joanne; THOMPSON, Judity; THOMPSON, Lorne; THOMPSON, Margaret; THOMPSON, Norm; THOMPSON, Shannon; THOMPSON, Sharon; THOMPSON, Suzanne; THOMSON, Blanche; THOMSON, Morgan; THORSELL, Irene; THOW, Kelli; THOW, Sherry; TIMKO, Mona; TIMLECK, Cindy; TIMLECK, David; TIMMS, Fae-Lynn; TIMOTEO, Frances; TISLAK, Annette; TISLAK, Caroline; TITHECOTT, Ronald; TITOSKY, Fran; TKACHENKO, Helen; TO, Dominic; TOBAR, Anna; TOKARYK, Lily; TOOLE, Susan; TOPOLNISKY, Metro; TOUPIN, Gloria; TOURANGEAU, Katie; TRACEY, Kim; TREIJS, Debbie; TREMAIN, Loretta; TREMBLAY, Margaret; TRENCHIE, Claire; TRENCHIE, Jeannette; TRENCHIE, Lauren; TRENTHAM, Gerry; TREVOY, Dorothy; TREVOY, Peggy; TRIPP, Kevin; TROTTER, Karen; TSANG, Lawrence; TUBIURLDAK, Emil; TUCHSEN, Ed; TUKOLAS, Sylvia; TUNG, Parrish Chi-Kin; TUPPER, Bill; TUPPER, Hope; TUPPER, Shelley Carmen; TURLEY, Donna; TURLEY, Janice; TURNER, Gail; TURNER, Gil; TURNER, Mary; TURNER, Steven; TURTON, Audrey; TYLER, Rob; TYMKO, Andy;

U

UGOTI, Claudette; UIF, Friedrich; UMBACH, Eve; UNGER, Diane; URSULAK, Dave;

V

VALENCIA, Hayson; VALENS, Margo; VAMITTO, Vera; VAN ALSTYNE, Merle; VAN BAKEL, Paul; VAN DE VLIERT, Garry; VAN DEN EYNDEN, Miriam; VAN HEMERT, Pauline; VAN STRAATEN, Christine; VANDENBERG, Jan; VANMAELE, Ann; VANONI, Albert; VANONI, Lois; VANZELLA, Christine; VARGAS, Marta Elaina; VARMA, Meena; VARMA, Neeraj; VEENSTRA, Debra; VEITCH, Joanne; VELT, Charles; VEN HEMEST, Jack VERBITSKY, Marilyn; VERHULST, Susan; VERMEULEN, Lorraine; VETTESE, Shelley; VICKORS, Katherine; VICTOOR, Dolores; VICTOOR, Elsie; VICTOOR, Sherri-Lynn; VINGE, Cheryl; VLCHEK, Violet; VOGELGESANG, Elsa Eleanor; VOGL, Joann; VOLLOB, Bruce; VOLLOB, Cheri; VON ZUR GATHEN, Teresita Jb; VONA, Peggy; VONEICKEN, Bert; VOUVE, Isabelle; VUKOVIC, Mary; VUNIOR, Keith;

W

WACHOWICH, David Joseph; WACHOWICZ, Teresa L.; WACHOWITZ, Yvonne; WADDELL, Lillian; WADLOW, Louise Diane; WAGAR, Ronon; WAGAR, Sandy; WAGNER, monica; WAKARUK, Rudy; WAKE, Joyce;

WAKEFIELD, Marty; WALDIE, Bruce; WALDIE, Gina; WALDIE, Heather; WALDON, Jan; WALDON, Lance; WALKER, Diane; WALKER, Greg; WALKER, Janet; WALKER, Kendall; WALKER, Lloanne; WALKER, Tony; WALL, Bob; WALL, Darryl; WALL, Lorraine; WALLACH, Craig; WALLACH, Joan; WALLACH, Shari; WALLER, Kelli; WALMSLEY, Gail; WALSH, Caroline; WALTON, Charlie; WAMSLEY, Gwen; WAMSLEY, Kenneth; WAMSLEY, Kerry; WANG, Shu Jie; WARCHOLA, Roman; WARITSKY, Marie; WARMAN, Margaret; WARMINGTON, Sylvia; WARNING, Joan; WARUNKY, Deborah Lynn; WARWARUK, Kathy; WARWARUK, Matt; WARWARUK, Vicki; WASELENCHUK, Debbie; WASLIW, Barry; WASYLYCIA, Elaine; WASYLYCIA, Lester; WASYLYNCHUK, Mary Ann; WATERSON, Richard; WATSON, Annette; WATSON, Lisa; WATT, Anne; WATT, Don; WATT, Dorothy; WATT, Joyce; WATT, Keith; WATT, Kevin; WATT, Penny; WATT, Wally; WATTERWORTH, Muriel; WATTS, Annike; WATTS, Jessica; WEATHERALL, Ann; WEBER, Denise; WEBER, Irvin; WEBER, Monica; WEBSTER, Daryl; WEBSTER, Fran; WEIDMAN, Teresa Lynne; WEINZIERL, Deanne; WEINZIERL, Deanne; WEIR, Ed; WEIR, Rita; WEISBERG, Deborah; WEISER, Thomas; WELCH, Jaqueline; WELCH, Juanita; WELCH, Lil; WELLS, Debra; WELLS, Laura; WELSH, Cy; WELSH, Jacqueline; WELSH, Kelli; WELSH, Sharon; WELSH, Shelley; WERSTIUK, Darin; WERTH, Lin; WEST, Gigi; WEST, Jim; WEST, Karen; WESTERMEIER, Angela; WETTERBERG, Donald; WETTERBERG, Donna; WETTERBERG, Shelly; WHERTON, Leslie W.O.S.; WHILLIER, Dave; WHILLIER, Dexter; WHILLIER, Oda; WHILLIER, Randy; WHISTANCE-SMITH, Andrew; WHISTANCE-SMITH, Douglas; WHISTANCE-SMITH, Lois; WHISTANCE-SMITH, Ronald; WHISTANCE-SMITH, Stephen; WHITE, Anna; WHITE, Carole Ann; WHITE, Christopher; WHITE, Elise; WHITE, Helen; WHITE, Joanne; WHITE, Mark; WHITE, Maurice; WHITE, Naomi; WHITE, Rita; WHITE, Ronald WHITE, Stewart; WHITESIDE, Marie; WHITEZEL, Sonja; WHITMAN, John; WHITNEY, Eli Marco; WICKEY, Andy; WIDGIZ, Sandra Louise; WIER, Mary; WILHELM, Jan; WILKENSON, Mary; WILKENSON, Sharon; WILKS, Cameron; WILLAR, Nancy; WILLAR, Robert; WILLARD, Linda; WILLERTH, Corinne; WILLEY, Christine; WILLIAMS, Brenda; WILLIAMS, Corinne; WILLIAMS, Dave; WILLIAMS, Della; WILLIAMS, Joanne; WILLIAMS, Lorna; WILLIAMS, Natasha; WILLIAMS, Roy; WILLIAMS, Susan Lee; WILSEN, Don; WILSEN, Helen; WILSEN, Mike; WILSEN, Stephanie; WILSON, Barry; WILSON, Brian; WILSON, Doreen; WILSON, Maureen; WILSON, Pat; WILTZEN, Hugh; WILTZEN, Janet; WILTZEN, Robert; WINCHESTER, Regan Stewart; WINFIELD, Lester; WINGROVE, Darcy Louise; WINTER, Frank Uwe; WITT, Rudy; WITT, Sharlene; WITTRUP, Gloria; WNUK, Ed; WNUK, Lu; WOJDAK, Sonya; WOLFE, Carole; WOLFE, Deborah; WOLFE, Donna; WOLFE, ROBERT; WOLOSHYNIUK, Marvin; WOLOSZYN, Betty; WONDERS, Lillian; WONG, Dorothy; WONG, James; WONG, Joseph; WONG, Kelly; WONG, Ken; WONG, Lambert; WONG, Mary; WONG, Rocky Ching-Kwai; WONG, Stella; WONG, Teck; WONG, Wendy; WOOD, Elizabeth; WOOD, Myra; WOOD, Sarah; WOODCOCK, Sharon; WOODGER, Jennifer; WOODHEAD, Sheena; WORONOWICZ, Donna; WORSFIELD, Gary; WOWK, Cheryl; WOWK, Leon; WOWK, Stephanie; WOWK, Todd; WOYWITKA, Karen; WOZNIAK, Kari-Lynn; WRAY, Lorie; WRAY, Wilma-Ann; WRIGHT, Kimberly Ann; WRIGHT, Kristine Elizabeth; WRIGHT, Nancy; WRUBLESKI, Jodi; WUAN, Evelyn Mary; WUAN, Lyle John; WUDIK, Pat; WULFF, Cliff; WULFF, Gary; WULFF, Joan; WUNDERLICH, Gerd; WUTZKE, Doris; WYGERA, Adele; WYGERA, Michael; WYRSTIUK, Denise; WYSOCKI, Linda;

Below: Flashcard holders who performed at both the Opening and Closing Ceremonies turned out 3,000 strong to volunteer their services for Universiade '83

YACHINEC, Izydore; YACHINEC, Marg; YAKABOW, Clayton; YAKABOW, Marrianne; YAKABOW, Marti; YAKABOW, Rhonda; YAKABOW, Ronald; YAKIMETS, Kay; YANO, May; YARMAK, Grace; YASKOWICH, Catherine; YAWARSKI, Cecilia; YEE, Elizabeth; YEE, Linda; YEE, Suey; YELLE, Lannie; YELLE, Mrgo; YEOMAN, Shaundra; YEUNG, Jupiter; YEUNG, Secanry; YODER, Arvilla; YODER, Ordilla; YORK, Dorothy; YORK, Ray; YOSHIHIRO, Maeda; YOUNG, Cam; YUN, Mellissa; YUN, Mina; YUNG, Bill;

Z

ZADECKI, Barbara; ZALESKI, Susan; ZAPF, Eugene; ZAPISOCKI, Angie; ZAPISOCKI, Ronal; ZAVISLAKE, Colleen; ZDNER, Teresa; ZELMAN, Karen; ZIELSDORF, Margaret; ZOTTENBERG, Dasha; ZROBEK, Caroline; ZUTZ, Elaine; ZWICKEL, Wendy; ZWOZDESKY, Christine; ZWOZDESKY, Christine;

Schools

Universiade '83 Edmonton Corp. expresses its profound gratitude to those magnificent young students from 44 Edmonton schools who devoted their time and enthusiasm as Field Performers during the Opening and Closing Ceremonies.

Allendale Elementary Junior High School
Archbishop MacDonald Catholic School
Archbishop O'Leary Catholic School
Avonmore Junior High School
Brittania Junior High School
Broxton Park School
Concordia College
Dan Knott Junior High School
Dickinsfield Junior High School
Donnan Elementary Junior High School
D.S. MacKenzie Elementary Junior High School
East Edmonton Christian School
Eastwood Elementary Junior High School
Elizabeth Seton Catholic School
Ellerslie Elementary Junior High School
Fort Saskatchewan High School
H.A. Gray Elementary Junior High School
Harry Ainlay Composite High School
Highlands Junior High School
Holy Cross Catholic School
Horse Hill School No. 266
Jasper Place Composite High School
Killarney Junior High School
King Edward Elementary Junior High School
Londonderry Junior High School
Louis St-Laurent Catholic School
McNally Composite High School
Ottewell Junior High School
Our Lady of the Angel School
Queen Elizabeth Composite High School
Riverbend Junior High School
Ross Sheppard Composite High School
St Alphonsus Catholic School
St Cecilia Catholic School
St Clare Catholic School
St Clement Catholic School
St Francis Xavier Catholic School
St Hilda Catholic School
Spruce Avenue Elementary Junior High School
Vernon Barford Junior High School
Wellington Junior High School
Westlawn Junior High School
Westminster Junior High School
Whitecourt Junior High School

Staff

ANTON, Tillie; ANQUIST, Nellie; ARMOUR, Laura; ARMSTRONG, Irene; ARTHUR, Linda; ASCHER, Don; ASHTON, Deanna; BAGSHAW, Bill; BALOG, Shawn; BAUDIN, Pierre; BEAULIEU, Joey; BELLINGHAM, Sheena; BEREKOFF, Bev; BEREKOFF, Tom; BLAKEY, Chris; BODNER, Tracy; BOEHM, Janice; BOURASSA, Laurette; BREITKREUZ, Bernard; BROCKS, Fred; BUKSA, Cindy; BUREAUD, Peggy; BURROWS, Roger; CHAFFEY, Barb; CHRISTIANSEN, Sue; CHRISTIANSON, Roger; CLEVELEY, Bruce; CLEVELEY, Dave; CREPIN, Richard; CUNNINGHAM, Lynne; CYR, John; DALLYN, Twylla; DAY, Bob; DEAKIN, Patricia; DEVEREUX, Sally; DIAMOND, Marlys; DOLINSKY, Betsy; DONLEVY, Jim; DZIEPAK, Karen; EVERETT, John; EWING, Diana; FALLOW, Adrian; FIELD, Peter; FLYNN, Alan; FORSTER, Molly; FRANCE, Bill; FRASER, Christine; FRASER, Jocelyn; FREEMAN, Pam; GALLANT, Linda; GAUL, Richard; GILFILLAN, Carol; GILFILLAN, Nadine; GRAHAM, Jim; GREENFIELD, David; GRIWKOWSKY, Con; GROUETTE, Jullie; HAMILTON, James; HAMILTON, Rebecca; HAMULA, Jeannette; HAYWOOD, Kenneth; HEANEY, Liana; HERRING, Elizabeth; HOLLINGSHEAD, Audra; ISHERWOOD, Suzette; JACKSON, Ken; JOHNSON, Ernest; JOHNSTON, David; JOHNSTON, Karen; KAMMINGA, Sandra; KAPTEIN, Winnie; KARAS, Lynn; KARPUL, Etta; KERR, Jan; KLEM, John; KMECH, Alice; KOENIG, Diana; KOO, Molly; KROETSCH, Richard; LABELLE, Michelle; LANG, Janet; LEAH, Judy; LEONARD, Heather; LINDSAY, David; LOVEJOY, Doug; MACDONALD, Paul; MACKENZIE, Catherine; MAIR, Pauline; MALAND, Dennis; MATHESON, Donna; MCAFEE, Elizabeth; MCCLENAGHAN, Gary; MCDONALD, James; MCDONALD, Michel; MCGAVERN, Don; MCGREGOR, Jim; MCKIE, Doug; MCLAUGHLIN, Loretta; MCNAMARA, Violette; MCVEIGH, Jack; MICHELIN, Lyn; MICHELS-BRITNER, Vicki; MILLER, Ernie; MONCRIEF, Henry; MORGAN, Bill; MORRIS, Steve; MUNAN, Joshua; MUNRO, Ross; MURRAY, Wendy; NELSON, Doug; NELSON, Russell; NEWTON, Paddy; NISATI, Susan; NORDIN, Idris; NOSEK, Joy; OLDENBURG, Rena; OLSON, Daryl; OLSON, Jo-anne; ORCHUK, Lynn; OSBERG, Roger; OUDSHOORN, David; PADDON, Bob; PAGNUCCO, Jackie; PALMER, Millie; PAPPES, Joan; PARIS, Claudette; PARSONS, Alan; PATTERSON, Jim; PETERSON, Bob; PIAUMIER, Stephanie; PLAISIER, Stan; PLUMB, Douglas; POLINSKI, Don; POTTER, Connie; POWLEY, John; PRELUSKY, Daniel; QUIST, Grant; RADFORD, Tim; RADKE, Claire; REHEL, Gladys; RICHARDS, Don; ROBERTS, Therese; ROBINSON, Carol; ROOKE, Tom; RUFF, Audrey; RUMOHR, Laura; RUSSELL, John; RYAN, Gail; SABULKA, Mike; SAMOIL, Larry; SANDULESCU, Rozalia; SAURINA, Edith; SAVOIE, Monique; SCHULHA, Dale; SCOTT, Aurilee; SHANKS, David; SHARPE, Sydney; SHAVER, Rick; SHORT, Gayle; SHULHA, Janet; SMITH, Debbie; SMITH, Murray; SOLOJUK, Lori; SOUTH, Barb; SPROULE, John; STANTON, James; STEADWARD, Bob; STELEY, Margaret; STOOCHNOFF, Jon; STRACHAN, Ken; STUART, Bill; STUTCHBURY, Rod; SWITZER, Carole; SYMINGTON, Tami; TATARCHUK, Hank; TYCHOLAZ, Edward; VANHOLDERBEKE, Luc; WAKEFIELD, Keith; WARWICK, William; WASYLIK, Bruce; WELLS, Audre; WIGELAND, Christine; WILLIAMS, Doreen; ZEMRAU, Ed; MORROW, David;

Government and Sponsors

The Organizing Committee for Universiade '83 is deeply indebted to the Government of Canada, Government of Alberta, City of Edmonton, The University of Alberta and the following sponsors and contributors whose generosity and support ensured the 1983 Summer Universiade was one of the most successful in its history.

We also wish to say a special Thank You to CBC Television for its invaluable contributions to the Games.

$100,000 and over

Sawridge Enterprises Ltd.

$50,000 to $75,000

Royal Bank; Alma Mater Fund; Bank of Montreal;
The Clifford E. Lee Foundation; The Recreation, Parks and Wildlife Foundation

$20,000 to $49,999

Nova, An Alberta Corporation; The Kahanoff Foundation;
R. Angus Alberta Limited; Canada Safeway; Atco;
Alberta Energy Company Ltd.; Canadian Imperial Bank of Commerce;
The Allard Foundation; Canadian Utilities Ltd.;
Chieftain Development Co. Ltd.;
Edmonton Civic Employees Charitable Assistance Fund; Ellis-Don Limited;
Province of Ontario; Principal Group Ltd.; Syncrude Canada Ltd.

$15,000 to $19,999

Bank of Nova Scotia; Max Bell Foundation; Interprovincial Pipe Line Limited;
PCL Construction Ltd.

$10,000 to $14,999

Strathcona Tri-Union Association; Canadian Commercial Bank;
Cormie Kennedy; Edmonton Journal; Genstar Corporation;
George Weston Limited; Great West Life; Gulf Canada Limited;
Northern Telecon Canada Limited; Oxford Development Group Ltd.;
John E. Poole; Dr. G.R.A. Rice; The Stephen B. Roman Foundation;
Toronto Dominion Bank; The Winspear Foundation; Woodward Stores .

$5,000 to $9,999

Imperial Tobacco Limited; TransAlta Utilities Corporation; RCA Inc.;
Consolidated-Bathurst Inc.; Continental Bank; The Brick Warehouse;
Canada Trust; Canadian Superior Oil Ltd.; Canadian Tire Corporation Limited;
Carling O'Keefe Limited; Dome Petroleum; Dow Chemical Canada Inc.;
General Foods Inc.; Interprovincial Steel & Pipe Corporation;

The Richard Ivey Foundation; Kraft Limited; County of Leduc #25;
Luscar Ltd.; Maclab Enterprises Ltd.; Merrill Lynch Royal Securities Limited;
Reed Stenhouse Limited; Sherritt Gordon Mines Limited;
Sun Life Assurance Company of Canada; Sunwapta Broadcasting Limited;
Wallace & Carey Ltd.

$1,000 to $4,999

Campbell, J.K. & Associates Limited; South Edmonton Rotary Club;
Nickle Family Foundation; Thorne Riddell; Royal Trust;
Horne & Pitfield Foods Limited; Imasco Limited; Mitchell, David E.;
Province of Prince Edward Island;
Richardson Greenshields of Canada Limited;
British Columbia Telephone Company; City of Camrose;
Esselte Pendaflex Canada Inc.; Milner & Steer;
National Trust Company, Limited; Pitfield Mackay Ross Limited;
Starlaw Holdings Limited; Westcoast Transmission Company Limited;
Banister Construction Group; Bow Valley Industries Ltd.;
Brooker, B.W. Engineering Ltd.; Canada Life;
Confederation Life Insurance Company; C.I.L. Inc.;
Dominion Construction Company Limited; Dun & Bradstreet;
Edmonton Motors Limited; Government of Yukon Territory; Lilydale Co-operative Limited; Manulife; The Mutual Assurance Company of Canada;
Nabisco Brands Ltd.; Nesbitt Thomson Bongard Inc.; Versa Services Ltd.;
Consumers' Welding Supplies Limited; AMCA International Limited;
Bank of British Columbia; Bryan Andrekson; Carthy Foundation;
Century Sales & Service Ltd.; Christianson, Dennis A., Architect Ltd.;
Carry, C.W. Ltd.; Gilbey Canada Inc.; Wood Gundy Charitable Foundation;
Lehndorff Property Management Limited; McGregor, Mrs. Eva;
Stuart Olson Construction Ltd.; St. Regis (Alta.) Ltd.; 3M Canada Inc.;
Mainland Crystal Glass Ltd.; Meubles Daveluyville Ltee.;
Acco Canadian Co. Ltd.; Alberta Natural Gas Company Ltd.;
Bow Valley Resource Services Ltd.; Brascan Limited; Burns, James. W.;
Campbell Soup Company Ltd.; Canada Cement Lafarge Ltd.;
Canada Permanent Trust Company; Canada West Insurance Company;
Ed Miller Sales & Rentals Ltd.; Edmonton Properties;
Everall Construction Limited; Fitch, Sanford T.; Fletcher's Limited;
Gainers Inc.; Guaranty Trust Company of Canada; Gyro Club of Edmonton;
Town of Hinton; Inglis Limited; Inter-City Gas Corporation;
The Italian Cultural Society of Edmonton; Johnston, S.C. & Son Limited;
Livingston, G.V.; London Life Insurance Company;
McDougall & Secord Limited; McLeod Young Weir Limited;
Miller Office Group; The Monarch Life Assurance Company;
Ogilvie & Company; Palm Dairies Limited; Pemberton Houston Willoughby;
Power Corporation of Canada; Prudential Steel Ltd.; Rice, Alison;
Roper Realty Ltd.; Royal Insurance Company of Canada; Sanyo Canada Inc.;
Scott Paper Limited; Transamerica Occidental Life Insurance Company;
Trizec Corporation Ltd.; Jack Walker Pharmacy Ltd.;
Walwyn Stodgell Cochran Murray Limited

Under $1,000

Facilities for the Future; Lawton, D.W.; The Leonard Foundation;
Credit Suisse Canada; Imperial Life Assurance Co.;
Pardee Equipment Limited; Investors Syndicate Limited;
Galactica Computers; Sinclair Supplies Ltd.; Singer, Millie;
Union Gas Limited; Clareview Village Centre; Miller McClelland & Co.;
Prudential Assurance Company Limited; Asamera Inc.; Avon Canada Inc.;
Bedford Bedding & Upholstery Ltd.; Belleco Rentals & Sales Ltd.;
Biltmore Chesterfield Creations Inc.; The Birks Family Foundation;
Bond Construction Group; Briggs Bus Lines; Bunting (Alfred) & Co. Ltd.;
Cadbury Schweppes Powell Inc.; Canada Malting Co. Limited;
Canadian Reinsurance Company; Town of Canmore;
Capital Packers Limited; Carsen, W. Co. Ltd.; Central Trust;
Colt Engineering Corporation; The Creperie; Dalby, Ronald N.;
Dillingham Construction Ltd.; Eastern Construction Company Limited;
Economical Mutual Insurance Company;
Energy & Chemical Workers Union Local 666 Celanese Unit;
Eric J. Clarke Insurance Agent Ltd.; Falconbridge Copper;
Fasco Rentals Ltd.; Fibreglas Canada Inc.;
Frieberg Family Charitable Foundation; General Distributors of Canada;
General Freezer Limited; Grand & Toy Limited; Halls Pharmacy;
Hardy Associates (1978) Ltd.; Heritage Savings & Trust Co.;
Hewescot Holdings; Hiram Walker & Sons Limited;
Home Oil Company Limited; Hughes, Doreen & George;

International Union of Elevator Constructors Local Union 122; The Keg; Lawson, Dr. A.K.; County of Lethbridge, No. 26; Marvel Hair Styling School; Mayson, Tom; Medigas (Alberta) Ltd.; Melcor Developments Ltd.; Mercantile Bank of Canada; Milner, Stanley; Milo Investments Ltd.; Mitsui & Co. (Canada) Ltd.; Mobil Oil Canada Ltd.; Northern Alfalfa Products Ltd.; Norwood Legion Ladies Auxiliary #178; Paludet, Dr. P.; Prudham Building Supplies (Alberta) Ltd.; Reitmans Inc.; Rentway Canada Limited; Roberts, Miss Annie C.; Smith International Canada, Ltd.; Town of Spruce Grove; Steelcase Canada Limited; Stirrat, Dr. James H.; Stollery, Robert; St. Paul Fire & Marine Insurance Co.; Thomson Newspapers Limited; Total Petroleum North America; Travelways Ltd.; Trimac Limited; Troister & Company Limited; Ukrainian Women's Association; Union Oil Company of Canada Ltd.; University Housing Joint Venture; Volume Sales (1970) Inc.; V.K. Mason Construction Ltd.; Western Caissons; Westgate Chevrolet Ltd.; Wilron Equipment Ltd.; A.V. Carlson Construction Corp; Clarkson Gordon; Smith Watson Textiles Ltd.; Alberta Investments Ltd.; Andiel, Fenrich & Co.; Arachnae Management Limited; Argus Machine Co. Ltd.; B & D Tire Town Limited; BBC Brown Boveri Canada Inc.; Brown & Root Ltd.; Campbell Sharp; Cohen, Dr. Harry; Consumers Glass Company Limited; Ecodyne Limited; Energy & Chemical EmmottWorkers Union; Finning Tractor & Equipment Co. Ltd.; First City Trust; Freeway Construction; Kosowan, Chief Judge C.A.; Mitsubishi Canada Limited; National Life Assurance Company; Ranger Oil; Ryder Truck Rental Ltd.; Bishop & McKenzie; C H Q T; Comco Distributors Ltd.; Consumers Distributing; Crown Trust; Ellis, St. Laurent, Govenlock & Company; Engineered Air; Hinchey, W. Grant; London Drugs; Lord, R.E.; Manitoba Bedding Company Ltd.; Midland Doherty Limited; Northern Life Assurance Company; Norwich Union Life Insurance Society; Pitney Bowes; Ramsey, Dr. C.G.; Rio Algom Limited; West Fraser Group; Kotow, K.J. & T.; Cheng, Gary; Akiyama, Mitsunobu; Alberta Grocers Wholesale; Arcese Brothers Furniture; Armstrong, John A.; Army & Navy Department Store Ltd.; Arthur's Restaurant; Associated Engineering Services Ltd.; Becker Milk Company Limited; Belcourt Construction Ltd.; Borden Consumer Products Canada; Bouey, Howard L. Architect Ltd.; Bovey, Edmund C.; Braemore Convertibles Ltd.; Brewers Warehousing Co. Ltd.; Bristol-Myers Products; Bylane Custom Builders; Calmont Leasing Ltd.; Cardinal Coach Lines Limited; Cardinal Industrial Electronics Ltd.; Carnation Inc.; Kelvinator; Corod Manufacturing; Cummins Alberta; Derrybard Service Station Ltd.; Dieleman, Carriere, Levine & Joly; Dunsmore, Lyle K.; Dunwoody & Company; Equitable Life Insurance Company; Evans Products Company Ltd.; Fame Furniture Co. Ltd.; Fidelity Life Assurance; Foulds, John R.; General Mills; GIII Ltd.; Gordon, John Peter; Graham, John Architects; Graschuk, Harry S.; Greschuk, Justice Peter; Grosser Parts Ltd.; Guardian Chemicals; Guthrie McLaren Drilling; Hertz, Lyla and George; Jaguar Canada Inc.; K-Mart Canada Limited; King & Company; Loveseth Ltd.; Michener, Rt. Hon. Roland; Morguard Investments; P & M Construction; Pan Alberta Gas Ltd.; Pankhurst, Ruth; Patrick, Bill; Pennock, Bruce; Pirelli Cables Inc.; Prairie Medical Ltd.; Prodor Construction; Reflections International Furniture Co.; Robinson Little & Company Limited; Ronalds-Federated Limited; Simcoe Leaf Tobacco Company Limited; Skandia Lodge #549; Taylor, Robert F.; Tkachenko, Helen; Travelers Canada; Wensley & Associates Architects; J. D. Furniture (Mfg.) Ltd.; Smith, David; Powell, A.; Argot Investment Corporation; Ashcroft, Durwood; BBT Geotechnical Consultants; Catalytic Enterprises Limited; E1 Ran Furniture Ltd.; The Engineers Collaborative; Foster Cathead (1975) Ltd.; Gourley, A.E.; Hayashi, Dr. T.; Heximer, G.; Kingston Ross & Co.; Kouri, Berezan & Heinrichs; Lewin, Dennis E.; Mitchell, George B.; Royal Canadian Legion Norwood #178; Shoctor, Hill, Mousseau & Starkman; Shugarman's Ltd.; Steintron International Electronics; Strang, Ian; Western Linen Supply Co. Ltd.; Wood & Gardener Architects Ltd.; Woods & Company; Wright, Wayne H. Architects; Caplan, Dr. Barry L.; Miller, Albert; Reimer, C. Neil; Walker, George; Bouey Bouey Rutledge & Partners; Spread, K.J.; Law Wives Curling Club; Millwrights Union; Allied Insurance Services; Alpine Forest Products; Altartic Engineering & Construction Ltd.; AMA Travel Agency; Aspen Engineering; Banister, Harold; Bargain Finder Press Ltd.; Barr, James; Bartz Auto Service Ltd.; Base-Fort Patrol; Bata, Sonja; Batiuk, Dr. Walter; Bell, Harold E. M.D.; Belmont Credit Union Limited; Belvedere Auto Parts; Bennett & Emmott Limited; Bentley, Newcombe & Margaret; Boake, Dr. R.C.; Bonar Packaging Ltd.; Burns, Robert A. Prof. Corp.; Campbell, James E. & Mary W.; Carborundum Canada Inc.; Canadian Corporate Management Company; Canvil Ltd.; Capital Steel Ltd.; Caravelle Foods; Carlton Cards Ltd.; Carney, Gordon; Cetinski, A.H.; Chinese Cultural Society; Chorny, Olga & Walter; Chow, Channy; Chuen, Norman; Claridge, Bruce G.; Clarke, Joe & Maureen McTeer; Clayton, Patricia; Clough, Mrs. Beatrice M.; Collins, Mary; Conroy, F.D.; Cormier, R.J.; Crown Well Servicing; C.I.L. Unit Local 666 E.C.W.U.; Delfi Investments Ltd.; DesBrisay, Ralph B.; Duncan, Dr. Neil F.; Durno, J.; Dykes, Dr. R.M.; Eacom Timber Sales Ltd.; Eid, T.C.; Electromed Services; Ellis, Dr. Roger; Energy & Chemical Workers Union Local 47; Energy & Chemical Workers Union Local 666; Energy & Chemical Workers Union Local 666 Vulcan Unit; Energy & Chemical Workers Union Alberta Area Council; Erickson, Vic; Fields Stores Limited; Flemming, Douglas; Fraser, Dr. & Mrs. R.S.; Frieson, David & Melitta; Fulkerson Professional Sales; Gay, Dr. Gary; Gerling Global General Insurance; Getty, Mr. & Mrs. Don; Gibson, Harold; Glover, Steven & Lesley; Goldsand, Dr. George & Judy; Gordon, Lorne; Green Forest Lumber Limited; Guild, Dr. J. & J.A.; Gusdorf Canada Ltd.; Hall, W.F.; Hamilton & Olsen Surveys; Hardin, Dr. Isidore; Harvey, John H.; Hassen, Lindsay; Heaton, Dr. P.B.; Hedinger, Mr. Adam S.; Henderson, T.; Hepburn, Alan; Heron Siegel Insurance; Hiebert, Theresa S.; Horricks, Bud & Barbara; Husco Industrial Ltd.; Hyde, Helen; Village of Hythe; Indal Limited; Inmont Canada Inc.; Jaffer, Shiraz, Shanaz & Nabil; Jet Marine & Sporting Supplies Ltd.; Johnson & Johnson Inc.; J. D. Nelson Radiator Co.; J. R. Paine & Associates; Kandler, Joseph; Kentwood Ford Sales; Kozdrowski, Peter; Koziak, Julian; Kruk, Jerry; Lakusta, Tom; Landmark Cinemas of Canada; Langley, Irene M.; Leduc Construction Co. Ltd.; Leong-Sit, Dr. F.; Leung, Ken Sunting; Lipinski, A. Eugenia; Lister, Alan L.; Lister, Ronald & Betty; Little, J.S.; London Life Insurance; Makar, Dr. Donald J.; Manuel, Ellen; Matheson, J.A.; Maytag Company Limited; McCullough, N.L.; McDermid, John, M.P.; McIntosh Workun & Chernenko Architects; McIntyre Mines; Mclean, Myrtle; McMahon, J.H.; Mikalonis, Sandra; Millar Western Industries; Miller, L.E.; Mitcom Industries Ltd.; Mowbrey Stout; Morris, James; Mulholland, William D.; National Concrete Accessories Ltd.; National Data Centre; Newson, Brigadier General & Mrs. W.F.M.; Noma Canada Ltd.; Northwest Drug Company; Northwest Hydraulic Consultants Ltd.; Northwest Industries Limited; Parry, J.D.; Pascal Family Foundation; Poole, Ian C.; Powlette-Job, Nina M.; Professional Property Management; Pulmonary Associates; Reber, Dr. Calvin R.; Reynolds Manufacturing Co.; Richards, Grant; Ritchie Texaco Service; Rogers Cablesystems Inc.; Rudolph, Mr. & Mrs. Louis; Samoil, Leo L.; Schaaf Bros. Construction Ltd.; Scott, David A.; Sewell-Huber Insurance; Shevin, Evan S.; Shipley, George & Marion; Sinclair, Warren; Skitch, Dr. C.; Smerek, Philip; Spittel, Dr. D.M.; Squirrel Investment Ltd.; State Farm Insurance; Stogryn Sales (Edmonton) Ltd.; Surveyor, Nenninger & Chenevert Inc.; Sylvan Properties; S. Thau Inc.; Taylor, Dr. Russell & Mrs. Cora; Taylor, Verna; Telesat Canada; Thorvaldson, T.B.; Toogood, John; Traub, Heather; UCS Group; Uncle Albert's Pancake House; Van Waters & Rogers Ltd.; Varvis, Dr. C.J.; Via Rail Canada Inc.; Victoria and Grey Trust Company; Vietnam-Chinese Association of Edmonton; Wachowich, Edward R.; Westburne Engineering & Plumbing; Wescab Industries; Western Credit Executive Forum; Whitfield, Leonard J.; Wing, Mr. David S.; Wosk, Mr. Ben; Woywitka, Dr. Nicholas; W. E. Greer Ltd.; Yakymechko, Dr. Mary; Yorkshire Trust Co.; Zolner, Mary; Atomic Developments Ltd.; Capilano Flowers; Habashi, Z.; Wild Ares & Murdoch; Browne, Beverley A.; Concord Engineering; Dhont, Margaret; Keogh, Catherine; MacArthur, R. Edith; Neilsen, A.R.; Polack Meindersma & Smith; Stewart Weir & Co.; Wickens & Wrozsek; Riverbend Junior High School; Acheson, Gary; Adler, Bernard; Amsterdam Tailors; Anholt, Dr. Leroy M.; Atlas Copco Canada Inc.; Bilous, Orest; Bolton, Hugh J.; Bothwell, Robert; Bowen, Peter; Buychuk, Gerald; Branham Augering Services; Brisbane, Richard; Brocklint, J.; Buchanan, Dr. D.M.; Canadian Liquid Air Unit ECW Local 666; Carbert, Beverley; Carlyle, Terry; Clarke, Dr. Kennketh & Elna; Davidson, A.M.; Town of Daysland; Devaney, Thomas B.; Ehlert, Reinhard; Ference, A.P.; Flamingo Steak House & Pizza; Fossey, Helen; Frazer, James S.; Friedrich, Elaine; Friesen, James R.; Gaetz, Robert; Gee, Gilbert E.; Goon, Dr. F.L.; Greek Ladies Philoptohos Society; Greenwood, Dr. Paul V.; Hankinson, Del; Harle, Gerald; Harryatt, R.D.; Hebert, Andre; Hembling, B.B.; Hennig, George; Henry, Howard; Hi-

Point Sales Ltd.; Hoh, Albert; Holub, H.F.; Imperial Optical Co. Ltd.; Jahrig Developments; Jespersen, Howard; Jespersen, Dr. Rueben; Johasson, B.; Kadis, Mrs. V.W.; Kettlys, Dr. H.; Kobie, Frank; Kuzyk, Bohdan L.; Langmaid, Ross A.; Lee, Dr. Michael; Leung, Dr. Anthony K.; Levitt, Irving; Lipinski, John M.D.; Lloyd, Donald; MacCormac, Ted; MacLellan, Peter Architects Ltd.; Matheson, Dr. James E.; McClelland, Richard; McDougall, Dr. D.; McLaughlin, Dr. Dennis; Miller, M.J.; Myrholm, Dr. Gunnar S.; Oilfield Consultants; Patterson, Dr. L.J.; Perdue, Aaron; Pooley, G.; Powell, Dr. Douglas, Preston, Mrs. V.J.; Provincial News; Rawson, Kenneth D.; Revell, Dr. Cliff; Robertson, Allan; Schwob, Elizabeth W.; Shewchuk, Michael E.; Shewchuk, W.; Siegenberg, Joe; Sirdar, Jerry F.; Smith, Michael; Starreveld, Dr. E.; Stegmanis-Greran, C.; Sundance Datsun; Takats, Dr. L.N.; Toupin, Dr. Henri; Tse, C.W. Architects; Turnbull, Lane; Wallington, Dr. G.A.; Wilkes, Dr. Gordon H.; Winter, R.W.; Wired Music (Western) Ltd.; Wood, Margaret L.; Workman, Paul; Wyness Architects; Young, Dr. J.E.M.; Allwest Institutional Furnishings; Armco Canada Ltd.; Metcalf, Mr. Malcolm S.; Sandy's Restaurant Ltd.; Kalmacoff, James; Sereda, M.; Docherty, Betty Lou; Dupuis, Mr. & Mrs. J.R.; Eskow, Elaine D.; Eykelbosh, George J.; James, Barry L.; Robblee, Norm.; Turner, Dave; Tymchak, Bernice; Airlite Neon Signs; Anderson, Kirk; Anderson, Miss Elinor; Armstrong, Edward L.; Beam Vacuum Systems; Bell, J.H.; Belvent Manufacturing Ltd.; Bokenfohr, Grce; Bowen, Phyllis; Brattland, Anita; Burdett, Mr. & Mrs. W.D.; Byington, M.; Cameron Interiors; Carmichael, Anne; Century 21 Executive Realty; Clark, John E.H.; Climate Master; Cooney, Cathryne; Cormie, Allison; Courcy, Mrs. L.; Cressman, Elizabeth J.; Cyr, Steven; Davies, Joanne; Diduch, Dr. Lawrence; Docherty, Margaret; Donahue, Joe Architect Ltd.; Dossetor, Dr. John B.; Driedger, Gordon; Edmonds Bros. Landscape Services (1979); Erdonnel Management Services Ltd.; Falkenberg, Mr. Rod; Graham, D.; Gregoret, W.; Haliki, Mrs. S. L.; Hansen, Karen; Hole, Elaine; Hole, Janice; Hontela, Dr. S.; Hunke, Erwin; Hunter, Edward F.; Ingram, Don; Summer Village of Itaska Beach; Jackson, Michael; Jewell, B.J.; Kennedy, S.E.; Kichok, Gerald J.; Kropp, Gary; Kudryk, Donna; Lemermeyer Architect Ltd.; Lindskoog, Mr. Ross T.; Livergant, Stephen; Lord, William R.; Love, Mr. D.P.; MacRae, Dr. Patrick; Mann, David L.; McClure, Ruth; McLean, William & Linda; McMillan, John; Mersereau, Grace; Mutter, Mr. & Mrs. J.H.; Nicol, William G.; Nobert, Dr. L.D.; Ong, Dr. Sit-Tui; O'Callahan, Pat; Parker, Gordon S.; Potter, Bryan; Prill, Kathleen; Reuvers, Dr. Hans; Richter, John; Rundle, Rev. Christine; Russell, D.B.; Sanders, John Architects; Schmidt, E. Kenneth; Scona Electric; Scragg, R.D.; Shanks, Phyllis; Shepherd, Murray; Shikazie, Grant; Shuler, L.J.; Simpson, Mrs. Anna; Skyview Auto Service; Smith, Helen; Splane, S.G.; Stuart, Alan; Szynkowski, E.; T & T Trucking (Alberta) Ltd.; Thompson, Effie C.; Tollic Foods Ltd.; Totman, R. Mary; Tredget, T.E.; Twa, Carol & Hugh; UAP; Vanderwell, Richard Architects; Veinot, Derrick; Venner, Mike; Venne, Dr. J.M.; Wetzel, Cherisse; Wilson, Jean; Wilson, Josephine Emmett; Wiltzen, Mark; Wolfe, Marke; Woloskyniuk, Gary; Wood, Rupert & Muriel; Wright, J.S.R.; Yelle, Ernest F.; Zaturecky, John William; Zukiwsky, Barbara; Chinchilla, Rosemarie; Coronet Developments Ltd.; Economy Drugs; Gee, Melvyn; Paulencu, Don; Ramage, Dr. Howard; Schlutter, G.K.; Stephen IU Architects Ltd.; Vecchio, Dr. Silvano; MicroSystems Ltd.; Williams, Anne; Austin, Richard F.; Carlson, Shirley; Dafoe, Charlotte; Fiddes, Dr. G.W.J.; Fort Road Confectionery; Fretz, Hon. Girve, M.P.; Masters, J., M.P.; Kotylak, Roy & Judy; Nerbas, John & Carolina; Samsung Electronics Canada Inc.; Stirling, Bob; Williams, Wendy R.; Robert, Mrs. Germaine

Official Sponsors:

Canon Canada Inc.; City of Edmonton; Digital Equipment of Canada; Government of Alberta; Government of Canada; G.W.G.; Kodak Canada Inc.; Molson Breweries of Canada Ltd.; Motorola Canada Ltd.; Omega Sports Timing; Pepsi-Cola Canada Ltd.; R.C.A. Sales Inc.; University of Alberta; Western Canada Lottery; Xerox Canada Inc.

Official Suppliers:

A.E.S.; Air Canada; ASICS Corporation; Atco Structure Ltd.; BCM/Jones; Canada Packers; Mikasa/Cooper Canada Ltd.; Converse Inc.; C.P. Air; Goodhost/Bunn-Omatic; Hewlett-Packard; The Ice Pedlar; Imperial Oil; Kuehne & Nagel International Ltd.; Mizuno Corporation; Nanton Water;

Petro Canada; Prieur Sports; Pacific Western Airlines; Reidmore Books; Shoppers Drug Mart; Spieth-Anderson Ltd.; Baldwin Pianos; Catelli; Penn; Simmons Limited; Amsterdam Tailors; McBain Camera; Todd Cleaners; Woodwards

Special Thanks to:

A.G.T.; American Hospital Supply Corporation; Auto Suture Canada Ltd.; Canada Safeway; Canadian National; Canadian Liquid Air Ltd.; Crown Zellerbach; Eatons; Davis & Geck; Edmonton Public School Board; Edmonton Safety Council; Edmonton Telephones; Electrical Workers' Union; Fisher Scientific; General Electric (Medical Division); General Motors; H.G. Caterers Ltd.; Harry Nash Agencies; Healy Ford; Hurtig Publishers; John Casablancas Modelling; Joseph E. Seagram & Sons Limited; Medtronic of Canada; Miller Office Group; O'Hanlon Paving; Precision Scales Co.; Purdue Frederick Inc.; RGO Office Furnishings; Scona Cycle; Joseph E. Seagram & Sons. Limited; Skelton, Alma; Speedfast Color Press Ltd.; Travelers Insurance; Underwood McLellan Ltd.; Union Carbide; Wardair; Westin Hotel; William Collins Sons & Co.

In Memorium

Sergei Shalibaswili

USSR

Student • Sportsman • Friend

Edmonton Alberta Canada

196